W9-BYR-072

DISCARD

The Politics of Autism

The Politics of Autism

Bryna Siegel, PhD

DISCARD

OXFORD
UNIVERSITY PRESS

OXFORD
UNIVERSITY PRESS

Oxford University Press is a department of the University of Oxford. It furthers the University's objective of excellence in research, scholarship, and education by publishing worldwide. Oxford is a registered trade mark of Oxford University Press in the UK and certain other countries.

Published in the United States of America by Oxford University Press
198 Madison Avenue, New York, NY 10016, United States of America.

Library of Congress Cataloging-in-Publication Data
Names: Siegel, Bryna, author.
Title: The politics of autism / by Bryna Siegel.
Description: New York, NY : Oxford University Press, [2018] |
Includes bibliographical references and index.
Identifiers: LCCN 2017053462 | ISBN 9780199360994 (alk. paper)
Subjects: LCSH: Autism—Epidemiology—Government policy—United States. |
Autism—Diagnosis—United States. | Autistic people—Education—United States.
Classification: LCC RC553.A88 S536 2018 | DDC 362.196/8588200973—dc23
LC record available at https://lccn.loc.gov/2017053462

9 8 7 6 5 4 3 2 1

Printed by Sheridan Books, Inc., United States of America

For David

CONTENTS

PREFACE

I worry that America is becoming a mob. Twitter, Facebook, Instagram, Google+, and similar well-subscribed sources for information entice readers to adopt articles of faith, sometimes in 140 characters or less. The Internet, the once un-potholed utopian information superhighway of the 1980s and 1990s, is now the place where one goes to become part of an in-group endorsing one's own ideas. One earns one's stripes as part of an in-group, posting black-and-white declarations of affinity. We are beginning to see a historical timeline of strong online identifications—with Trumpism, and the Freedom Caucus, to Black Lives Matter and #MeToo, to Alt-Righters, to recruiters for ISIS. Not coincidentally, we experience divisiveness about immigration, guns, abortion rights, climate change, and growing racial divisiveness though many hoped Obama had left us a postracial America. How we know and understand things has fundamentally changed: Articles of faith that underpin such groups are just that, and not infrequently, inconvenient data are damned.

What's good, and what is bad about how we learn things these days? My microcosm for exploring these kinds of disturbing developments is the politics of autism. I've spent my professional life trying to help children and families living with autism, but always with an eye to influencing social policy. I'll discuss the expansion and seeming popularity of the diagnosis of autism, the hysteria around vaccines and autism that have impacted pediatric public health, and the mystique of the autistic savant and how misconstruction of what autism is has thrown up barriers to effectively planning for the limitations the vast majority of adults with autism inevitably face.

Social media and ratings-driven TV have made sound bites of what we are told we need to know. Colorful brain images on PBS or cover page stories in *Time* or *Newsweek* about autism lift spirits by suggesting what is possible or may be possible soon, but may turn out not to be true. Such sound bites direct us away from understanding the sea change needed to improve the lives of people living with autism, as well as many other neuropsychiatric disorders. It redirects our attention from the poignancy of families striving to do their best with less-than-perfect children, and who find little succor in what brain imaging or genetics may tell them—someday. The vulnerability of truth combined with American optimism may have led us to the edge of a crevasse where many families of children with autism stand as they gaze toward their child's adult years. We've not built them a bridge or a road to travel onward. This book is an effort to figure out what we need to do, how to build some new roads, so the future of children with autism and their families is better.

Key references appear at the end of each chapter. More extensive references appear at the end of the book, organized by chapter, with references for each chapter divided into two sections: The first section for each chapter is citations from popular media—books, magazines, newspapers, television, or URLs. The purpose is to illustrate where and how ideas about autism in the general culture are formed. The second section for each chapter lists scientific writing organized by major subtopics to highlight what is or is not yet known from research. This organization of the references is designed to facilitate use of this book as a reference for college and graduate coursework and to further scholarly investigation. Where possible, both chapter Notes and the References organized by chapter at the end of the book include a URL for the citation; a PDF of these references can be downloaded (http://www.brynasiegel.com/politicsofautism/), and the links to the references are available on the website.

INTRODUCTION

I met my first child with autism when I was a 19-year-old undergraduate, in about 1972. I am now in my early 60s. The most recent family with a child with autism is probably someone I met earlier today or yesterday. In all that time, the "autism" landscape has changed: In 1972, autism had not quite emerged from its Dark Ages. In the Dark Ages of autism, mothers were strongly suspected of an early, profound, unconscious rejection of their infant, and that the ensuing failure to bond resulted in the solipsistic autistic aloneness with which the child faced the world.

Leo Kanner, an American child psychiatrist, was the first to describe "early infantile autism," a condition where the child acted as if others were not meaningful to constructing his or her emotional life.[1] *Early infantile* was meant to refer to the earliest stages of infancy when the infant "takes," but has not yet developed a capacity to "give" in his or her social contact. While Kanner himself did not argue that parents were the cause, he acknowledged that many parents who sought out his academic expertise were not the warm, fuzzy parents he felt had "the right stuff" to naturally break through their child's self-isolation.

Others, like Bruno Bettelheim, a professor of mine, who I talk about more in Chapter 3, did frankly posit that "refrigerator mothers" caused autism. Bettelheim, in his book *The Empty Fortress*, opined that these distant, unemotional parents that Kanner had described had in fact caused their child's difficulties, and interventions like "parentectomy" (basically residential placement) were the child's best chance to achieve wellness.[2]

This was basically where the state of our understanding of autism was in 1972—when I first met children with autism. I'd grown interested in autism as a way to explore the themes guiding the study of psychology of the day—"free will" versus "determinism," specifically—in child psychology, this boiled down to "nature" versus "nurture." A determinist would argue that the behavior that made for autism was pure nature or biology; a humanistic viewpoint, on the other hand, argued that nurture or the application of psychotherapeutic-induced change could make all the difference. Autism, it was thought, was the most extreme example of nurture gone awry. I wanted to see that for myself.

So, in 1972, I got a summer volunteer position at Creedmore, a New York City welfare hospital, at a children's inpatient psychiatric unit. These children were like none I had seen: Just like in *The Empty Fortress* that I had read months earlier, these children danced on their toes, twirled in circles, flapped their hands, and talked only in echoes. My attempts to help with simple activities like joining a group for a story time, coloring, or even eating with utensils were met with vacant stares, even with getting up and just sprinting away. I wanted to understand why. At lunchtime, I was allowed to read their medical records. One girl was the seventh of nine born from different fathers to a schizophrenic mother. Another had been found after being abandoned by his drug-addicted parents. "No wonder they created their own worlds!" I thought at the time.

Fascinated, I wanted to learn more, so I signed up for a 3-month teaching internship at Elwyn Institute, a long-established, well-funded private residential school for the developmentally disabled outside Philadelphia, Pennsylvania. This time, the children in my class did not come from the poorest parts of New York City, but the wealthiest. These children were a lot better dressed than the kids at Creedmore, but they too danced on their toes, twirled in circles, and flapped their hands. Elwyn pupils came from intact, well-off families with siblings who were high achievers in school. How could I reconcile the "refrigerator mother" hypothesis—as Dr. Bettelheim had put it? By January, I returned to college, determined to write my senior thesis on the etiology of early infantile autism in order to read much more about causes of autism so I could really understand whether evidence supported autism as nature or nurture.

Making a long story short, I researched and wrote my thesis. I decided the etiology of autism was biological, that we were a long, long way from understanding the specific cause(s), and if I was interested in studying nurture more than nature, which I was, the field of autism was probably not a great place to spend more time.

I changed tactics. I did a PhD in (normal) child development at Stanford, focusing on another much more clearly nature-versus-nurture problem, early mother–child attachment, and whether it was disrupted by the use of significant early nonparental care. By the late 1970s, the feminist movement supported women who chose to return to work shortly after childbearing. It is hard to believe now, but then the idea of day care for infants was new. Like questions that had motivated me to learn about autism, there was concern that leaving infants to nonparental care would disturb mother–infant attachment, the prototype for all later secure social relationships. Interested in the earliest aspects of nurture, I took a master's degree in early childhood education, then finished my PhD—in child development/developmental psychology, writing my dissertation on the early effects of day care.

Then, I was 27 years old, with a young daughter, a Stanford PhD (and a year of postdoctoral training in biomedical statistics) under my belt. I had a contract to write my first book—a book for parents on what research said about how to choose developmentally beneficial day care. But, I needed a "day job." Luckily, I happened to give a talk about my new book at Stanford's child psychiatry department. The department head, Dr. Tom Anders, had just started his youngest child in day care that week. He really liked the talk and wished he could hire me, but the only open position was to run an autism research project.

Based on my earlier teaching experience, a teaching credential for autism, my senior thesis on autism, and my training in statistics, I convinced him to hire me. What I thought would be a day job became my career.

As I grappled with the Stanford autism data, I realized that what had changed for me was that I could now view the symptoms of autism with a developmental "lens." Nobody was thinking, talking, or doing research in child psychiatry on "developmental disorders" from a developmentalist's perspective. I was intrigued and saw a new path for myself. Then, within a year, I was left completely in charge of Dr. Anders's autism research project as he and the rest of his lab left to join the faculty at Brown University.

I then began collaboration directly with the autism project's other principal investigator, Roland Ciaranello, a bright, ambitious biological child psychiatrist. But he, like many professors of psychiatry I would meet in my future work, didn't want to have to see children with autism, just receive biological specimens after I'd confirmed the diagnosis. Ciaranello was an early entrant into the race to find an autism gene: Working with Dr. Ed Ritvo and Dr. B. J. Freeman of the University of California at Los Angeles (UCLA) to do a total population ascertainment of all the multiplex families (families with more than one child with autism) in the state of Utah, I got to ski Alta and Park City and see families with three, four, and five children with autism. Ciaranello, then short-listed to head the National Institute of Mental Health, predicted we would have "the gene" for autism in 5 years. Thirty-five years on, he did not live to see his early prediction fail to be realized or to participate in the twists and turns in psychiatric genetics—still far from any clinically meaningful genetic markers for any psychiatric disorders. (In Chapter 9, I visit the field of autism genetics today, viewed through my 35-year lens in that game.)

By 1989, wanting my own clinic and lab, I accepted a faculty position up the road from Stanford at the University of California, San Francisco (UCSF), joining my closest Stanford clinical collaborator in my autism work, Dr. Glen Elliott, who had just become UCSF's director of child psychiatry. By then, I had published research on trying to statistically model subtypes of autism[3] and participated in the *Diagnostic and Statistical Manual of Mental Disorders* (3rd ed., revised; *DSM-III-R*) field trials, an international research effort to standardize the way autism was diagnosed, and had proposed improved statistical modeling for it with the late Dr. Robert Spitzer, who had headed the *DSM-III-R* effort.[4,5]

From my early work on subtyping, it became clear to me that there were many dimensions of autism, many present in some children but not others, and that severity varied as well. On top of this, as a developmental psychologist, I worried that in child psychiatry diagnoses there was no meaning given to "developmental" in the psychiatric term *developmental psychopathology*. Psychiatry lacked a model for factoring in that a child was a developing child first, not just describable by the signs and symptoms of his or her disorder. In autism, and in fact in any neurodevelopmental disorder, some tracks of development could be proceeding on time, while others might not be. Impairment in the brain's language center would, not unexpectedly, hamper language development, but usually also impede "downstream" development in interdependent realms like play—because the capacity to narrate play with language would be hampered when there was little or no receptive or expressive language capacity. I began to see children with autism not just as a checklist of symptoms as psychiatrists did, but clinically as a developmentally driven interplay of their individual strengths and weaknesses. Eventually, this work led to my 2003 book, *Helping Children With Autism Learn*,[6] which applied my autistic learning disabilities/ autistic learning styles model to educating children with autism.

At the same time, I had also became increasingly involved with the effects of autism on the family. As a field, we now all understood that parents did not cause autism, but it did not take much to see that autism caused some families to struggle. In 1994, together with Dr. Stu Silverstein (a pediatrician and older brother of Mark, a man with autism), we published *What About Me? Siblings of Developmentally Disabled Children*.[7] Just as a gauge of the times, our original publisher, also publisher of the only scientific autism journal at the time, wanted our book to have examples of developmental disorders other than autism and for the title to reflect that because the autism "market" was seen as so small.

Soon after, the "sibling" project was finished, I published *The World of the Autistic Child: Understanding and Treating Autistic Spectrum Disorders*.[8] This was the first book I know that used the term *spectrum* in the title along with *autism*. In the research community, we had begun talking about a spectrum as a way of characterizing what was coming to be realized as a very broad range of expression for signs of autism, though the term *autism spectrum disorder* was not used in formal diagnostic terminology for another 17 years.

The *World of the Autistic Child* described how autism could alter how a child with autism understood things in his or her world. It included a chapter based on some of my empirical research, on how getting the diagnosis of autism provokes grieving for the loss of the hoped-for child, and what "healthy" versus more prolonged, complicated grieving looked like based on what we know about grieving in adults who lose spouses prematurely. This work struck a chord when I spoke to parent groups, and I began to realize how urgently the psychological lives of parents of children with autism needed to be addressed. Most important, I could see that parents did better if they could see themselves as able to help their children improve. This is still a key focus of my current work—parent training for families with children with newly diagnosed autism.

Back in the mid-1990s, publication of *The World of the Autistic Child* opened the door to invitations to speak to parent groups throughout the United States, Canada, and abroad because it spoke to their issues from the moment of getting their child's diagnosis to the challenges of going through life trying to make sure each decision on behalf of their child was as fully considered as it could be. In traveling, lecturing, and meeting parents from all over, I realized just how needy parents were for guidance to help their children and how, outside the "ivory towers" of academia, few evidence-based programs existed.

In the 1990s and 2000s, my direction in autism treatment work was guided by two powerful mentors, Dr. Eric Schopler and Dr. Ivar Lovaas, who, to my mind, were working toward the same goals but were flip sides of the same coin, the former aiming to improve the quality of lives and the latter aiming to "cure."

Prior to 1987, the only nationally disseminated treatment program for autism was TEACCH, developed by Schopler, at the University of North Carolina, Chapel Hill. A giant figure, and a pioneer in the field of autism treatment and research, Dr. Schopler was founding editor of what originally was the *Journal of Autism and Childhood Schizophrenia*, today the *Journal of Autism and Developmental Disorders*. His work, dating back to the early 1970s, profoundly influenced my own, being the first to define teaching for children with autism as needing to focus on the child's likely autistic learning strengths, such as the ability to rely on visual schedules and on routines. These learning strengths became systematized in my own work that I just described—as "autistic learning styles," juxtaposed with common autism-specific learning deficits that I classified as "autistic learning disabilities."

My second mentor, Dr. Ivar Lovaas, had in 1987 published a paper that rocked the world of autism by suggesting that intensive application of behavior modification principles could recover 50 percent of children with autism.[9] Of course, everyone instantly wanted his therapy for their child. A couple of the patients from the autism clinic I had just started at UCSF in 1989 made it down to the UCLA Lovaas Clinic and came back very much improved. One seemed no longer autistic; another was talking and playing with toys—both new developments from several months earlier, when this same child had been completely withdrawn, actively avoidant, and preverbal. The parents of this second boy recruited me, along with Dr. Tristram Smith, then head of Dr. Lovaas's clinic, to testify at an educational due process hearing against the child's school district and the state of California in order to compel the boy's pubic education authority to pay for treatment with the Lovaas method—called DTT (discrete trial training). Tris Smith and I helped the parents prevail, and the case, known as *Smith v. Union School District*, set federal precedent for subsequent cases that proliferated across the country over the next few years, compelling school districts to fund or offer Lovaas's methods of intervention.

I was thrilled with the outcome of the *Smith* case, as the alternative for this boy would have been just 3 hours of "Mommy and Me" classes per week—which was basically all schools did for young children with autism in the 1980s and the first half of the 1990s. Over time, however, I began to accrue a local sample of children receiving DTT, and not all benefitted nearly as much as the first two I had seen who had received DTT at UCLA—even though most were treated by students Lovaas had personally trained.

In 1998, one of my then graduate students, Dr. Stephen Sheinkopf, and I published on this sample, finding that DTT was significantly better for children than "treatment as usual" (like a Mommy and Me class), but that there was considerable variation in treatment outcome.[10] We also had preliminary data to suggest that further studies examine whether 25 hours per week of DTT rather than the recommended (and obviously more costly) 40 hours per week were comparable. This suggestion for "further research," standard operating procedure for the concluding paragraphs of any research paper, became a flashpoint, and conflict began between those with interest in the science of applied behavior analysis and those who reified Dr. Lovaas's study and magically believed that anything less than 40 hours per week of treatment was an unfounded risk. (Today, most children treated with this method receive something more like the 25 hours per week Sheinkopf and I wrote about more than 20 years ago, so research has supported what we then suggested be studied.)

In Chapter 5, I talk more about Drs. Lovaas and Schopler, but for now the point is I learned a great deal from the work of each man. One looked at autism as a problem with learning, the other as a problem with behavior. The work I do to this day emphasizes that things must be taught in developmental sequence (thank you, Dr. Schopler) and must be taught using behavioral techniques (thank you, Dr. Lovaas).

My perspective, distilled from these two men and from many others, has underpinned how I have tried to help families understand their child's autism, as well as influenced what I wrote in *Helping Children With Autism Learn* and a further volume, *Getting the Best for Your Child With Autism*,[11] in 2008.

Some of the other work I did during my 24 years at UCSF drew on my statistics and psychometrics background and honed my diagnostic expertise, such as participation and analysis data from the American Psychiatric Association (APA) *Diagnostic and Statistical Manual* (DSM), *DSM-III-R* (revised, third edition)[4] and then *DSM-IV* (fourth edition)[12] field trials for autism—the latter leading to the psychiatric diagnostic criteria that were in place from 1994 until 2013. The mixture of politics and science that I saw going into creating APA diagnostic criteria led to what I talk about in Chapter 3. In another line of my work, because of my psychometrics training and developmental background, I spent several years standardizing the Pervasive Developmental Disorders Screening Test II (PDDST-II), a screening test for autism for infants, toddlers, and preschoolers.[13]

Becoming an expert in autism diagnosis, as well as having written about autism treatment, has often drawn me into education litigation around the need for autism-specific education—which I write about in Chapter 2, where I examine whether there really is more autism today, and in Chapters 4 and 5 on educational methods for autism such as inclusion, as well as in Chapter 6 on autism health economics. Along the way, my growing familiarity with autism in the legal area drew me into what I call "the vaccine wars," which I look at in Chapter 8.

At the end of 2013, I retired from UCSF after 24 years of running an autism clinic, doing research on identification and diagnosis, writing and lecturing for parents and teachers, and collaborating with colleagues in genetics and neurology, who someday, I hope, will achieve the holy grail of autism—prevention or medical remediation. But I knew I was not done yet working in the field of autism: My heart was in helping families better parent their children with autism and developing a model for an "autism home"—a place families could come back to for continuity of care, where the clinicians know them and their child (or now teen or adult), and know what had worked and what hadn't worked. Too many families I knew felt that they were on their own after the diagnosis, when in fact their need for support and guidance was just beginning. I knew that if the diagnosing clinician never saw a child again after giving the family a diagnosis of autism, that clinician would be in a very limited position to discuss prognosis. To provide prognosis, you must be able to factor in treatment response. Presently, there is not much out there in the way of continuity of care for families living with autism. Parents need a place to get continuing care—so they know if they are doing the right thing, if their child's treatment regime is all it can be. Parents need to know if their child is not improving as much as ideally hoped and why that might be. Parents need a relationship with a professional who has seen where their child has come from and what has been tried, who can say what else should be tried or can say, "You're doing all you can do and doing it incredibly well." Believe me, without that support, the guilt of believing there must have been something missed exists in every parent with a child who carries a diagnosis of autism.

In 2013, I founded the Autism Center of Northern California (http://www. acnc.org) to create a model for a place families could go for help—to learn how to teach their children, to learn to deal with behavior difficulties, and to come back at each new stage of development—including adulthood. I am convinced from research and experience that interventions that integrate developmental and behavioral principles are foundational to the most effective approaches we have today for ameliorating the difficulties caused by autism. I'll leave the curing of autism to my medical colleagues.

In popular media, the autism "voice" that is most often heard is that of a handful of the very highest functioning people with autism and a subset of parents of individuals with autism who have been incredible advocates for a range of autism causes. However, a large number of parents are too immersed in day-to-day life with their child with autism, or are disenfranchised due to their own socioeconomic barriers, to voice their child's need for more supports. The "autism" I talk about here is the whole "autism spectrum." Sometimes, there will be reasons to call out those better described as having "Asperger's disorder" or "high-," "medium-," or "low"-functioning autism. Mostly, I try to speak to the issues of those with autism who have no voice of their own—which is basically everyone with medium- or low-functioning autism and quite a few identified as high functioning.

This book is about many aspects of the American experience of autism. *The Politics of Autism* provides a window into how Americans deal with a most often lifelong disability. On some level, *The Politics of Autism* is also a cultural anthropology of autism. In *Far From the Tree*, journalist Andrew Solomon explored involuntary cultures—of deafness, Down syndrome, dwarfism, autism, and many more. He described how these individuals would live lives more identified with others of their disability group than with their families of origin.[14] Using Solomon's definition, people with autism, and often also their family members, are shaped by this culture of autism. Today, the culture of autism certainly not only provides some supports, but also provides what can be disinformation, mostly with good intention, leaving parents of less able children envious of the accomplishments of more able ones and leaving parents of more able children fearing their children may develop the problems of the less able ones.

The autism culture is based on an inherent contradiction: "Cure" is much more valued than "palliation"—though palliation is what most get most of the time. Inclusive education is promoted as an end in itself, rather than as a means. Academic education in middle and high schools provides a smoke screen for future adaptive and vocational limitations parents often don't face up to until the day after high school graduation. We can do better, but policy change is needed. Today, the culture of autism lacks supports as robust as those that have been extended to people in wheelchairs and people who are deaf. I am hoping that an inspection of the politics of autism will provide impetus to better support this culture of autism.

Notes

1. Kanner, L. (1943). Autistic disturbances of affective contact. *Nervous Child, 2,* 217–250. Reprinted 1968: *Acta Paedopsychiatrica, 35*(4), 100–136.

2. Bettelheim, B. (1967). *The empty fortress: Infantile autism and the birth of the self.* New York: Free Press/Simon & Schuster.

3. Siegel, B., Anders, T., Ciaranello, R. D., Bienenstock, B., & Kraemer, H. C. (1985). Empirical of the autistic syndrome. *Journal of Autism and Developmental Disorders, 16*(3), 475–491.

4. Spitzer, R. L., & Siegel, B. (1990). The *DSM-III-R* field trials for pervasive developmental disorders. *Journal of the American Academy of Child and Adolescent Psychiatry, 26*(6), 855–862.

5. Siegel, B., Vukicevic, J., & Spitzer, R. L. (1990). Using signal detection theory to revise *DSM-III-R*: Reanalysis of the *DSM-III-R* field trials data for autistic disorder. *Journal of Psychiatric Research, 4,* 301–311.

6. Siegel, B. (2003). *Helping children with autism learn: Treatment approaches for parents and professionals*. New York, NY: Oxford University Press.

7. Siegel, B., & Silverstein, S. (1994). *What about me? Growing up with a developmentally disabled sibling*. Boston, MA: Da Capo Press.

8. Siegel, B. (1996). *The world of the autistic child: Understanding and treating autistic spectrum disorders*. New York, NY: Oxford University Press.

9. Lovaas, I. (1987). Behavioral treatment and normal educational and intellectual functioning in young autistic children. *Journal of Consulting and Clinical Psychology*, 55(1), 3–9.

10. Sheinkopf, S., & Siegel, B. (1998). Effects of very early intensive behavioral intervention for autistic children. *Journal of Autism and Developmental Disorders*, 28(1), 15–23.

11. Siegel, B. (2008). *Getting the best for your child with autism: An expert's guide to treatment*. New York, NY: Guilford Press.

12. Volkmar, F., Klin, A., Siegel, B., Szatmari, P., et al. (1994). Field trial for autistic disorder in *DSM-IV*. *American Journal of Psychiatry*, 151(9), 1361–1367.

13. Siegel, B. (2001). *The Pervasive Developmental Disorders Screening Test–II*. San Antonio, TX: Psychological Corporation.

14. Solomon, A. (2013). *Far from the tree: Parents, children and the search for identity*. New York, NY: Scribner/Simon & Schuster.

The Politics of Autism

The Politics of Autism

In the more than 40 years since I first met a child with autism, I have strived to use my voice as a professor, researcher, writer, and lecturer to talk to parents, teachers, fellow autism scientists, therapists, and even judges—to convey what is and what is not known about autism. This book is intended to "tell it like it is" about the world of autism. My goal is to balance what often is reported in the media about autism against what one learns through "life in the trenches" (as an autism basic scientist who deals only with blood samples, genes, cells, or mice might describe the way my day-to-day labors are different from his or hers). Academic colleagues whose work I admire most have encouraged me in my writing of this book, urging me to "get it out there," but also have annotated their encouraging words by noting I am "brave" for doing so. I don't think truth-telling should necessarily be an act of bravery, but rather guided by ethical imperative. I state this as a prelude to the conflicts and controversies I cover here. I see the truth about autism as vulnerable: vulnerable to clinicians who don't follow children with autism and don't know whether recommended treatments work or not; vulnerable to educators offering diluted "core curriculum" rather than teaching critical life and social skills; vulnerable to scam artists, who promise results from unproven treatments; and even vulnerable to researchers, who raise millions for what is basic science, falsely claiming it is autism science that will help those with autism.

This book is certainly about autism, but it also is an attempt to position what we hear about autism in the media as an object lesson in what is happening to our ability to apply science and clinical experience to social policy and, more broadly, to discerning what's "real news" and what's "fake news." The politics of autism, like many things these days, is shaped by an unorthodox amalgamation of knowledge and beliefs that permutates every "byte" of information we assimilate. New media, from partisan television stations to "news" via satirists, social media, and the Internet in general make it increasingly difficult to know what you know because you want to believe it and knowing something based on objective facts.

In graduate school at Stanford, I was taught psychometrics and charged with the ethics of not "lying with statistics." Boy, are we light years from that simple caution today. On the air, conservative radio host Rush Limbaugh describes mainstream media as folks who "just make it up."[1] We have a president who tweets "facts," indistinguishable from what he just happens to find expedient to believe at the moment or just saw on a random website. And "facts" can now be "walked back." Who knew facts were ambulatory creatures?

Exploring the politics of autism can, I believe, teach us something about who we are, how we think, and what we value as Americans. Yes, this book may be most interesting to those whose lives have been touched by a person with autism, but I am hoping the general reader, intrigued by why so much about autism is in the media, will want answers to whether the things he or she has read are really true. We are bombarded by information—about autism, about other disorders like attention deficit hyperactivity disorder (ADHD), about mental illness, about the promise of mapping the brain, and about the promise of genetics. All these fields intersect with "autism." If autism facts can be walked back, one might assume that facts about these other conditions and areas of research can also be walked back. Mainstream media presents science as facts, not "work in progress." As a result, one week we are told of the risks of daily wine consumption, a year later, that a glass of red wine now and again might not be bad, and even might be good. Do we just stop listening and believe what we want to believe? How and when can we trust the interface with the science that we get from media to make difficult moral, ethical, and financial decisions around mental health care and physical health care, not only for individuals with autism, but also for individuals with other cognitive and mental handicaps and especially for ourselves?

"Information" Versus "Knowledge"

We have a surfeit of information these days—about everything. I will argue that knowledge, by contrast, has not kept pace. Information is what you can get from Google, from Wikipedia. The data available to us in this form are, let's face it, often just sound bites. Knowledge, by contrast, emerges only when information is used to test a hypothesis, the hypothesis can confirm a theory, and the theory guides action effectively. If the information you rely on is false or a partial or irrelevant truth, any hypothesis you believe you have confirmed, any theory you have developed, any action you take based on it risks being insubstantial or wrong.

Not long ago, *New York Times* columnist Ross Douthat wrote about "Facebook's Subtle Empire."[2] He lucidly pointed out the obvious—that when we search the web, what we find predisposes what we will subsequently find. He questioned whether finding things you "like" is really learning or mainly self-reassurance about views one already holds. Information thus gleaned is not only recursive, but also arguably steps us further away from objective knowledge.

The comedian John Oliver[3] has ravaged (in a humorous way) crowd-sourced science, noting how many TV and press outlets take real scientific findings that have been distilled into press releases and distill them further—resulting in pronouncements that two thirds of a chocolate bar is good for you when pregnant or three glasses of champagne a day keep the cancer away. He quoted a *Today Show* host, who noted, "You find the scientific study that best supports your view, and go with that." This dissemination of scientific findings quickly degenerates—much like a preschooler's game of "telephone"—only the resulting distortions can lead folks in directions that aren't so funny.

Our Information About Autism

We have a lot of information about autism. We get it from the Internet, newspapers, magazines, TV, and hearsay. As someone who has labored in the field of autism research and treatment for quite a while, I am often surprised to see yet another article in a newspaper or a story on TV about autism. I am often surprised by what that article asserts, what TV programs choose to show about autism. Such content is often heartwarming, but as I think about it, it is not infrequently a self-possessed point of view or is full of assertions that just happen to be unsupported by existing research. Mostly, as someone who tries to keep up on "real" autism research, it often does not further my knowledge about autism. I find myself wondering what drives these politics of autism, why the media talk about the very peculiar things they do when it comes to autism. Indeed, there *are* more than a few stories of savants and success stories of winning that foot race that ring true. There *are* brave mothers who fight for their child's rights, gain what they seek, and achieve a much happier ending than if they had not pressed on. These vignettes provide us with terrific, inspiring narratives.

But, with ringing exceptions, this public window on autism is not the autism that most of us who work in this field, who are, in fact, down in the trenches with families and their children, experience day to day. There is a political filter on what makes select stories on autism into "news." For me, it is a case study in what it says about America in the age of information technology. We are in an age of more information and less understanding: The politics of autism are the slant that filters information and provides us with what we will probably "like."

American Autism

The thesis of this book is that the politics of autism in America have led to misguided priorities that have left behind the real needs of most individuals and families living with autism. This is despite congressional hearings, millions of research dollars, proliferation of autism journals, an international autism research society, and so much more public "autism awareness." The bulk of *treatment* dollars goes to preschoolers, a stage of life that is about 3% of the life span of a person with autism. The bulk of *research* dollars goes to study the brains and the genes of children with autism and their families. Seldom spoken of is that this research offers no real hope of improving the quality of lives of those being studied. Instead, parents, therapists, teachers, and whole "villages" involved in raising children with autism just do what they can to provide the best education, support, and care—this despite very limited funding to engineer programs that could support the best possible quality of life for those with autism and their families.

Autism Realpolitik

Most families who have an infant, toddler, or preschooler diagnosed with autism will someday have a little or a great deal of responsibility for an adult with autism. In America, despite our "every child can be president" optimism, there is no well-lit road to autistic adulthood, no road map, and there are few resources for most of the developmentally less able people with autism. Whether able enough to have once deserved 5 minutes on the *NBC Nightly News* or still needing help with activities of daily living, few adults with autism are likely to have received most of the help they needed or still may need. All mothers and fathers of a child with autism dream of a future where they can be secure in knowing their beloved child will have had the opportunity to actualize his or her potential and have a life with meaning after they are gone—just like everyone else.

About 90 percent of adults with autism spectrum disorders, including the intellectually most able ones, are unemployed as adults.[4] Why? They are unemployable. We have failed to prepare them for jobs where they can succeed. Much of special education for individuals on the autism spectrum in middle and high school is inadequate. Teachers can have their heads in the sand when it comes to where they believe their pupils will ultimately be able to go—even though teachers have the clearest idea of what a given child knows and what it takes to teach that child. Educational administrators prevaricate to parents and set unachievable benchmarks with unrealistic goals. Doctors very often equivocate and sidestep questions about prognosis, even when parents directly ask about their child's future capabilities. There are many children with autism who are painstakingly taught academic subjects for years and years by the most excellent and caring educators and therapists—though it is plain to any truth teller that such a child will never get to the point where he or she can take a place in a society that requires real reading comprehension, writing composition, or the math needed to manage income or a household. Imagine being a child, then a teen, then a young adult drilled incessantly in things you can't fully understand or remember, rather than being allowed to develop relative strengths and talents as a way of finding your niche.

Outside America, where academic education is not considered a birthright or a prerequisite for a good life, individuals with autism and other disabilities may actually have *more* opportunity to take part in meaningful societal activity—from work on a farm or in a factory to community-based centers of care for the young, disabled, and elderly. In many places outside America—some places with as many resources as in America, some places with far fewer—raising a child with a disability is not all about getting the child academically trained. Such children may be trained to care for themselves first, then to participate in family and community life, and then to participate vocationally, as they can, if they can. This is simply accepted to be what is possible.

In America, we do a disservice to individuals on the autism spectrum by often teaching children with autism things that are unbearably hard for them to learn. When it seems they can't learn it, we say they are inattentive and can prescribe a medication for that. When we keep trying to teach those same things, still beyond the individual's capacity, and they become angry and agitated, we also have a medication for that. We just keep trying to teach things the individual shows little inclination to learn. Meanwhile, we ignore the teaching of more simple skills that improve a person's independence and thereby the quality of daily life—like taking care of personal needs, preparing the foods they eat, caring for the place where they live, and developing a range of healthy leisure activities. As we keep trying to teach things that are insurmountable, we risk making the individual feel like a failure, anxious, or depressed. We risk having parents feel they have failed their child and that the system of care they depended on has also failed them because the system has not delivered on its promise to teach their child to read, write, and do math. These parents are infuriated, and there is no one to reassure them when, in fact, most often they have done their best by their child, maybe even more than for their typically developing children, who may have not seemed to need them so much.

Americans care a great deal about helping those less able. Absolutely, everyone deserves a chance to get better. There are a tremendous number of us who want to help in whatever way we can. Altruism is very American. When we are 10 years old, it makes us Girls Scouts and Boy Scouts. When we grow up and go to war and win, it leads us to "nation building" to affirm that our victory is meaningful to the conquered.

However, altruism alone does not necessarily lead to success: Only a small number with autism will get "better" enough to make decent adjustments and find a niche for themselves in life. A few will thrive. This book really is not about those more fortunate individuals. Honestly, enough has been said by them and about them. This book is to give voice to the rest, the vast majority of families and individuals who will always be living with autism. We examine many ways we, as a society, can try to help and explore whether we could be thinking about some issues—from autism awareness, to autism diagnosis, to autism education, to medications, to prioritizing research—differently—if we really want to help those presently living with autism.

Politically Incorrect?

Your reaction to any examination of the politics of autism may be that it is politically incorrect to say anything that might be construed as lowering expectations for any child. If that's how you feel, I am sorry. I hope you will keep an open mind and read on. I am not trying to lower expectations for children with autism and their families, but rather introduce realism to our discussion about what autism is for most families and what can be done to instrumentally help children and their families living with autism in America today.

We have had rainbow-high horizons in autism for a long time now. We've been chasing the pot of gold, the cure for autism, for a good 30 years, but the cure still is not in sight. I'll argue here that for families living with autism today, their lives will not be shaped by any cure at any time in their lives or the life of their child. Rather, we need to turn attention to "saying it like it is," and then doing something about what "it" is. This means parents need to know both what to do and what may result from the help they provide. A child's prognosis can be ascertained to some degree with increasing detail as different treatments are given, response to those treatments is examined, and the child continues to develop. The hard truth of this, of course, it not all children will benefit equally from the same treatment. The overall severity of the child's outcome will likely play a more determinative role than what exactly is done for the child. Outcome is not only a roll of the dice, but also a complex interplay of at least three things: First is the symptoms and severity of a child's autism, what he or she "brings to the table," that child's potential. Second is treatments administered. Third are the parents and caregivers who will be placed in the critical role of cementing treatment and maturational gains in how they support their child's habilitation in the child's daily activities.

Autism Family Wellness

"Autism family wellness" is what I call this third factor: Parents need to know what they should be doing to help their child beyond being the selector of treatments and the chauffer between therapies. Parents need an "operating manual" for their child with autism because the way that their child operates is clearly not the same as typically developing children. Parents need to be trained and supported as they learn to parent a child with autism. The involved parent becomes an informed consumer of therapies and therapists that work best and what strategies of their own are most effective. For a trained, informed parent, his or her child's development is no longer a roll of dice, but something the parent can control as much as possible. There is good reason to believe this filters down into less personal anxiety and depression, a better marriage or significant relationship, and a better family life for siblings.

Conclusions

Ways of addressing some of the political challenges that arise from having a child with autism are rooted in lack of information or a misunderstanding of what the disorder is, what can be done about it, and what happens to people with autism when they grow up. This is a problem that, I would argue, is best addressed from the grassroots. The grassroots are the parents of children with autism, making sure, from the day their child receives a diagnosis, there are strong educational supports to help them understand the disorder, what can be done about it, and what their own role in their child's habilitation can be. This is identical to saying that a newly diagnosed cancer patient needs quickly to learn about his or her disease process, treatment alternatives, prognoses associated with each kind of treatment, as well as what medical insurance will pay for and the social safety net that may provide work leave, disability insurance, and so on. As a society, we have come to better terms with the politics of cancer, as a potentially life-threatening physical disease, than we have with autism or other conditions that threaten the lifelong integrity of our children.

Social Policy Recommendations

Beginning in this chapter, and in each subsequent chapter, I provide social policy recommendations that stem from the chapter's content. For me, these provide a venue to say what we might do about problems I've highlighted, making constructive the critique I've offered. The social policy changes discussed in this chapter include (1) the need for parent training and (2) the need for better family leave policies to help parents who are trying to help their children.

RECOMMENDATION 1: TRAIN PARENTS TO BE ACTIVE AGENTS OF THEIR CHILD'S HABILITATION

Research clearly shows that parents who read to their children, take them to the library, talk to them over dinner, and take them to museums and cultural events have children who do better in school than children who come from families who watch TV through dinner or each plug into their electronic device of choice. The same is true for children with autism, only parents need to learn how to reach them differently if they are to provide a comparably rich upbringing. The observation that the child with autism does not seem able to learn the same as siblings, cousins, or neighbors is what typically leads parents to have their child evaluated in the first place.

In this vein, research such as the JASPER program at the University of California at Los Angeles (UCLA)[5] or PRT parent training at the University of California at Santa Barbara[6] provides great examples of how parents of children with autism who are taught to understand and work with their children themselves have kids who do better and also do better themselves (are less depressed, less anxious, possibly less vulnerable to quackery). One of my own current clinical efforts is a parent training program called JumpStart—Learning to Learn.[7] Parent training may focus on social skills, communication, behavior, or all of these, but it is a new direction in autism treatment.

Interestingly, applied behavior analysis (ABA) programs (one-to-one behavior modification for autism that I critique in detail in Chapter 4), which are now the single most costly element in autism treatment, began with the work of Dr. Ivar Lovaas—and actually included parent training. When Lovaas first founded a treatment program based on his research, he initially required one parent (over the course of the child's first year of treatment) to become their child's senior interventionist and program manager. There were no commercially available ABA programs in the 1980s as there are now, so this was practical, but more important, the parent involved in the ABA home program knew exactly what the child was learning, how well the child knew it, and what it took to elicit use of newly acquired knowledge. The synergistic effect of this was that when the mother, as lead interventionist, took her child for needed grocery shopping after a daylong intervention program, she would quite naturally prompt the child to label colors of canned goods (if the child had been learning colors) or to point out vegetables (if learning words for foods) or ask the child to verbalize yes/no choices when she came to the breakfast cereal isle. The mother was part of the intervention team, so she knew just how to orient the child's attention and how much to prompt and was sure to reward a correct answer.

This essential ingredient, teaching the parent how to be integral to his or her child's ability to progress (and requiring it), has largely been lost from home-based ABA today, as well as from special education. Instead, parents "help" their child by spending much time driving from intervention to intervention, on the phone fighting with insurance companies, making appointments for assessment after assessment that may not yield further direction for treatments, preparing for meetings with schools, and then fighting with schools when they are anxious that what has been offered is wrong or not enough. Preparing parents to be integral to their child's learning, in the style of late 1980s ABA programs, needs to be restored. A child's parent is not uniquely qualified to be his or her chauffer or secretary; rather, parents are uniquely qualified to know most about what their child can and can't do and what motivates the child.

Parents already lose much time from work just doing the work needed to organize school and therapy appointments. Often, the home ABA programs don't really know how to help parents actively collaborate with the rest of their intervention team; even such collaboration can add a unique voice. Sometimes there is the concern that the mother might want to do things her own way or might ask challenging questions about working with her child that the low-level "line staff" who provide 80 percent of ABA hours are not trained enough to answer. Truthfully, most often, schools don't want the parents around much either. So, many parents of children with autism have filed lawsuits that many special education directors can readily envision a parent visit as a lawyer-directed opportunity to gather data that can be turned into legal complaints. As a result, parents often are cut off from learning new ways to help their child through their children's therapists and schools. What can we be doing instead to ensure parents have the skills to help their children themselves during all the hours no therapists, tutors, or teachers are around? Even a child with 40 hours per week of therapies has another 40–50 hours per week awake, not in therapy, and in the charge of parents or other caregivers.

The Case for Parent Training

The key ingredients for high-quality parent training is that parents must receive individual instruction around *their* child—not come to generic autism training classes where they will be scared by hearing about children with problems more severe than their own or depressed to hear about children with fewer problems than their own. Children with autism are too different and families are too different for efficacy to be associated with such generic training—and experience with parent training programs supports this.

We need more programs that train parents, providing them with an individualized psychoeducation tailored to their own child. Parent training consultants can focus on developing parents' competencies in teaching through the activities of daily living, communication, and play that occur in all homes in the hours when there is no school or therapy. These staff have to be professional-level behaviorists, speech and language pathologists, play and social skills therapists, specialists who understand development and learning, not just entry-level technicians as in home-based ABA programs.

This type of individual parent training should be paid for by medical insurers or by state developmental service agencies just the way ABA programs are. When we consider bang for the buck and the very high cost of home ABA programs, parent training is a better economic value compared to the same dollars applied to more direct service from minimally trained ABA line staff. For example, a month of salary just for line staff in a 30-hour ABA program might cost $4,000. A full-time, week-long parent training program with one family, 1:1 with one professional at a time, might cost about the same. Parents who have been coached to apply behavioral, communication social skills, and play techniques that fit their child's developmental level can then fill in the 40–50 nontherapy hours each week with "teachable moments" that naturally immerse the child in wraparound learning.

Policy Concerns: Parents Have Rights—And Responsibilities

I have served as an expert in over 100 educational due process hearings about access to ABA for children with autism, appearing on whichever side I understood to best represent a plan in the best interest of the child. In one early hearing of this sort, in New York City, the public authority was to provide ABA but required the mother to do "line staff" work about 10 hours per week herself. The family, represented by the child's father, who was an attorney, argued that requiring his wife to work in the program was tantamount to slave labor. The research we have today that demonstrates the positive relationship between parent training and child outcomes did not yet exist, though we did know that children at the Lovaas Clinic at UCLA, where ABA for autism had started, required a parent to become a "senior therapist," who, while providing more therapy hours, also would learn a lot about how the child could learn. You can surmise from what I've said about parent training that I testified that this child would be better off if his mother *did* spend 10 hours per week working in her child's ABA program, just as the Lovaas Clinic parents had. I supported this parent having to take some personal responsibility for her child's progress, not mainly to save the state of New York the money, but because it could be expected to be linked to a more immersive learning experience that her child could then have in nontherapy hours.

From the start of special education planning for a child with any learning difference, educators provide parents with a written copy of their rights under the Individuals With Disabilities Education Act (IDEA) prior to every individualized education program (IEP) meeting and review it with them. Parents sign that they have received it and understand their rights.

What about parental responsibilities? Under any updates to IDEA, there should be consideration that parents receive either parent training in their child's disability (not only autism, but also think of parents of deaf children) or learn through classroom volunteering or participating in supervised education sessions with school staff, the child, and a parent. We know from research that generalization of taught material will be broader if parents are able to provide practice and reinforcement of new skills outside the school day. Let's put something "special" into special education and define responsibilities as well as rights for parents since parent involvement is correlated with better outcomes.

Create Mentorship Roles Between Teacher and Parent

Individualized parent training can serve as an "operating manual" for parents of a child newly diagnosed with autism. However, learning how to support their child's development becomes a task for parents throughout the child's school years. Attracting teachers to special education can be challenging. Keeping trained teachers in place is another challenge. One problem is that teachers trying their best can feel unduly criticized by parents. When parents are critical of teachers, it may be they don't understand why things are done as they are. Teachers trying their best with too few staff, or too many children, are less likely to have a good chance to show parents what they can do. It goes without saying we need more teachers, better paid teachers, more paraprofessional aides supporting those teachers, and better trained paraprofessionals.

Another approach to the need for both parent training and high-quality special education is to bring parents into the classroom as paraprofessional teachers. The familiar parent–co-op model used by preschools is a template: In a cooperative preschool, parents help where the teacher directs them. In a special education program, as with a paid para professional aide, the teacher should be responsible for on-the-job-type training of a parent serving as a paraprofessional. The result of such a relationship can be the parent learning more about teaching children with autism, learning skills that can be taken home to further teach their own child, and maybe even new respect for the their child's teacher as a trained professional.

Conceivably, some such positions could be paid ones as schools chronically lack a pool of qualified paraprofessionals, and this might be helpful to lower income families where the caregiving parent is losing the opportunity to earn a living by spending time with his or her child with autism. Since the basic qualifications for being a paraprofessional aide in a public school classroom are so low, a parent, just by virtue of parenting experience, could scarcely be less qualified than most other paid paraprofessional aides. The aims of any program to bring parents into classrooms should be to educate the parent in how his or her child can learn, as well as to build a culture of more collaborative relating between parents and teachers.

This model for a child's teacher to also be the parents' teacher is obviously a fit for the early years of intervention and education. The early years are where a parent's foundation for understanding autism is laid; well laid, it can continue to guide parents as their child's decision-makers.

RECOMMENDATION 2: REVISE THE FAMILY MEDICAL LEAVE ACT FOR FAMILIES LIVING WITH AUTISM

Parents Need Time to Help Their Child With Autism or Disability

Mothers who qualify to receive public assistance may get additional Supplemental Security Income (SSI) for a child with a disability and may also get an exemption from welfare-to-work obligations. This is one case where the economically disadvantaged parent has some advantage over the working parent. When a typical nonindigent, two-earner, working-class family has a child with a significant disability, the family may expect to take on more debt because of the lost income of the caregiving parent. In addition to direct loss of income from not being able to work, many family leave policies under the minimal US federal Family and Medical Leave Act (FMLA)[8,9] are guaranteed only unpaid leave. American family leave policy is a dinosaur left from the age of fathers as the sole wage earner. Lack of consideration for the time it takes to parent a child with a developmental disability like autism is dwarfed by the lack of federal support to all families with young children.

Becoming a part-time worker in order to care for a disabled child plus coordinate and participate in the child's services may also limit future income growth because part-timers generally do not advance as quickly as full-time workers.[10,11] In addition to passive income loss from not being able to work, families of children with autism spend money directly on therapies that require copayments and therapies not readily covered by public education or medical insurance—even when some clearly are evidence-based treatments.

First, it is shameful that the United States stands out as a modern, Western society that does not universally require employers to provide paid leave at the birth of a child. The current FMLA that guarantees 12 weeks of unpaid leave is both too short and too costly for many parents to access as it is. It is even less supportive of families facing the extra time and cost of a child with autism or any developmental disorder that only will be diagnosed long after birth leave has been used.

The FMLA should support ongoing paid leave with federal subsidy, not employer burden alone. By developing a program that would give parents of some children small amounts of time off from work on certain days each week for specific and limited periods of time, we could create opportunities to increase the gains made across special schools and therapies, as well as help parents develop needed special skills of their own to foster their child's development. Such leave would need to be carefully tied to actual time a parent needs to access treatment or partner with treatment providers.

For example, think about a parent who needs to leave work at 4:00 p.m. rather than 5:00 p.m. to take his or her child to speech therapy, observe the speech therapy session, and meet with the therapist to learn techniques to practice at home until the child's next visit. We know that follow-through on speech therapy goals multiplies its effectiveness over the benefit accrued from the session itself—much like when you or I might go to physical therapy for a sports injury. Opportunities for outside practice of newly taught skills are critical. As a parent learns to provide this bridging care, it is almost a given that the new teaching skills will be used with the child in other situations at home. As another example, think of the parent with a child with a home ABA program each afternoon who comes home in time to touch base with program staff and maybe even has time to try out home applications of the therapeutic strategies they are using. That parent can start to use skills so that the child can make meal choices instead of throwing a tantrum until he or she gets what he or she wants. When parents learn to use therapeutic techniques—and can see them making their lives easier—the most challenging times at home can become teachable moments.

What I do not envision is FMLA funds to take a child to soccer practice because it is probably good for his social skills (as it is for all typically developing children) or for full-time pay for part-time employment of a parent who would prefer to pick their teen up after school and bring the teen home rather than enrolling him or her in nontherapeutic after-school care or study hall. The after-school care may likely not be therapeutic, but it also may likely not be detrimental. We need parental leave that allows the child's day to be construed in his or her best interest given the disability, but not function as a pension for the child's parent.

Notes

1. Peters, J. W. (2016, December 26). Wielding claims of "fake news," conservatives take aim at mainstream media. *The New York Times.* Retrieved from https://www.nytimes.com/2016/12/25/us/politics/fake-news-claims-conservatives-mainstream-media-.html

2. Douthat, R. (2016, May 21). Facebook's subtle empire. *The New York Times.* Retrieved from http://www.nytimes.com/2016/05/22/opinion/sunday/facebooks-subtle-empire.html

3. Singal, J. (2016, May 9). John Oliver took on junk science on *Last Week Tonight,* and it was great. *New York Magazine.* Retrieved from https://www.thecut.com/2016/05/john-oliver-took-on-junk-science-last-night-and-it-was-glorious.html

4. A. J. Drexel Autism Institute. (n.d.). *National autism indicators report series.* Retrieved from http://drexel.edu/autisminstitute/research-projects/research/ResearchProgr aminLifeCourseOutcomes/IndicatorsReport/#sthash.WqMvOWCQ.dpuf

5. KasariLab. (n.d.). *JASPER.* Retrieved from http://www.kasarilab.org/treatments/jasper/

6. Gevirtz School, Graduate School of Education, University of California at Santa Barbara. (n.d.). *Pivotal response treatment.* Retrieved from https://education.ucsb.edu/autism/pivotal-response-treatment

7. Siegel, B., & Bernard, A. (2009). JumpStart Learning-to-Learn: First intervention and training parents to promote generalization of children's early interventions. In C. Whalen (Ed.), *Real life, real progress for children with autism spectrum disorders: Strategies for successful generalization in natural environments* (pp. 149–172). Baltimore, MD: Brookes.

8. Wage and Hour Division (WHD), US Department of Labor. (n.d.). *Family and Medical Leave Act.* Retrieved September 15, 2016, from https://www.dol.gov/whd/fmla/

9. US Department of Labor. (2015, December 9). *FMLA (Family & Medical Leave).* Retrieved September 15, 2016, from https://www.dol.gov/general/topic/benefits-leave/fmla

10. Leigh, J. P., & Du, J. (2015). Brief report: Forecasting the economic burden of autism in 2015 and 2025 in the United States. *Journal of Autism and Developmental Disorders, 45*(12), 4135–4139. http://doi.org/10.1007/s10803-015-2521-7

11. Buescher, A. S., Cidav, Z., Knapp, M., & Mandell, D. S. (2014). Costs of autism spectrum disorders in the United Kingdom and the United States. *JAMA Pediatrics, 168*(8), 721–728. http://doi.org/10.1001/jamapediatrics.2014.210

2 }

The Politics of Autism Diagnosis

Is There More Autism?

After I'm asked "What kind of work do you do?" the next question invariably is "Do you really think there's more autism than there used to be?" This question can be answered as "Yes," "Maybe," or even "No." Where you stand on whether there is more autism these days depends on where your interests are vested, your "read" of the data, and which data you read. This is true, however, not only of autism prevalence, but also of many aspects of autism a person may "research" on the Internet. Ask the right question until you get the right answer. By this I mean that there are websites attributing the rise in autism to all sorts of causes—most of them unproven, most often not even linked to any causal mechanism. Even genes linked to autism account for a small percentage of cases (about 15 percent),[1] and work on how they cause autism is speculative.

Figure 2.1 indicates the data concerning how many more cases of autism have been diagnosed each year between 1996 and 2007.[2] The most up-to-date data are reported periodically by ADDMN (Autism and Developmental Disabilities Monitoring Network), with 2016 data being the most recent. The good news is that there is no evidence that some unseen pathogen is causing this. The bad news is that the rise in incidence is poorly understood, and there are all sorts of speculative explanations. This is what we'll explore in this chapter.

You may be able to think of a child, teen, or adult you have known who you learn has just been given an autism diagnosis, or maybe you have heard the child is "on the spectrum" or has Asperger's syndrome. It may be someone you did think had "problems"; it may be someone you considered just shy, anxious, or awkward.

There clearly are many more cases of autism diagnosed now than 10, 20, or 30 years ago. In this chapter, I'll explore the politics of an autism diagnosis: shifting diagnostic boundaries, changing diagnostic practices, increasing public "autism awareness," and increased service access with an autism

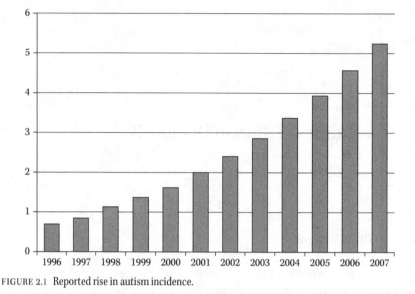

FIGURE 2.1 Reported rise in autism incidence.

diagnosis. The factors I'll discuss here are the nonbiological ones. Unproven biological or environmental factors that have been considered include vaccines (discussed in Chapter 8), interactions between genes and environment (epigenetic factors), and teratogens in our air, water, or food. To date, none have been confirmed to raise the incidence of autism, though there are a number of folks out there looking.[3]

"Autism" Over the Years

I'll start with three graphic figures designed to show that what "autism" encompasses has changed: These figures lay out concepts I'll introduce in this chapter and will return to and elaborate throughout this book. Figure 2.1 shows that what is meant by "autism" has changed in the last 30 or so years. For one thing, there is a widening definition with an increasing number of associated new descriptive terms. In the early 1980s, autism was a diagnosis mainly given in university medical centers, often referenced back to the early cases described by Dr. Leo Kanner, who used the term *early infantile autism*. By this, Kanner meant that many of the children he had grouped under this term had an air of aloneness and self-absorption, not unlike the early infantile period where the infant is basically self-contained until a smile, tickle, or some other strong sensory or social stimulus catches the infant's attention. Initially, Kanner said little about whether these children also had intellectual disability (then called mental retardation), but he did note "islets of preserved functioning"—some things these children could do well despite not doing other things that were developmentally comparable. In the 1970s and 1980s, it was realized that some children with at least a few Kannerian symptoms were primarily disabled by their intellectual disability (e.g., not being able to talk was more of a handicap than hand-flapping) and were often termed *mentally retarded with autistic features* (Figure 2.2), a term that has fallen completely from use. We still, though, have children with autistic signs who also meet criteria for intellectual disability on IQ tests. The link between autism and intellectual disability is no longer "popular" however: Presently, the American Academy of Pediatrics propounds use of the term *global developmental delay*, rather than *intellectual disability*, if a child is under age 6 and showing signs of being significantly behind others the same age. Most American children who receive autism diagnoses do so before age 6, so intellectual disability, if it is present, often is never counted in.

By the late 1980s, the *Diagnostic and Statistical Manual of Mental Disorders* (3rd ed., rev.; *DSM-III-R*)[4] had been published and used the new term *pervasive developmental disorder* (PDD) to refer to the fact that there were many children who had some but not all signs of autism. This seeded the "autism spectrum" concept and parenthetically ended talk of "autistic features" in those arguably most handicapped by their intellectual disability. These children could now accurately be described as "PDD." This was just one "flavor" of PDD; other variants encompassed symptoms of other neurodevelopmental

Widening Autism Diagnosis "Circle" and "Autism First" Diagnosing

→ 1980s
Rarefied group diagnosed mainly in academic medical centers = Narrowly defined

→ 1990s
Autism = "spectrum" + mentally retarded with "autistic features"
= either Autistic disorder or PDD, NOS

2000s →
Some autism + anxious, or avoidant, or under-/poorly socialized with a touch of "neuroatypicality," e.g., learning disorder, ADHD, borderline IQ, "sensory processing disorder"
= Autism spectrum disorder

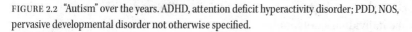

FIGURE 2.2 "Autism" over the years. ADHD, attention deficit hyperactivity disorder; PDD, NOS, pervasive developmental disorder not otherwise specified.

conditions: After *DSM-III-R*, reported autism incidence continued to rise, as the numbers and types of associated symptoms, including features of language disorders, attention deficit disorder, learning disorders, and sensory processing problems were noted in children with autistic features now classifiable as PDD. As each new associated symptom was noted, at times, to also occur in children with autism, more children with these associated symptoms (language problems, learning problems, etc.) became more likely to be counted as belonging on the "autism spectrum." Increasingly, if a child was seen as having both a language problem and autism, arbitrarily autism would more likely be designated as their first diagnosis. This might help the child receive more services.

There was another big reason autism would be labeled first: Autism symptoms may or may not co-occur with intellectual disability—which was a label more dreaded than autism. PDD in *DSM-III-R* did not imply intellectual disability the way "mentally retarded with autistic features" did, as was common during use of *DSM-III*. Diagnosing autism first (under age 6) and global developmental delay second in the youngest children tended to obviate consideration of intellectual impairment—though that diagnosis could be established by the time the child was 5 or 6. Why would parents return to their diagnosing clinician when the child was 5 or 6 years old to ask if autism was the wrong primary diagnosis and intellectual disability was the right one instead? It didn't happen.

A downside of assigning autism as the primary diagnosis was then, and continues today, to not only steer away from the consideration of intellectual disability, but also steer away from the consideration of other things that may need different or additional treatment. These may include significant difficulties with attention, learning, and language that may need different or additional treatments than what the child receives with "only" an autism diagnosis.

As autism has become a preferred diagnostic label, the deficits conferred by other developmental delays and by intellectual disability basically have been subsumed as part of an autism spectrum disorder (ASD). Figure 2.3, for example, shows how between just 2011 and 2013 and then 2014 the increase in ASD was approximately the same as the decrease in cases of intellectual disability and of other developmental disorders.[5] There is no reason for these other conditions to have declined. The most parsimonious explanation is that individuals in such cases were increasingly diagnosed as having autism (Figure 2.3).[5]

THE "SPECTRUM" AND INCREASED "AWARENESS"

Figure 2.4 focuses on how many children were given the diagnosis of autism over the last 30 or so years simply through changes in terminology, measurement, and a social destigmatization of "autism" as it was increasingly disassociated with comorbid (co-occurring) intellectual disability and other conditions that limit the individual's potential.

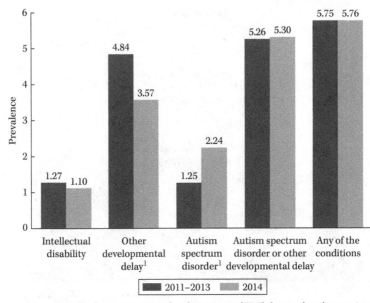

FIGURE 2.3 Using Centers for Disease Control and Prevention (CDC) data to show how autism became a preferred diagnosis. [1] Indicates a statistically significant difference ($p > .001$) between 2011–2013 and 2014.

Source: Zablotsky, B., Black, L. I., Maenner, M. J., Schieve, L. A., & Blumberg, S. J. (2015, November 13). *Estimated prevalence of autism and other developmental disabilities following questionnaire changes in the 2014 National Health Interview Survey*. National Health Statistics Reports No. 87. Retrieved from https://pdfs.semanticscholar.org/92c2/2987bdb4397ef53b8e2b0b8a7bda432a0900.pdf

A label such as "autism" is phenomenological. The more autism that has been reported, the more autism has been the diagnosis considered first. In the 1980s, almost all children with autism I met had been tested for hearing loss first. This is because in the 1980s, more children were reported to have hearing loss than autism. As popular awareness of autism has grown, more early difficulties are considered features of autism, although early failure to talk, for example, can be due to a range of minor to major things: a short frenulum ("tongue tied"), an ear infection, a language disorder, a hearing loss, or intellectual disability. Increasingly, however, parents now quickly associate delayed language with autism and take their 18-month-olds to their pediatricians and ask about autism rather than any of these other conditions.

Sometimes, the diagnosis is a matter of "seek and ye shall find": The typically developing child who hand-flaps when mad, doesn't like long sleeves, loves Thomas the Tank Engine, or has a preference to brush teeth *after* getting in pajamas suddenly can look suspiciously autistic. Isn't this love of Thomas a "narrow interest"? Isn't that bedtime routine an example of "inflexible adherence" to a routine? These otherwise-benign 2- and 3-year-old behaviors readily become part of the autism symptom count. Woe be it to the 2- or 3-year-old who is very shy of the diagnosing clinician, looks down, and refuses to speak

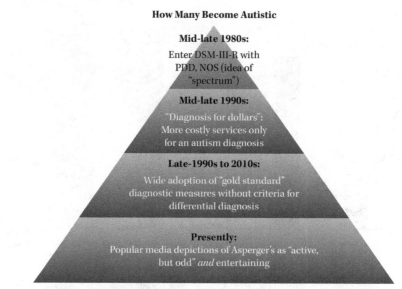

How Many Become Autistic

Mid-late 1980s:
Enter DSM-III-R with
PDD, NOS (idea of
"spectrum")

Mid-late 1990s:
"Diagnosis for dollars":
More costly services only
for an autism diagnosis

Late-1990s to 2010s:
Wide adoption of "gold standard"
diagnostic measures without criteria for
differential diagnosis

Presently:
Popular media depictions of Asperger's as "active,
but odd" *and* entertaining

FIGURE 2.4 The "spectrum," the Autism Diagnostic Observation Schedule (ADOS), and increased "awareness." DSM-III-R, *Diagnostic and Statistical Manual of Mental Disorders* (3rd ed., rev.); PDD, NOS, pervasive developmental disorder not otherwise specified.

when spoken to or is upset because the autism examination is taking place in the same room where he has received many shots. I can tell you I have seen many such children diagnosed with autism or deemed "at least" to be "on the spectrum."

"PIE CHART" CHILDREN

The next problem is what I call "pie chart" children: While some individuals clearly are challenged by symptoms of autism first and foremost, or even exclusively, many, many more have additional difficulties more closely allied with one or more other neurodevelopmental or behavioral diagnoses. Arguing which of several diagnoses is really more fitting, which is second most fitting, and so on can be similar to counting angels on the head of a pin. More important, when autism alone is the assigned diagnosis in a pie chart child, there can be failure to develop comprehensive plans to treat all that child's difficulties. Figure 2.5 shows some of the other comorbid conditions not infrequently seen with autism. Parents of such children often encounter obfuscation, going from one diagnostic center to another, with each concluding the child *does* have features of the condition in which they specialize, often implying early diagnosticians missed the boat.

If a slice of that child's pie is autism, it is often the preferred diagnosis for seeking services, widely associated with a higher level of treatment. A final word on autistic pie chart children: They not infrequently grow up to be pie chart adults, with the autism slice of the pie sometimes only first identified in

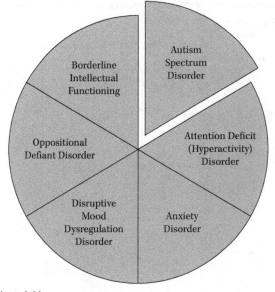

FIGURE 2.5 Pie chart children.

adulthood if earlier diagnoses date from when autism was not yet seen as a spectrum disorder (Figure 2.5).

AUTISM IS INCREASING

Yes, there are data to support that there are more cases of autism than there used to be. The changes I have just explained have to do with historical trends in diagnostic practices, changing diagnostic terminology, and how autism's comorbid signs and symptoms and their presence in other disorders some-times result in that individual, epidemiologically speaking, being counted in as autistic. Data from the Autism and Developmental Disabilities Monitoring (ADDM) Network show that counts of autism have increased from 1:150 in 2000 to 1:68 in 2012 (Table 2.1).[6]

"DIAGNOSING FOR DOLLARS"

Not only is there more autism, but also there are, largely, better early interven-tion provisions specifically for autism in toddlers and preschoolers. There are also more autism-specific school programs for school-aged children. Autism definitely is a growth industry. I even receive calls from investment bankers from time to time, asking me if autism is the type of growth industry where they should be figuring out how to invest.

Increased service provision is often tied to getting a bona fide diagnosis of autism first. This phenomenon can be thought of as "diagnosing for dollars,"

TABLE 2.1 } Autism Prevalence: Identified Prevalence of Autism Spectrum Disorder, ADDM Network 2000–2012, Combining Data From All Sites

Surveillance Year	Birth Year	Number of ADDM Sites Reporting	Prevalence per 1,000 Children (Range)	This is about 1 in X children ...
2000	1992	6	6.7 (4.5–9.9)	1 in 150
2002	1994	14	6.6 (3.3–10.6)	1 in 150
2004	1996	8	8.0 (4.6–9.8)	1 in 125
2006	1998	11	9.0 (4.2–12.1)	1 in 110
2008	2000	14	11.3 (4.8–21.2)	1 in 88
2010	2002	11	14.7 (5.7–21.9)	1 in 68
2012	2004	11	14.6 (8.2–24.6)	1 in 68

ADDM, Autism and Developmental Disabilities Monitoring.

a result of political pressure to count difficulties as "disorders" in order to get (paid for) help with those difficulties.

Autism has become such a talked-about diagnosis, and has so many powerful advocates, that it has accrued more funding for treatment than its Cinderella sisters—intellectual disability, language disorders, learning disabilities, or even attention deficit hyperactivity disorder (ADHD). If you want a high level of service for a child, a high per pupil expenditure (PPE) in school, autism is the diagnosis you will want. So, is this *also* driving diagnostic rates?

ARE THERE BIOLOGICAL FACTORS CONTRIBUTING TO A RISE IN AUTISM?

The sociological and political reasons for more autism are my focus here, but there are a few factors it would be remiss not to also mention to round out the picture of rising autism rates: First, increases in all developmental disorders—autism included—with increased maternal and paternal age at the child's birth. The Centers for Disease Control and Prevention's (CDC's) National Health Statistics show that age at first pregnancy has increased by 5 years in the last 45 years. Across ethnicities, the biggest increase in first-time pregnancies is to women over 35 years old. This means, of course, that a mom who was 35 or older when she had her first child was even older than that at the birth of any subsequent children.[6]

Second, information from large population studies in Scandinavia suggested there is an additive autism risk in those using in vitro fertilization, which, let's face it, is designed to counter natural selection. Many healthy babies are born from in vitro pregnancies, of course, but there appears to be some small increased risk, possibly from in vitro procedures that select sperm (intracytoplasmic sperm injection, ICSI) that would not have made it under their own steam.[7]

AUTISM AS A WANTED DIAGNOSIS

How can autism be a wanted diagnosis? Recently, a 13-year-old boy from a monolingual non–English-speaking family was sent to my center for a reexamination of his autism diagnosis. He hadn't been evaluated since his original autism diagnosis at age 2½ years, when he was clearly language-delayed and very anxious. The examiner who had seen him at 2½ years old had speculated he *might* just have a language delay, but because of the boy's anxiety, rendering him especially fearful of his English-speaking examiner, and because he was not yet speaking, this examiner decided to call what she saw autism, noting the picture might "clarify" as he received services and developed language. At 13, this boy was bilingual, speaking well, and relating well in both English and his first language. He genuinely seemed to enjoy his assessment, readily asked and answered questions, asked his examiners about themselves and their interests, and gave no impression of autism. What had come to pass was what the original examiner had speculated—that with the development of language, this young man would become better socially adjusted. The assessment team concluded he did not currently meet criteria for autism, but still did have anxiety, as well as a mild intellectually disability. We told the mother he no longer met criteria for autism, but rather was being held back by his slower ability to learn and by his anxiety. The boy's mother, through an interpreter, expressed that she was clearly disappointed to hear we did not think he had autism any longer.

Don't you think this would be good news? Instead, it turned out that the boy's mother was concerned that he would lose various special education and developmental disabilities services for which he qualified. After being reassured he would not lose these—because he would continue to qualify based on his intellectual disability, she was somewhat reassured. When she and her son left for the day, our interpreter expressed puzzlement. She often also translates in our toddler parent training program and has seen, first-hand, how hard it is for parents of toddlers initially to accept their child has autism. "Why, then," she asked, "isn't this parent glad when you say you think he no longer has autism?" I told her this was pretty typical. Early age of first diagnosis, no rediagnosis after the child developed language, limited ability or opportunity for the parent and clinician to communicate clearly, and a parent's understanding that autism brings more help made "autism" the problem this mother had come to focus on as the name for *all* of her son's difficulties. The language interpreter had just identified a case of "diagnosing for dollars" in a parent concerned that removal of the autism diagnosis would result in removal of help for her son.

The diagnosis of autism has become associated with more services and more costly services than those for other childhood neuropsychiatric disorders.[8] Is this a good thing or a bad thing? Children should get access to evidence-based treatments. But what factors may distort fair distribution of treatment dollars and access to needed treatment resources?

NOT A LEVEL PLAYING FIELD

Diagnosis for dollars is not a game just anyone can play. There is an underclass of families with children with autism who still struggle to get help, even *with* an autism diagnosis. This is not just an economic inequality issue. There can be many reasons some families are unskilled and unsuccessful navigators of resources. Parent level of education, parent mental health, parent intelligence, and many family and cultural factors provide barriers: These families include some single parents, parents with many other children, some dealing with two or more children with autism, and some with unclear immigration status, fearful to call attention to themselves. These vulnerable families are often the most overwhelmed and immobilized by the weight of the autism diagnosis. Some are families with English as a second language (ESL), unacculturated non-Western families where guilt and shame at having a disabled child decrease their child's likelihood of service.

Personally, I want to make sure there are ways to help these families as much as there are ways to help the families with skillful, well-educated parents. I love nothing better than spending the day with an educated, well-informed, motivated, sensitive family with all the "right stuff" to help their child. I am less fond of parents who jockey for resources that both research and experiences make clear will unfortunately change little. Often, the squeaky wheel needs to get the grease. But being squeaky doesn't mean you are inherently right: The most costly program may not be the best program for every child. If the most costly program is not appropriate, it does not mean nothing else will help, though in American culture, it is pretty easy to assume that more, or more costly, is better, and that if it is being denied to your child, it is in your rights to experience it as a personal affront. I do try to be empathetic and remember what these parents must be feeling. I know such parents just want what is best for their child—though what was best for another child may not be best for theirs. They deserve to understand the research behind a "why not," rather than capitulation. While giving parents whatever they want can seem therapeutic, it can set a bad precedent. The real problem we face is that the resources we have to treat autism are not unlimited. How do we curtail diagnosing for dollars so that resources are fairly allocated?

WHY EARLY EDUCATION FOR AUTISM IS SO COSTLY

Autism has become the most costly developmental disorder. There are more special education "autism resources" than special education "ADHD resources." Further, the fields of education and medicine use different criteria to define *autism*, leading to an even broader and less well-defined understanding and further confusion about who can and should access autism services.[8,9] There are more autism resources than therapeutic supports for the shy, anxious, or slow-to-warm child. If your child has a language delay, there is speech therapy. If your child has a language delay and has autism there is speech therapy—and much more. Some families will say there is more hope if your child has autism than if the child has intellectual disability—although many children with autism have both, and parents may speak of only autism and not the intellectual disability. The diagnosis of an ASD, wielded well, is the ticket to a lot of help. So, if you had a child with a difficulty that anyone had suggested might be autism, why wouldn't you want to try to go with that?

AUTISM SERVICES IF A CHILD DOES NOT HAVE AUTISM

One difficulty we face is that if a child does not have autism, would it hurt for that child to receive certain forms of autism help anyway? My position is that pushing for an autism diagnosis to receive more services "just in case" is harmful because sometimes such parents actually end up believing their child has autism and telling their child he or she has autism when the child does not. Then we are dealing with a child whom others may see as more handicapped than he or she is. This may seem like an unlikely scenario, but it is not.

How does access to services that may not be needed occur? This can easily happen when a young child has a few signs of autism (which may just as likely be due to another diagnosis), like limited, repetitive language or hand-flapping, but a parent or even a clinician is aware that much more help will be forthcoming with the autism diagnosis in place. The conundrum is that if the nonautistic-in-the-first-place child improves with autism services, it is very unlikely anyone involved in helping the child will believe improvement would have been comparable without autism services. This is not to say anything bad about that child's parents, the therapists, or the recommender of the service in question. Getting better while receiving treatments that may be unneeded is, some might argue, what the whole vitamin industry, antiaging cosmetics industry, and GMO (genetically modified organism) food industry is all about. But what if these things *have* helped? There is virtually no way to know from a single case.

"DIAGNOSING NORMAL"

In the next chapter, I talk about some of the ways in which we, as a society, seem to want to diagnose "normal"—as posited by psychiatrist Dr. Alan Frances, who headed the development of the American Psychiatric Association's (APA's) fourth edition of the *DSM* (*DSM-IV*),[10] which provided the version of psychiatric diagnoses in place from 1994 to 2013. As you let your fingers do the walking through the *DSM*, all sorts of innocent behavior can seem "not so normal." Such not-so-normal behavior can be viewed as just harmless, or even amusing, quirks. Exactly how much eye contact is not enough? (When does it become "lack of nonverbal communication"?) If you are a 3-year-old boy, can you be too interested in Thomas the Tank Engine? (Is it a "narrow interest" if you reject Brio trains in favor of Thomas and his friends?) Is it the sign of a disorder ("a ritual") if you insist on buttering your bread before you toast it, or is it just a quirk (Box 2.1)?

A number of years ago, a set of satirical diagnostic criteria for a disorder titled "diagnosis of childhood" circulated among many of us concerned that the APA's diagnostic criteria might be too inclusive of normal aspects of child development, and that this might lead to overdiagnosis not only of autism, but also of any number of psychiatric disorders first evident in childhood. The criteria for diagnosis of childhood were structured to look like diagnostic criteria for any psychiatric disorder in the *DSM*, with mandatory, alternate,

BOX 2.1 } Diagnostic Criteria for Childhood (Satirical)

A. Individuals meeting diagnostic criteria for Childhood must be below age 10, with onset of symptoms frequently reported from the earliest years. If comparable symptoms are present in an individual between ages 11 and 18 years, the diagnosis of Adolescence should be strongly considered.

B. At least 4 of the following 6 symptoms must be present (at least 2 from I and 1 from II): Classically, symptoms are easily observed across most settings where the individual socializes, though symptoms are often reported to occur with greatest frequency in the individual's home environment.

I. Social:

1. Marked and rapid mood swings in response to minor antecedents (may go from crying to giggling in seconds).
2. Irritable temperament, especially with familiar adults.
3. Frequently makes irrational demands of caregivers.
4. Egocentric thinking marked by either
   a. Frequent refusals (e.g., "No!") of suggestions of others, especially authority figures.
   b. Uncontrolled emotional outbursts if contradicted.

II. Somatic:

1. Small physical stature.
2. Frequent refusal of unfamiliar foods.[a]
3. Hypomanic denial of need for sleep.

[a] A food challenge may be employed, and bulimic symptoms secondary to challenge can be considered confirmatory of this symptom.

---

and affiliated signs. I frequently used this slide in my course on typical child development taught to child psychiatry residents.

Increasingly, we, as a psychiatric disorder–consuming public, are seeing many quirks as positive signs of the presence of some disorder or other— whether or not these quirks confer impairment in day-to-day living for that quirky individual. How often do ideas like "diagnosing normal" and "quirks equal symptoms" play into diagnosing ASDs? How broadly or narrowly should each individual criterion for autism or any other disorder be interpreted? Does the subjectivity of judging "how much is OK" cut into what little science of diagnosis there is? Does it open the diagnostic process to evaluate a fairly normal or slightly quirky behavior as abnormal to open the door to giving help that will be only available *with* an autism diagnosis, not without it?

BOUNDARIES OF NEUROTYPICALITY

Subjectivity in diagnosis has become an increasing issue as the autism spectrum has grown broader: One big step in this direction was in 1994, when *DSM-IV* added, for the first time, a separate PDD diagnosis of Asperger's disorder, characterized, more or less, as autism without verbal intellectual disability. Quickly, there arose a group of normally intelligent, or intellectually gifted, individuals now diagnosed under the *DSM-IV* as having this new condition of Asperger's disorder. Intelligent "Aspies" not infrequently acclaimed their lack of neurotypicality as a form of superiority. However, many Aspies want it both ways: They want Asperger's acknowledged as a disorder, too—if it's needed as a back pocket note to request extra time on tests, accommodations in the workplace, or an explanation for why their verbosity should not be judged as boorish behavior. Every year I meet more and more people who refer to themselves as having Asperger's disorder or talk matter-of-factly about this relative or that friend who has Asperger's. If I ask where the individual was diagnosed, the answer is usually that the diagnosis is simply well understood, much like saying someone is depressed or bipolar.

WHERE DOES THE SPECTRUM END?

As signs of the autism spectrum have come to be visualized in the more mildly impaired and in more normally intelligent people, the diagnosis gets easier and easier to be seen in behavior previously understood to be within normal limits, though marking a particularly quirky, colorful, or difficult personality. Social insensitivity, through a clinical lens, may be seen as "lack of social reciprocity." It becomes quite possible to construe boorishness as a "social-pragmatic communication disorder" (a diagnostically close cousin of the autism spectrum in *DSM-5*) marked by an inability to understand rules of conversation.

An individual beset by an interest shared by relatively few others can readily be seen as meeting criteria for having a "narrow" or "obsessive" preoccupation. Franklin Delano Roosevelt was a stamp collector, a philatelist. Is it a sign of Asperger's disorder that his biographers should now ponder? When can we agree that some individuals with such traits are "neurotypical"—or should we just go ahead and say they are on the spectrum? What if these traits are benign (stamps only collected in private)? What if these traits annoy others (the individual talks about his stamp collection despite lack of interest from listeners), but his collecting does not confer adaptive dysfunction (e.g., success as president of the United States)? Can we then be dealing with a diagnosable psychiatric disorder? As autism has become viewed as a spectrum disorder, we have basically failed to characterize a point beyond which we are, in Dr. Alan Francis's words, "diagnosing normal."

It's not just autism: Problems with agreement recognizing boundaries below which an individual does not have a psychiatric disorder are intrinsic to the subjective nature of psychiatric diagnosis. These problems are endemic to diagnosing childhood psychiatric disorders where *delays* in one aspect of development can readily be mistaken for *atypicality*, especially if these delays affect functioning in another domain. For example, a boy with language delays may not respond readily when addressed by a peer on the playground because he can't summon a verbal reply, not because he is uninterested in joining in. When is a very, very active 5-year-old boy considered really energetic, and when might his teacher refer him for assessment for ADHD? In psychiatry, we often deal with continuously distributed variables: Picture a bell curve representing the activity level of one hundred 5-year-old boys, each wearing a pedometer for a week. The data may well not show a distinct second, smaller "bell" to the right of the main one—meaning the child with ADHD may not be "off the charts" but rather just on the far end of a normal distribution. So, would it be OK just to call the top 10 most active kids as "at risk" for ADHD—because ADHD is reported in 10 percent of American boys?

The same is true for autism. The prevalence of 1:68 is often cited as the rate of ASDs in the population. If we have 680 children, should we identify the 10 quirkiest ones and classify them as at risk for autism? That is essentially what has happened with how the public has come to view autism and other childhood neuropsychiatric disorders.

DIAGNOSTIC OVERSHADOWING AND INCREASED AUTISM PREVALENCE

How do these issues play out when it comes to assessing a child (or an adult) for a possible form of autism? When is it autism? When is it something else? When do we call a quirk, a quirk? When is it nothing? When (as with the early diagnosis of autism) is what we are seeing just a transitory developmental delay in language or social development? When might it be something else that calls for very different interventions than those for autism—like a reactive attachment disorder in an ex-preemie who, on top of his birth delays, is not cared for very consistently by his drug-using mom? The help she will need to be a successful parent is very different from what a parent of a comparably aged child with autism likely needs, though both babies may be reported to cry inconsolably and be angry if picked up when it is not wanted.

On top of ASDs getting confused with behavior that may be due to a different problem or even may be within normal limits, there is the problem of children who may actually have more than one psychiatric diagnosis. When should one diagnosis, like that of an ASD, come first? Always? What if other conditions, such as the child's level of hyperactivity, seem even more impairing for the child than the child's autism—should that be diagnosed first? By saying what comes "first" or "second"—or even "third," or "fourth," I am talking about the pie chart children in Figure 2.5 of this chapter. Does it matter etiologically or, even more importantly, in terms of the treatments the child will need which diagnosis comes "first?"

This has been a big battleground in psychiatry. Not everyone has agreed, but the diagnosing manual from the APA (the *DSM*) has made rules about what can be diagnosed with what as a way of (at least as they see it) defining who can be in which studies, get which drugs, and get which services. During the 1994–2013 sovereignty of *DSM-IV*, ADHD was *not* to be diagnosed along with any ASD—period. That's what the manual said. Many clinicians nevertheless "voted their conscience" and would diagnose both when presented with a very hyperactive, highly distractible child with autism. Neither hyperactivity nor distractibility are diagnostic features of autism. Diagnosing autism might help this child get a one-to-one aide in school or get placed in a smaller class with a more experienced teacher trained in special classroom supports. However, diagnosing ADHD instead would likely result in neither of those. With ADHD as the primary or only diagnosis, that child might only be allowed the dispensation of sitting in the front of the class, staying close to the teacher as an "accommodation" to his or her inattention—but be given nothing to address the autism—because the rule book (the *DSM*) said the child could not have both.

Which do you think clinicians would diagnose? The answer is, probably autism. The autism classroom with more resources would be more likely able to call in a school psychologist who could come up with a plan to address hyperactivity and inattention. Did *DSM-IV* inadvertently help more children with features of both be seen as autistic because it was a pathway to more substantial service? What about primarily diagnosing an ASD when anxiety or a language problem appears as prominent as autism symptoms? I would argue that the habit of coding (diagnosing) autism first when features of many difficulties might be present was inadvertently promoted by the way *DSM-IV* imposed limits on what could be diagnosed at the same time rather than issuing more flexible criteria that acknowledged some children might experience multiple handicapping symptoms of several disorders simultaneously. The *DSM* is not inscribed on stone tablets, but more about that in the next chapter.

Interestingly, since the fifth edition of the *DSM* (*DSM-5*)[11] replaced *DSM-IV* in 2013, the restriction on diagnosing autism and ADHD in the same child has been removed; now, some studies have shown that as many as a third of cases meeting criteria for an ASD *also* meet criteria for ADHD. The term *diagnostic overshadowing* has been used to refer to when one diagnosis is considered more "important" for some reason, maybe more important because more costly services come with its assignation. In terms of treatment dollars, there is no question that autism overshadows any other childhood psychiatric diagnosis that can assigned.

If we could give as many diagnoses as seemed relevant and assign "pieces of the pie" to each of a child's apparent diagnoses, how many children classified as autistic might actually be better described as a pie chart child who actually meets full or partial criteria for many different diagnoses? Then, among those multiple diagnoses, for how many is autism really the main or most marked aspect of their overall picture? We don't know, but I would guess it would lower prevalence rates.

THE LENS OF THE CLINICIAN AND AUTISM PREVALENCE

So, diagnosing autism is not so simple politically, as the clinician knows that what is diagnosed will influence what services the child will likely receive. The next problem likely influencing prevalence is the "lens" (discipline and experience) of the person doing the diagnosing: For example, if this is an "autism expert" who has treated a hundred kids with autism, has he or she *also* had the experience that will enable him or her to know a meth baby when he or she sees one? And, what do clinical psychologists and psychiatrists really know about diagnosing children with a primary language disorder?

THE ADOS LENS

How many of today's autism diagnostic experts can go beyond saying "It's not autism because a better explanation is some combination of developmental delay, language disorder, intellectual disability, or learning problems, compounded by unsuccessful parental attempts to deal with these difficulties?" In my experience and the experience of most parents I meet and many colleagues, an "autism evaluation" these days means an assessment where autism was "ruled in" or "ruled out," not an assessment where there was interviewing or testing to consider other diagnoses as well.

Much autism diagnosis in the last 20 years has included training in, and use of, a structured clinical interview called the ADOS (Autism Diagnostic Observation Schedule) and sometimes the ADI-R (Autism Diagnostic Interview–Revised).

The ADOS, in particular, is often referred to as the "diagnostic gold standard" for ASDs. These tests originally were developed as research tools to characterize autism for researchers interested in autism genetics. It is perhaps for this reason that neither the ADOS nor the ADI-R have scoring that might show when another "pie chart" problem may be contributing to a child's difficulties. Said another way, the ADOS lacks a way to indicate likelihood of a "differential" (different or additional) diagnosis; rather, it can only indicate how autistic a child is.

The ADOS is simply an interview with standardized tasks and standardized scoring. It requires that administrators receive training to "criteria," which means the administrator has shown that she or he can derive the same scoring as an ADOS trainer. However, the way a given child happens to react during the hour or so of an ADOS interview can be strongly influenced by whether an examiner has rapport with the child and whether the child decides he or she likes or dislikes the examiner, does or does not want to be cooperative, and so on. Turning pages, writing things down, talking too fast, not getting the child's attention before beginning a new activity, and not waiting long enough for a response may leave a child looking "worse" than the child may have seemed with a different examiner, in a different setting, or on a different day. If the child looks "worse" on the ADOS (that is, less engaged), it tallies up to the child looking more autistic.

Clinicians can buy an ADOS kit, take a weekend seminar to learn to use their test kit, establish agreement with the test developers on what they see on ADOS interview videos, and become bona fide autism diagnosticians. There is enough autism diagnosing work to go around (given that 1:68 are reported autistic) that many with ADOS certification can specialize in autism diagnosis but know little else about diagnosing other related disorders the child may have instead of, or in addition to, autism. ADOS scoring makes it hard for an uncooperative child, a nonverbal child, an anxious child, or a very intellectually disabled child not to look somewhat autistic. With no scoring to show how autistic an average anxious child looks on the ADOS, an average score for how an autistic and average severely intellectually disabled child looks on the ADOS, and so on, as expected from the overall lack of specificity (uniqueness) of individual autism symptoms, there is a lot of autism detected with the ADOS. The ADOS was first developed in the early 1990s. Epidemiologically, the dramatic rise in autism tracks closely with the adoption of the ADOS as a "diagnostic gold standard."

Gatekeeping Versus Opening the Floodgates

There is always the question of why an assessment for autism is being sought. Is the purpose of diagnostic assessment to cast a broad net, ensuring that all those that *might* benefit from extra "autism" help receive it? Or, is it to be a "gatekeeper"—making sure individuals *without* a form of autism aren't inadvertently let "in"?

We know that higher functioning children with autism respond better to virtually every evidence-based autism treatment than lower functioning children. Are diagnosticians more likely to "see" autism in higher functioning children who will be less resistive in treatment and more likely to make more notable changes than children who are more obstreperous and lower functioning? Could that have anything to do with why more and more children identified as being on the autism spectrum are intellectually higher functioning than ones recognized before there were intensive services available? Since the availability of applied behavior analysis (ABA) to treat autism, epidemiological studies have reflected a shift: Children diagnosed with autism using criteria in use before 1989 included 70 percent with intellectual disability and 30 percent without,[4] compared to the present rates, with diagnoses of 30 percent with intellectual disability and 70 percent without.[6] (These numbers are imperfect because it is unclear how many of the present 70 percent are truly without intellectual disability, because if diagnosed below age 5, "intellectual disability" would not have been coded, and most with intellectual disability are first assessed below age 5, as discussed previously.)

OF BUS SHELTERS AND BILLBOARDS

What about national advocacy groups that widely "advertise" that autism is underdiagnosed, and that early diagnosis is key, that we all need is to be more "autism aware"? All over America, on the walls of bus shelters, sides of buses, and billboards and in full-page ads in the *New York Times*, are telling us that *your* toddler is more likely to have autism than to become the next Tommy Hilfiger. (Tommy Hilfiger is a parent of a child with autism and is an active advocate for autism, so he really deserves kudos for promoting that example.)

Is autism awareness driven by advocacy efforts mainly objective, or is it also fearmongering? In a very recent billboard from this same advocacy group involved with the Hilfiger ad, a cartoon shows a small child impinged on by a cacophony of sounds covering his ears. The caption informs us that auditory hypersensitivity is a sign of autism. Yes, but auditory hypersensitivity is not by a long stretch unique to autism. Is there such a strong push to identify new cases that we will begin wondering whether the toddler waiting with his mom in a bus shelter with this just-described autism awareness advertisement might have autism because he is covering his ears as a fire engine goes by? Are we maybe getting a little too "aware"? Do "false positives" raise prevalence? Yes.

WHO DO YOU TRUST?

Once a parent has suspicions that his or her child might have a form of autism, who can or should that parent trust to learn more? How does a parent learn anything about who may diagnose well, versus overdiagnose or misdiagnose? Should you start with information from a national organization that spends a significant portion of its budget not serving people with autism, but on plastering ads in bus shelters and advertising in the *New York Times* about how much autism you should be aware there is out there?

In a sociologically interesting way, autism advocacy groups have their own skin in the game. It might be argued that advocacy groups for autism are governed by the same in-group culture as advocacy groups for other problems— like Alcoholics Anonymous. "Admit you are one of us, and then you can come in and we'll take care of you." "Come see who else is here; folks just like you." "Admitting you belong here is the first step." This logic is a tempting call-out to any parent with a child who has *something* wrong, and who wants to feel that their family belongs somewhere. (A concrete example of this is parents at a first diagnostic assessment who have already started their child on a gluten-casein–free diet, sufficiently self-convinced their child does have autism and have read this diet will help.)

Hearing numbers like 1 in 68 will send you running to look for more children with autism. Advocacy groups and their advertising connect to anxious parents in ways that are, without question, critical to helping families who do have children with autism get on the road to needed help. However, the problem may be that for every family who needs help, hundreds more parents, their relatives, and well-intended neighbors also become autism aware, "autism sensitized," and "autism anxious." While the autism awareness movement can serve to destigmatize autism, it may also serve to make its presence seem more likely. The information carefully crafted by public relations agencies to make us autism aware has been so effective that it has left many in the lay public feeling they understand more about recognizing autism than they do.

BLIND MEN WHO FEEL ELEPHANTS

I've already talked about clinicians who learn to diagnose through the lens of the ADOS. The *DSM*, the APA's standard, is the main standard designed for use by psychiatrists and clinical psychologists and also by all sorts of other clinical professionals, like neurologists, pediatricians, school psychologists, clinical social workers, marriage and family therapists—and their various trainees. In addition to an assessment tool like the ADOS, the "lens" can be focused by both the experience and the disciplinary orientation of the professional assessing the child. As a diagnostician, your profession will guide what you look for.

Diagnosing autism is not merely a matter of googling the "autism spectrum disorders" page of *DSM-5* and reading each criterion like a slip of paper inside a fortune cookie. With the advent of Internet medicines, we all google our latest symptoms, with a few of us invariably convincing ourselves that our cough is sign of a dreaded disease, others that the cough needs only a spoonful of honey in some herbal tea. Googling autism symptoms is much the same. One might call this the "subjectivity of concern."

In addition to the subjectivity of concern, each professional looks at ASDs through the lens of their training, and what they see, or do not not see, can be quite different from what a colleague in a different discipline sees. To explain to parents why their neurologist, their pediatrician, and their speech therapist all seem to be saying different things about their child, I often find myself using the parable of blind men feeling an elephant. Are they all looking at the same thing? No, they are not. Each is applying different objective criteria (from their training) as well as adding personal subjectivity of concern. But there is just one elephant. Each child with autism will have many difficulties, and those difficulties may look like different things to different examiners: For example, a child who flaps his hands, covers his ears, gags at the sight of certain foods, and can't tolerate tags on his clothes might seem very autistic to an occupational therapist or even a neurologist. But if the examining clinician also spent time to learn that this child has a best friend and is academically more advanced than others his age, the child might start to seem less autistic. Some more examples are given next.

The Pediatric Lens

The American Academy of Pediatrics has procedural standards for pediatricians to use in diagnosing autism; these standards ultimately end in comparing all available data to *DSM-5* ASD criteria. The pediatric standards endorse autism-screening checklists and ask about the absence of expected milestones in speech, social smiles, peer interests, and the like. These are questions that a good primary care pediatric practitioner readily can fit into a 15-minute or shorter well-baby check at 18 and 24 months of age while preparing a half-naked toddler for a vaccination. However, the range of the child's behavior at that time may be limited to what most half-naked children fearing an imminent shot behave like. They may be apprehensive or outright fearful, and their overall demeanor will not be very representative of how smiley, talkative, or playful that child can be. If concerns about autism do come up, the primary care pediatrician usually only has time to focus on reassurances that vaccines do not cause autism (which they definitely do not). The pediatrician gives the shot, then exits the exam room, leaving the now-screaming, just-vaccinated child to be dressed by his mother. This means the pediatrician has no opportunity to collect further data on the child's repertoire of typical behavior. The pediatrician's opportunity to directly observe and evaluate the child's behavior is limited to a parent report questionnaire, which may be influenced by parental anxiety, mastery of English, or being a first-time parent. The typicality of the child's observed behavior at the pediatric well-child visit is, unquestionably, skewed by the shot.

The Lenses of Psychologists and Psychiatrists

The American Academy of Child and Adolescent Psychiatry (AACAP) has procedures for child psychiatrists to use in diagnosing autism; the standards end in comparing all available data to the *DSM-5* ASD criteria. But what about child psychiatry training? How much training in diagnosing autism does the average child psychiatrist receive? AACAP requirements have child psychiatrists in training focusing almost exclusively on the child over 5, some younger children who are "repeat offenders" (expelled from a succession of preschools), and a much smaller number of toddlers seen because of mother–infant attachment disorders, early abuse, and neglect—where much of the diagnostic and therapeutic focus is on the parent, not the young child. Even a trainee child psychiatrist with a strong interest in neurodevelopmental disorders will have seen few children under 5 years old because ADHD, learning disorders, and disorders of childhood mood and conduct are generally not recognized until the early school years. Even in the University of California at San Francisco (UCSF) child psychiatry training program where I taught for 24 years, and where I ran a large and active autism clinic, a child psychiatrist in training spent only 8 to 12 days of their 2 years of specialty training in my clinic. A child psychiatrist's training prepares him or her well to focus on family psychiatric history, pregnancy and birth history, and other indicators the child might need to be seen by a collaborating geneticist or neurologist or be treated with psychoactive medications. Fewer have any chance to develop expertise in very early developmental progressions and how lines of social development, communication, and play should be typically intertwining in the first 3 or 4 years of life. Maybe this is another reason the ADOS has become highly depended on to diagnose autism in children under 5.

Child psychologists often use a lens much like that of child psychiatrists but tend to focus less on genetic family history or neurological soft signs. Training in behavior and development may prepare them better than child psychiatrists to detect patterns of atypical behavior that are indicative of an ASD as opposed to ADHD or a language disorder. Increasingly, clinical psychologists adopt the lens of neuropsychology, identifying themselves as clinical child neuropsychologists (though relatively few are board-certified pediatric neuropsychologists). Neuropsychology may be a more profitable specialty than psychotherapy and puts the focus not on talking to the child or observing but on giving standardized tests, sometimes a great many tests. One concern is that most of these tests require training in the test, not in autism per se, allowing autism to be diagnosed by any clinical psychologist who uses many different tests, whether or not they have ever actually trained in a setting for diagnosing or treating autism. Another concern is that such testing is subject to the same errors of parent reporting, and the child's cooperativeness and motivation, as something like that seen with the ADOS or ADI-R. However, the more you test, the more you are liable to find things (like an ASD) that are "wrong"—though what to do about these things in a child with autism often requires the expertise of a special educator, speech and language therapist, or occupational therapist, so there often is a disconnect between neuropsychological testing and what to do about any positive findings.

Converse to diagnoses being given by psychologists and psychiatrists with little or no direct training in autism are those given in ASD-specific clinics by those who may or may not be testing for other possible conditions when a parent brings a child in for an autism assessment. With these clinicians, too, lack of consideration of other diagnoses, of transient developmental delays, or of stages of normal early child development can cloud their lenses.

The Lens of Speech and Language Pathologists

The professional standards of the American Speech and Hearing Association (ASHA) counsel speech and language pathologists to leave diagnosing to psychologists and child psychiatrists, but speech and language pathologists are often the first to treat a child with autism, even before the child's diagnosis, and often are the ones to refer the child to the psychologist or child psychiatrist for autism diagnosis. Not surprisingly, an experienced speech and language pathologist who has sent off many clients for diagnostic assessment for autism and sees which ones come back with an autism diagnosis has a pretty good lens for knowing which child will be diagnosed as having an ASD. ASHA does not have procedural standards for diagnosing autism because its members are experts in speech, language, and communication—not the activities, interests, and possible sensory and motor problems that also need to be considered to diagnose autism. Returning to the "blind men feeling the elephant" analogy, there are children with echolalia (repeating what has just been heard) who are autistic—*or* who have other auditory-processing problems. Echolalia alone, or lack of age-appropriate language alone, does not make for an autism diagnosis but certainly may be part of it. As said previously, the same is true of auditory hypersensitivity. Any language difficulties considered without the fuller picture of whether a child has "joint attention" (shares interests with others, even if just nonverbally); has unusual interests, routines, or motor movements; and has other "autism problems" can lead to any child with echolalia, auditory hypersensitivity, or very delayed language development being seen as likely having autism.

The Occupational Therapist Lens

In addition to speech and language pathologists, in the last 10 years, more and more children with autism see occupational therapists for what is termed "sensory integration" or "sensory-processing disorder" (not a validated diagnosis in any field). I meet an amazing number of occupational therapists these days who also feel they know autism when they see it, though their professional training lacks any procedural standards for diagnosis used by pediatricians or child psychiatrists. Maybe because of the lack of professional guidelines about diagnosing autism, occupational therapists often tend to be less conservative than speech and language pathologists, more ready to judge that "of course he's on the spectrum," though an occupational therapist focuses not on core symptoms such as communication (like a speech and language pathologist does); not on social deficits (like a psychologist or psychiatrist does); but on activities, interests, and sensorimotor perception—just one part of the autism spectrum's symptoms sometimes referred to as the "RRBs" (routine and repetitive behaviors). An occupational therapist will not "really" diagnose autism but will at times attach an ASD moniker. Then it becomes a game of "telephone" as the message that "he's on the spectrum" is repeated to other professionals, who may be influenced by what has already been said—though originally, the "diagnosis" came from an occupational therapist, perhaps the most "visually impaired" when it comes to "feeling the elephant."

Teachers Have a Wide-Angle Lens

Educators belong to another profession that is involved in recognizing, diagnosing, and treating autism. Ask a teacher, and he or she likely will say that the child he or she suspects of having autism doesn't listen and doesn't behave like the others—but knows those problems can be due to all sorts of things. Teachers, unlike clinic or hospital-based professionals, actually see the child with possible autism as he or she interacts with peers (or doesn't) and negotiates the "real world" of social demand (or doesn't). The teacher can see whether the child does or not does not pay attention to verbal and nonverbal cues where the press for communication might be planned, might be incidental, might be spontaneous, or could be elicited.

Teachers have a better, more naturalistic laboratory for observing a child's capacities that most other professionals can only learn about by asking parents—who often are not at school, preschool, or day care much, if at all. Though teachers are not trained in using *DSM* diagnostic standards, they too have a "lens," with a much wider angle than anyone else's. While diagnostic standards for psychiatrists, pediatricians, and psychologists all emphasize the importance of looking for validation that each diagnostic sign is present across all the places a child spends time, more often than not the child's teachers and the child's diagnosticians do not even speak to one another. The diagnostician is also unlikely to make a home visit or review a home video to see if what is said about behavior at home or school seems to be as parents understand it. (These days, with basically everyone having a video camera in their cell phone, it is easy enough for clinicians to ask parents to make brief videos of their child's concerning behaviors in different settings and bring them along to any diagnostic visit.)

Misdiagnosis and Informant Bias

The picture of a child's difficulties will likely be different, depending on the lens through which the child is viewed. For each clinician I've just described, the whole clinical picture he or she gets can become overrepresented by the aspects of autism (or whatever clinical disorder) that clinician's training has taught him or her to focus on. I've talked about how the time, place, and informant can have a great deal to do with how facts make it into a diagnostic formulation— or not. In an ideal situation, all the "blind men" would feel the elephant at the same time and then sit down and have a case conference. A group discussion might be the best way for each participant to appreciate the perspective of the others—and incorporate further information into his or her own point of view.

In reality, diagnostic assessment seldom works this way: Every one of these blind men—the psychiatrist, the psychologist, the teacher, the speech–language pathologist, the occupational therapist, the teacher—are busy people. Usually, a child is seen by each of these professionals individually. After each visit, the parent presses: "So, do you think he has autism?" Most professionals will acknowledge who else has an opinion that must be counted, but most, understandably, may forge ahead and offer their best estimate of the child's diagnosis based on their own data. What if their own data are missing something critical? Is such practice likely to raise or lower prevalence rates?

DIAGNOSIS THROUGH THE DEVELOPMENTAL LENS

We have seen how, aside from teachers and parents, pediatricians, psychologists, and psychiatrists rarely get a natural picture of how the child plays with peers, or how the child lets others know when he or she wants something or is excited about something new. But age is also critical: If you are diagnosing an 18-month-old or a 24-month-old, "play with peers" does not have the same meaning as when you are watching 3- or 4-year-olds. (If you've had a child at these ages, you know what I mean.) Early play for typically developing 18- to 24-month-olds is not yet truly about the mutuality with the other little person who is there. Young toddlers don't yet have the capacity or the sustained interest to go back and forth with their play partner in the same way that evinces shared enjoyment—as seen in typical development by age 3 to 4 years.

For some clinicians without children of their own or without training in typical developmental stages, this distinction can be easily lost. Without expertise in the relevant distinctions about peer play, a typical 18-month-old's play with another child could be mistaken for "autistic"—which indeed it might be if that child were playing in the same way but was a 4-year-old instead. If you don't know much about analyzing interactive peer play (because you are a neurologist, a psychologist, or a psychiatrist who hasn't been around typical young children much), accurately analyzing the child's developmental level of peer play might not seem critical, and you may decide to diagnose a child's lack of play like a toddler as actual lack of play, even if the child is 14 months old, when sustained interested in playing with others has not yet emerged. In this way, such a clinician risks supporting a false-positive diagnosis of autism. Further, if one does not consider that a 2½-year-old might be playing like a 14-month-old because he also has moderate intellectual disability and not because he has autism, it may lead to overdiagnosis of autism in young children with intellectual disability.

Another phenomenon that may be raising autism rates is a kind of intellectual race to see who can diagnose at the youngest ages (when developmental considerations are most critical to differential diagnosis). Presumptively, you can feel yourself to be a better clinician if you "call" it "autism" at 10 months or 14 months rather than at 18 or 24 months of age. (There is excellent research on early detection of autism, but findings of such work are not yet widely applicable for community clinicians, who tend to lack equipment like eye trackers or facilities for electroencephalographic telemetry.) Over the years, I have run into a handful of clinicians who consistently overestimate their powers of autism detection. Typically, the errors made are blind-men errors, focusing on one part of the elephant and not feeling around for indications supporting the suspect behavior as normal, given the child's stage of development. There is also an interesting kind of machismo around being able to "see" autism where others might miss it. To my mind, this often can involve ignoring a full evaluation of a child's strengths in favor of emphasizing the child's weaknesses.

ONE MAN'S RAINDROPS ARE ANOTHER MAN'S DELUGE

In doing diagnostic assessment, certain signs of autism like over- or under-responsiveness to certain sensory stimuli (which can be contributory, but not diagnostic) must be taken at the parents' word. The child who is reported to coves his ears to a loud restroom hand dryer will not present this way in the child psychiatrist's playroom or the pediatrician's exam room because no hand dryer is likely installed on the wall. Professionals therefore have to rely on a certain amount of parent report of lower incidence events. Parental "subjectivity of concern" readily can lead to increased false-positive diagnoses.

Nevertheless, factoring in a parent's report is a key element in diagnostic assessment—and should be. No one knows the child better than his or her parents. But there will be the parent assiduously avoiding the autism diagnosis who may underreport his child's terror of the restroom hand dryer. On the other hand, there will be the parent concerned her child will not receive services unless she endorses every atypical behavior about which she is asked. There are first-time parents who simply do not know what is to be expected when you take a cranky child into a public restroom and a lot of people are using hand dryers. Then there are parents who lack comprehension, vocabulary, or education to appreciate the distinctions being queried. These parents are flummoxed by what the hand dryer in a rest room could possibly have to do with this doctor's appointment and wish they had asked to have a translator.

These things become a real problem when relying on a parent's report if it is all, or even most, of what the clinician has to rely on to arrive at a diagnosis.

One might suppose this mostly happens *outside* university medical centers, where clinicians are less likely to be specialists, data are not being collected via standardized assessment procedures, and there is less time available for each child seen.

These days, most children seen in a university specialty clinic for autism are there specifically to "rule in" or "rule out" autism—with much less effort put into what the child "has" if he or she doesn't have autism. For example, the ADOS, which I described previously as a possible contributor to the rise in autism incidence, is used in the vast majority of autism research clinics internationally and only gives you a score on how autistic (or not) the child is—but not how the child's pattern of scores might better line up with a language disorder, ADHD, an intellectual problem or learning disability, or even test anxiety or separation anxiety. Might having only a score that references how autistic the child is bias overall assessment conclusions? If a child is one "point" shy of the "cutoff" for an ASD on the ADOS, is it fair to say the child has a touch of ASD? What about two points below that cutoff? What else is it then, if the child had almost enough points to be considered definitely "on the autism spectrum"? The ADOS won't tell you, and chances are the child's medical insurance has only authorized enough hours to test for autism, not anything else. Might this raise estimates of autism prevalence?

Most clinicians in the "helping professions" want, not surprisingly, to help. Most clinicians I know would rather err on the side of overdiagnosing than underdiagnosing autism, especially to open otherwise-closed doors to more services. For community clinicians hoping for more referrals, overdiagnosis may help earn a reputation as someone who can help get more services. For me, the "why not" for such practice is that "more" services will be autism services, which perhaps are not best fitted to the child's learning needs. Additionally, inclusion of increasingly different kinds of children under the diagnosis of autism can hinder research looking for neurobiological correlates of an ASD diagnosis. (There is more discussion about that in Chapter 9.)

SCREENING CHECKLISTS

As a clinical researcher who has published a screening test for autism,[12] I am completely clear regarding the difference between a screening test and a diagnostic test, but it seems like not every professional out there who uses one is. A screening test, just like a screening test for any other medical problem, is just that—a first step to determine whether it is justified to proceed with a more extensive and costly diagnostic assessment. Mammograms screen for breast cancer. The prostate-specific antigen (PSA) test screens for prostate cancer. Hemoglobin A_{1c} screens for diabetes. Most screening tests for ASD involve parent self-administered measures prone to subjective reporting, which we have already discussed. This is not terrible, though, since ASD screens, like medical screening tests, are devised to yield more false positives over false negatives. If you have a "positive" mammogram, it doesn't mean you have breast cancer, but that it is worthwhile to come in for further studies. The goal of mammograms is not to miss any potential cases of breast cancer. Similarly, autism screeners that give a positive score do not mean the child has autism, only that the child should now receive a workup for autism.

Screening is OK if everyone involved understands that a screening test is *only* a screening test. After 30 years of talking to parents and teachers who have brought me the results of every screening test for autism that has ever been developed, I can safely say that only a very small proportion understand that a positive screening result does not mean a child has autism. Even though, I think, most people do know that a positive mammogram does not mean you have breast cancer, screens for psychiatric disorders seem to be taken more at face value. Maybe this has to do with the lack of any biological marker to confirm a positive diagnosis for autism, unlike for some forms of cancer. This may relate to the overall subjectivity applied to how autism is portrayed in popular media. If someone (a scriptwriter) says this TV character has autism, the character does.

What are the ways a screening test for autism may be positive and the child *not* have autism? One issue is that many conditions that cause symptoms of autism aren't autism. These cases get caught in the screening tests' broad net. For example, the average child who runs from public restrooms with mechanical hand dryers is not autistic. But a screening item that mentions hand dryers might receive a positive score. On one screening test for autism called the M-CHAT (Modified Checklist for Autism in Toddlers), most cases with moderate-to-severe intellectual disability screen positive along with most autism cases. That's OK because the M-CHAT is a screener, and further assessment is aimed at deselecting cases where intellectual disability is the main issue. However, once a child is found to have a "positive" result on the M-CHAT (or another screening test), the autism finding often "sticks" and is passed on to future assessors, who may or may not appreciate that the autism result came from a screening test and not a diagnostic test. Might this result in more autism-only testing, in more reports of more cases of autism?

Positive screening test scores for autism may influence diagnosticians doing a full ASD workup to look more carefully for autism than for other conditions: A child who is language delayed—like a toddler with autism—should really receive a workup for a language disorder, as well as for autism. A toddler not interested in peers—like most toddlers with autism—may be that way because he is very anxious and fearful and may need to receive a workup for an anxiety disorder or a problem in parent–child interaction as well as for autism. Another toddler who ignores peers may grow up antisocial, not asocial—like a child with autism. A toddler who handles change poorly, like many with autism, may do so because he or she still lacks language to ask what will happen next or may even have an incipient obsessive–compulsive disorder.

One of my mentors, Professor Edward Ritvo of the University of California at Los Angeles (UCLA), a very wise child psychiatrist, taught me that in a very young child "the brain only has a few ways to say 'ouch.'" It took me a while, but I realized he was quite right: The repertoire of a toddler's behavior is much less differentiated than that of an older child—and the first signs of what may later develop look much more similar in a 2- or 3-year-old than in an older child.

Some screening tests are falsely positive simply because parents tried their best to answer the questions but did not produce an answer that matched more detailed information gathered later. I worried a lot about this when I was developing the Pervasive Developmental Disorders Screening Test II (PDDST-II) for autism. Parents fill out the PDDST-II, and if the screener is scored positive, the administering clinician pulls out a "glossary" of questions that come with the test kit and asks further verbatim questions to verify whether the parents understood the questions as intended and whether the severity and examples the parent had in mind were the same as what a clinician would rate positive. Even with safeguards such as these, screening tests may well have served to increase the numbers of children classified as having some form of autism.

QUALIFICATION FOR EARLY INTERVENTION

Screening tests for autism are most often used when a child is very young. That's when getting a child into early intervention services (Part C of the Individuals With Disabilities Education Act [IDEA]) is critical. During this period, it can be clinical practice (as we discussed in looking at how the American Academy of Pediatrics does things) to focus more on getting help started than on a definitive diagnosis that will likely be more clear as the child develops and has a chance to respond to treatments. Children under 3 years who are served as "at risk for autism" based on screening test results may find autism becoming their diagnosis if, after age 3, they continue to receive services designed for children with autism, like ABA programs. Some of those children, as presciently predicted by American Academy of Pediatrics practice parameters, will no longer screen (or test) as autistic. Some are still "counted" as autistic, especially if the goal is to retain services initiated because of an earlier autism diagnosis. This practice may also be raising autism prevalence rates.

A PARTICULARLY AMERICAN PROBLEM WITH IDENTIFYING AUTISM . . .

As we have talked about identifying, screening, and diagnosing autism, the implication is that we have been talking about what the various versions of the *DSM* have called autism; PDD; PDD,NOS; and Asperger's. But if you are reading this book in England or Australia, you might have in mind what the

International Classification of Diseases, 10th edition (*ICD-10*) calls autism—still basically in the same ballpark as the various *DSM* "autisms." However, in the United States, we have an additional difficulty: What the US Department of Education calls autism and what each state decides to call autism are different from any *DSM* or *ICD* designation. In the United States, most special services for autism that are available to individuals between the ages of 3 and 22 years old are mandated and funded under IDEA. This is a federal law that makes sure that every American child with special educational needs receives a free and appropriate public education (FAPE).

The educational definitions of "autism" found state to state are very often more broad compared to the *DSM*: Some do not even use the term *autism* per se, but rather "autistic-like" or "autistic-like learner (AUT)." The US Department of Education guidelines end up providing a very well-attuned way to attain autism-specific special services for those who learn differently (and need to be taught differently) due to signs of autism. The clinical diagnosis, even in the *DSM*, should be all about understanding what autism does to the child's functionality, so we can help a child use innate skills (his or her autistic learning styles) to develop compensatory learning strategies to bootstrap the weaker skills that, educationally, are their "autistic learning disabilities." (I think this functional approach might be better than that of the *DSM* for genetic and neuroimaging research in autism also, but more about that in Chapter 9.)

However, because a state's educational autism definition under IDEA is that of an autistic-like learner, that child may or may not have *DSM-5* autism. Educators seldom explain to parents that "their" diagnosis is not the same as a medical diagnosis of autism. It often is not explained to parents of a child qualified for special education as autistic-like that their child may not, in fact, be found to have autism if a psychologist or psychiatrist were to be asked if the child met criteria for *DSM-5* ASD. Generally, the educational diagnosis of autism is broader than a *DSM* diagnosis, so parents can be surprised (and confused) if a clinician says their educationally "autistic" child does not actually meet *DSM* criteria for autism. Schools typically don't explain that "their" autism might be different from the standards used by the child's doctor. Conversely, many physicians and psychologists I meet are unaware that schools don't rely on their *DSM* diagnoses to qualify a pupil for educational autism services.

SCHOOL AUTISM AND CDC AUTISM

To make matters worse, the prevalence and incidence studies of autism that have been carried out in the last 10 to 15 years by the federal CDC in Atlanta, Georgia, often count cases where autism is the diagnosis the child has received in schools, as lower income families may rely completely for diagnostic evaluation on their school's psychoeducational diagnostic services mandated procedurally as part of the child's qualification for special education.

The last 25 years of scientifically sound work on autism treatment has created an obligation for IDEA to provide more costly FAPE to pupils with autism (AUT) than to any of education's other diagnostic categories. Other educational diagnoses can include severe language impairment (SLI), intellectual disability (ID), or learning disabilities (LD), and so on. The designation as an autistic-like learner can be seen as a ticket to more services, with, presumably, an improved chance at the best possible outcome for that child.

ATTAINING THE "BEST" CARE

As ABA took hold as the most promising of autism treatments and schools were litigated into paying for it, not surprisingly, I began to see more individualized education programs (IEPs) with AUT coded as the primary special education eligibility classification. Throughout the 1990s and 2000s, departments of education throughout the United States reported rising rates of AUT as the primary IEP eligibility classification. In fact, most states code a primary and secondary handicapping condition, but I don't think I have ever seen an IEP with two diagnostic codes where if one is AUT, it is not coded first. Parents and their legal advocates were quick to understand that costly ABA services would be rationed by educational authorities only if the child's primary educational classification was AUT. Might this have increased reported autism prevalence?

REPRISE: IS THERE MORE AUTISM NOW?

I revisit the question raised at the beginning of this chapter in considering why there may be more autism today. Autism, simply put, is a "popular" diagnosis. There are the many success stories in the media, books by self-advocates, and the idea that if you have autism, you "can't" also have an intellectual disability. All this drives the popularity of an autism diagnosis. As one who regularly participates in assessing children for autism, not a small number of parents are disappointed if you don't think their child has a form of autism. The parents themselves may have really not considered other possible diagnoses or explanations: You say: "He's social, looks to you to see what you think, makes up stories with his toys. We don't see that in a child with autism." The parent counters, concerned about observations you may have overlooked: "What about the fact that he lines up his Thomas the Tank Engine toys on the track— over and over, and then lies on the floor and looks at the track as they roll by?" Well, based on this observation alone, this might be a typical 3-year-old boy. It is hard not to line up trains if you use your tracks. These parents are bombarded by what they read on the Internet about autism—"Don't miss the early window of opportunity to treat" or that most boys who love Thomas the Tank Engine are autistic (not true!). Alone at night in front of a glowing computer screen after a 3-hour battle to get a 3-year-old to stay in bed, a parent can be worn down and worried there must be something wrong with that child. The credibility of a blogger insisting that autism is a key reason for sleep problems in 3-year-olds might be more than in the light of the morning.

I have come to realize that, for many parents, their first reaction to "it's not autism, and it's not a form of autism" is often as if one is saying that all the difficulties experienced with the child are not "real," just in their imagination. This is certainly not the case. There are many kinds of developmental delays, neurodevelopmental atypicalities, and just badly behaved kids who may benefit from behavior modification, special school plans, family therapy, individual therapy, or psychoactive medications to get better. There are parents who have come to the understanding that if their child doesn't have autism, the child will receive no special help. Amazingly, it sometimes seems that "autism" has overshadowed all other forms of difficulty for which a child might need help in school or from a therapist.

Resetting Priorities

In this chapter, I've set out many reasons why we may be seeing and hearing so much about autism these days. I am not directly challenging the CDC's statistics that point to autism in 1 out of 68 children, but I am saying there may be reasons for many false-positive cases. The more we hear about autism, the more autism becomes the first thing to be considered when a child is seen as having something wrong.

If a child has autism, has symptoms that we have reason to believe will benefit from autism-specific help, then by all means, let's go for it. But if the child has additional or different problems, those must be considered instead of, or in addition to, autism treatments. What can we do to reset priorities in how we help families deal with receiving a diagnosis of autism? Should we be using suggestions such as these as a template for how we respond to the needs of families with children with other developmental disorders also?

Social Policy Recommendations

In this chapter, recommendations focus on how medical care for autism should not begin and end with diagnostic assessment but continue, because autism, like other neurodevelopmental disorders, most often is a chronic condition requiring ongoing service.

THE NEED FOR HELP BEYOND THE DAY OF DIAGNOSIS

Most autism treatment dollars go to expensive one-to-one ABA therapy programs for children under 5. The idea of ABA's unitary efficacy in autism treatment has been marketed so well that it has gobbled resources that arguably would be better spread over later childhood and adulthood. The "buy-in" for ABA programs is that the child might "lose" his or her diagnosis this way, though most experts agree that only a single-digit minority do. It's dice most parents are willing to roll as they set down the autism road, betting this will be their way "out" of autism. This is totally understandable from a parent's point of view.

But, ethically, expensive autism treatment programs need to be weighed in terms of both benefit to the child who receives it *and* the effect of drawing down resources for, basically, every adult and child over age 5 with a diagnosis of autism. This uneven allocation of resources is driven by the most hopeful, altruistic, optimistic motives. Autism advocacy is very largely about early intervention. Great, but how can this advocacy for early intervention be counterbalanced in a way that acknowledges the need for treatments for most who will continue to have autism beyond age 5 or 6? How do we create a system of care different from the one we have now, where autism specialists mainly deal with the diagnosis of children under 5 and seldom see children again once the children have been diagnosed? There is a crying need for follow-up care that can be focused on adjusting treatments according to treatment response. Many professionals are trained in diagnosis, but relatively few in the developmental course of autism. Parents essentially have nowhere to turn but the Internet to figure out what they might being doing to help their child after early ABA programs end, usually by the time the child is 4, 5, or 6 years old. At that point, parents either can rely almost entirely on the special education system or can put together an amalgam of treatments based on things they have read and heard about—usually with little input from a professional who can opine whether the new treatments being considered have an evidence basis or are (yet) developmentally appropriate for that child.

Further, the way it is now, there is little obligation for professionals to speak of prognosis over time, as it is unlikely they will ever see a family after the day they give the autism diagnosis. Parents lack access to professional psychoeducation to understand what their child's progress means for what he or she may or may not learn in the future, compensatory strategies that might be effective, let alone long-term prognosis for adult independence.

Most diagnosed with autism in childhood face outcomes somewhere between "indistinguishable from normal" and "institutionalized," but the pain and fear associated with being less than "normal," compounded by very few ongoing case management services for families living with autism, have resulted in few supports for families beyond when the child is the age of early intervention programs. A child's intellectual capacity as well as changes in the child's autism symptoms have to be monitored to refine treatment plans and prognosis. If a parent is not told at the time of diagnosis to come back when their child is 5, 8, 16, or 22 years old to learn more about what then can be done, why would they come? If a parent holds on to false hopes about a child's outcomes, it detracts from helping that child become prepared for the future he or she will face.

Medical insurance for autism care is much more likely to cover diagnosis than any ongoing monitoring of progress. This is just wrong and inadequate. A neurologist would not diagnose and plan treatment for a seizure disorder in one shot. A cardiologist would not treat heart disease that way. An endocrinologist treating diabetics would not encourage patients to rely on the Internet, deciding for themselves whether one new diet regime or the other was right for them—without monitoring, individualizing, and educating. We need to be able to do something like this for individuals with autism.

Many specialty clinics for autism are set up as diagnostic centers with no capacity for follow-up treatment planning, case management, or even services to assess for further diagnoses or revisit the autism diagnosis as the child grows. There are a few reasons for this: (a) The prototypes for autism specialty clinics are tied to research programs where their raison d'être is to funnel autism-positive cases into research protocols. (b) The clinics are run in medical departments like child psychiatry, pediatrics, and neurology, where "treatment" ends with psychopharmacology and does not embrace education or behavioral methodologies—which comprise much of autism treatment but are outside the expertise of physicians. (c) Medical insurance often covers autism diagnosis, but not continuing care or even treatment planning, especially if the treatments that are planned are behavioral or educational. In recent years, ABA therapies for autism increasingly in many states are covered by medical insurance as "medically necessary." It's a start. I would argue that it is more a priority to monitor and limit ABA services, limiting them to those for whom it is more effective than less intensive treatments—and consider redistributing funding to the "medically necessary" task of management.

Since my retirement from UCSF in 2013, I have established a nonprofit organization (the Autism Center of Northern California, ACNC) with the mission of "serving families living with autism from diagnosis through adulthood." At ACNC, we are piloting a model to address this in an "autism home clinic." This is based on the "medical home" model that exists for many chronic medical disorders—putting together coordinated, comprehensive special education plans, development of social skills and leisure activities outside school, investigating what kind of education and job skills training is well suited, how to support transition to adult living, and how to bolster family functioning.

Over time, following an individual with autism allows a professional to determine (a) if he or she still meets criteria for autism, (b) what treatment approaches fit best given learning history, (c) whether presence of additional conditions may indicate the need for additional treatments, and (d) whether detecting intellectual disability or a very splintered intellectual profile (e.g., visual-spatial skills much better than language skills) might inform treatment plans. The biggest issue here that affects treatment planning is intellectual disability. At the time of autism diagnosis (if it was under age 5 or 6 years), most parents are told their child is "developmentally delayed" (a temporary condition implied), but not told intellectual disability (a permanent condition) may exist. Indeed, some children *are* just temporarily delayed. For many, delay persisting beyond the preschool years needs to be reinterpreted as a permanently altered and slowed trajectory in some or all areas of development. When parents are not educated to understand that intellectual disability is not the same as autism, parents of children with mild or even moderate intellectual disability often conclude their child's delays are entirely a part of autism. When they hear of wonderful adult outcomes in the media, like young people with autism going to college, they have no way of knowing that young person is not like their own. Without follow-up care and support in understanding a child's response to intervention, it can be very hard to develop an operationally useful picture of where a child may be able to go in the future.

Some families don't receive follow-up care, but nevertheless intuit what the future holds and proceed to plan with realistic notions of their child's future. Others just avoid thinking about it. With professionals often absent from the process of ongoing reappraisal of the child's progress and treatment planning, this shouldn't be surprising. It is time that public policy support ongoing care for autism.

What's Next?

We've talked about what autism is to parents and diagnosticians. But, how did autism become autism? The process of defining what gets to be called autism is much more political than scientific. Basically, the same can be said for virtually every *DSM* psychiatric diagnosis. There is some science, but is it enough? Is it the right kind of science to advance our understanding of the causes and treatments of psychiatric disorders? In the next chapter, I pull back the curtain of soft science that cloaks *DSM* by tracing how autism came to be, how it changed, and where today's autism seems to be going.

Notes

1. Huguet, G., Ey, E., & Bourgeron, T. (2013). The genetic landscapes of autism spectrum disorders. *Annual Review of Genomics Human Genetics, 14*, 191–213.

2. Christensen, D. L., Baio, J., Braun, K. V., Bilder, D., Charles, J., Constantino, J. N., . . . Yeargin-Allsopp, M. (2016). Prevalence and characteristics of autism spectrum disorder among children aged 8 years—Autism and Developmental Disabilities Monitoring Network, 11 Sites, United States, 2012. *MMWR Surveillance Summaries, 65*(SS-3), 1–23. doi:http://dx.doi.org/10.15585/mmwr.ss6503a1

3. Iwata, K., Matsuzaki, H., Takei, N., Manabe, T., & Mori, N. (2010). Animal models of autism: An epigenetic and environmental viewpoint. *Journal of Central Nervous System Disease, 2,* 37–44. Retrieved from https://www.ncbi.nlm.nih.gov/pmc/articles/PMC3661233/

4. American Psychiatric Association. (1987). *Diagnostic and statistical manual of mental disorders* (3rd ed., rev.; *DSM-III-R*). Washington, DC: APA Press.

5. Zablotsky, B., Black, L. I., Maenner, M. J., Schieve, L. A., & Blumberg, S. J. (2015, November 13). *Estimated prevalence of autism and other developmental disabilities following questionnaire changes in the 2014 National Health Interview Survey.* National Health Statistics Report No. 87. Retrieved from https://pdfs.semanticscholar.org/92c2/2987bdb439 7ef53b8e2b0b8a7bda432a0900.pdf

6. Centers for Disease Control and Prevention (CDC). (n.d.-a). *Autism spectrum disorder: Facts about ASDs.* Retrieved September 15, 2016, from http://www.cdc.gov/ncbddd/autism/facts.html

7. Centers for Disease Control and Prevention (CDC). (n.d.-b). *Reproductive health: Data and statistics.* Retrieved September 15, 2016, from http://www.cdc.gov/reproductivehealth/data_stats/

8. Educational vs. medical autism diagnosis. (2013, June 27). *Spectrums Magazine.* Retrieved from http://spectrumsmagazine.com/educational-vs-medical-autism-diagnosis/

9. CAR Autism Roadmap. (n.d.). *Medical diagnosis vs. educational eligibility for special services: Important distinctions for those with ASD.* Retrieved from https://www.carautismroadmap.org/medical-diagnosis-vs-educational-eligibility-for-special-services-important-distinctions-for-those-with-asd/. Last updated June 15, 2016.

10. American Psychiatric Association. (1994). *Diagnostic and statistical manual of mental disorders* (4th ed.; *DSM-IV*). Washington, DC: APA Press.

11. American Psychiatric Association. (2013). *Diagnostic and statistical manual of mental disorders* (5th ed.; *DSM-5*). Washington, DC: APA Press.

12. Siegel, B. (2004). *Pervasive Developmental Disorders Screening Test-II.* San Antonio, TX: Psychological Corporation/Harcourt Assessment/Pearson.

3 }

The Psychiatric Diagnosis Industry

THE APA AND ITS *DSM*

Autism Is a Disorder

Autism, like all conditions described in the American Psychiatric Association's (APA's) "bible," the *Diagnostic and Statistical Manual* (*DSM*) describes the difficulties of certain people who will be called autistic or be described as on the autism spectrum. These people will have problems adjusting to life, and a label is presumed to be useful in guiding them to appropriate help. The diagnosis of any form of autism, just like other *DSM* diagnoses, is an amalgam of problems that tend to appear together and are referred to as a *disorder*. The boundaries of these psychiatric amalgams shift as research suggests additional problems that further define a given disorder. This is critically different from a diagnosis of a *disease*, where there are physiological delimiters called *biomarkers* determined through measurements like blood tests, imaging, and the like, and where the presence of a disease then can be spoken of in more absolute terms.

Without biomarkers, psychiatric disorder boundaries shift with the words describing the symptoms. "Dose" matters: A little obsessive–compulsive disorder (OCD) might make you a good accountant. A little attention deficit hyperactivity disorder (ADHD) might help you on the floor of the New York Stock Exchange. Gifts and talents may correlate with certain psychiatric symptoms. Did Mozart have bipolar disorder? Did Van Gogh have schizophrenia? I'll leave that to their biographers. Mozart and Van Gogh were recognized as excellent at their pursuits because of their strengths, quite possibly enhanced by their psychiatric disorders, which arguably also hastened the mortality of each. In the late 1960s, the psychiatrist R. D. Laing made a case for recognizing all mental illness as a potentially positive variant of sanity. Laing sought to destigmatize schizophrenia by referring to it as on a continuum with "normal." His work later extended to destigmatizing many mental disorders and helped place discussion of psychiatric disorders on the same plane as discussion of physical diseases, conditions that were not the patient's "fault."

Some see autism as a condition endowing benefit the way Laing saw schizophrenia as potentially endowing benefit. "Geeks" and "Aspies" become admired as savants for monomaniacal focus on a topic of their interest. Autistic savants who draw with great accuracy are seen as even more impressive than neurotypical artists who draw the same way. Being able to draw in detail when you can't speak enough to hold a conversation is indeed mystifying. For those with high-functioning autism who can speak well, social malapropisms can be seen as curious, but valid self-expression, and not as failure to be able to consider the perspective of another. While this kind of reframing can serve to decrease stigma and help one to see the cup "half-full" rather than "half-empty," it rails against the purpose of psychiatry, which is to identify disordered behavior and alleviate psychic pain the individual may experience from his or her perceived distortions of reality.

I am not a "Laingian" when it comes to understanding autism. Rather, I see autism as a collection of "autistic learning disabilities" in social motivation, direction of attention, affiliative drive, sensory processing, and the like. These create barriers to successful adaptation as a social and societal being. The definition I use does not see autism as an endowment or a gift, but as an impairment, though gifts of artistic ability or visual spatial prowess may relate directly to the attenuated visual and non-social lens through which some with autism see and process the world. Many autism self-advocates have come to see what others have told them is their disability as their strength. Narrow interests spoken about perseveratively, a conversational style limited by the inability to read nonverbal cues that you have said enough or too much, and the insistence on one's own way of doing things (despite a parent or work supervisor's preferences) are all problems and need to be seen as part of the disorder. Self-advocates who have very high-functioning autism or Asperger's write about themselves and their experiences in a way that frames these traits as enabling unique adaption. This has helped "autism" become a desirable diagnosis for some people, as explicated in the autism self-advocacy poster in Figure 3.1. I will argue this is more politics than science.

This chapter explores how the diagnosis of an autism spectrum disorder (ASD), along with other *DSM* diagnoses, often is framed politically, at least as much as scientifically. A case in point is how politics influenced the coming (in 1994) of the diagnosis of Asperger's disorder and its going (in 2013).

Growing Grass

The whole idea of autism, along with all other childhood-onset psychiatric disorders, is modern, though there are historical records for what was likely

Always
Unique
Totally
Interesting
Sometimes
Mysterious

FIGURE 3.1 Contemporary autism advocacy poster.

autism in centuries past. Schizophrenia also has been described for eons across cultures and social classes. A more modern idea has been to map psychiatric disorders *developmentally.* Mapping of any psychiatric disorder's "developmental psychopathology," of its symptoms (the weeds) sprouting alongside typical development (the grass), is pretty new. Weeds can choke out grass (over time, psychopathology can take over); weeds can be cut back so they don't make the grass look ugly (symptoms suppressed with medicines); or weeds can be pulled out by the roots (the promise of therapies that leverage neuroplasticity).

Important to diagnosing autism and other conditions first evident at very early ages is that all problems look much the same the younger one looks for them: If you are a toddler and can't talk, you may be autistic, but you also may be deaf, be hard of hearing, have a language-processing problem, be intellectually disabled, or may even be traumatized. The brain only has so many ways to say "ouch" when you can't yet talk and are not yet expected to provide for your own daily needs. We therefore expect those earliest "buds" of childhood psychiatric disorders to look most like one another in toddlers. Symptoms will become increasingly differentiated in children as they grow—once they should be able to talk, play, and form friendships. When the brain grows to adulthood and capacities for abstract reasoning emerge, there is even more differentiation in the behavioral repertoire, so we then get "weeds" we call psychoses. With development, fuller expression of psychopathology is supported by a brain that may be organizing in increasingly atypical and impactful ways. (The "seeds" for schizophrenia are likely present all along, but "look" different in the context of less mature developmental acts.) This conceptualization places emphasis on the fact that psychiatric diagnosis in childhood necessarily will be limited by how the *forme fruste* (early manifestations) can be expected to overlap.

Not surprisingly, though we have lots of research on what autism looks like in very young children, we lack a decent descriptive taxonomy for what adults who will go on to develop schizophrenia, bipolar disorder, severe mania, or severe depression acted like when they were 2, 3, 5, or 10 years old. Undoubtedly, some of what we see today in toddlers and fit into autism, ADHD, and the other childhood-onset neuropsychiatric disorder classifications may instead be the first glimmers of those adult disorders expressed by brains that cannot yet think and act based on more abstract reason. Nevertheless, *DSM* enumerates diagnostic criteria for childhood disorders as if they were as nondevelopmental and static as adult disorders.

With this in mind, let's explore the history of how what we now call autism and ASDs have been recognized and diagnosed across the history of *DSM*. The goal of this investigation is to uncover how autism as well as other diagnoses arguably are more a reflection of political forces than empirical data with a neurobiological basis (which we basically don't have). To me, this supports the idea that if there is no medical basis for constantly changing criteria for psychiatric disorders, maybe we shouldn't be constantly changing them, especially for conditions first diagnosed in childhood where behavioral specificity is lowest.

Autism, Asperger's, and a Brief History of the *DSM*s

The concept of "autism" did not exist before 1943. In that year, Dr. Leo Kanner wrote an academic paper describing "autistic disturbances of affective contact," naming this problem and associated symptoms "early infantile autism."[1] By this, Kanner meant that these children with early infantile autism related to others like infants, focused on satisfying their own needs rather than taking pleasure from social reciprocity. There was enough interest in Kanner's work that when the APA first published standards for psychiatric diagnostic classifications in 1952, they included "early infantile autism," and variants of early infantile autism have been included in each version of *DSM* since. The current version is the fifth edition, *DSM-5*.[2]

The term *autism* was coined in the heyday of psychoanalysis. Psychotropic medications were just making the scene. Treatment for everything psychiatric was largely talking therapies, even for autism, where getting "refrigerator parents" talking was seen as key to warming up their cold, aloof children. Today, we have moved a long way from seeing autism and other psychiatric disorders as caused by parental treatment. Most diagnostic criteria of today's *DSM-5* disorders have roots in the original 1952 *DSM*. Like the diagnostic criteria for autism, the criteria defining each disorder have been refined with each new edition of *DSM*. Today, it is widely accepted that most psychiatric disorders originally considered psychogenic are now seen as caused by faulty neurobiology. But, in psychiatry, unlike other fields of medicine, today, as in 1952, there are no defining biomarkers for psychiatric diagnoses as there are in other fields of medicine.

One theme of this chapter is that psychiatry, in general, has some barriers to becoming a hard science. Diagnosis for autism and diagnosis for most childhood and adult psychiatric disorders are simply descriptive of behavior. Psychiatry considers itself a field of medicine, but none of its disorders is diagnosed by biological markers—the way cancer is, heart disease is, or, really, everything else we think of as medical. Without biomarkers defining a diagnosis, the *DSM* process of frequently changing boundaries of psychiatric diagnoses can be argued to be nothing more than an annoying moving target for researchers looking for genes or neural substrates in preferably nonmoving target population cases or for clinicians looking to validate effective treatments.

THE SOFT SCIENCE OF PSYCHIATRIC DIAGNOSIS

Essentially, psychiatric diagnoses lack validity. Validity for psychiatric diagnoses would be a biological substrate—a gene, a region of the brain—with a characteristic defect linked to a descriptive diagnosis. Without validity, psychiatric diagnoses can strive only for *reliability*—a statistical term meaning that one group of clinicians or researchers can all agree that a particular group of people have autism (or ADHD or whatever) and then train others to use their standards in the same way to reach the same diagnosis. All the agreement among standardizing clinicians means is that it's an agreement. The *DSM* can be continually redrafted to reflect changing agreements—as long as there still are no biomarkers for the newly refined diagnoses either.

Fast forward a half-century or so from the first 1952 diagnostic manual: The APA has revised its criteria for mental disorders several times. Why? One might posit that the revisions to *DSM* have been spurred by sociological and political, rather than purely scientific, reasons: The best example of this is the 1973 change in the second edition (*DSM-II*) wherein homosexuality was no longer considered a psychiatric disorder. Do you think the discussions that led to the decision to no longer consider being gay a disorder were data driven or political and sociological?

THE MOVE TO MEDICALIZING PSYCHIATRY

A countervail to politics sneaking into psychiatric classification has been the medicalization of psychiatry supported by the move away from psychogenic to neurobiological causes for its disorders. Arguments that psychiatric disorders are not psychogenic, but rather have biological underpinnings have propped opened the door for medical health insurance to pay for psychiatric care, which has been a boon for adults needing psychiatric care and for families needing psychiatric care for their children.

It has also opened the door for Big Pharma's willingness to produce a drug for every new or newly revised psychiatric disorder that *DSM* enumerates. In childhood psychiatric disorders, the hand-in-hand partnership of diagnosis and drugs plays out a bit differently than for adults because parents tend to resist psychopharmacology for their children in ways they do not resist it for themselves. This is for good reason. Children have developing brains in a way that adults do not. We have a poor understanding of how psychopharmacological agents that alter neurochemicals in the brain may alter subsequent brain development in a child. Most parents don't think in such explicit terms, but generally get this on some level.

This pendulum swing in psychiatry from psychogenic to biological causes has led to some occasionally frightening reports about psychiatric care for children; psychopharmacology is especially frightening for toddlers and preschoolers. A December 2015 *New York Times* article documented children *under age 2* being prescribed antipsychotics.[3] The brain is developing rapidly, and there are simply no safety or efficacy studies (and no medical ethics board would even approve studies of them) in such young children. When children this young are prescribed antipsychotics, it is fairly certain that a psychiatric diagnosis has been given that child. While there may be evidence that the drug fits the diagnosis, it is less clear that any psychoactive drug fits a toddler. Medicalizing psychiatry and then labeling very young children with psychiatric disorders gives cover to medically treating a very young child who may well have a psychogenic (or "behavioral," the now-preferred term) antecedent—that may be effectively treated (behaviorally) without brain-changing chemicals. The field of psychiatry has done a deal with the devil: In exchange for medicalization of undesired behavior, any behavior that is undesired can be seen as subject to medical (pharmacological) treatment—even in toddlers. But, giving a toddler Risperdal, a powerful antipsychotic, is not the same as giving a toddler cough medicine for a cough.

PSYCHIATRIC DIAGNOSIS AND OFF-LABEL PRESCRIBING TO CHILDREN

Nevertheless, off-label prescribing of psychiatric drugs (tested in adults) to children continues to increase. There are not enough studies—partly because funding agencies and medical ethics committees balk at the needed randomized clinical trials with very long-term follow-up that would be needed to really know not only what works, but also what is safe to start and at what ages. This is particularly concerning because, as I have already discussed, a diagnostic label for a very young child is subject to misinterpretation: The younger the child is, the more similar behavioral disturbances look across diagnoses. A major parent-intolerable tantrum in a child with autism, a child with ADHD, and a child with a future diagnosis of bipolar disorder may look much the same. The drug to treat that tantrum may differ according to which label that young child already carries: For example, if the child was thought to be autistic and having a tantrum about something being imperfectly ordered, the child might be given a selective serotonin reuptake inhibitor (SSRI). If the child was thought to have ADHD, the tantrum might be seen as overactivation and treated with a psychostimulant. If the child was thought to have a bipolar disorder, he or she might be given a mood stabilizer to quell the tantrums. None of these classes of psychoactive drugs is explicitly approved for use in any 2- or 3-year-old—not exactly precision medicine.

The politics of off-label prescribing for young children are influenced by the scarcity of child psychiatrists, relatively few pediatricians with specific training in psychotropic medications, and parents who need to keep their jobs but have badly behaved children who are kicked out of day care after day care. One real concern is that prescribing a medicine is quicker and less costly than analysis of potential sources of anxiety, mood, aggression, or hyperactivity. Parent training and behavioral treatments are very costly alternatives to medication and most often not in the toolbox of medical doctors. A 2013 article in *Pediatrics* reviewed US trends in psychotropic medicines for children over the prior 15 years.[4] About 15 percent of 2- to 5-year-olds with an ASD were medicated with one or more psychotropic medicines. For children that age diagnosed with a mood disorder, it was 66 percent and with ADHD, 58 percent. APA's classification of childhood disorders termed neuropsychiatric or neurodevelopmental (like autism or ADHD) places a focus on the nervous system (rather than, say, experiential adversity or bad parenting). Is that formulation based on data, or is it better characterized as a hypothesis?

THE ORIGINAL *DSM*

The 1952 first edition of the *DSM*, now sometimes referred to as *DSM-I*,[5] was then "supplemented" in 1965 to line up with the then-current 1949 *International Classification of Diseases* (*ICD-6*),[6] the rest of the world's manual for classifying different psychiatric and other medical conditions. If you think about it, it took a certain hubris to create a separate and purely American and purely psychiatric classification system in the first place, when Americans and the rest of the world already were subscribing to a system put in place by the World Health Organization.

DSM-II

In 1968, there was the second *DSM* edition, *DSM-II*[7]—in retrospect, the first realization by APA that there was a business in rolling out updates to diagnostic nomenclature. The diagnosis of "Autism" appeared in tandem with

"Childhood Schizophrenia," as, at the time, it was thought that possibly most children with autism were also suffering possible cognitive deficit, while those with childhood schizophrenia were mostly appearing more able cognitively. The first scientific journal to publish research on autism appeared in 1971, the *Journal of Autism and Childhood Schizophrenia*.

DSM-III

In 1980, the year I received my PhD, the APA really got busy in the psychiatric classification business with publication of *DSM*'s third edition, *DSM-III*.[8] This was only 7 years after the last notable *DSM* changes in 1973 with the sixth printing change to *DSM-II* (in which homosexuality was removed as a disorder).[9] In *DSM-III*, childhood schizophrenia was dropped, considered rare anyway, not necessarily related to schizophrenia in adults, and questionably related to autism. Autism itself was subsumed under a new descriptor, "pervasive developmental disorder." The *Journal of Autism and Childhood Schizophrenia*, keeping up with the times, changed its name to the *Journal of Autism and Developmental Disorders*. (With that change, research on childhood schizophrenia pretty much ended.) Research on *DSM-II* had shown that, clinically, doctors might disagree on childhood psychiatric diagnoses up to 50 percent of the time, so the goal of *DSM-III* was to be more reliable (use criteria on which all evaluators could agree).[10]

DSM-III-R

DSM-III was still fairly new in 1984, but studies that would lead the *DSM-III* to change into *DSM-III-R* (*R* for "revised") in 1987 began to ramp up.[11] I have to say I rode the wave: The goal of a new *DSM*, we were told, was to incorporate new data to build a more empirical *DSM*. As a junior researcher, I was invited to participate in the *DSM-III-R* field trials for autism (at the Stanford University site where I was doing my research at the time), so I had a very inside view of the process of making new *DSM*s as a field site coordinator. As a young scientist with a statistical bent, I tried to make sense of what this process really was trying to accomplish. My job was to think about statistical reliability. Everyone emphasized how important it was to making *DSM* statistically reliable. It was still years until it would dawn on me to be bothered by the lack of validity. As it was in 1987, *DSM* was all about reliability (agreement) and still today pays way too little attention to validity (whether signs or symptoms correlate with a causal factor or even a treatment response).[12]

With psychiatric diagnoses getting more reliable, though, we could, at least, all use *DSM* criteria to agree on who did and did not have autism, now called autistic disorder, or a partial form of autism, now called PDD, NOS (pervasive developmental disorder, not otherwise specified). Autism, like many psychiatric disorders, had an NOS subclassification for individuals with a subset of symptoms who did not seem to be as fully affected as others meeting more full criteria. (Adding that "NOS" to all sorts of *DSM* disorders helped improve reliability for many classifications. It also created a new problem for autism and other disorders—having an NOS form of something tended to obfuscate lower limits below which an individual could no longer be considered affected. Today, this persists as a major problem in determining where symptoms are few or mild enough so as *not* to be "on the spectrum.") When *DSM-III-R* was published, there was not yet outright recognition of an "autism spectrum," but some researchers, including myself, were starting to find it a more helpful description than PDD, NOS, an awkward mouthful that meant little to end users, who most often were parents of a newly diagnosed child.

The Politics of APA and the National Institute of Mental Health

At about the same time that publication of *DSM-III-R* was under consideration, the National Institute of Mental Health (NIMH) had begun talking in similar terms about establishing RDC (Research Diagnostic Criteria) for use by researchers of psychiatric disorders so that those investigating causes or treatments of psychiatric disorders would have reliable diagnostic criteria to use in research studies—which perhaps would stay stable for longer than the prior four sets of *DSM* criteria, and could look more microscopically at behaviors of interest. The thought was that RDC might have had advantages over *DSM* as they could have included specific signs of disorders that a researcher was studying: A researcher advocating for RDC might want a criterion for, say, "hand-flapping" if there was reason to suspect a specific neural etiology separate from other repetitive motor movements. In *DSM,* by contrast, it was seen as more easy to establish agreement (reliability) on the presence or absence of repetitive motor movements if hand-flapping was simply lumped in with all other repetitive motor movements.

I remember at the time thinking that the RDC were a great idea and just what researchers needed. But, basically, the NIMH's RDC threatened to compromise the very existence of, the very need for, the APA's *DSM*. For example, if a drug or other therapy's efficacy was validated on research carried out on an RDC-defined sample, clinicians in practice would want to know whether the patient for whom he or she might use that treatment was like RDC-defined study participants rather than like what *DSM* was calling a case with the same disorder. What happened? APA effectively co-opted the NIMH's agenda to develop more researcher-friendly criteria by including the same researchers who could have worked on the NIMH RDC into the *DSM* field trials.

Duck or Platypus?

While *DSM-III-R* did have reliability field trials, definitely a move in the right direction, something RDC advocates could endorse, the veneer of "science" for *DSM* diagnoses still was only skin deep: The diagnostic classifications were now more reliable (key scientists could all agree to call a "duck," a "duck,") but the classifications had no more "validity" than before. Validity would be like agreeing a duck should be classified as a bird because it can fly—like other things we call birds. With *DSM-III-R*, we could all agree on who had which label, which diagnosis, but had no idea whether those diagnoses meant anything in terms of unitary cause (or unitary treatment response). We did not know, for example, whether HFA (high-functioning autism) and LFA (low-functioning autism) were both ducks. For all we knew then, for all we still know, HFA may be a duck, and LFA might well be a duck-billed platypus (an egg-laying mammal some people think is a bird). Lumping forms of autism together (like high functioning and low functioning) moved people away from considering how they might be separate disorders and instead arbitrarily placed emphasis on similarities—common "autistic" symptoms—rather than on differences like intellectual level.

Changing Criteria, Changing Prevalence Rates

In moving from *DSM-III* to *DSM-III-R*, another peculiar thing had happened. Just by changing the wording and the thresholds for pervasive developmental disorder (meaning either autistic disorder or PDD, NOS), about one third more of reported cases turned out to meet *DSM-III-R* criteria but had not met *DSM-III* criteria.[12] Between *DSM-III* and *DSM-III-R*, some wording had changed, but perhaps most important, while a certain number and type of symptoms had to be present to be diagnosed with autistic disorder, there was no lower threshold specified for the number or type of symptoms needed to be diagnosed with PDD, NOS. This, I'd argue, was one factor at the beginning of the "autism epidemic." By the publication of the fourth *DSM* edition, *DSM-IV*, this lack of a specified lower cutoff for PDD, NOS was "corrected," but the idea that PDD, NOS meant just *some* symptoms of autism still could be a form of autism had taken hold.

DSM-IV

The idea, on publication of *DSM-III-R*, was that criteria could be further modified once there were biomarkers to validate the boundaries of these disorders. *Did* APA wait? No. Five years later, in 1994, *DSM-IV*[13] was published following much the same procedures as *DSM-III-R* with no new biomarkers to increase validity (like gene markers, neuroimaging findings, or drug responses). The biggest change for the autism classification was that Asperger's disorder was added as a new subtype of PDD, though the old PDD, NOS continued as well.

As no surprise, the incidence of autism again increased as cases previously "not autistic enough" to have autistic disorder or PDD, NOS were found to have Asperger's disorder. In particular, the inclusion of Asperger's turned the case-finding focus from mainly toddlers and preschoolers to school-aged children, teens, and even adults who might now be included under the Asperger's classification. Additionally, the inclusion of less severely affected individuals (that is, those now diagnosable with Asperger's) had the effect of lowering the PDD "bar" overall. Most notable was that the inclusion of Asperger's pushed the recognition of autism symptoms in those without intellectual disability like never before. The reported epidemiology of autism at the publication of *DSM-IV* was that 30 percent had normal intellectual functioning and 70 percent some degree of intellectual disability. By the time Asperger's had been added to the autism spectrum for the 23 years of *DSM-IV*, this ratio had flipped, with 70 percent of those on the autism spectrum now appearing not to have intellectual disability, while 30 percent were still rated as having it. Was *this* the "epidemic" or just new individuals who previously did not meet *DSM-III-R* criteria now counted as having a form of autism, largely because of the addition of Asperger's?

DSM-IV was arguably a rearrangement of the deckchairs on the deck of the ship (which did not sink) but moved no closer to its beautiful destination. During the time *DSM-IV* was in place, new studies showed autism incidence continuing to rise. Fears about new etiologies sprang from everywhere. (We'll get to vaccines in Chapter 8.) The addition of Asperger's and increasing scrutiny of school-aged children, teens, and adults for Asperger's or for more mildly expressed symptoms of ASD were virtually never tagged as possible contributors to this new "autism epidemic."

DSM-IV-TR

The fourth edition of *DSM, DSM-IV*, was followed by its millennium doppelganger, its "text revision," *DSM-IV-TR*,[14] in 2000. Asperger's disorder was where all the excitement was about for "the autisms" in *DSM-IV-TR*. The concept of ASDs had, by this point, become widespread. As more individuals with normal IQ were diagnosed with Asperger's, there were more people "on the spectrum" who could speak and advocate for themselves. The very qualities of what was considered core to autism of the 1970s, 1980s, and 1990s inexorably shifted. More people in the general population had heard of autism as more people were found to be on the spectrum. More people had the impression that many with autism were exceptionally smart. *Autistic* and *Asperger's* became adjectives in common parlance to describe odd, eccentric, quirky, boorish, asocial friends, family, and coworkers. The boundaries between a disorder and a personality variant thinned.

DSM-5

The next edition of the *DSM*, the fifth, is called *DSM-5* (and not *DSM-V)* because the Roman numeral system was eliminated so that future revisions could be made more like software updates. Envision a future *DSM-5.1, DSM-5.2,* and so on. So, what propelled *DSM-5* into existence? By 2010 or so, there was a new crop of researchers who had never been in a field trial for *DSM*. Even if we set aside methodological concerns about the lack of validating biomarkers, the thought of a *DSM-5* brought up other concerns: It seemed not unrealistic to fear that with a new *DSM*, cases might again be added.

My concern was that a new definition using the term *autism spectrum disorder* might embrace everyone with poor social skills and ADHD, those with a language problem that caused it to be hard to make friends, and those with anxiety, and a slow-to-warm temperament, who weren't badly behaved enough to be considered to have a mood disorder. I dreaded to consider it. I was hoping the *Autism Diagnostic Observation Schedule* (ADOS), widely used as the "gold standard" diagnostic assessment at this point, would come out with a new version geared to a *DSM-5*. It did, but still lacked criteria for assigning a diagnosis other than autism. With the new ADOS standards, more of the nonautistic kids I had in mind would surely be considered on the spectrum.

Why was I concerned? Any change to who was included on the autism spectrum could wreak havoc with ongoing research study samples already partly comprised of *DSM-IV* cases. When *DSM-5* was introduced, all of the large national and international biobanks held carefully diagnosed *DSM-IV* cases. If *DSM-5* criteria brought some new cases in, or kicked some cases out, these researchers and clinicians would now be studying or treating something a bit different. At this point, I was working closely with researchers interested in autism genetics and autism neuroimaging at UCSF, and their concerns, along with my own, were palpable and understandable.

What actually did happen when *DSM-5* replaced *DSM-IV-TR* in 2013? Part of what I worried about did come to pass: For example, removal of the restriction of diagnosing autism in a child with primary signs of ADHD led to more cases of children being diagnosed with both, essentially a new variant of autism. The best part, for me, was eliminating PDD, NOS as an arbitrarily "partial" form of autism, as well as eliminating the superordinate term *pervasive developmental disorder*, which had often been confused with PDD, NOS. We now had the term *autism spectrum disorder* instead. There were no subtypes of autism like Asperger's disorder or PDD, NOS, but rather varying degrees of severity noted for each of two autism symptom domains: social communication symptoms and routine or ritual behaviors. *DSM-5* brought in the idea of severity ratings: 0 if the symptom was not marked; 1 if it was mild; 2 if marked; and 3 if severe. Those meeting all three social communication criteria (symptoms) and showing at least two of four symptoms of restricted, repetitive patterns of interest or activity would be diagnosed as having ASD. Strangely, the *DSM-5* manual states that if you had a *DSM-IV* PDD or *DSM-IV* Asperger's disorder, it is OK to just go ahead and say you have *DSM-5* ASD—without

TABLE 3.1 } *DSM-5* Criteria for Autism Spectrum Disorder (Adapted)

A. Persistent deficits in social communication and social interaction across multiple contexts (must meet A.1, A.2, and A.3)

1. Deficits in social–emotional reciprocity

2. Deficits in nonverbal communicative behaviors

3. Deficits in developing, maintaining, and understanding relationships

Severity level (0 = not marked, 1 = mild, 2 = marked, 3 = severe)

B. Restricted, repetitive patterns of behavior, interests, or activities (must show at least two of four of B.1, B.2, B.3, B.4)

1. Stereotyped or repetitive motor movements, use of objects, or speech

2. Insistence on sameness, inflexible adherence to routines, or ritualized behavior

3. Highly restricted, fixated interests that are abnormal in intensity or focus

4. Hyper- or hyporeactivity to sensory input or unusual interest in environmental sensory input

Severity level (0 = not marked, 1 = mild, 2 = marked, 3 = severe)

Source: Adapted from *DSM-5* criteria for autism spectrum disorder.[2]

applying the new *DSM-5* criteria. This made little sense as some diagnosed with Asperger's in *DSM-IV* might not have the *DSM-IV* symptom profile that can map onto *DSM-5* ASD. The distinction between those with a full set of symptoms equaling autistic disorder in *DSM-IV* or a partial set as in *DSM-IV* equaling PDD, NOS or Asperger's has been removed. Everyone is now on the spectrum together (Table 3.1).

In the continued absence of biomarkers, *DSM-5* created something that essentially hypothesized that all the cases had some form of the same thing—were all somewhere on the spectrum. This was a committee decision, not an evidence-based one. It is unclear that *DSM-5* is a scientific improvement for investigators of etiology or treatments for autism, but it is fair to say that the deckchairs have been painted, reupholstered, and rearranged again.

The ESSENCE Alternative

Increasingly, researchers share a consensus that when a causal agent, gene, or brain region is found to be highly linked to autism, it will correlate most highly with a fairly specific symptom or symptom cluster, and not as strongly to the diagnosis of autism per se. For example, we are coming to understand that dysfunction in certain neural circuits correlates most strongly with specific information-processing problems (like slow auditory processing speed, slow habituation to auditory or vestibular stimulation)—which on a broader symptom level can be expressed as signs of autism like echolalia (repeating things as heard without necessarily fully comprehending them) or auditory hypersensitivity. My own work has been informed by this framework, operationalizing autism symptoms as autistic learning disabilities and autistic learning styles. But the researcher whose work is most outstanding in this regard is Dr. Christopher

Gillberg of the University of Gothenburg in Sweden, who has proposed reconceptualizing all childhood neurodevelopmental disorders as ESSENCE[15] (early symptomatic syndromes eliciting neurodevelopmental clinical examination). Under the ESSENCE umbrella are all signs and symptoms, not statistically aggregated in ways that specify different disorders, but rather enumerated separately to promote investigation of pandiagnostic constructs like lack of a social affiliative drive, lack of capacity for imitation, lack of affect recognition or nonverbal communication, speed of auditory processing, or other sensory processing threshold abnormalities that can be present in not only ASDs but also other child psychiatric disorders.

ESSENCE could be codified by returning to the idea of RDC as was proposed in the 1990s, with characterization of traits with expression likely closer to gene or brain functions than clinical diagnostic groupings. This is discussed again in Chapter 9 of this book in the context of new strategies to promote research on autism causes.

Initial Community Response to *DSM-5* Autism Spectrum Disorders

Back to the politics of *DSM-5*: The Asperger's self-advocacy blogosphere went ballistic when it got around that Asperger's as a separate diagnostic classification (which had appeared for the first time in *DSM-IV*) was being dropped from the new *DSM-5* ASDs. No longer would these quirky souls have their very own label, but they would be lumped with often less able individuals with rather different variants of ASD. From a community mental health perspective, this made some sense, but it has been ego wounding for the Aspie community, many with average or above-average intellectual capacities. They can experience much of the world they wish to access like an elusive brass ring on a merry-go-round. Diagnosticians might rate their *DSM* ASD symptoms as a 1 (mild) compared to others on the autism spectrum, but their *own* experiences of their barriers often are *not* experienced as mild but as severe when they compare themselves to peers they describe as "neurotypicals."

Dissension Among Autism Researchers Over *DSM-5*

At the 2012 International Meetings for Autism Research (IMFAR) in Toronto, Canada, just before *DSM-5* was published in May 2013, the APA's appointed *DSM-5* Autism Field Trials panel was met by a largely hostile room of about 500 of the world's top autism researchers. The APA's proposed *DSM-5* ASD criteria had already been posted for comments for months. The panel chair let us know that more comments had been posted on the *DSM-5* ASD page than for any other field-trialed classification for *DSM-5*.

The *DSM-5* Autism Spectrum Disorder Field Trial panel came to IMFAR to "sell" their new diagnostic criteria for ASD to the constituency for whom it had been constructed. Few, if any, words of praise were heard. One main concern was about those who might lose services due to removal of the diagnostic classification of PDD, NOS, and that the newly created diagnosis of social (pragmatic) communication disorder (SCD) was an effort to "kick" those with mild PDD, NOS "off" the spectrum. It didn't happen. The SCD diagnosis has not been widely adopted. Many former PDD, NOS cases either were shoehorned into *DSM-5* autism or were simply described as "on the spectrum," returning us again to the situation in *DSM-III-R* where there is no well-specified lower cutoff.

Most vocal about *DSM-5* during its review period, not surprisingly, were blogging adults with Asperger's—who announced that they certainly had Asperger's, not autism, and always would. As this IMFAR meeting to present the new *DSM-5* criteria for ASDs proceeded, it became clear that the panel intended no reexamination of the criteria based on anybody's comments, and that APA's posted comment period had served as a straw man for a done deal.

Politics of *DSM-5* Changes

The IMFAR panel had offered that eliminating Asperger's from *DSM-5* would put the kibosh on further inflating of incidence numbers as *DSM-III-R* and *DSM-IV* had. Certainly in my own experience, there were lots of adults with all sorts of psychiatric illness being drawn to Asperger's as a somehow less stigmatizing label. These adults, most newly diagnosed with Asperger's in adulthood, were often quite dissimilar from the standardization sample that had met criteria for Asperger's disorder in the *DSM-IV* field trials. It was clear, however, that such individuals would still hew to their Asperger's label, focusing on one or two criteria they did meet, ignoring the diagnostic requirement for autistic disorder that they needed to meet additional criteria as well.

Diagnostic No Man's Land: Social (Pragmatic) Communication Disorder

There was serious concern about "falling off the spectrum" for the *DSM-IV* PDD, NOS cases who did not have any atypical routine or repetitive behaviors, now required in *DSM-5* to meet ASD criteria. In *DSM-IV*, a substantial number of cases receiving the PDD, NOS diagnosis did so specifically because they had much the same social and communication difficulties that any child with autism might have, but lacked oddly routinized or repetitive behavior—mandatory for getting that *DSM-IV* full-syndrome "autistic disorder" label. These individuals might have the social and communication problems associated with autism in spades, and in those respects be indistinguishable from any other child clearly meeting full criteria for autistic disorder, but did not do things like lining up toys, flapping hands, or covering their ears. *DSM-5* requires such cases be exiled from the autism spectrum to a new diagnostic no man's land called S(P)CD (also known as SCD).

Nobody has wanted to be the parent of the child who is diagnosed with SCD instead of ASD. No clinician I know wants to give the diagnosis to a child with autism symptoms the clinician feels may benefit from autism-specific services—but just happens to lack routine, repetitive behaviors. I've seen several children who have meet SCD criteria who are more severely autistic than some bona fide cases who can be considered to be on the spectrum with much milder difficulties. Should we be sneaking such children onto the spectrum by questioning a flicking of the wrist that might pass as a bit of hand-flapping (a qualifying motor stereotypy) or give the opinion that a 3-year-old boy can be loving Thomas the Tank Engine a little too much (and so qualify as having a narrow interest)? Given the lack of reliability or validity for SCD (let alone ASD), it is so much madness, as well as negligence, to deny such children any services known to benefit children with the social or communication problems that other children earning a place on the spectrum have.

The Politics of Getting That *DSM* Autism Diagnosis

The *DSM* as a piece of "intellectual property" has grown with each revision. As *DSM*'s prominence in defining psychiatric illness has increased, it arguably has become more political as some diagnoses are buoyed by how they have an impact on an individual's access to resources to support functioning in one or more settings: Among childhood psychiatric disorders, for example, we have diagnoses such as ADHD (to help with problems in school), oppositional defiant disorder (ODD; to extrajudicially address problems in interaction with authority figures), and (formerly) Asperger's disorder (to address problems in social and employment situations). The implication is that the diagnosis encapsulates a panoply of interrelated problems, not individual symptoms. By clustering problem behaviors together into diagnoses, we accept we are treating disorders, not individual symptoms.

Why is this a problem? When we talk about "autism treatment," it basically implies autism treatment will aid all components of autism. A child with autism can be subject to treatment strategies for component symptoms such as lack of nonverbal communication, presence of sensory sensitivities, and so on. Conversely, then, anyone with problems in nonverbal communication, anyone with sensory sensitivities, and so on might be seen as needing autism treatment. If a child might benefit from a component of autism treatment for a particular symptom, isn't that child then on the autism spectrum?

This is backward thinking because almost all symptoms of childhood psychiatric disorders, including those of autism, can occur in children with other *DSM* diagnoses. Such children may not seem fully autistic but may have the very notable presence of one or two signs—such as lack of eye contact. Other children may seem to more clearly have all the symptoms of another disorder, like ADHD, but cover their ears in response to high social or auditory stimulation. *DSM* has conflated diagnostic categories with symptoms of diagnoses as if we have a basis to conclude that something like auditory hypersensitivity correlates more strongly with the neuropathology of other signs of autism than other disorders. *DSM* is basically implying that if auditory hypersensitivity is a sign of autism, then shouldn't we be seeing any child with auditory hypersensitivity as a little bit autistic? What about a very verbal social child who covers her ears when fire engines go by? A little bit autistic? No. This should give a flavor of just how "soft" *DSM* diagnoses really can be.

DSM: THE HUB OF PSYCHIATRY'S WHEEL

Needing a diagnosis has become key to medical treatment, behavioral treatment, educational treatment, and advocacy organizations. Without the label of ASD, a child won't get medical services with codes approved for autism treatment and certainly won't get an applied behavior analysis (ABA) program, approved virtually only for autism. Children with a need for treatments considered mainly autism treatments can be out of luck: The child may have anxious agitation (just like a child with autism, who might be prescribed Risperdal), but the child with ADHD may be given a psychostimulant because that's what is designated as first-line treatment for ADHD. A 3-year-old child with no learning readiness might benefit from ABA but will not receive it, though a child with autism and no learning readiness will. A child with expressive apraxia might benefit from a very visually supported, high-routine classroom designed for children with autism but may not be placed there without an autism diagnosis.

You get the picture: The imprimatur of a *DSM* diagnosis of autism more readily opens the door to needed help than simply having the same symptoms but no *DSM* diagnosis of autism. Do you think this drives autism prevalence?

AUTISM STAKEHOLDER NO. 1: BIG PHARMA

Naturally, for drug companies who make an agent approved to treat autism, the more who are diagnosed with autism, the better. A prize for a pharmaceutical company would be Food and Drug Administration (FDA) approval for one of their agents to treat autism. Then the agent can be specifically marketed for autism treatment, irrespective of which specific symptoms of autism may be the treatment target. The *DSM* label of autism can then become more important than the target symptom in a prescribing decision. This results in things like 2-year-olds newly diagnosed with autism being prescribed Risperdal because it has been approved to treat autism, as I mentioned previously.[7] In autism, the *DSM* diagnosis is especially useful in medication marketing to nonspecialist clinicians less likely attuned to which symptoms an autism-approved drug might best target.

DSM, Autism, and Off-Label Prescribing

Much autism psychopharmacology is off-label treatment with agents that have not been well studied in autism, or not studied well in children, period. From a marketing point of view, it is no matter really, because physicians are free to prescribe agents as they feel is indicated by existing research, clinical experience, or the pitch they heard at an industry-sponsored dinner last week. (At an industry-sponsored lunch, I once was given a tennis ball–size spongy gray "brain," promoting Prozac. It goes without saying it was designed to remind one that if your patient needs an SSRI, why not start with Prozac?)

Big Pharma can't help but hope their newest psychoactive agent gets picked up as an off-label drug for autism, like Prozac (originally for OCD), propranolol (a beta-blocker, originally for heart conditions), or haloperidol (an early atypical antipsychotic). Big Pharma even will push academic researchers hungry for grant money into doing trials on a drug like Namenda (which is approved for dementia) with or without much of a mechanistic hypothesis of why it might work. What matters to Big Pharma is if it works for *DSM* autism cases—well, there's another market. In autism, which can present in so many different ways, it's a roll of the dice whether something like Namenda might help one of the many autism symptoms that some subset of individuals with autism can have. There are so few approved "autism" medicines, so much demand for ready (drug) treatment, that it really is the Wild West out there.

Chapter 7 discusses the alternative medicine culture in autism, which arguably has benefited from the substantial practice in off-label prescribing for autism: Parents, fearful of giving their child an agent designed for "something else," may turn to homeopathic prescribing that is even less data driven. Big Pharma's access to autism treatment may be most active among family physicians who, unbeknown to parents, are often not as highly trained in child psychopharmacology as pharmacology for physical diseases. Physicians who lack tools other than a prescription pad to respond to a parent's request for a doctor's help in treating their child's autism seem most likely to resort to drugs rather than behavioral or educational treatments that are even farther afield from their expertise.

DSM Diagnosis and Being First in Line for New Medicines

Big Pharma has made its way into the autism market with the cockeyed logic that if a drug may have helped one symptom in one child with autism, it might be worth trying for any/all symptoms in any/all children with autism. An early example of this is secretin (a pancreas stimulant) that made a big belly-flop in the autism treatment world in the mid-1990s. (Secretin will also be reprised in Chapter 7.) The first thing that happens when word of new agents (like secretin) hits the autism "grapevine" is a push even by those without a confirmed autism diagnosis, even with just a few symptoms, to get into the treatment trial queue. However, when you do an FDA-approvable drug trial for autism, everyone will need a current *DSM* diagnosis to get in. This, among other things, may be helping to drive rising autism incidence reports (as we discussed in Chapter 2) as parents eager to try anything new may push for a *DSM* autism label if it will help gain access to a new treatment. Having been involved in identifying subjects for drug trials for many years, I can say from my own experience this is true.

Looking with a more wide-angle lens beyond autism, the partnership between the APA with its *DSM* and Big Pharma is predicated on mutual benefit: If APA makes a new *DSM* diagnosis, Big Pharma can get to work making a drug to treat it.

AUTISM STAKEHOLDER NO. 2: AUTISM TREATMENT PROVIDERS

Getting a bona fide *DSM* autism diagnosis is also important to those seeking behavior therapy for autism: providers of these behavioral services who have made impressive political inroads in lobbying for behavior-based therapy as "medically necessary" for autism. As of this writing, over 40 states mandate behavior therapy as medically necessary for autism. This means a medical insurance company must pay for behavior therapy (ABA) in 40 states. This push for medical coverage of ABA started with research that showed that early and intensive, one-to-one use of very directive ABA methods were effective in establishing early skills, essentially learning readiness for the youngest children with autism. If someone is going to pay for what you do and what you do is costly—like a comprehensive ABA therapy program that might run $60,000 per year—there will be gatekeepers for the entity doing the paying. Having the exact *DSM* diagnosis of autism has served this gatekeeping purpose.

Parents of children with intellectual difficulties, learning difficulties, attention problems, and anxiety have all questioned me regarding whether I think intensive ABA might help their child. I respond, "Of course it might!" The parents then ask, "Can it be recommended for my child then?" Of course, the answer is "no" when parents have a child who lacks a *DSM* diagnosis of autism. "Can we have that diagnosis then?" they might ask.

Why Are Costly Programs Only for Autism?

This is important: There is nothing about autism that is so unique that it might be predicted that ABA would not work with others with some overlapping symptoms. As far as I know, there are no studies of intensive ABA, say, to teach reading versus traditional classroom-based methods of teaching reading. If you told me there was a study of typically developing 5-year-olds who had received intensive ABA methods to learn to read versus "treatment as usual," and that the ABA group read better after 6 months, I would not be surprised, not at all.

The more cases identified with autism, the more potential clients that the behavior interventionists will have. This is where things get messy. There are *symptoms* of autism that can be mitigated with behavior therapy even in individuals who do not meet full *DSM* diagnostic criteria for autism. But the gate shuts on those without that bona fide *DSM* ASD diagnosis. Might there be clinicians who give ASD diagnoses so a child has more treatment options?

AUTISM STAKEHOLDER NO. 3: AUTISM ADVOCACY ORGANIZATIONS

Another constituency that benefits from there being more autism is autism advocacy organizations. The more autism there is, the more of an argument that can be made for devoting increasing resources to helping autism. No wonder the National Institutes of Health's Interagency Autism Coordinating Committee (IACC) has pushed for study after Centers for Disease Control and Prevention (CDC) study that slices and dices autism epidemiology, always showing growing prevalence. Parent advocacy groups have been heavily involved in this effort, as they should be.

On a federal level, ever more autism funding has been supported by the occasional US senator, US congressman, National Football League quarterback, or Hollywood celebrity with a son or grandson with autism. (My all-time favorite was actress Rene Russo sitting at a long table giving US Senate testimony on the need for autism funding while senators, perched on their dais above, peered down her décolleté. On the one hand, this is wonderful. The woman was willing to do whatever it would take to convey her message that autism is a big problem.)

AUTISM FIRST IDENTIFICATION

In these politically correct times, we in the developmental disability community speak in "person-first" language, not "disability-first" language. No longer do I talk about an "autistic child," but rather about a child with autism. (I have noticed, though, that parents of children with autism sometimes publish things about their autistic child, but never me, I can assure you.) Autism has also become the diagnosis of first identification: Parents with severely intellectually disabled children, even parents of some severely physically handicapped children, tend to refer to their child as autistic, leaving off other, more diagnostically and prognostically meaningful, adjectives that are *more* true.

NOT THE WHOLE ELEPHANT

Public autism advocacy has been so effective, we all are now so "autism aware" that everyone who is a little "off" is likely to be said, by someone, to have autism or to be "on the spectrum." It seems everyone now knows of a relative with autism or knows of *someone* with autism. Autism, I am often told by people I meet in various informal social situations, is something most people now know when they see it. As chit-chat, I find people will volunteer who they know to be autistic and why they are sure they are. I would be a rude guest to suggest a full diagnostic assessment might precede such a statement.

The general public awareness of autism, and apparent corresponding ability now to recognize it when it is there, has all sorts of folks getting identified as autistic and sneaking into the autism tent under the back flap. My own experience is that laypeople who "know" that one person or another *has* autism is generally focusing on a single "quirk"—and not "feeling the whole elephant." Advocates want us all the more autism aware so we will recognize the importance of attending to those with real autism. Inadvertently, autism awareness has increased the perception that even mild quirks and singular difficulties are autism. After all, what else could it be?

The stakeholders we have just discussed have an investment in there being more *DSM* autism as it promotes their agendas. Being counted "in" using the *DSM* diagnosis leads to opportunities for treatment services that will not be available if you are not in. Not wonder there was such angst when *DSM*-5 was first presented to the professional community for review at IMFAR in 2012.

The Autism Gatekeepers

"MEDICAL NECESSITY" AND POLITICAL LEAPFROGGING

I previously mentioned how the most costly autism treatment services (ABA programs) require a *DSM* diagnosis of autistic disorder. Increasingly, state after state in the United States is compelling private and public medical insurance providers to provide what has been deemed medically necessary autism treatment.

I served on the California Autism Advisory Task Force, formed to recommend guidelines for implementing a California State Senate Bill, SB946, guaranteeing medically necessary autism treatment. The idea behind "medical necessity" is that clinically effective autism treatment is understood to be "habilitating" the brain the way various therapies "rehabilitate" the brain of a stroke patient. A treatment, then, is medically necessary if it evokes positive changes to neural organization. Because autism is a *DSM* diagnosis, and a *DSM* diagnosis of autism implies a biological cause, our task force was asked to see our way to specifying just how and when medical insurers should have a role in funding autism treatment as "medically necessary." I discuss this in more detail in Chapter 6 when I cover cost shifting in autism health economics.

DSM AND DIAGNOSING THE BRAIN

The business the APA does, of course, is not just autism business. It's not just autism that some want diagnosed more. Every diagnosis in the *DSM-5* has its own political backstory of who made it, who shaped it, and why. A little background on who gets diagnosed with what, when, where, and by whom mirrors the story of what does or does not fall within the bounds of an ASD these days.

We hear constantly about how psychiatrically classified disorders are illnesses of the brain. Yes, they are, but the brain is not just any organ. Bones and blood don't think and feel. Changes in the function of the brain are very sensitive to changes in social interaction, environment, mood, and self-reflection—all subject to great change from contact with others—both therapeutic and everyday experiences. In the early days of psychiatry, psychodynamic psychiatry did what it could to alter mental states through social change, with the presumption that this was the best way to change brain function that might underpin behavior.

But, psychotherapy has never really been a field of medicine. Yes, Freud was an early psychiatrist, a neurologist even, and student of the brain. He never explicitly talked about changing the neurology of his patients but felt he might be doing that with his "talking cure." Following Freud, most psychoanalysts were physicians, almost all were psychiatrists, though many prominent psychoanalysts (like his daughter, Anna Freud) were not because, honestly, you did not need to be in order to understand the principles of psychoanalysis. Most psychoanalysts acknowledged they were treating the mind—which strictly speaking did not require having attended 8 or so years of medical school and psychiatric residency training. (These days, psychoanalytic training for psychiatrists is often completed separately, and *after* medical school and residency training.) All this is to say that there is a murky relationship between what is psychiatry, what is the brain, what is the mind, and what kinds of treatments are psychiatric and truly medical. There are more hypotheses about how we can change the brain with talking or behavioral therapies than data showing that the brain is, in fact, changed.

HOW USEFUL IS THE "SPECTRUM" CONCEPT?

Where is the demarcation between "autistic disorder" and "on the autism spectrum"? Where is the demarcation between "quirky, nerdy, really geeky" and on the autism spectrum? Today, one may hear speculation that every geek is "probably" on the spectrum. The *DSM* does prudently indicate that to cross the line into psychopathology (in this case, to being on the autism spectrum), there must be adaptive dysfunction associated with symptom expression. If you are a geek who (a) concentrates very well on writing efficient computer code, (b) can earn a low six-figure salary, (c) drive a BMW, (d) have an administrative assistant who organizes your work life, and (e) have a spouse who organizes your home life, where's the adaptive dysfunction? What about if you only have achieved two of those five things? Might you be on the spectrum then?

DR. ALLEN FRANCES AND *SAVING NORMAL*

Saving Normal[16] is a fascinating book, part mea culpa, part a straightforward, very well-explicated contribution to stemming the runaway self-aggrandizement of the APA, which arguably becomes more central the more people there are with psychiatric conditions.

Saving Normal shows how there are now so many diagnoses for everyday mental aches and pains that virtually everyone can be said to meet *DSM* criteria for something. Interestingly, its author, Dr. Allen Frances, chaired the *DSM-IV* task force that created the APA's *DSM-IV*. (Like me, Dr. Frances is now retired from academia and safe from the academic backlash.) In *Saving Normal,* he argued that almost everyone can qualify for a diagnosis these days.

Through medicalization of mental distress, he argued, there will be a drug for what ails you. Not only does Big Pharma clean up financially by more *DSM* diagnoses and more people with *DSM* diagnoses, but also, more importantly, he argued, many essentially "normal" people are left feeling there is something fundamentally wrong with them after receiving a *DSM* diagnosis. He argued that diagnostic labeling supports justification to obtain a drug for any mental ache or pain. Further, he noted, medicalizing a problem with a *DSM* diagnosis helps to get one's insurance company to pay for psychotherapy around a divorce, career dissatisfaction, or a kid lost to street drugs, not to mention coping with getting a diagnosis of autism for one's child. No one would say these are brain disorders, but the *DSM* diagnoses are all broadly under the rubric of neurochemical imbalance that can be rebalanced with a psychoactive agent.

We are not talking here about the schizophrenic who, on medications, feels normal after he or she stops having command hallucinations. We are talking about how *DSM* has also created classifications of "cosmetic" psychopathology, paving the road for medication being offered to a shy person who is OK with being shy and doesn't like being told he will be more normal if he takes an anxiolytic or an obstinate worker being told he probably has Asperger's and should get help.

HOW MANY AMERICANS HAVE A PSYCHIATRIC DISORDER?

I'm asking how many Americans have a psychiatric disorder to highlight that the increasingly broad and parochial use of "autism," "on the spectrum," and Asperger's mirrors other trends in American psychiatry. Among Americans, approximately 6 percent of children and 20 percent of adults take psychoactive medication at some point in their lives. Another way to look at it is that if you take a psychoactive medication, you have a *DSM* diagnosis—given to you by whoever wrote that prescription. So, according to this, the answer to the question of how many Americans have a psychiatric disorder is one in five adults and one in twenty children. This means that in every elementary school class, at least one child is probably on a psychoactive medication or has been tried on one. These numbers reflect an approximately 20 percent rise in the last 10 years.

Here's what diagnosis of mental disorders in America looks like today: Numbers in Table 3.2 are estimates drawn from a range of nationwide studies, always shifting a bit, but you'll get the idea. Once the *DSM* diagnostic label has been affixed, in psychiatry it tends to stick; is transmitted to the next mental health professional, who may agree—or add another diagnosis or maybe also another medicine. Someone who has beat cancer will say they are cancer free and a cancer survivor. Once a child is labeled with a form of autism or ADHD, the label tends to stick for a lifetime: The signs of ADHD may be gone, that is, the problems paying attention during school years is gone; the adult may be a successful stock trader but will still say, "It's my ADHD that makes me good at what I do!" Yes, but then it's not a disorder now, is it? What about the geeky 10-year-old diagnosed with Asperger's who has more computer applications than friends on Facebook? When he gets a job at Facebook at age 25 with a degree in electrical engineering, does he still have Asperger's? If "symptoms" are not maladaptive, can they be counted as "symptoms?"

TABLE 3.2 } Common Prevalence Estimates of Neuropsychiatric Disorders

Common Estimates Within US Population

Childhood-Onset Diagnoses

Autism spectrum disorders (ASDs)	1.5%
Attention deficit disorders (ADHD/ADDs)	10%
Intellectual disability (ID)	0.9%
Learning disorders	4.7%
Language disorders	2.8%
"Emotional disturbance" (CD/ODD/IED)	0.8%

"Lifetime" Disorders of Adults

Generalized anxiety disorder	3.1%
Social anxiety disorder	6.8%
Obsessive-compulsive disorder	1.0%
Dysthymia	1.5%
Major depressive disorder	6.7%
Bipolar disorder (BPD)	4.4%
Schizophrenia	1.2%

ADD, attention deficit disorder; ADHD, attention deficit hyperactivity disorder; CD, conduct disorder; IED, intermittent explosive disorder; ODD, oppositional defiant disorder.

CAN AUTISM BE "CURED"? IMPLICATIONS FOR THE *DSM*

The medicalization of a psychiatric disorder can create the impression that there is a permanent physical difference in the brain of a *DSM*-diagnosed individual. (This is complex, as we begin to consider if a *DSM* disorder is associated with an abnormality of gene expression because we know genes don't change.) Still, we also speak about brain plasticity and transfer of function may be compensating for the bad programming of the bad gene. If there are no longer behavioral signs of abnormality, is that what it takes to achieve a psychiatric equivalent of a cure?

What are the implications? I would argue that when an intervention in autism can seemingly exploit brain plasticity, it is fantastic! We should stop calling it autism. We should also delist these children from epidemiological counts—though the preference for cross-sectional rather than longitudinal methods by epidemiologists won't reflect this. There are two other problems: (a) Do we know how much of psychiatric treatment is clinically brain changing and how much is simply the result of learning or education, as happens for all other children? (b) What should we do when a child is close enough to normal that he or she no longer meets *DSM* criteria for autism, although there may still be signs of *something*? (In *DSM-III*, that *something* was called "residual state autism," but like Asperger's disorder, it has slipped from the nomenclature.) Politically, we think, once autistic, always autistic, because who knows? Maybe something will happen and we will want to call that label to the fore again.

WITHIN NORMAL LIMITS

A theme of Dr. Alan Frances's *Saving Normal* is that sometimes diagnosing normal might spare some individuals who may be more harmed than helped by a diagnosis. Though not studied, as far as I can tell, once a child or adult is presented to a mental health professional with symptoms of concern, the person seems to almost always leave with a diagnosis. Certainly, in my 30 years of running autism clinics, I had more than one tiff with our medical billing department, which let me know that if we could not diagnose the child we'd seen with *something*, the parents' insurance company would likely not cover the visit. *DSM* has had one special *V* code (V71.09) that indicates "no diagnosis." There *are* diagnoses such as "adjustment *disorder*," but again, this is medicalization of what might be bad behavior or a transient reaction to a normal stressor (like a child's reaction to the birth of a sibling).

In the 1940s and 1950s, before *DSM* had the relevance to American psychiatry that it does today, badly behaved children were commonly blamed on badly behaved parents. Often, psychiatry went so far as to suggest that for the child to get better, it was the parents who would need therapy. A great example of this is that, in the 1960s, a former professor of mine, Dr. Bruno Bettelheim, was the standard-bearer for "refrigerator mothers," cold, rejecting mothers who he insisted had caused their children to be autistic because of their wholesale rejection of them from infancy. (He and I never agreed on that, but I did learn a lot of other things from this brilliant man.)

Today, with the medicalizing of *DSM*, the tables have turned 180 degrees: If it is the child who shows the symptoms, it is obviously the child who has the illness. Emphasis on mental disorders as based in brain dysfunction can make parents less guilty, but it does not make it impossible for parents to induce psychiatric symptoms in their children. In reality, the truth of psychiatric dysfunction lies in the confluence of brain and behavior: Say we are talking about a very badly behaved child who ends up diagnosed with disruptive mood regulation disorder (DMRD). Receiving this diagnosis can provide big relief to parents who feel steamrollered by a kid who my grandmother, who raised eight kids, would have called a "bad seed." However, it is hard not to react to such a child in ways that can make his or her behavior even more unmanageable. Until we can change parents' responses to the DMRD bad seed's behavior, we won't know how much of that bad behavior really is biologically driven and how much is inflamed by ineffective parental responses to it. Similarly, we might be talking about an immature "not-as-smart-as-siblings" 5-year-old who was kicked out of a couple of tony private schools as having inattentive-type ADHD. A medicalized *DSM* diagnosis says this is "not his fault, not mom or dad's fault; let's get him tested to see what's wrong with his brain." How much are this child's ADHD symptoms fueled by biology and how much by parental disappointment that their long-awaited son is more a jock than bookish, like dad? Should he be given Ritalin so he can pay better attention in class or a couple of hours of afterschool sports instead of Kumon (math tutoring), along with some counseling to help his parents cope with a student who receives a B⁻ in math?

Saving Autistic Normal

In 1960, aloof, "autistic" (from the Greek *autos* for "self") children were seen as socially rejecting of others because their refrigerator mothers had rejected them. We now know there is an incontrovertible biological basis to autism. But where does that biological basis become exacerbated by parental practices? When is a child "normally" aloof, reserved, quirky?

There is an autistic normal to be saved. These are individuals who seem to lack social attunement so that the specter (or diagnostically speaking "spectrum") of autism is raised. We might be talking about an anxious, shy young nerd who would rather be assembling his 4,000+-piece Star Wars Death Star than spend time with a play date his mother arranged with her best friend's son. This sounds like Asperger's, right? Maybe yes; maybe no—not everyone spending over $1,000 on a Lego kit this large has autism.

AUTISTIC NORMAL, SHADOW SYNDROMES, AND THE BAP

A fascinating 1997 book, *Shadow Syndromes,*[17] by John Ratey (an ADHD authority) and Catherine Johnson (psychology scholar and mother of an autistic son) takes off on the idea that the biology of psychiatric disorder, personality, and responses to atypical biology, as well as life events in general, all play a role in clinical profiles that may not warrant a *DSM* diagnosis but "shadow" them. Normal people have real problems, and the way they cope has roots in biological predispositions. Among parents of children with autism are parents with autism "shadow syndromes." A behavioral geneticist might describe such an individual as having the "broader autism phenotype" (BAP)—emphasizing the biological underpinnings. Mostly, these are individuals who have excellent-to-adequate lives, sometimes only becoming aware of their "autistic-like" traits when reflecting on their child's difficulties as not entirely unlike their own experiences. Recognition of one's own shadow syndrome can become the basis for identification with their unusual child and even self-identification as being on the autism spectrum as well.

HYPE, HOPE, AND HYPERBOLE

There is barely a week that goes by without a media story, TV character, or movie that brings a new autistic media darling to our attention. It might be a sitcom about perennial physics graduate students or a good doctor who is autistic, a savant, and a surgeon. It might be a *New York Times* column on one mom's brave fight against the system for her child with autism to be included in mainstream classes. It may be a dramatic TV episode with a *Rain Man*–like savant who unwittingly provides the detective with all the clues he needs to solve the murder (while inadvertently getting himself killed before the end of the episode). It might be a movie abouta Nobel laureate physicist with a beautiful mind made more beautiful by his schizophrenia (but that actually leaves him disabled and unable to be productive). It might be a real story about a shooter, a seemingly psychotic murderer of 20 little children and 6 adults who might have had a neurochemical imbalance that was recognized but was not "yet" certified in a way that would restrict his civil right to access guns. All these stories seem to resonate a fascination with mental illness, and certainly with ASDs.

What is the peculiar American fascination with autism? Many non-Western families I meet will nervously tell me they are not sure if there is autism in their family tree—because if there is, they are sure no one will have spoken about it. For Americans and other Westerners, I have sometimes thought an idealized version of autism tweaks a nerve first hit by Jean-Jacques Rousseau, the 1700s philosopher who wrote of the "noble savage," the resident of the true state of human nature. This savage man was free because he did not follow the rules of any society, because he was presociety, and so was the ideal of a free man. We

Americans idealize an individual's freedom, and in certain ways it *is* saluted in the asocial, self-centered ethos of the person with autism. People with autism may appear closer to living in that "state of nature" because they prefer to follow their own presociety rules rather than our own social ones. Rousseau's noble savage is an idealization of living life without societal constraints, living much as a child with autism who has never been "civilized" by trading away an asocial preferred activity for a tangible reward.

The Politics of an Asperger's Diagnosis

AUTISM SHADOW SYNDROME VERSUS ASPERGER'S

As someone who has taken family histories to look for Asperger's long before "official" Asperger's disorder appeared in *DSM-IV* in 1994 (and continues to look today, even though Asperger's is no longer official), I can tell you there are a lot more people who are *thought* to have it than people who *really* do have it. (I base my "really" on the fact that I was a *DSM-IV* field trials investigator, meaning my ratings became part of the "gold standard" for the criteria for diagnosing Asperger's disorder.) Many parents assert they just *know* that this relative or that "has it." In doing developmental histories as part of an assessment for children who might have ASD, I receive reports of relatives with Asperger's about half the time. When I ask where this individual was diagnosed and when, I hear that it is simply that my informant (or all family members) just *know* that their father, grandfather, or eccentric uncle has it or had it.

Asperger's, in particular, for some reason, is a condition that people seem to feel is subject to self-diagnosis or diagnosis-by-astute-family-member, no professional expertise needed. So, what would you think? Would this raise or lower the reported incidence of Asperger's? Would it result in fewer or more inaccurately "diagnosed" cases?

ASPIES, NEURODIVERSITY, AND DOUBLESPEAK

There are many self-diagnosed people with Asperger's disorder out there. Many like the name *Aspies* for themselves. Some very intelligent people who are bona fide or self-designated Aspies proudly make a case for what they call their "neurodiversity." The concept of neurodiversity can only be described as classical Orwellian doublespeak, that being handicapped by whatever handicaps them as an Aspie is actually not a handicap but a beneficial endowment. Some posit neurodiversity as savantism, even if the neurodiverse individual has no special talents derived from his or her neurodiversity. Self-identified Aspies not uncommonly deride "neurotypicality" (the opposite of neurodiverse) as just not as interesting and may be found wearing the ribbon in Figure 3.1.

DOES VLADIMIR PUTIN HAVE ASPERGER'S?

Asperger's is a label thrown around for all sorts of reasons: A couple of years ago, I was fascinated to learn that a Pentagon think tank "diagnosed" Vladimir Putin with Asperger's.[18] Other involved professionals opined he had "some sort of autism"—at least. Did these individuals interview his mother? See videos from his first 3 years of life? Do a clinical diagnostic interview with him? Of course they did not.

Is Putin a cool cucumber? A fascist? A dictator? Does he lack variation in facial expression? The answers are maybe, probably. Does that mean he cannot understand how others think, that he lacks theory of mind? More likely, he does not *care* how other people think. Why should he? He finds it socially reinforcing to be seen as a fascist dictator. Did the pundits wielding an autism spectrum diagnosis for him consider these other characterizations?

DOES ASPERGER'S LEAD TO CRIMINALITY?

I have met many a young budding sociopath with truly lovely parents who cannot understand how they managed to germinate such a bad seed. The child's siblings are fine, except that they cower in the presence of their "oppositional defiant" brother. *Oppositional, defiant*, and *disorder* are not nice words. (ODD is also a *DSM* diagnosis.) So, instead of ODD, how about Asperger's? There we go—a much more neutral word. Their budding sociopath (the lovely, kind parents opine) must not understand that others have emotions; if he did, why would he be so mean? He doesn't have empathy, they posit. They have read a lot and figured out it must be Asperger's because people with Asperger's lack empathy.

Typically, these children—who don't have Asperger's but do have early signs of sociopathy—are indeed insensitive to the feelings of others. Are they unaware of what makes one feel bad? Absolutely not. Just ask such a child what makes *him* (or her) feel bad. You'll get a litany of slights about being denied a promised TV show because he didn't finish homework on time or because he just gave a cross-eyed look to his younger brother, who cried and ratted on him, and claimed he was going to get beaten up. No, that's more like incipient sociopathy. Maybe he'll grow up to be a criminal—or if he has an IQ way above average, he will realize he can steal more money with a briefcase than with a gun and become a sleazy type of investment banker. It's not that he does not understand others have feelings; he doesn't care. I have never been worried about being physically harmed by anyone with Asperger's. Interpreting the countertransference, I have always felt this means that people who really have Asperger's are the opposite of sociopaths.

Does this mean someone with Asperger's or an ASD can't commit a crime? No; it can happen.[19] I recently worked as an expert in a case where a middle-aged man with a heretofore undiagnosed ASD shot and killed an intruder to his mobile home. The intruder, an ex-lover of this defendant's roommate, had dropped by to physically assault his roommate. The defendant considered his roommate to be his first and only true friend, so he shot and killed the assaulter. (The fellow whose life the defendant saved was actually freeloading off him—not such a true friend.) The defendant, the man with Asperger's, was, mercifully, acquitted on the grounds of self-defense. The defendant's primitive understanding of friendships, and his lifelong failure at them, had made him particularly vulnerable to the imprecations of his roommate, who had often taken advantage of him for money and housing, without him realizing it.

In contrast, in another case, the defendant's attorney sought a diagnosis of Asperger's as a justification for why his 20-year-old client did not understand that joyriding in someone's car until he wrecked it or stealing $35,000 of computers from a university computer lab was wrong. The defendant's attorney was hoping the judge could understand that this young man—with a history of learning disabilities and special education services—had been diagnostically "missed" all along, and that Asperger's was why he had not been able to understand these actions were wrong—convenient. This young man had feelings: He cried when I asked him if he had thought about the fact that he might do time, though he expressed no remorse for the wrecked car or for students who might have had projects on the computers he had stolen.

IT'S NOT ME: MY HUSBAND HAS ASPERGER'S

Sometimes at my autism center, I am asked to consider a request from a wife referring her husband to be assessed for Asperger's. For starters, I ask her to call back and find out what the husband thinks of his wife's concerns. Sometimes, it is the other way around: A husband initiates a call because he thinks their marriage problems might be due to his Asperger's. Where do you think there are more "false-positive" cases: the fellows who think they might have Asperger's or the fellows with wives who think they do? If the individual himself is concerned that he has traits that function maladaptively in his marriage or work and those traits sound like they have to do with social misunderstanding, over-literalness, inflexibility, or a narrow solipsistic view of the world, then by all means, this individual might have Asperger's and maybe we can help.

What about if it is the wife's complaint? I recently got an e-mail from a frustrated husband telling me how his wife had convinced her therapist that he had Asperger's. What was her chief diagnostic complaint about her husband? He watched too many *Seinfeld* reruns (among other comedy reruns). Eventually, after his wife insisted repeatedly, the husband met with his wife's therapist. The therapist was not impressed that her patient had been correct in her diagnosis.

What happened? First, it turns out, not surprisingly, that this man's wife had not been trained in Asperger's diagnosis. Second, it is fairly likely the wife's therapist had not been trained in Asperger's (or any ASD) diagnosis either, but sensed this fellow was not "off base" in an autistic-like way. Fortunately for the gentleman who wrote to me, his wife's therapist had good differential diagnosis chops—and in this case was able to "save normal."

ASPERGER'S ONLINE

So, what's happening? Why is everyone an Asperger's expert these days? Well, if you don't know about something, you can undertake to study it and learn. In the olden days (say 1980), this meant that if you were interested in autism and things like it, you might start by going to a medical library and getting a librarian to show you to the shelf with back issues of *JADD* (the *Journal of Autism and Developmental Disorders*) and peruse it for a couple of days. Today, it means googling "Asperger's" for 15 or 20 minutes. Mostly, we are not even talking Google Scholar-ing it.

Say you are online, googling around, and you see a questionnaire that tests for Asperger's. If you think you, a loved one, or an obstreperous friend might have Asperger's, just take a test on the Internet and find out! There are some good (i.e., scientifically well-developed) tests for Asperger's online, and there are some phony ones. There really is no way for most Internet travelers to know which is which.

Importantly, when a nonprofessional fills out a questionnaire online, it is difficult, if not impossible, to know what the threshold for a positive symptom is supposed to be. Is loving *Seinfeld* reruns a "narrow interest," or is amassing information about South American rail tracks and their lengths, their gauges, and the types of equipment that run on each? For me, *Seinfeld* reruns are not so narrow an interest. South American rail lines and how wide they are are just a bit more narrow an interest. But—and this is the interesting part—to the person filling out the question about narrow interests on himself, his love of rail gauges may not seem at all narrow, but tied to the fascinating history of colonization of South America; to the development of steam, coal, and electric train engines; and to many other things he and his online friends all find intriguing. On the other hand, a wife thinking her husband's interest in *Seinfeld* is narrow will positively endorse this questionnaire item, while the extreme rail buff may not. If the rail buff came into my clinic, handed me his completed questionnaire, and in response to my polite chit-chat about having traveled from Panama City to Colon on an antique French rail line excitedly monologued like a runaway locomotive about similar South American train routes until his wife stopped him, I'd change his response on the questionnaire item to "positive." All this is to say that the motivation, knowledge base, and subjectivity of the questionnaire's respondent has everything to do with the score. In the end, there *are* folks out there with Asperger's syndrome. Some can identify themselves; some cannot. Some stand falsely accused.

THE IMPRECISION OF PSYCHIATRIC DIAGNOSIS

Today, maybe we should refer to all of those with Asperger's as having "once and future Asperger's disorder." I say this because, for now, Asperger's has been removed from the *DSM*, really just as arbitrarily as it was first included. Maybe it *does* have some etiological differences from other ASDs, maybe not. We certainly can't test that if the diagnosis is deleted. On the other hand, we may be much more likely to find biomarkers that relate to psychophysiological thresholds, sensory processing differences, attention and memory measures, neurological signs, and the like than to any arbitrary *DSM* diagnostic label, so probably, we shouldn't worry. When can we expect *DSM-5.1*?

Resetting Priorities

WE NEED RESEARCH DIAGNOSTIC CRITERIA FOR AUTISM

The diagnostic system used to identify individuals with autism, as I have put forth, is not helping us gather the fine-grain data we need to do a better job of knowing which treatments work for which individuals with autism. More important, the *DSM-5* diagnosis of ASD is not helping us get closer to understanding the cause(s) of the myriad symptoms of autism, like genetic causes or brain region differences tied to specific symptomatic behaviors.

What we have in *DSM* is a diagnosis designed by a committee. It is arbitrary, based on lists of symptoms people can agree on rather than any neurobiology or genetics. Fifty years of autism research on a shifting set of diagnostic criteria enumerated in *DSM-III, DSM-III-R, DSM-IV/DSM-IV-TR*, and now *DSM-5* has just widened and shifted boundaries that include more, and slightly different cases identified as autistic, providing a moving target for anyone studying biomarkers, not only in autism, but also in any psychiatric disorder.

We need RDC as first proposed in the 1980s and more recently suggested again by Dr. Tom Insel, when *DSM-5* was published in 2013 and he was director of the NIMH.[20] Until there are biomarkers to delineate autism from other conditions or to delineate among different forms of autism, there is nothing really to be gained from changing the definition of autism or ASDs. Dr. Insel's comments about fixed RDC for scientists not only pertained to autism but also are obviously relevant to *DSM*'s methodology.

What Kind of Diagnostic Criteria Do We Need?

The RDC for ASDs should be planned by stakeholders from both the clinical treatment and biological psychiatry fields. From my point of view, the RDC for ASDs should be multitier. On the innermost tier, there should be characterization of basic behavioral endophenotypes. By *behavioral endophenotypes*,

I adopt the term from genetic epidemiology here to specify behavioral symptoms hypothesized to have a clear genetic connection rather than an environmental etiology. These behavioral endophenotypes would be constructs that can be hypothesized to have a clearer neuroanatomical connection or genetic connection than the kind of diagnostic criteria we have now. Candidates for measurement as behavioral endophenotypes might be readily characterized psychophysiological thresholds, sensory processing differences, attention and memory measures, or other neurological signs. In other work, I've taxonomized behavioral endophenotypes such as these with the terms *primary* or *innate disabilities*. In and of themselves, these behavioral endophenotypes would not be intended to be diagnostic signs or specific to autism alone, but would be more readily testable for their relation to a specific gene's expression or a specific neural response.

Then, there should be a second descriptive tier: distinctive clinical symptoms. What I call behavioral endophenotypes can be understood as interactions with more intact neuropsychological functions that form self-compensations (e.g., autism symptoms like echolalia, which could be tested as the possible result of a behavioral endophenotype like delayed auditory processing) interacting with more intact auditory memory, which might result in echolalia such as we see in autism but might also occur in a language-impaired child for the same etiological reasons. Importantly, these second-tier symptoms might not be unique to autism either but would produce a clinical description potentially more useful for both clinical treatment and biomedical research on causation.

The RDC should be put together by NIMH with input from clinical researchers, neurobiologists, geneticists, and statisticians. Any RDC will need to consider the sensitivity of first- and second-tier symptoms, rather than struggling to artificially aggregate sufficient numbers of symptoms to create artificial superordinate categories—like autism or ADHD—by gaining specificity through some additive collection of symptoms.

Put another way, it really is as obvious as the nose on our face that any single case of autism will have some signs that are the same as could be seen in another childhood neuropsychiatric condition. Many basic behavioral endophenotypes cut across many disorders—so how is it useful to say that one case (tactile sensitivity, for example) is due to autism and not ADHD, not sensory processing disorder, or not intellectual disability? How is it useful to say that "repetitive motor movements," "repetitive speech," or "repetitive routines" are all cut from the same cloth given that speech, movement, and kinesthetic memory have differing neural substrates? That is, should all three of these forms of repetitive behaviors be considered signs of autism, when in one case repetitive motor movements may co-occur with other indicators of Tourette syndrome; in another case, repetitive speech may co-occur with other indicators of a language-processing disorder; and in a third case, repetitive routines may co-occur with other indicators of an OCD. A useful RDC would allow these clinical traits to be more readily characterized and studied individually and (secondarily, as far as I am concerned) as parts of *DSM* disorders.

AUTISM AWARENESS, PREVALENCE, AND DIAGNOSIS: ENOUGH IS ENOUGH

Relative to other possible autism priorities, tremendous resources have already been expended on autism awareness. Constantly increasing rates of autism incidence definitely promote justification for greater research and programmatic expenditures. On one level this is admirable; we do want more programs, but we already have identified a tremendous number of individuals not adequately served via early intervention, education, and adult services. There is real concern that the earlier we diagnose, the more false-positive diagnoses there will be, parents forever changed in their view of their expectations for their child because between 14 and 32 months, someone prognosticated the child was "probably" (or definitely) autistic. No one forgets if they have once been told their child has autism, even if later it no longer seems apropos.

The largest autism advocacy organization spends a not insignificant amount on autism awareness. Now pediatricians may think of autism before they think of a language disorder, deafness/hearing loss, or sometimes even an ear infection if a child doesn't talk at 18 months old or behaves badly toward other toddlers. Children are referred to "rule out" autism, often using diagnostic tools like the Social Communication Questionnaire (SCQ), which are not geared to indicate a probability of risk for any other conditions. By default, any positives on these measures can be construed as autistic-like and seen as on a spectrum with no lower bounds.

In Chapter 2, I talked about a billboard of a young child covering her ears, surrounded by a cacophony of sounds. The caption asked whether autism should be considered. Many normal children can be auditorily hypersensitive and many children have all sorts of sensory threshold issues. This type of autism awareness raising has great potential to misguide the public. As more cases are referred and considered based on single symptoms like auditory hypersensitivity, public awareness does grow. This also drives the demand for prevalence and incidence studies (Table 3.2). Such studies that use references to autism in a school or medical record are very likely to overestimate cases, as such references will appear in the records of any child referred for an autism "rule-out." An autism rule-out may be suggested if a parent, relative, or kindly neighbor/former teacher sees the billboard linking auditory hypersensitivity and autism and helpfully insists to a new parent she get her child checked out for autism. I'd argue we are a little too aware of autism and now need to turn our resources to doing more about it.

What's Next?

So far, we have talked about the diagnosis of autism and how it is made. We've discussed how the diagnosis of an ASD can be a gateway to services of various types. Most services that most individuals with autism will receive for their autism are educational. These services are delivered between age 3 and age 22 from a system of public entitlements. At age 22, educational services come to a screeching halt, as I touched on in Chapter 2. Chapters 4 and 5 discuss the politics of educating our children with autism. Chapter 4 focuses largely on one peculiarly American trend—which is educational inclusion, the practice of educating children with disabilities among typical peers, but surrounding them with special supports. When is this effective, and when is it pie in the sky? In Chapter 5, I tackle the problem we Americans have in facing the fact that almost all children with autism grow up to be adults with autism, and that Americans are pretty much failures at preparing these young people for the future they face, no matter how high or low functioning they are.

Notes

1. Kanner, L. (1943). Autistic disturbances of affective contact. *The Nervous Child, 2,* 217–250.

2. American Psychiatric Association. (2013). *Diagnostic and statistical manual of mental disorders* (5th ed.). Washington, DC: APA Press.

3. Schwarz, A. (2015, December 10). Still in a crib, yet being given antipsychotics. *The New York Times.* Retrieved from http://www.nytimes.com/2015/12/11/us/psychiatric-drugs-are-being-prescribed-to-infants.html

4. Chirdkiatgumchai, V., Xiao, H., Fredstrom, B. K., Adams, R. E., Epstein, J. N., . . . Froehlich, T. E. (2013). National trends in psychotropic medication use in young children: 1994–2009. *Pediatrics, 132*(4), 615–623. http://doi.org/10.1542/peds.2013-1546

5. American Psychiatric Association. (1952). *Diagnostic and statistical manual of mental disorders.* Washington, DC: APA Press.

6. World Health Organization. (1949). *International classification of diseases* (6th ed.). Geneva, Switzerland: Author.

7. American Psychiatric Association. (1968). *Diagnostic and statistical manual of mental disorders* (2nd ed.). Washington, DC: APA Press.

8. American Psychiatric Association. (1980). *Diagnostic and statistical manual of mental disorders* (3th ed.). Washington, DC: APA Press.

9. American Psychiatric Association. (1974). *Diagnostic and statistical manual of mental disorders* (2nd ed.). Washington, DC: APA Press.

10. Mattison, R., Cantwell, D. P., Russell, A. T., & Will, L. (1979). A comparison of *DSM-II* and *DSM-III* in the diagnosis of childhood psychiatric disorders II. Interrater agreement. *Archives of General Psychiatry, 36*(11), 1217–1222. doi:10.1001/archpsyc.1979.01780110071008

11. American Psychiatric Association. (1987). *Diagnostic and statistical manual of mental disorders* (3rd ed., revised). Washington, DC: APA Press.

12. Spitzer, R. L., & Siegel, B. (1990). The *DSM-III-R* field trials for pervasive developmental disorders. *Journal of the American Academy of Child and Adolescent Psychiatry, 26*(6):855–862.

13. American Psychiatric Association. (1994). *Diagnostic and statistical manual of mental disorders* (4th ed.). Washington, DC: APA Press.

14. American Psychiatric Association. (2000). *Diagnostic and statistical manual of mental disorders* (4th ed., text revision). Washington, DC: APA Press.

15. Gillberg, C., Fernell, E., & Minnis, H. (2014). Early symptomatic syndromes eliciting neurodevelopmental clinical examinations (ESSENCE). *Scientific World Journal, 2014*, 710570. doi:10.1155/2013/710570. eCollection

16. Frances, A. (2013). *Saving normal.* New York, NY: Willam Morris/HarperCollins.

17. Ratey, J. J., & Johnson, C. (1997). *Shadow syndromes: Recognizing and coping with the hidden psychological disorders that can influence your behavior and silently determine the course of your life.* New York, NY: Pantheon Books.

18. Locker, R. (2015, February 4). Pentagon 2008 study claims Putin has Asperger's syndrome. *USA Today.* Retrieved from http://www.usatoday.com/story/news/politics/2015/02/04/putin-aspergers-syndrome-study-pentagon/22855927/

19. Katz, N., & Zemishlany, Z. (2006). Criminal responsibility in Asperger's syndrome. *Israel Journal of Psychiatry and Related Sciences, 43*(3), 166–173.

20. Insel, T. R. (2014b). The NIMH Research Domain Criteria (RDoC) Project: Precision medicine for psychiatry. *American Journal of Psychiatry, 171*(4):395–397. http://doi.org/10.1176/appi.ajp.2014.14020138

4 }

Autism Education and the Illusions of Inclusion

The Individuals With Disabilities Education Act (IDEA) along with the Individuals With Disabilities Education Improvement Act (IDEIA) allow parents to choose to have their child with autism taught in a class designed for nondisabled peers. This is called *inclusion*. The child with autism is given needed supports but spends the majority of his or her time in a general education classroom with other children of the same age and grade level.

When is inclusion educationally effective? When might inclusion thwart addressing the legitimate educational needs of that child? Are parents ever *falsely* led to feel that educating their child with autism alongside "neurotypical" peers is the right thing to do? Actually, few data support inclusion as a differentially effective academic method for most children with autism most of the time. There clearly are children with autism who can benefit academically by access to curriculum provided in general education settings and *at their developmental level*.

When is it that inclusion may be a cost-saving smokescreen? When is it that inclusion may be just palliative for the wound of an imperfect child? Having one's child with autism educationally included is what parents of all children with ASDs hope can be achieved. The law does say any child can be included (as long as the child does not create a detriment to the learning of classmates). But what if the law, on the one hand, and educational programming construed to educationally benefit the child, on the other hand, point to different things?

What are the ethics of educationally including the child with autism in a mainstream class if there may be educational disadvantages accrued by the typical learners because of disproportionate teacher effort directed to curriculum adapted only for the child with autism? How much time should a general education teacher spend with an included pupil with autism if that child has a full-time, one-to-one paraprofessional with him or her and the teacher is the only instructor for the other 25 or 30 pupils?

Millions of dollars are spent on inclusive education with virtually no evidence that it helps further meaningful long-term goals of special education, such as greater independence, greater academic advancement, or workability (i.e., the academic plus social skills needed for employment). If a child with autism isn't being helped by inclusion, even if the law says he or she has a right to be there, are we failing that child if the child could be doing better by being in a class with a qualified special education teacher? Children with autism educated alongside nondisabled peers often do have a one-to-one aide, but commonly, this individual will have no more than a few units of community college credits reflecting a few courses in child development or education. But when that aide essentially is regarded as that child's "teacher" and the classroom teacher as the teacher for the others, what "special education" does that child with autism really receive? Is inclusion a good "bang for the buck" for the parents who selected it? How often is it either effective education for the child with autism or in some way a benefit for the child's classmates?

The Naked Emperor

Twenty years ago, I published a public policy monograph with the Society for Research in Child Development, "Is the Emperor Wearing Clothes? Social Policy and the Empirical Support for Full Inclusion of Children With Disabilities in the Preschool and Early Elementary Grades."[1] In it, I pointed to the lack of data demonstrating benefit of inclusion for moderately to severely educationally handicapped pupils. There also weren't even many good data on academic advantages for mildly handicapped pupils, especially in secondary education.

It wasn't a popular point of view then; it is not a popular view now. Since then, the trend to educate mild-to-moderately handicapped children with age-mates has really caught on. But there still are no significant data that support the increasing trend for inclusion for children who are not yet ready to learn the same things as their classmates. Just to be clear, much inclusion involves placing a child with autism (or another educational handicap) in classrooms with chronological age-mates who typically are farther along academically than the child with autism. This may create further disadvantage as the child included is unable to fully comprehend academically or keep up socially with what is going on.

I believe inclusion has become a civil rights issue more than an educational issue. It is no longer about "the best interest of the child." Parents are often supported in focusing on their child's civil right to be educated in the same classroom as nonhandicapped peers. Instead, the priority should be identifying which *methods* are in the child's best interest—methods available in an inclusive setting or methods available in a special education setting. While general education curriculum is often "adapted" for the educationally included child with autism, the adaptations (like less homework, shorter class, preferential seating, a peer tutor) are often of little meaning if the curriculum is above the special education pupil's academic level or if, simply, the fact of being in a classroom space with 30 other children is overwhelming.

Before Public Law 94-142 (Education for All Handicapped Children Act)

Here's the irony: We are no longer neglectfully denying children with special needs a special education, as was all too common before Public Law (PL) 94-142, which was the first federal law to guarantee universal special education, passed in 1975. It was 1975 when the Handicapped Children's Act was enacted, then it was revised in 1990 as the IDEA. Prior to PL 94-142, there was only Section 504 of the Rehabilitation Act of 1973, which provided for a few "accommodations" in general education classes, but no guarantee of special education classes. Today, children who do not have significant enough learning differences to qualify for an individual educational program (IEP) under IDEA still may qualify for a 504 plan—largely accommodations in a mainstream class and, sometimes, differentiated instructional services (DIS) like speech and language therapy.

The period before PL 94-142 was grimmer. Parents could simply be told that there was not enough demand for any special services their child might need. Parents could be told that their child could stay home or come to a regular classroom, but there were no guarantees for meaningful accommodations based on disability. Prior to 1975, schools were more or less unencumbered by any mandates to create special education programs. Often, an educational authority might offer nothing more than one classroom for all special education pupils within the school's catchment area. Deaf and blind children were often shipped off to specialized regional boarding schools. Kids with obvious forms of mental retardation that were lifelong, like Down syndrome, were more likely to be institutionalized—and parents counseled to just have another child. Before PL 94-142 (which is when I first worked in special education), better public special education programs simply tracked pupils as either educable mentally retarded (EMR) or trainable mentally retarded (TMR). Goals were not individualized as they are today. Rather, the goal for those classified as EMR was to learn self-care and then simple rote skills that could be useful around their homes; for those classified as TMR, it was simply self-care.

Clearly, educational entitlements are substantially better now. However, in a certain Kafkaesque way, we have come full circle: We now don't give the inclusion pupils with special needs either special education classes or special education teachers but instead put them with others who do not need special education—and call that their special education. General education teachers, as well meaning and devoted as many are, are not trained in special education methods, the way credentialed special education teachers are.

Trickle-Down Education

Twenty years after PL 94-142, in 1995, a volume, *The Illusion of Full Inclusion: A Comprehensive Critique of a Special Education Bandwagon,* was written by James Kauffman and Daniel Hallahan.[2] They wrote in response to the Reagan-era cuts in education that brought us what was essentially trickle-down education (a political bedfellow of trickle-down Reaganomics). The new federal education creed, sold to child disability advocacy groups, was that what children who were hard to teach really needed was not specially trained teachers using special teaching methods but just an opportunity to copy how other children who didn't have difficulties did things—no special education classrooms with special education teachers needed. This was, and still is, completely illogical: If special education children just could learn from their nondisabled peers, they wouldn't have special educational needs in the first place. Many children in special education have plenty of time with typical peers—siblings, neighborhood and family friends, and peers in day care. If they could simply learn by emulating peers, there would be little need for special education.

This inaccurate construction of presumed mechanisms of benefit for inclusion persists today and has been especially damaging to our pupils with autism spectrum disorders (ASDs)—for whom lack of imitative ability or lack of imitative drive is often a hallmark of their learning difficulties. Children with ASDs are the least likely to learn spontaneously by just being around peers. Another critical barrier to their learning is that most children with autism, even high-functioning children with autism, have play and social skills that are developmentally less advanced than those of their peers—so same-age role models usually are doing things developmentally "out of reach." (If you, the bright 4-year-old with autism, like to fill and sift a sand bucket, and the other 4-year-olds in class are wetting sand, pouring it into buckets, and molding castles, you are not at the same developmental level, and what they are doing doesn't make as much sense or seem as fun as what you are doing.)

If Not Inclusion, What?

In the special education community, it is often so politically incorrect to rail against inclusion that the knee-jerk reflex of many special educators is to quickly avoid discussion of its possible lack of benefit for specific students. If a special educator thinks inclusion is not appropriate for a given pupil, the hope is that either the parent will say so first or the parent will just not ask for it. In some locales, special educators have never sat in a meeting for a student's special educational planning where first-line consideration of inclusion was anything but a given, irrespective of the pupil's learning readiness. Doesn't that seem amazing? Every pupil is entitled to an IEP, and indeed, there is a mandate to include a child if the child is likely to accrue educational benefit. But, when a child is not yet developmentally in spitting distance of peers, how could anyone see it as logical that the child will be able to "access" anything from such a curriculum? More important, that special education child with autism deserves, like every other special education child, to be taught what "comes next" in developmental sequence, and if a child is sight-reading single words, the child will not get far in a mainstream class where others already are writing sentences.

INCLUSION IS A METHODOLOGY, NOT A GOAL

The practice of inclusion in American special education today is but the tip of the iceberg. What is also "frozen" is any real examination of the value in teaching "core curriculum" to students with autism with overall impairment that endows them with mild, moderate, to severe learning handicaps. (Issues of educational inclusion may play out differently for children on the autism spectrum with overall intelligence that is average or above average if it is used as a selective method for targeted curriculum. Such children are not the focus here, but rather the vast majority with ASD diagnoses and significant disability in language ability or overall ability.)

To be clear, I am not "against" inclusion. Rather, I see inclusion as an educational strategy that should be used to achieve specific goals—if it is the strategy most likely to succeed in teaching those goals. Inclusion, really, is just one tool in a special educator's toolbox, especially for pupils with mild-to-severe intellectual disabilities along with an ASD.

Inclusion is a methodology, not a goal. Similarly, teaching core academic skills may benefit some special education pupils some of the time but, arguably, not all of the time. For some pupils, inclusion may not be beneficial at all if autism and intellectual disability are so marked that the academics being taught to mainstream classmates will consistently be developmentally beyond their reach. A second grader functioning at the preschool level is missing out on things he or she should be learning (basic phonics and numeracy) if the child is spending most of school time included in a second-grade general education class where everyone is reading and writing. What about the 10th grader functioning academically at the third-grade level, placed in a high school class where everyone is doing algebra or another class where everyone is studying civics from a textbook written at the 10th-grade reading level?

Just so the reader understands what goes on in American schools today, there are 15-year-olds with paraprofessional aides who take them to the toilet on a schedule and then take them to their American history class. There are 8-year-olds who neither read nor speak who go to their third-grade reading group and with an aide's hand-over-hand help, touch an icon to indicate whether the protagonist of the short story the teacher just read was "good," "bad," "helpful," or "mean."

I find this painful to watch. Each of these special education pupils deserves more liberty. By liberty, I mean the ability to reach into a new area of learning and add just a little more to his or her established understanding of something rather than being "motored" through something the people on his or her IEP team (the child's educational planners) feel the child should be able to do by now. Each of these pupils deserves to be taught things he or she can really learn, is ready to learn, and pays attention because what is being taught "fits" with what he or she already knows. The other 15-year-olds do not need help going to the toilet—because they mastered that more than a decade ago. The other third graders do not need hand-over-hand assistance to point to an icon because their receptive language and conceptual development enable them to formulate the oral response the teacher expects. To my mind, these children are being denied the special education they deserve to master skills meaningful to them—"academic" or not.

TRAINABLE AND EDUCABLE

Some parents, advocates, and even educators cannot imagine what can be taught if core (academic) curriculum is not taught to every child. Actually, it is not hard to image at all: Historically, pupils with moderate-to-severe conditions that had a pervasive impact on learning, including a portion of those on the autism spectrum, were considered *trainable* rather than *educable*—per those terms used prior to PL 94-142. A trainable pupil was taught needed life skills other children were able to incidentally acquire in the context of the family—using utensils and managing hygiene, home safety, and housekeeping tasks. They did not spend 10 years learning to order the letters of the alphabet or numbers between 1 and 10, activities now common in both elementary and high school classes for severely handicapped pupils.

At this earlier time, the governing philosophy was that the dignity of self comes from independence. Introduction to recreational skills like singing, making music, and making art were also cultivated as educational activities—to enhance quality of life in the daily living these trainable pupils would have when they reached adulthood.

For individuals with milder disability (formerly classified as educable), the goals were higher, helping others as well as oneself: Between the world wars, the heralded Italian early educator Maria Montessori developed the idea of the "housekeeping corner" in each early education classroom as a place that less able children could be trained to eventually take on needed household tasks like bathing babies and washing dishes and laundry—tasks that some family member in those big Italian families of her time would have to do.

Americans now have a peculiar shame and avoid discussion of teaching activities that comprise mainly unpaid physical labor done at home—like cooking, cleaning, laundry, gardening, and caring for animals. Somehow, it has become illegitimate for these to be the focus of instruction in schools for handicapped learners, unfortunately only taught when it is agreed that it is time for academics to be basically "given up." It needs to be acknowledged that no one failed and "gave up," but rather, unrealistic goals were adopted in the first place. We now have many modern home conveniences to help us with the household tasks of Maria Montessori's time. However, these activities still can connect an individual to a greater sense of independence, as well as prepare him or her to be a member of a household or community where his or her efforts have value for others as well as for him- or herself personally.

THE EARLY YEARS OF MAINSTREAMING AND FULL INCLUSION

As we delve into controversy about how we should most effectively be educating children with autism, a definition of terms helps delineate the key issues: The term *inclusion* was historically hitched to the adjective *full*, with *full inclusion* meaning full-time placement in a general education classroom as opposed to a segregated special education classroom or special education–only school. In this scenario, fully included pupils receive accommodations (like a classroom aide, shorter or simplified work assignments, technology to assist expressive communication) as well as DIS like speech therapy (to understand and speak as well as others in the same grade) or occupational therapy (to, for example, improve handwriting to grade-level expectations).

Inclusion basically means *primary assignment* to a general (non–special education) classroom designed for pupils of the same, or approximately the same, chronological age. The underlying assumption of full inclusion was that the pupil with special needs required specific support in a few areas to access the same education as others of the same grade level. Under the earliest implementations, full inclusion was mainly used for pupils on the higher end of the autism spectrum deemed not to need help with reading, writing, or speech. At that time, children with some degree of intellectual disability along with their autism went to what are called fully self-contained classes (FSCs).

In the late 1970s, 1980s, and even early 1990s, few DIS services existed specifically to address the social difficulties that formed a barrier between pupils with high-functioning autism (HFA) and classmates. Then and also now, these children are the ones most likely to be meaningfully fully included. In the early days of autism special education, such HFA pupils were simply fully included with a hope the pupil would swim rather than sink. Today, speech and language pathologists in schools do more than promote good pronunciation—they work on "language pragmatics," which are the skills involved in initiating and maintaining conversation. Occupational therapists in schools now deal with more than poor handwriting; they also try to develop accommodations that will mitigate problems with attention. These supports have been critical to improving outcomes for children with HFA.

However, there has been a great deal of "mission creep" in the special education of children with autism: These DIS services used for children with HFA are increasingly also used for those with mild-to-moderate intellectual disability to support *them* in full inclusion, too. There are few data to support that this will be helpful, as these children can be so much developmentally "younger" than classmates. General education pupils readily recognize their developmentally mismatched special education peer as early as kindergarten and tend to "mascot" them (treat them as "cute" because they are immature); ignore them; or on some occasions, sadly, when the teacher isn't looking, bully them. Any child who is a mascot to some classmates will be at risk to be bullied by some others. For parents, this is painful because they desperately want their child to be included socially, but the same traits that provoke a caregiving response in some or even most classmates also announce the child with autism's social vulnerability.

MAINSTREAMING VERSUS INCLUSION

The term *mainstreaming* originally referred to pupils *primarily* being educated in a special education classroom but also having some regular time slots for joining general education classes or activities (in the "mainstream"). Mainstreaming for pupils with ASDs has often been quite inside out: The first move is usually to mainstream the child for nonacademic times—like lunch, recess, and physical education. Developmentally, the autism spectrum pupil is most behind peers in social milestones. That's what makes the child autistic. Lunch and recess can be elementary school free-for-alls with everyone shouting and running around outside. Maybe William Golding got background material for *Lord of the Flies* by watching how 10-year-old boys behave at recess. Children with autism mainstreamed for recess often end up alone by choice or by default.

If an adult facilitates interaction for a child with ASD at recess, children can be seen orienting to the facilitating adult in a bid to please him or her, rather than to strike up a true friendship with the "aided" child with ASD who can be hard to befriend. There are of course exceptions to this, but spend a few hours on school playgrounds at recess watching mainstreamed children with autism, and you will see what concerns me. What would be better?

Pupils with ASDs who are mainstreamed for activities like lunch and recess, in the best cases, are assigned a shadow paraprofessional to oversee playground activity, an assigned peer buddy in the cafeteria, or a "lunch bunch" to join. In my experience, it is a rare adult who can pull back in a way that allows the typically developing peer (who may appreciate the opportunity to act altruistically) to make a genuine connection with a classmate with autism.

FROM HOME ABA THERAPY TO INCLUSION: PROBLEMS ON THE PERIMETER

Home-based, intensive, one-to-one teaching using methods of applied behavior analysis (ABA) swept the world of autism early intervention in the early 1990s. Parents who had litigated against educational authorities and won ABA for their children as the newest evidence-based treatment for autism were radicalized with respect to their children's education. After being the first to get ABA in their school districts, such parents were not ready to stop fighting their schools for what they wanted next—which, quite often, was inclusion: The state of inclusive education, especially for pupils with autism, began to shift in the mid-1990s when children exiting home ABA programs headed for their first group-based education—preschool or kindergarten. ABA providers who had focused on one-to-one training of imitation skills with discrete trial methods ("Touch your nose!" "Good touching your nose!") wanted, next, to generalize these imitation skills to copying everyday things their pupil with autism would see nonautistic classmates doing.

For many, the shift from responding to a specific prompt (like "Touch your nose!") to copying something a peer did was too big a leap. One-to-one home tutors came into classrooms and tried to achieve successful imitation of peers by turning what they wanted the child to do into a discrete trial, just like they would do at home: "Get the pink crayon!" "Good!" "Color the bunny with the pink crayon." If this sounds like it would look artificial in a preschool class, it does. Some children with autism, though, were able to do this and fake it until they made it. Others would end up looking like they existed in their own little one-to-one classroom inside their real classroom.

Despite the limits of essentially bringing discrete trials into classrooms, parents began to demand, and receive, the right to have one-to-one home ABA tutors replace a school's one-to-one paraprofessional as the child with autism's support staffer in the inclusion classroom. Many ABA tutors have more years of education than the school's paraprofessionals, but their training vis-à-vis the child with autism is behavioral and not educational, centered on one-to-one teaching, not group instruction. This has set up a bad dynamic where the teacher may feel the ABA tutor's style impinges on his or her teaching of the whole group, and the ABA tutor may feel the teacher is failing to appreciate the necessity of the ABA tutor's one-to-one teaching. The ABA tutor and the classroom teacher often end up lacking respect for the teaching methods of the other.

There also is a long history of ABA-trained aides criticizing the general education teacher for not calling on "his" or "her" pupil more often and then reporting these complaints to the parent. Generally, certified teachers have not taken well to being second-guessed by young ABA tutors with no education background, whom the teacher considers a guest in the classroom. From the teacher's point of view, the less well-educated, school-hired paraprofessional aides who *are* meant to take direction from a *teacher* may be preferred.

MODERN MAINSTREAMING EQUALS "INCLUSION"

Over the last 10 to 15 years, placing children with autism among typical peers has proceeded apace—driven, I would argue, as much by political considerations as pedagogical ones: The term *mainstreaming* has largely been thrown over in favor of the term *inclusion*. For some, mainstreaming is tainted by the implication that when not being mainstreamed, the child is out of the mainstream (in a special education class) and so in a less desirable condition. For this reason, the term *mainstreaming* is increasingly less used. Today, inclusion usually is considered the more politically correct term, even when not "full."

ARE YOU "NEUROTYPICAL"? HAVE YOU EVER BEEN NEUROTYPICAL?

In a related political and psycholinguistic turn of the screw, the oxymoronic term *neurotypical* has come into the special education/inclusion lexicon. *Neurotypical* is an antonym for "atypical," promoted to mitigate the implied stigma of being "atypical." Parent advocacy websites for developmentally atypical children are introduced to the term *neurotypical* as the politically correct way to refer to the normally developing siblings of their child with autism, as if receiving and not receiving special education is similar to differentiating which of one's children is a budding pianist or is a soccer-playing fanatic. The sobriquet *neurotypical* also has been promulgated in the autism community by higher functioning adults with ASDs who are cognitively "typical" (or above average) but are hampered solely by their difficulties in social understanding. These individuals see themselves as cognitively as good (usually, as better than) others, just less able socially, as if that were the same thing as being less able athletically. In their taxonomy, being neurotypical is the opposite of being *neurodiverse*, another politically correct designation discussed in Chapter 2.

While the use of neurotypical or neurodiverse may be dismissed as bend-over-backward political correctness, it masks a societal discomfort at being up front about the fact that atypical learners can most often be expected to obtain fewer desirable outcomes, compared to neurotypical learners.

DISENGAGING FROM THE CORE CURRICULUM

I argue that much of the money spent on implementing educational plans (IEPs) for mildly, moderately, and severely intellectually disabled pupils with autism is a waste of money. Much effort either is spent teaching academic content the pupil will never need to know and will never use or is spent teaching things he or she will not understand in any meaningful way. This is the core of the problem in special education today that needs to be brought front and center.

The majority of lifelong special education's atypical learners will not achieve the same range of outcomes as adults as peers never in special education—no matter how concerted the effort to break down the core curriculum and teach it in small bits and with special techniques. Instead, I would argue, we need to teach them "news they can use."

First is an example of what I mean by wasteful teaching. Here is what "curriculum" can look like for a mild-to-moderately intellectually disabled child with autism: A 10-year-old came to visit our school consultation clinic with his mother recently. The mother started off saying she had come because her son had been grabbing his backpack and running out of the classroom, sometimes getting off campus. The school would call her to come pick him up. She felt they were abrogating their responsibility to educate him every time they called her. The school agreed to develop a "behavior support plan," an action required under educational law in response to such a situation. After much study, and as no real surprise, it was concluded that this young man ran from his special education classroom when he eschewed the instructional content of the moment (often math). This boy, about to enter his sixth-grade year, had IEP math goals as a focus of remedial learning—for the last 5 years. His mother endorsed that, at home, he still couldn't tell you if he had three magazines and got two more how many that would be. (Hoarding magazines to look for certain pictures was a major leisure activity of his.) I suggested it was time to stop teaching him math in contexts he did not care about and saw no use for. An example of a worthless worksheet for this boy would be one querying if you have two oranges plus two apples, how many fruit do you have? His mother agreed that her son learned nothing when it lacked personal relevance. We talked about "functional math"—like measuring quantities to make a simple food he liked such as a cheese sandwich (two slices of bread, two of cheese). Forget the apples and oranges. This made sense to her as a new way for him to learn math. This is what I mean by "news you can use."

The same problems existed in how this boy was being taught all his subjects. His mother told me how each year, a general education teacher from his grade level explained the "core curriculum" (this year, for sixth-graders), but with "accommodations" available to her son. The "accommodated" math goals he had failed to meet in fifth grade would be replaced by accommodations to the sixth-grade math curriculum. And, if sixth-grade history was going to cover Spanish colonization of South America, his accommodation would be that *he* would be "learning" it by coloring in maps of South America, learning names of South American countries, names of South American animals, and other things that might be taught to kindergarteners learning about South America.

Special Education Doesn't Have to be a Waste of Money

To my mind, such an accommodated curriculum is a waste of time and of educational resources and accrues no knowledge this child will ever use. He learns very slowly. The school knows that; they retest his cognitive levels every 3 years as they are mandated by law to do. So, what of it? What should they do instead? If he likes burritos, maybe his mother and teacher could work together to make a "visual recipe" for very simple burritos and weighing and measuring ingredients would be his math curriculum. Work in some reading (words under a pictorial recipe) and writing (copying the recipe to do again) and you have three worthy curriculum goals. It is well understood that children with autism tend to be intrinsically motivated to learn to do preferred activities for themselves. As a side note that reinforces this, as I was talking with this 10-year-old's mother, a staff member played with him using action figures. "What did he want to play?" I asked. "He made one figure, put it on his backpack, and ran away from school so his mom could come pick him up." Is escaping the school day filled with meaningless tasks a reinforcer? Never underestimate a child with autism when it comes to him getting what he wants! Let's teach such children things they want to learn.

A RADICAL PROPOSAL: A LIFE SKILLS TRACK FROM AGE 10

We need reassessment at age 10 (prior to fourth-grade age) to determine if a child has a severe developmental disability. This can be simply defined by broad cognitive testing, for children with and without autism. By the time a child is 10, we know he or she will very, very likely remain nonverbal if not yet talking. We know that if that child has mostly a picture-facilitated vocabulary, this child will very likely continue to communicate this way. We know such a child will still be struggling to bathe, toilet, dress, and eat independently—and will continue to do so—unless someone at school teaches the child these things instead of practicing to write his or her name or write numbers 1 to 10 next to corresponding quantities. Such a child should be assigned to a daily living skills track. This means a curriculum where tasks of daily living are taught, and there is little or no emphasis on reading, writing, and mathematics unless it is linked with multimodal, multisensory curriculum materials (pictures, voice buttons, etc.).

In the United States today, there are very few of these programs. This is largely because teachers don't want to "give up" on what they have habitually taught and reexamine whether they actually believe what they are teaching will someday be meaningful to their pupils. Further, educators may be either unwilling or disinterested in engaging parents in planning for where their child's disability will leave the child in 10 years. But planning tied to curriculum is what they should be doing. Many parents do want the truth about what their child can learn and what the child won't learn. They also want their 10-year-old to be toilet trained and to be safe riding in a car.

Parents with severely disabled children know they are severely disabled, but often don't know anyone who will tell them what it is very likely to mean in the future if they do not start early in the teaching of skills needed for as much lifelong independence as that child can achieve. Such parents can see their children are not going to acquire activities of daily living naturally, as their other typically developing children have. It flummoxes me why schools most often do not address this problem head on. Not only does persistent teaching of skills that can't be mastered unnecessarily frustrate a child, it leads to behavior incompatible with instruction, such as hitting, running away, and property destruction—which then result in unneeded behavior plans and medications to control behavior that might be better addressed by teaching pupils things that interest them.

ANOTHER RADICAL PROPOSAL: A FUNCTIONAL ACADEMIC TRACK BEGINNING IN MIDDLE SCHOOL

A tier above those with severe disabilities that need to focus on learning life skills from age 10 are those with moderate disability (autistic or not). Such children should be assigned to a functional academics–vocational track. A functional academics–vocational track needs to begin in middle school, when core curriculum in mainstream education turns to the development and implementation of abstract reasoning. These moderately disabled pupils are the ones who may read simple sentences and match sentences to pictures. They cannot compose their own narrative. They may read better than they can extract meaning. They may do rote math worksheets for addition, but can't recognize numeracy in the most basic functional equations. For such pupils, schooling needs to be redirected to (a) ensure that independent self-care skills and personal safety skills are in place (many have gaps) and (b) teach simple tasks that someday may translate into helping at home or in a vocational activity that has a high level of routine components (institutional food preparation, gardening, janitorial activities, housekeeping). Like more severely handicapped pupils, pushing children with moderate disability to learn things that are very difficult for them runs the risk of pushing maladaptive behaviors to the fore as the pupils try to avoid work they dislike because it is incomprehensible and intrinsically uninteresting.

One difficulty here for parents is that these are the children with autism who may have very low language skills but may have "splinter" nonverbal skills (copying 250-piece Lego designs in a short time, drawing with great graphic accuracy), making it all the more difficult to reconcile that, to some extent, the chain may not be much stronger than its weakest social link.

A THIRD PROPOSAL: BRING BACK VOCATIONAL EDUCATION TO HIGH SCHOOLS

In the tier above those who have severe or moderate disability along with their autism are pupils without significant limits in their activities of daily living who have borderline-to-low average intelligence in addition to whatever social and communication difficulties come from their autism. Such pupils learn more slowly than average, tend to be more concrete thinkers, may know many facts, but have poor "executive functioning," which is to say they struggle at putting 2 + 2 together at times that it would be a helpful equation to solve. Such pupils with ASDs can prefer things to be routine and predictable. Today, most such pupils track through high school with some general education and some special education classes or resource specialist program time, may succeed marginally in their mainstream classes, but manage to graduate. Such young people often lack direction as they head into their postsecondary years. Over the last 20 or so years, community colleges have developed learning assistance centers as clearinghouses for college coursework plans for such young people; these plans often are filled with remedial high school academics that prove no easier to master at 19 years old than at 15 years old.

I would argue that it is past time for "remedial college" to be the main alternative for entry to adulthood for these young people. Unlike when teens without disabilities enter college, the world is not at their feet. Instead, opportunities to struggle at the same academics they struggled with at high school lay before them. Unsurprisingly, courses they might hope to take are barred by the high school–level prerequisites they cannot pass. Many become depressed or anxious about leaving their homes. When there is no more mandatory school they must attend, they drop out of college courses no one can force them to take. There is no IEP or 504 plan anymore. Parents become frantic about the future their teens face. After taking a small number of community college classes, failing as many as they pass, many then drop out completely after a few years, with few job training or independent living support options for them to pursue. Parents feel there are no alternatives but to cajole them to try again. This seldom makes either party happy. What a waste!

What could be happening instead? To begin, such young people need an opportunity to engage in vocational training *in high school*. They need the opportunity to gain job-holding social skills—in high school. Such young people should be able to enter a vocational high school track. High school–level vocational education in the United States—for both special education pupils and typical learners—has atrophied in favor of community college education, which only occasionally provides certificated employment tracks like being an x-ray technician, dental assistant, or auto mechanic—many such jobs still out of reach for the group I am concerned about here. In the next chapter, Chapter 5, we will talk more about how vocational education and other modifications to core curriculum may best serve these pupils in high school, focusing more specifically on transition to adult living. For now, the point is that for parents of some high school–aged youth, it is time to consider a different sort of high school experience than we mostly see these days in the United States and use what we know about the likely developmental trajectory to plan this different sort of high school experience instead of indulging in the pretense that somehow things will be finally set right if only a high school graduation certificate is in hand.

SHOULDN'T EVERYONE WITH AUTISM WHO WANTS TO GO TO COLLEGE GO?

I don't think everyone with autism who wants to go to college should go. It is critical to create alternative pathways because each young person deserves a chance to learn something that will leave him or her feeling more masterful. That's what we want for all our kids. We know that there is a relatively small group of teens with ASD who test with overall average intelligence and above who can succeed in college and, even then, need many special supports. We will come back to them in a moment. If a high school pupil with an ASD demonstrates average to above-average intellectual capacity, only *then* should the pupil be educated in a high school track with others who have postsecondary educational goals. There definitely are people with autism who can succeed in college—if, like all other people with autism, they find something they are really motivated to learn. In Chapter 5, I focus on transition to adulthood in teens and young adults with autism, but to set the stage, the model I advocate is not to push pupils into things they will very likely not master, things where they will struggle—whether because they are severely intellectually disabled and autistic or even intellectually above average and autistic.

We think so much of autism as a neurologically based disorder that we can forget that individuals with autism, like anyone else, are subject (even more at risk, really) to depression and anxiety when things do not go as planned. While it may sound dismissive to say that for individuals with autism the sky is not the limit, it is really true for all our children. We are unlikely to encourage our typically developing C students in high school to apply to Ivy League schools, but we are more likely to do so if they score at or near the 800s on their SATs.

First to consider for this different high school curriculum I will describe is that group of teens with ASDs often called "high functioning," but who are not as high functioning as those with above-average IQs who are rightfully college bound. These high-functioning high school pupils *are* high functioning, but relative to those who are "medium" or "low" functioning. I am speaking here of the teens who not only have ASD, but also have either low average IQ (75–85) or borderline intellect (IQs of 65–75) or have "splintered" IQs, meaning poor communication abilities although relative talents at visuomotor, visuospatial, or orthomotor skills. These are the guys and gals who can do things like put together massive puzzles or huge Lego assemblages or draw cartooned figures with uncanny expressiveness, but cannot talk as well as they can draw or build.

These young people deserve the opportunity to access social skills training, independent living skills training, vocational training, and functional academics programs (in approximately that order) in high school. This is because, as it will turn out, the chain will only be as strong as its weakest link: If you leave high school not yet able to do the things that other high schoolers were able to learn incidentally (like order a burger with your own money, take public transit, or use an ATM), you will not be well prepared for any real transition to adult independence.

I meet many such young people who might be called "lower" HFA: They continue to live at home through their 20s without much capacity or motivation to engage in social lives of their own; they are unable to organize their own meals or maintain their living spaces, are largely unemployed, and are without plans to move on. My colleagues at our autism center and I describe these young people as "failures to launch." Their lifestyles are painful for their families and, most often, not happy for them. They did not get the high school experience they needed, which was one that would have provided independent living skills, vocational training, and functional academics—in lieu of what they did get: an IEP filled with accommodations to get though Algebra I, accommodations to get through English language arts, plus an hour in a resource specialist class at the end of each day for time to get started on their uninteresting, unmotivating homework in Algebra I and English language arts.

EDUCATIONAL TRACKING AND AMERICAN CULTURE

Assigning high school curricular tracks for individuals on the autism spectrum by intellectual level and symptom severity is likely to be reliable by age 10, well before high school. Why age 10? By age 10, about the age when we begin to plan for middle school, IQ has become fairly stable. By age 10, the most adaptively impairing levels of autism signs either remit or moderate with age and intervention. We can say a thing or two with decent reliability about an individual's likely developmental trajectory going forward from there.

This is the age school authorities should be dedicating part of IEP planning to identifying a middle school or middle school program that can provide a developmentally geared and comprehensive program. Initiating discussion of such assignment should not be regarded as laying down some immutable truths, but realistic planning for the modification of curriculum so pupils are taught what they are most likely to learn, retain, and use. On the other hand, not acknowledging a pupil's likely developmental trajectory, arguably, does not do the child, the child's parents, or society much justice. Instead, it prolongs a reckoning apparent to seasoned educators (though not always to younger educators who have not yet encountered 12th-graders they first knew as kindergarteners).

It is disturbing for parents with a child at any level of disability to face a school career that is anything but the typical one. In American culture, the practice has become to put off as long as possible any discussion of realistic trajectories and expectations. We now are guided, as codified in educational law, to wait until age 16 to work with parents to understand whether their young person will receive a certificate of completion from high school and not a diploma, as such. This is way too late. With each year of middle school and high school that a child with "lower" HFA is not given curriculum that works on social skills and independence in activities of daily living and introduces prevocational and then vocational alternatives alongside functional academics, the greater the barriers to eventual independence.

For some of these "lower" HFA pupils who stay largely on the high school academic track and do manage to graduate from high school with IEPs that still enumerate many one-to-one services, the possibilities of life without an IEP's support may never be discussed between educators and parents. This is really unacceptable as it helps no one. It certainly does not help that child fulfill his or her adult potential. It arguably makes worse that moment when parents face dashed unrealistic expectations that their child is not really "college material."

When that moment comes, and it does, parents often experience a sense of having failed their child. Parents recriminate themselves for academic "roads not taken" that they now worry could have helped their child to achieve goals (which they were never told were unrealistic in the first place). Educators are not going to be the ones to pony up and let the parents know that it was not Mom or Dad who failed this child, but it was them. They taught the wrong things. I don't blame educators personally. Virtually all who are "down in the trenches" didn't make the significant educational or social policy decisions that could have mitigated this failure.

I do feel badly for parents who reach this point. But I empathize most with their child: Years of education that fail to accrue expected gains leave *the child* at risk to feel like a failure. If a young person has not mastered what he (or she) has been taught at school, what parents have told him he can do, it is likely he will not have succeeded at jobs he was told to try either. Entering the workforce as a young adult with lower HFA and no prevocational or vocational job training or work habits predisposes failure. By their mid-20s, many youth with ASDs and other disabilities have given up trying to obtain the type of employment they have been told to try to get (often entry-level service jobs that require on-the-spot social interaction like bagging groceries or being "on the floor" of a big box store. Failing at what you have been told is an entry-level job is depressing for anyone, whether you have a developmental disability or not. Often, the young person has no emotional reserve left to regroup or to think about a different form of employment or a different kind of life course. It is not his or her fault to be at this point. The system has failed this person.

This unhappy state of affairs is a natural outgrowth of that American "can-do" attitude. There is a terrible disconnect between what we know about a young person's intellectual, social, and emotional capacities and what parents can come to believe might be "good" for him or her—with educators sometimes absolving themselves of any responsibility to connect the two. Many overburdened educators "check out" and burn out after writing very repetitious 3-, 6-, 9-, and 12-month IEP goals for a pupil year after year. We need to reset curriculum for that majority of pupils with autism who will not succeed at college. (Even the ones who eventually succeed at college are likely to struggle in predictable ways, but we'll get to them in the next chapter.)

SETTING ACADEMIC STANDARDS FOR MODERATELY TO SEVERELY HANDICAPPED PUPILS

Let's consider standards for reforming the education of more impaired children with autism first. What data do we rely on? When a pupil is tested, and special education law does require psychoeducational retesting triennially, test results typically yield a development "age" or, in education, "grade level" of academic skills. If a child's intellectual capacity is 50 percent of others', this indicates the expectation of a half-year of curriculum gain in a year of schooling. However, cumulatively, after 10 years of growing at half the rate of typically developing peers, a 15-year-old may still be learning concretely and in a rote fashion, like a first- or second-grader. In fairly rare cases, a child's rate of learning may improve, which could be due to improved behavioral management, for example; then, expectations for the child's learning also should be upgraded. However, as most pupils approach puberty, brain capacities are becoming mature to the extent that while more will certainly be learned, capacity for more complex operations are rather unlikely to emerge, although the fund of knowledge at a more concrete level will continue to accrue.

As an example, if a 5-year-old who has received 3 years of intensive behavioral intervention for autism is functioning overall at the 2-year level, the child is extremely unlikely to be functioning beyond the 5- to 7-year level when 18 years old. This means the child will be able to develop very basic literacy and numeracy, like recognizing his or her name and some other words for things the child likes, or functional numeracy like using a preloaded debit card to pay for supervised activities outside the home. What will promote learning is being taught skills for self-determination and even "pay" (earning access to preferred activities as motivators). I am talking here about teaching skills that most children learn at home without special instructional techniques—like brushing teeth, bathing, and dressing, as well as skills for home life, like preparing simple foods, making a bed, doing laundry, cleaning around the house, and gardening. Typical teenagers will not want to master doing the laundry or taking out the garbage either, but also will work for pay or privileges. Teaching for individuals with LFA should be construed to teach needed work habits no differently. For those with LFA, none of these basic skills is likely to be incidentally acquired just by watching others but will require the skills to be broken down and taught step by step with good behavioral technique. The curriculum needs to be derived from the sequence these skills are learned in a typically developing child. Presently, many moderately and severely disabled students with autism mostly have curriculum goals aimed at learning the alphabet, spelling, basic writing, and doing rote math. These are all activities divorced from any meaning for the child's daily living. This is pretty much the picture I see, no matter where in the United States I have visited an elementary school class serving such pupils.

If you think about this, it is gut wrenching; the learning problem really is not with the child but with the people who are supposed to be acting in his or her best interest, but who continue to teach things the child can't learn. In the absence of being taught things that seem meaningful or useful, children become frustrated, inattentive, or aggressive. They are treated for attention deficits, "sensory problems," and other problems that reflect their inability to absorb what they are being taught. Rather than reconsider that the curriculum is inappropriate, a first-line treatment is often "functional behavior analysis," bringing a behavioralist into a classroom who is charged with identifying the antecedent of an undesirable classroom behavior that is incompatible with instruction. Such analyses seldom consider whether overly complex, developmentally not yet appropriate curriculum might be the antecedent. When the behavior analysis fails to innovate improvements to the pupil's classroom behavior, medication is typically the next step. This may include psychostimulants, anxiolytics, or, not uncommonly, antipsychotics—all agents that may induce medical and other behavioral side effects.

MORE HIGH-FUNCTIONING PUPILS WITH AUTISM

As the prevalence of ASD has increased, the proportion of affected individuals who are reported to have co-occurring intellectual deficits has decreased to the point where presently about 70 percent are reported as without intellectual disability, 30 percent are affected with it; this is a reversal of the ratios reported 25 years ago when autism was estimated to occur in closer to 1 in 800 cases. (I talked about this in the previous two chapters.) Despite all the prevalence studies, we still don't know how much of today's 70 percent of those with supposed HFA have untested or unreported mild or borderline intellectual deficits. Children served educationally as having autism may also be tested to meet criteria of mild intellectual disability or borderline IQ. Parents are told "borderline," but not always what border the child is on. If there is a strong skill and a weak one, educators tend to emphasize the strength as they review test findings, not the finding that places a skill in the intellectually deficient range. Educational practice is almost as if educators don't explain what numbers reflecting low intellectual potential mean, they might go away on their own. As I have said, this is unlikely in a middle schooler or high school–aged pupil.

Ignoring the role that intellectual disability as well as specific learning disabilities may play in limiting what some can learn has, in American education today, promoted the unrealistic goal of expecting virtually everyone not explicitly diagnosed with some level of intellectual disability to obtain some college education. This is because we promote the idea that as many as possible should be on the college track. As a result, we find that 90 percent of adults with autism are unemployed or underemployed. Many have some college education or even college and graduate degrees. But they cannot, or do not, work because they lack viable job skills. To push out the timeline of what high school educators should be talking about with parents, one need look no further than a person with Asperger's with a master's in philosophy hard-pressed to find a job in his or her chosen field because there are non-ASD unemployed individuals with *PhDs* in philosophy who will do a better job interviewing because they can understand why the interviewer asks certain questions. Teaching in general, even teaching things like high school math or chemistry or supervising a computer lab, tends to be hard for a person with HFA to achieve success because of a poor ability to figure out what a student needs explained. These are not hypothetical examples. I have met with smart young people who personify failure at teaching these topics. Each was pushed through college and sometimes beyond with the idea that his or her lack of social skills, the weakest chain in the link, would simply not matter or would disappear at some point—and did not.

WHERE TO GO FROM HERE

Special education needs to prepare children with mild, moderate, and severe disabilities for their future, not ignore what that future will be. We don't know exactly what each child with an IEP or 504 plan will eventually learn, just as we don't know which typical sixth-graders will go to law school or medical school and which will work in the fast food industry—but we have an idea. American special education is sorely in need of putting such ideas on the table as curriculum is planned and parents are advised.

To sum it up, some children will not learn to speak, even with 18 years of IEPs aimed at accomplishing that. Some children will not learn to read or write, even with 18 years of IEPs aimed at that. Some children will have marginal literacy and marginal numeracy that will preclude independence at managing many of their own tasks of daily living. Some children will talk, read, write, but never do so better than most second-graders—or fifth-graders. Herein lies the problem: How do we, as a society, have an honest dialogue that can lead to ways that realistically support the best future for which we can educate our children with autism? The truth in special education is a very vulnerable commodity.

Resetting Priorities

BUILDING RESPONSE TO INTERVENTION INTO SPECIAL EDUCATION FUNDING

Response to intervention (RTI) is an educational concept that supports empiricism in special education planning. It goes without saying that research-based instructional strategies and curriculum should be used whenever possible. But, critically, data should be collected on goals (which is what IEPs require), *and* then the collected data should drive decision-making about the future curriculum. If you are at all scientifically minded, the idea that I am proposing is to use tested teaching tools, see if the selected tool works to help the child reach a developmentally set goal, and then decide what to do next based on results. This probably does not sound radical. Yet, in special education, what I have just said is really radical. Goals are often more wish lists than developmentally set objectives. If goals are not achieved, the same curriculum with the same goals is often used again without reexamination of the goals or of the selected curriculum content.

When looking at children with neurodevelopmental disorders, RTI is positive if the individual improves as much (or more) than can be expected developmentally. *Expected developmentally* can be defined as predictable change given the child's starting developmental level. If, for example, a 3-year-old scores 50 percent below expectation for expressive language (i.e., at the 18-month-old level), then in a year's time, the child should have improved at least 50 percent maturationally (i.e., to the 24-month level when 4 years old). If the child actually did better and improved so that delays were now only 25 percent below expected levels for age, expectations can be raised, and goals for the following year can now be set higher, and expectation for 9 months, not 6 months, of progress can reasonably be expected in the following 12 months (i.e., functioning at the 2¾-year level when the child is 4 years old).

If RTI is low and that 4-year-old child progressed less than the 50 percent expected, then the developmental appropriateness, intensity, or targets of intervention should be reconsidered or recalibrated. Maybe *what* the child is being taught is wrong developmentally, like alphabet recognition when the child does not yet consistently respond to his or her name or discriminating a picture of his or her mother from one of his or her father. Typically developing children are expected to recognize a picture of their mom before they recognize the letter *A*, but since teaching you to recognize a picture of your mom is not part of preschool curriculum, the alternative is to go straight to teaching *A*. But maybe *how* the child is being taught is wrong—not intensive enough or reliant on undeveloped imitation or social skills. Using an RTI model should ensure that a child (a) gets enough developmentally appropriate and methodologically effective intervention and (b) doesn't just get more of an approach that is not proving effective.

When There Is Too Little Early Intervention

For a given child, there may be not enough early intervention for all sorts of reasons: (a) In some areas of the United States, there simply aren't resources, or parents may be uneducated about available help and think their delayed child is still "not ready" for school. (b) In some locales, parents who themselves are survivors of childhood neglect or abuse are traumatized, caught up in intergenerational cycles of neglect, physical abuse, and drug use, and produce more than their share of prenatally drug-exposed offspring. Such parents are not good at helping themselves and tend not to do a good job at getting help for their kids. (c) There are parents in denial of the significance of their child's signs and symptoms of autism. (d) There are parents, both working incredibly long hours, with children in the care of caregivers or grandparents who do not know, or do not complain, that a child's development seems increasingly derailed.

Another, more pernicious, reason we do not have enough intensive early intervention for autism is that there are those who argue that the best special education is essentially no special education. I'm returning to this chapter's title—an illusion of full inclusion. In this model, very young children with autism are integrated with typically developing children by educators arguing that role-modeling and socialization are the most important things for learning. However, early hallmarks of autism include limited imitation and limited affiliative drive, so intervention that depends on learning from role models is a really poor fit. This is why the strongest treatment responses for young children with autism can be expected to come from individualized and intensively delivered early intervention. To do otherwise ignores the principles of basing curriculum and method on empirical data.

Too Much Early Intervention

There are some children who get too much early intervention. I have met parents who, having read that 40 hours a week of ABA is needed, no matter the age, keep 2- or 3-year-olds from napping. Some children who are in Year 4, Year 6, or even Year 8 of an ABA program (no longer "early intervention") continue because parents can point to developmentally infinitesimal gains (like recognizing three more letters of the alphabet after a year of 40 hours per week instruction) and falsely consider ABA (which is available because of research on its efficacy as *early* intervention) the only way their child can learn. If we followed an RTI model, a child not making developmentally meaningful gains would be tried on a different methodology (i.e., not one-to-one teaching), a different curriculum (i.e., not learning the alphabet), or both. If a child has developmental skills at the 14-month level, curriculum should be dictated by what a 14-month-old learns—names for objects, ways of requesting things, concrete play.

Guidelines for Resource Allocation

Resource allocation can be inequitable in American special education largely because of access to due process litigation for educational services. To be sure, this litigation is a two-edged sword—moving the ball forward on creating a mandate for newly emerging evidence-based programs but also resulting in outcomes of "spoils to the victor." Squeaky wheels are greased, while children who may benefit from more modest exposure to intensive early training are passed over—because their parents are themselves uneducated, don't speak English, are immigrants and afraid to "ask," or are poor and don't know there may be public funds to help their child.

The spirit of fighting for one's child is nothing but admirable. However, in the absence of strong RTI principles in special education, there is no mandate for equitable distribution of resources among children with different kinds of autism. Parents who "insist" most often get, even if there is lack of developmentally expected RTI.

Acknowledging That Quality Resources Are Finite

Resource allocation in early intervention is tough because no one wants to curtail programming to a very young child who is getting all the help that indeed may greatly benefit some children but is not benefitting this child nearly as much. These children are the ones with parents most at risk of turning away from mainstream treatments (as we'll talk about in Chapters 7 and 8). For them, the truth they believed was that intensive services would make all the difference. When it did not, the concept of what really was the truth became vulnerable to believable lies.

Quality one-to-one services are finite, and not all children benefit equally. In California, we experienced the consequences of the pretense that service availability was infinitely elastic: When SB946 (a California law mandating early ABA for most young children with autism) went into effect, Kaiser Permanente, the largest medical insurer in California, tried to create about 2,000 new ABA programs overnight to meet new guidelines from the California Office of Managed Health Care. They contracted with Easter Seals, an excellent national organization serving young children with developmental disabilities—but that had never provided even one ABA program for a child with autism in California. Easter Seals got on the job, but unsurprisingly was unable to put together a quality workforce overnight. ABA early intervention quality plummeted. Not only did parents feel snookered, but also motivated young college graduates who took the Easter Seals jobs in large numbers quickly quit in large numbers. There weren't even enough qualified staff to train them. Newly minted interventionists simply did not know what to do with the children they were assigned once they were in the child's home. Parents, while not faulting them, did not want them around their child. The parents wanted the promised therapy. As California was about the 27th state to mandate third-party insurance-paid ABA, the same lesson was being learned all over the United States—just on a bigger scale. A political entitlement to services is no guarantee for access to quality help as access will be limited as the autism-diagnosed population continues to grow.

A similar thing had happened about 10 years earlier in Ontario, Canada. ABA was approved for all children with autism but had to be relinquished around age 5 to create service availability for the next cohort of even younger children with autism. The problems were that parents who got ABA for their children did not want to relinquish services that were effective when their child aged out. There were families who had been waitlisted for services for months and had only just begun to receive ABA when their child hit the disqualifying age, or worse still, families were waitlisted throughout their child's entire eligibility period and never received intensive ABA services. In both the United States and Canada, these problems were partly due to lack of research on alternatives to early intensive ABA, or even research on who was likely to respond best or least and at what "doses" (hours per week).

One solution to finite resources of an intensive costly service is guidelines for moving children from more to less intensive programs based on how they respond to treatment with it. This could help more fairly allocate the more scarce resource of intensive programming and also ensure that children moved out of intensive services do not lose ground, by monitoring them for any decline in learning rate. Research already shows that children who do not make strong gains in highly intensive early therapies learn at comparable rates in less intensive therapies. Further, after children with autism gain learning readiness skills such as imitation and response to social reinforcers through early intensive ABA programs, they are more amenable to (more naturalistic) early intervention, where all children learn by participating in group activities and where they are called out and praised for their successes, a response they can develop in ABA.

Potemkin Villages

I've made the case that one way that a tremendous amount of money spent on special education is wasted can be because intensive ABA programs continue as long as someone will pay for them, irrespective of RTI. In a way, early costly ABA programs set the tone for what parents of children with ASDs come to expect as their children enter special education classrooms: They expect more services, more dollars spent, and that one-to-one teaching must be better than learning in a group. It might be better—or not. I am not implying the money spent on intensive special education services should not be spent; rather, often it is being spent on treatment not tied to outcomes. Underpinning this waste is a very American optimism that special education ideally is not palliative but, rather, curative. This fuels the idea in autism special education that if a child is learning slowly, one-to-one teaching (just like in ABA) might pick up the pace of mastery because "more" has got to be better.

Here's an example that anyone who has ever been involved in special education can readily envision: I visit a preschool where a 3-year-old child with autism is receiving hand-over-hand assistance to trace his name on top of a large template of 2-inch letters. I visit a second-grade classroom where a similar 8-year-old is receiving physical prompting to hold a pencil with appropriate grip followed by verbal prompts to trace his name over a template of 1-inch letters. I visit a high school class for moderately to severely handicapped pupils where I am told the pupils are practicing writing their name on a mock application page that says "Name" in the upper right-hand corner. With five or six verbal prompts, the 17-year-old pupil writes a more-or-less legible version of his first name. For such children, what is the point of 14 years of practice in writing one's first name? None of these classes is giving these children the special education they need to become more functional adults, but it is a costly charade. Each of these classes is a Potemkin village—an impressive façade designed to hide an undesirable condition. (Potemkin, a Russian general, fooled Catherine the Great into thinking much rural redevelopment had been achieved by lining riverbanks with portable wooden mock-ups of villages so she would think her subjects lived better than they did.)

The Human Rights of the Child With Moderate-to-Severe Disability

Regarding the 14 years of practice in writing his name, why put the student through this? Will he ever need to fill out a job application to get a job? Why do we pretend? Much more important, would you like school if *you'd* been constantly pushed to do basically the same things for 14 years? Would it be an environment where you still were interested in learning, or a place to practice work-avoidance strategies?

Each child has the right to be directed to learn things he or she has a capacity to learn. Each child needs to learn things that have the potential to increase self-efficacy and independence. I would argue that for the type of 17-year-old pupil I have just described, it might be much more meaningful for him to learn to use a hot air popcorn popper than to have an IEP goal to increase accuracy of spontaneously writing his first name on a faux job application. I can guarantee you that if he likes popcorn, he will master the popcorn maker plus any related tasks that involve measuring, pouring, and cleaning up more quickly than learning any writing task. Let's acknowledge that we must play to a child's strengths, not what we choose to have the child learn under the guise of making him or her more "mainstream."

We Need Educational Tracking for Children With ASDs

How do we shift the culture of special education where the goal is for each pupil to fulfill his or her potential for independence and not to fail to learn a watered-down version of the general education core curriculum? I am speaking here of moderately to severely handicapped pupils who are not able to make academic gains in mainstream high school classes but continue to be educated in fully self-contained classes.

Presently, IDEA mandates that a child with an IEP be assessed at age 16 to determine (a) whether he or she will be able to earn a high school *graduation* certificate or qualify for TAL services after high school (ages 18 to 22 years) and earn a high school *completion* certificate. Age 16? This is way too little, way too late. (TAL determination used to be at age 14 but was unfortunately raised to 16 a few years ago—just in case anything prognostically major might happen in those 2 years—talk about mixing politics and special education.)

SPECIAL EDUCATION VOUCHERS

Why We Need Special Education Vouchers

No one is more motivated to help a child than his or her parent. No one has the potential to understand a child like his or her parent. Sometimes, parents may look at all the public special education resources offered in their community and feel nothing can provide the kind of developmentally appropriate, evidence-based programming that would mesh with their child's unique needs. Sometimes, teachers have tried; a school has tried. Sometimes, the school authorities conclude that the needs of a particular pupil are just too unlike those of other pupils or too multidimensional (e.g., both developmental and mental health) or self-endangering or endangering to others for the pupil to be served in their public system.

We have long had nonpublic special education schools that have met this need for pupils the public education system feels it cannot serve. Mostly, parents and their lawyers have opened the door to these schools for such pupils, because in fact, it is more often that parents request such placement than it is that schools offer them. These nonpublic schools usually are fairly expensive, the lawyers are expensive, and only occasionally are the parents doing the litigating for such programs rich. Assuming the cost of litigation is a scary burden for a stressed family of a hard-to-serve child. But some put many family resources on the line to get more help or different help for their child. Is there a better way?

While Americans have universal and mandatory public education available, parents of typically developing children have the right to pay for alternative education—private schools. Some feel that such parents of typically developing children should have educational vouchers—so they can chose the education they want, more like the way they choose the house or car they want. Non–special education vouchers basically mean buying your preferred schooling minus the cost of what you could have had for free (public education) but were given in a cash-value voucher to apply toward a private school.

What about for special education? Per pupil expenditure (PPE) is a little harder to evaluate as each child has an IEP that will cost something different based on the numbers, types, and frequency of services the child requires. However, it should be fairly straightforward for any local school authority to estimate the cost of education for any one special education pupil given the student's IEP service profile. Why not give parents a voucher and let them select special education outside the public schools? Yes, the special education schools parents could select should be licensed and should use evidence-based practice, but this would allow parents more control over the child's programming—a good thing psychologically for parents of children with autism, as having a child with autism makes many things in one's life as a parent not very "under control." Importantly, a voucher school choice would allow parents to seek a chance to do things they might feel are critical but are not being done in the school—like a specific reading program, incorporation of computers into instruction, or a program where physical exercise is used as counterpoint to seat work. There are endless possibilities.

The availability of vouchers (which parents could add money to) also should incentivize development of a wider range of nonpublic school alternatives, not only for children with autism, but also for all children requiring special education. The main downside risk would be the lack of equity if vouchers were available to special education but not general education.

REVISE SPECIAL EDUCATION DUE PROCESS PROCEDURES

We Need Arbitration

I have been qualified as an expert witness in about 125 educational due process hearings in the last 30 years—maybe 4 hearings per year, some years more, some less; sometimes on behalf of parents, sometimes on behalf of school authorities; always to advocate for what the best available research says will likely meet the federal standard of a free and appropriate public education (FAPE). I have appeared before local administrative judges, state judges, and district court judges in several states and in Canada before provincial court judges.

Special education matters are usually court hearings before a judge, administrative judge, or hearing officer (no jury) who hears evidence by a plaintiff (parents on behalf of their child) going against a respondent (usually a school authority). Due process actions in special education have been a very active

114 { The Politics of Autism

venue for establishment of special education entitlements for children with autism over the last 30 years.

But, for me personally, this is very much a two-edged sword: There have been times (in the early 1990s) when the average level of service that schools gave to 3- to 5-year-old children with a bona fide diagnosis of autism was a few 2-hour Mommy and Me classes each week. It is well supported by research that these early years are the most critical to establish learning readiness through intensive treatments at home and school. Models such as one-to-one ABA were shown by early researchers, including myself, to be more beneficial than what schools were doing at the time. I was an expert witness in *Smith v. Union School District*, the first fair hearing of these new methods as children I followed received them at the University of California at Los Angeles (UCLA) Young Autism Clinic, headed by Dr. Ivar Lovaas, who developed the methods. The UCLA clinic family whom I helped prevail at their hearing received the first school district–funded home-based ABA program in California (perhaps the United States). These parents put a lot on the line as advocates for their son. They paved the way for many others.

After *Smith*, many educational authorities were, one by one, compelled to provide similar services or at least provide more comparable and intensive services. I testified on behalf of many similar families. However, as more children with autism were treated with these intensive services, it became clear that not all responded as robustly as the "Smith" boy treated at UCLA. In fact, research only a few years later came to show that for children with autism and more marked intellectual disability, these more costly programs yielded few measurable additional gains compared to the children receiving much less intensive, more conventional special education.[3] I then began to appear as an expert for school authorities at further fair hearings to explain this new research when there was a petition for intensive help that research did not support would be helpful. I appeared opposite parents who could afford the lawyers but could not accept that their child was one of the ones very unlikely to respond to further costly treatment, but rather might benefit more meaningfully from learning picture communication, becoming potty trained, and learning to use silverware. Schools had begun to develop these sorts of programs for children who could not differentially benefit from more costly programs. Stories in the media focused on amazing improvements from ABA/Lovaas therapy, so that's what parents understood to be the best.

Related to this was that while special education law *does* guarantee a FAPE, it is not obligated, under FAPE, to offer the "best" education: Parents of typically developing children can opt to pay for a "better" private education, but parents of children with autism have been left to argue that the "best" (an ABA/Lovaas therapy program) was the only "appropriate" education, especially if their school had begun to offer some version of intensive services for children with autism but not at-home one-to-one ABA.

RESOURCES ARE SCARCE

The bottom line is that we do not have enough skilled interventionists to give every child *with* autism everything he or she may need to have the best shot at fulfilling his or her potential. There is something bittersweet about being asked to endorse allocation of scarce resources to a child who has had them and who has benefited only marginally from them.

There are hard choices to be made. The special education system almost totally lacks external accountability, meaning objective third-party checks to see if the agreed method to reach a specific goal has turned out to be valid. If the child does not improve as much as hoped, parents can threaten to sue and receive more—even if the child's autism severity and response to intervention so far strongly suggest that more costly services are not likely to be differentially beneficial. It is personally wrenching for me when I see a child of well-meaning parents, who are savvy advocates, get things for their child when I know many more children, also with loving parents, who could be doing much better if only they got one good teacher, a good aide for half a year, or a home program a few hours a day for a year or so. These are the children of parents who can't, won't, don't leverage the system.

Simply *more* of what is not working well is seldom the way to improve a child's outcome. It is never the case that a child with autism can't be helped or that we as professionals should just "give up" on that child. But that is often how it feels to parents who are told the treatment or more treatment they happen to want will not be made available for their child. Instead, it becomes a matter of how success can be redefined. Sometimes the child's parent cannot, will not, hear what kind of limited success their child will likely obtain in the long term, even with services that meet criteria of "no stone left unturned." It may be that when the child was first diagnosed, parents were either given false hope or not disabused of it because letting them believe what they wished about their child's future was seen as a temporary salve. A child's failure to achieve is personal; often, it is experienced by parents as their failure to get the right things for their child, rather than the reality of their child's limitations.

The politics of giving bad news is discussed in further chapters, but for now, the point is that more is not always better. Resources are scarce. We need accountability. We need honesty. We need Plan B for those children with autism who cannot benefit from Plan A. Plan B is not going to be more Plan A. Important to the discussions in this chapter, seeing a child as autistic when the child's primary disabling limits may derive from intellectual disability is not going to put the child in the ballpark of the more positive outcomes we may see in children with autism but without intellectual disabilities.

I remember one year in San Mateo County, California, near where I live and work in San Francisco, a wealthy family obtained day- and nighttime services for their child; these services were funded by the school district—to the tune of

3 percent of the special education budget of the county (about $250,000) when the average child with an educational diagnosis of autism was receiving about $16,000 of services. A good number of children in this Silicon Valley county are from well-educated and wealthy families, some of whom can even choose to fund the private education of their children with autism. But many publicly educated children with autism in San Mateo County come from homes with undocumented parents who clean the homes, build the swimming pools, and tend the gardens of the wealthy families. Such parents, as well as others who are legal immigrants from authoritarian Asian countries, are unlikely to consider standing up for their child's educational rights. Some children have parents simply too trusting of the education system to realize their own child's needs were being pillaged by one child making minimal gains with $250,000 of help. If the $250,000 child had been rightfully recognized to have intellectual disability that was as handicapping or more handicapping than the child's autism, allocation of resources might have left more in the pot for others who were needier.

In Hawaii, I have been involved in several cases for which parents won residential placement for their lower functioning children with ASDs; per child, these placements cost the state over $200,000 per year with tuition, transportation, and family visits. These children were very difficult to keep at home—partly because a skewed look at the wrong research seemed to suggest they should be able to do much better than they were doing with the special education they were receiving in their home state. The couple of million dollars Hawaii spent on out-of-state residential placement for a handful of children diminished resources for the rest. This is another example of how emphasis on autism, and not on intellectual disability when it is a child's major handicapping condition, can misallocate resources that could have been beneficial to other children fitting the profile of those with autism who benefit from intensive therapies.

The families of these Hawaiian children who did receive the costly residential services were still in pain about their child's status. Although they had been given everything they had asked for, their children were still significantly disabled and showed few benefits that would have not been expected in good-quality local programs (which existed).

Whose job was it to help these parents learn what to expect given their child's dual handicaps of autism and intellectual disability? What did they expect? How can parents be helped to develop an appropriately calibrated measure of their child's successful growth? If that calibration is informed by random success stories in the media, most parents are bound to be disappointed when their child does not do as well. They may feel they have failed their child in some way—with guilt compounding despair. It shouldn't be this way.

I believe parental angst about whether treatments are right, or are enough, needs to be met by realism. I have colleagues who shy away from being realistic at the time of diagnosis, especially raising the possibility of intellectual disability. I have heard it said, too many times, that this parent or that "couldn't handle it." That's paternalistic medicine at its worst. Being supportive and truthful with parents, being clear on what is known and not yet known, what is likely and what is not likely is the ethical high road. No, clinicians don't have crystal balls, but if they read the research, they should know some things about how most with autism are likely to develop. Holding out autism as a mysterious disorder with all sorts of outcomes may not be wrong, but it may not be right either. Parents deserve the truth.

How Special Arbitration Could Replace Due Process

I am proud to have played a positive role in access to the first school-funded ABA programs, but I have found that sometimes what the school offers is indeed appropriate and what the parents want is sometimes beyond what evidence would support to be "just" appropriate. Increasingly, I am brought in by schools just for an opinion on what is appropriate (FAPE), where the school authority's goal is to work with me and the family to understand the research and to appreciate differences that may exist between "FAPE" and "best," for which the school is not obligated to pay. On the Internet, I have read this misconstrued as my being "for" the school rather than the child. Autism special education due process matters seem to have a way of bringing out the worst in each opposing side by nature of the adversarial nature of due process adjudication.

The adversarial nature of legal due process really is completely opposite of what the involved parties need to be doing to build a collaborative relationship that will allow the parents to seek guidance about the child from school authorities. Parents may do a good job of burning their bridge to their local school authority by suing them. If the family plans to stay in their district, or has other children in the district, this suing for special education services can be a poor strategy. A courtroom with a judge with no special training in autism is not an efficient venue for adjudicating what is FAPE, for what is the "standard of care."

Two ways the use of judges to decide on FAPE could be curtailed would be with a process akin to binding arbitration by a panel of experts (e.g., three) to review evidence presented by both sides; hear oral summations; have a list of possible witnesses, including further experts that could be called at their discretion; and then adjudicate plans for resolution that ideally give some choice of implementation to both sides. These expert panelists could be qualified by interview with existing panel members regarding their expertise in evidence-based treatment and developmental individualization of IEPs and then be paid for their work in a manner that neither incentivized being quick or being laborious. This idea is also discussed further in Chapter 6 on autism health economics because the due process hearing procedures as they now exist siphon much money away from the actual special education services so many with ASDs need.

Presently, in the adversarial legal scenario, both sides can submit overwhelming numbers of often irrelevant or outdated exhibits that bog down administrative judges, who are not content experts on autism. Exhaustive parades of witnesses are hauled in. These can include school staff very peripherally involved with the child, arguably done strategically by plaintiff's counsel to disrupt the school's staff scheduling and ability to serve others, perhaps in hope the school will settle rather than endure these disruptions. Teachers, speech therapists, school psychologists, and the like who have no experience in the legal process are often stressed and intimidated by having to testify, feeling they are being accused of having done something wrong when they feel they are just doing the job they have been hired to do. This stress of having to testify, unfortunately, has led a number of well-trained special educators I have known to flee from the field of special education.

Reduce "Beyond Reasoned Limits" Lawsuits

There are many, many actions brought by parents that reflect their hopes and wishes for what their child may be able to learn. The school may have agreed to goals that were not developmentally realistic and then failed to meet them or may refuse to sign on to such parent-proposed goals in the first place. Parents or their advocates may request methods, curriculum content, or practice that is not evidence based. I would hesitate to use the term *frivolous* here as is used to refer to frivolous lawsuits in other sectors because no one's hopes for their child are frivolous. Perhaps a more accurate term should be something more like "beyond reasoned limits" or "not reasonably construed to accrue benefit to the child." However, if parents file for services a judge or panel can deem as not reasonably construed to confirm benefit based on research, such parents should be liable for litigation costs accrued by the school. This could dissuade angry, acting-out parents to think twice before filing nuisance suits, including those for unfound damages and requests for compensatory education that would be aimed at goals beyond the child's expected capacities. Sadly, I have seen more than a few of these, and these actions often clog special education due process calendars for years and do nothing but further embitter certain families.

Overall, the numbers of educational due process hearings involving children with autism have risen, which can be a bad thing, just as autism-specific programs have increased, which is largely a good thing. Access to these high-quality autism-specific programs can be attenuated, however, when a school district needs to set aside $50,000–$150,000 or more each year to cover potential litigation—money that really should be directed to programs.[3]

What's Next?

In this chapter, I focused on how programming for many children with ASDs is poorly calibrated to accrue viable long-term outcomes given the nature of each child's disability. Every case of autism is different with respect to the number, type, and severity of autism symptoms and also with respect to the strengths and weaknesses inherent in each individual's cognitive profile. There is much work to be done in dropping the misconception that inclusive education is inherently preferable. It may not be the best place for certain pupils to learn and feel successful if they cannot meaningfully access the curriculum or fit in socially without feeling bullied. In the next chapter, I turn my attention to how this plays out in secondary education and in preparing individuals for their lives as adults with autism.

Notes

1. Siegel, B. (1996). Is the emperor wearing clothes? Social policy and the empirical support for full inclusion of children with disabilities in the preschool and early elementary grades. *Monograph of the Society for Research in Child Development, 2/3*, 2–17.

2. Kauffman, J. M., & Hallahan, D. P. (Eds.). (1994). *The illusion of full inclusion: A comprehensive critique of a current special education bandwagon.* Austin, TX: Pro Ed.

3. Pudelski, S. (2016). *Rethinking special education due process: A proposal for the next reauthorization of the Individuals With Disabilities Act.* Alexandria, VA: AASA, the School Superintendents Association.

5 }

Educating Youth With ASDs for Their Future

When it comes to understanding how well our nation is helping
youth affected by autism, our situation is like driving a car
through the fog with no dashboard. We know we're moving. We
can feel the gas pedal under our foot, the steering wheel in our
hands. But we do not have many indicators to tell us how fast we
are going, whether we're getting close to our goals, or what kind
of mileage we are getting from the resources fueling our trip.

> —Paul Shattuck, PhD, Director, A. J. Drexel Autism
> Institute, *National Autism Indicators Report, 2015*

The Special Education Folie à Deux

I believe the effort of preparing adults with autism spectrum disorders (ASDs)
for adulthood begins with educating parents about the nature of their child's
disability. It continues with educating educators about the nature of their
student's disabilities. If neither parents nor educators know what to expect,
how can appropriate goals be set or reached? Failure of doctors to be realistic
with parents about autism from the get-go fuels hopeful but unrealistic parent
expectations for both higher and lower functioning individuals and everyone
in between. Yes, some kids will do amazingly well. Some kids will come a long
way, overcome seemingly insurmountable early problems in social relating,
communicating, and adjusting. Some will achieve what has been described as
"optimal outcomes." Some will definitely lose their ASD diagnoses. With "best
practice" interventions, virtually all will do better than what most parents fear
in their darkest moments.

Generally, a realistic picture of variable outcomes, and of lingering signs of
autism even for most with high-functioning autism (HFA), is not the picture
painted for parents when they first learn of their child's diagnosis. Instead, little
to nothing is said about the long-term implications of this child's diagnosis of
autism. The appointment is too short, the clinician knows how to use standard

measures to diagnose but lacks long-term personal experiences, or the clinician simply doesn't want to broach discussion of the future.

It's not that parents don't want to know: Instead, parents read information on the Internet to learn what the long term may look like. They read heart-warming stories of success. They also may read or hear about young adults with persisting and severe problems. If no one is there to help a parent fit these images to his or her child as that child grows and develops, a mentally healthy person may well hope for the best—which is a good thing, but is based on hope, not data.

With this lack of direction, parents are left with short-sighted, rudderless special education practices that mostly never look more than a year ahead. Good educators are always hopeful, but hope, I argue, does not always navigate parents in the direction that may serve the child's best interest. Educators try to aim for the goals parents hope for. This is a very good standard of practice when a child is receiving his or her first years of help. However, professionals (educators and others) can see that adaptation to life with persisting difficulties is part of a child's future by the time the child reaches 5 or 6 years old, if by that time the child has received 2 or 3 years of decent treatments. The child who will lose his or her diagnosis or be classified as having achieved an "optimal out-come" is pretty much known by the early years of primary school education.

How much difficulty, and what kind of difficulty, may persist will, of course, vary from child to child. No one has a crystal ball. But we are not blind, either. We usually have data that show whether children are responding robustly or in a limited manner to their earliest years of intervention. Nevertheless, the school years most often continue as if mastering some version of the core ele-mentary and secondary curriculum will be possible (and meaningful) for any-one. Nevertheless, by age 5 or 6 it is clear that at least half of those with an autism diagnosis will plateau before learning to read, write, or do math better than most third- or fourth-graders—something that is evident by examining individual education program (IEP) goals (what is aimed to be taught) to most fourth- though twelfth-graders with autism.

As I talked about in Chapter 4, much special education is not geared to a de-velopmental sequence of learning, starting with self-help and social skills typi-cally learners acquire outside of school. Special education often is not modified according to data from assessing response to intervention, but it stumbles on as paler and paler imitations of curriculum for age-mates (watered down seventh-grade algebra leads to watered down eighth-grade algebra, even if principles of seventh-grade algebra are nowhere near mastered). This means that many youth with autism hit major roadblocks when they complete secondary schooling at age 18 to 22 years old because they have spent a great deal of time being taught things they can't learn or have learned but do not link to any functional skill. Most often, the teaching of basic social or daily living skills related to age-appropriate independence has simply been left out of the curriculum, especially for children with low-functioning and medium-functioning autism (LFA and MFA, respectively).

WHAT DO LONGITUDINAL OUTCOME DATA TELL US?

The best data on adult outcomes in autism come from the work of Dr. Paul Shattuck (quoted at the beginning of this chapter) and his colleagues at the A. J. Drexel Institute at Drexel University in Philadelphia, Pennsylvania.[1,2] Their work shows that during high school, over half of youth served as autistic will be receiving combinations of help like speech–language therapy, occupational therapy, social work or case management, a personal paraprofessional educator, and transportation (Figure 5.1).

The day these youth graduate from high school, these services end. The Drexel group noted that by young adulthood, 26 percent were unemployed or not in higher education and received no services—such as vocational training or training in independent living skills. This was not because families didn't want it, but rather because such services are scarce and funding poor. Overall, only 42 percent of young adults with autism worked for pay. Only 1 in 5 lived independently in their early 20s. Figures 5.2 and 5.3 are graphs from the A. J. Drexel National Longitudinal Transition Study that clearly indicate the current situation.

It has been difficult to bring change to this picture. I argue it is because the opportunity to introduce vocational skills and adaptive behavior training in high school was abrogated. While the number of youth with autism seeking help from state vocational rehabilitation agencies is on the increase (e.g., almost

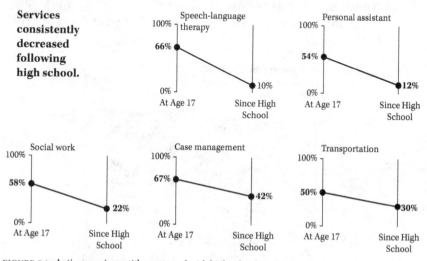

FIGURE 5.1 Autism service entitlements end with high school graduation.

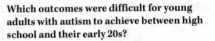

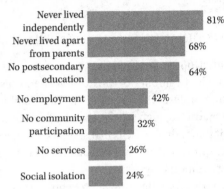

FIGURE 5.2 Young adult outcomes in autism.[2]

Source: National Longitudinal Transition Study-2.

50 percent between 2009 and 2014), it is stymied by the corresponding decline in all kinds of support services enumerated in Figure 5.1. When postsecondary youth with autism do get jobs, it is in a miscellany of activities, not the result of systematic vocational aptitude testing or training. More data from the A. J. Drexel report are shown in Figure 5.4.

STARTING OVER

I examine where we are going in special education for autism—with the goal of redesigning secondary education for children with autism so that there is opportunity to maximize the adult potential of every child with an IEP.

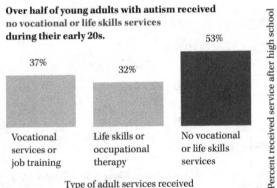

FIGURE 5.3 Lack of postsecondary vocational or adaptive skills training for youth with autism.[2]

Source: National Longitudinal Transition Study-2.

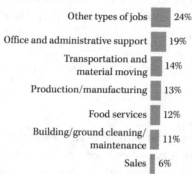

What type of jobs did young adults with autism tend to have?

Other types of jobs — 24%

Office and administrative support — 19%

Transportation and material moving — 14%

Production/manufacturing — 13%

Food services — 12%

Building/ground cleaning/ maintenance — 11%

Sales — 6%

Percentage of adults with autism who worked (at their current or most recent job)

FIGURE 5.4 Jobs for youth with autism reflect ad hoc opportunity, not systematic aptitude testing and training.[2]

Source: National Longitudinal Transition Study-2.

Very few children diagnosed with autism in early childhood, and who remain autistic through the school years, will grow into what members of the autism community consider "neurotypical" adults. We need to acknowledge this and provide much, much more developmentally directed curriculum during the school years. How do we help such youth find their métier, their niches where they can be as successful and fulfilled as possible as adults, like the rest of us? We need a combination of teaching what skills can be expected to emerge next in developmental sequence and what is especially motivating to a given individual with autism because it is so well understood that individuals with autism learn what interests them so much more readily than learning what we think they should be interested in (but are not interested in). Autistic self-determination can be a big part of the adaptive impairment conferred by autism—at whatever overall level of functioning. Today, we are indeed "driving through the fog," as Dr. Shattuck asserted, when it comes to knowing what will be best for supporting the transition of young adults with autism into the adult world of independent living and work. His research group argued convincingly for more resources to study models and efficacy of adult services. He spoke accurately of most pupils with autism "falling off the service cliff" when they graduate from high school or transition to an adult living program.

Several million dollars in research to test curriculum models that lead to greater adult independence for teens with autism would be nice, but first, we need direction for that research. For starters, we already know what we do now is not working particularly well: In data drawn from the National Longitudinal Transition Study–2,[2] the data looked actually a bit rosier than that from other sources, but it was found that over one third of adults with ASDs never get a job or further their education after finishing public education; more than 40 percent never work for pay, and about 80 percent continue to live with families at least through their 20s. Virtually all identified educationally as autistic at the end of high school were still receiving some special services. Over a quarter then transitioned to receiving nothing, no services, in their 20s.

WHEN IDEA IS DONE

Just picture this: An 18-year-old with ASD earns her high school graduation diploma with the help of a one-to-one aide or 2 hours a day in a resource room, where her curriculum is "adapted." This often means the curriculum is truncated to the point of questionable utility—like reading a synopsis page and answering five multiple-choice questions, instead of reading a 20-page chapter and writing a 3½-page essay response. She has a social skills support group at lunch time—her "lunch bunch" friends who come to the resource room to eat with her because the larger campus is not a place she can navigate independently. What about the week after high school graduation? There is no bus to school in the morning and no structure to get the day going. The rule about no videos or Internet surfing until after homework is moot. There is no one, nothing, to cause one activity to end and another to begin.

Obviously, when this day arrives, it is not because parents of these youth, who had attended countless school and other service meetings for years, had suddenly stopped caring. On the contrary, most often there is simply nothing any longer for them to get for their children. How does this happen? All the guarantees of the Individuals With Disabilities Education Act (IDEA) to a free and appropriate education (FAPE) are in the past and are over.

In a wonderful movie about a successful adult transition model for some very high-functioning youth with autism, *Programming Hope,* the father who has initiated an inspiring computer programming workshop-cum-startup company talks about his own despair for his son the day he realized the "short yellow school bus" was not going to be stopping at his home any longer. As the program becomes established, developing and patenting video games, the youth working there make friends among coworkers, who accept each other's quirks, form their own congregate living arrangements, develop social lives together, and generally make a better adjustment than many parents worried they might not.[3]

THE HOLLAND-NOT-PARIS STORY

With apologies to the Dutch, there is an old chestnut of a story that has been retold at countless parent–special educator conferences and conventions throughout the United States. The speaker is virtually always the parent of a child on the autism spectrum. He or she says something like this:

> When my son was born, I imagined his future as having a boundless horizon. I imagined the places he might go someday. I, myself, dreamed of someday seeing Paris—as the most perfect, interesting, sophisticated place in the world. Then, one night, just after I learned my son had autism, I had a dream. In my dream, I thought I finally was on my way to Paris! But, when we landed, I discovered I was in Holland. I had never thought much about going to Holland. But finding myself there, I discovered its small pleasures, windmills, tulips, canals. When I awoke, I realized the dream would be the story of my life: I would not see Paris with my son, but he and I could experience Holland together.

Whenever I hear a parent of a child with ASD embark on this parable, I feel a bittersweet joy. I am happy this parent has processed the unbidden news that his or her child has autism in a way that holds a future full of happy things to anticipate, even if that future is not "Paris." I know this parent will work better with special educators planning for his or her son than the one who thinks special educators are all French travel specialists but are holding out on offering that deal to go to Paris.

HOW TO GET TO HOLLAND

Not infrequently, early childhood special educators meet a parent who optimistically posits the belief that in his first year at school his or her preverbal 3-year-old with autism will learn to say his first words, declare "Mommy I love you!" be toilet trained, and stop throwing tantrums.

Would that it were true! Who will reach out to the parent to make it clear that this particular child is on a different developmental trajectory? What happens in 3 years when this child only has 10 words, simply says "Open" when he wants something, and is schedule trained for the toilet but still not requesting to "go"? It is meaningful progress, but not what was originally hoped and, I promise you, not what was originally promised by the educator. Arguably, special educators can become caught up in a parent's false hopes—admiring the parent's optimism and positive energy and so unintentionally reinforcing unrealistic goals by not countering them. It is hard not to feel the pain of parents facing the likelihood that "this" will not be "over" by the time their child goes to kindergarten. Are such parents (maybe most parents of children with autism) being set up for a harder fall than if the specialist had bucked up and found a way to be more frank from the beginning? I've been pondering how to get this right for years.

THE ETHICS OF PROGNOSTICATING IN ASDS

When a child is diagnosed with autism at age 2 or 3, whose job is it to speak about the future? Diagnosing autism is not exactly like diagnosing a terminal cancer, where the recipient of the bad news takes a deep breath and asks, "How long do I have?" For cancer, the answer may be somewhat mitigated by what kind of cancer it is, how progressed it is, the general health and age of the patient, and the effectiveness of treatments for this particular cancer. That's basically also true for autism. The overall capacities of the child and the availability of best practice treatments will make a great deal of difference in outcome.

REALISM

Even if a clinician can broach the topic of variability in prognosis, it does not begin to handle the answer to the deeper existential question that the parent really wants: "How can I possibly handle this?" Most doctors I know "punt" when they see this level of parental pain. I try not to punt, but some days, I punt a bit—and am not proud of it. It is absolutely true we do not know exactly how things will turn out, but would we be doing a better job to inculcate realism from the beginning? I remember a father, years ago, asking—in these few words: "Do I save for college, or do I save for a home where my son will always have someone to live with him and help him? Just tell me." Another asked "College or a special needs trust?" It is much easier for professionals to be realistic with a "just tell me" parent than a parent who does not utter such words. So, professionals not only fail to engage in conversation over prognosis but also may feel it is best practice to "take the high road" by simply telling another professional that this parent is not "ready" to be told, a paternalistic practice.

In the bad old days of highly paternalistic medical practice, it was considered fine for the doctor to take the high road: In one of the last episodes of the popular TV series *Mad Men*, one of the female protagonists, Betty, collapses and is brought to hospital. Only after her husband arrives does the doctor address the husband, while Betty stands aside; her husband is told she has terminal lung cancer. The culture at the time gave the doctor permission to make it less stressful on himself by addressing the bad news to the husband, assumed to be calmer and more rational than the patient herself, who was right there and fully capable of understanding him.

What about today? Do doctors do things to avoid stress for themselves when they diagnose? As with cancer, an insurance company is not going to be eager to expend resources on a costly treatment with few data to support its efficacy. When a doctor limits discussion to the best treatment responses and a correspondingly better prognosis, he or she may be hoping it will help get an expensive treatment covered, even if it seems unlikely to be all that helpful. Similarly, many terminal cancer patients receive costly treatments unlikely to work because there is no other choice than no treatment at all. In oncology, it is called "compassionate care."

But we do not even talk about compassionate care when we talk about autism treatment. Rather, we just pretend we have no idea how effective the treatment likely will be for a particular child. Often, we pretend the treatments associated with highest outcomes are the *only* treatments. Autism treatment providers often fail to provide the probabilistic success data as routinely as oncologists do to let the patient decide if he or she wants a certain treatment or treatment at all.

I believe that is where the impetus for some of educational inclusion comes from. If you are "included," you must be doing better than if you were receiving education in a more "restrictive" setting. *Included* is a positive word. *Restrictive* is a negative word. Not offering to carry out a child's education in an inclusive setting sometimes is interpreted to mean that all hope for a really good outcome will be lost if we were to place that child in a special education program even though specialists in this setting are trained in how the child learns and what the child should be taught. Neither inclusion nor supercilious adaptations of the "core curriculum" should be standing in as an autism version of compassionate care when there are other skills the child may actually be able to learn with the more skilled support available from a credentialed special education teacher.

This is the folie à deux first set up between diagnosticians and parents. Often, it becomes the folie à deux between parents and special educators. Parents hope their child is in the best outcome group and so should receive what children who will have the best outcomes receive. (I get it: If I had cancer, I would want to believe I was like those with the best prognosis, and that I would respond to the same treatments the way the best responders are known to respond.)

When any parent, irrespective of the severity of their child's ASD, feels their child should have the same treatment as the best responders, that is when parental expectations for an offer of intensive one-to-one applied behavior analysis (ABA) programs, one-to-one aides, and inclusive education, with all possible supports, become the norm for everyone—which indeed is considered the standard of care by many. If not offered, parents are counseled by advocates and parents who have gotten "better" offers to hold out. Educators, knowing these parents will be spoiling for a fight, are more likely to go along if parents are seen as litigious. This only reinforces unrealistic expectations. Ultimately, it can destroy the parents' faith that the educators really know how to help their child if the child doesn't achieve hoped-for (but unrealistic) outcomes.

Certainly, there are children on the autism spectrum who do much better than others. The hard part here is that any clinician who says he or she has no way to know who has a better prognosis and who has a poorer one is being disingenuous (or may be very inexperienced). For the pupils who truly are among those who may obtain the best outcomes, we have evidence that many forms of special help can be absolutely critical, so the allocation of resources is justified. When there are data to support that a child with certain pretreatment characteristics can reasonably be expected to benefit from such services, I am the first to volunteer to write a letter or testify at a due process hearing to see that the child gets the needed help.

Problems arise when data suggest a particular child may not derive as much benefit from the same high level of service and, in fact, can be expected to do about the same with less costly service. Special education is not required by law to offer "compassionate care" IEPs. They are not even required by law to offer "the best" education. The law requires only that they offer an "appropriate" program, FAPE. But, there is more to it than that.

A folie à deux takes two. The special education system not infrequently abnegates its responsibility to bring the parent to the table and to consider realistic programming actually calculated to be appropriate for a child. Instead, it is standard operating procedure in most American educational jurisdictions simply to offer adaptations of the child's grade-level core curriculum as what will be taught—even when the child lacks prerequisites (e.g., reads at a second-grade level but will "learn" concepts designed for eighth-graders). This charade of adaptations to age-level core curriculum can extend through a pupil's entire school career without anyone from the school "telling it like it is" to parents of children who are not developmentally in reach of the adaptations being offered to them. The whole notion that special education curriculum should be adapted from the age-mates' same-grade core curriculum, rather than geared to the child's present levels and personal rate of learning, is pretty far-fetched when you think about children who developmentally are 3, 4, 5, or more years behind age-mates in language comprehension, reading, and math.

COMING OFF THE CORE CURRICULUM

As a psychoeducational specialist of sorts, I can tell you this "coming off the core curriculum" is pretty hard to talk about with parents: Recently, parents of a minimally verbal 13-year-old were disappointed when I told them it really was time to stop drilling their son on identifying colors because every time he had "mastered" them since age 6, he had forgotten them again if they were not re-reviewed every few weeks. To me, teaching this boy his colors was going nowhere. Inevitably, such academic drilling is part of a larger picture of a child lacking much earlier developmental skills. Teaching this young man to be 100 percent toilet trained (which he was not), including initiating going to the toilet on his own, should be more of a priority, as well as "mastery" of other skills that reflect what most 3-year-olds can do for themselves. What should a clinician do in this circumstance? For one thing, such a 13-year-old with autism is, by definition, one who also has moderate-severe intellectual disability.

AUTISM WITH INTELLECTUAL DISABILITY

For those children who can be thought of as having "low-functioning autism" or even "medium-functioning autism," the "low" or "medium" designation is more closely tied to level of concomitant intellectual disability, not the severity of autism symptoms. It is well understood by clinicians, though seldom emphasized to parents, that level of concomitant intellectual disability will be at least as prognostically determinative as the autism itself.

Some autism advocates argue that it is not possible to diagnose intellectual disability in autism, that failure to answer questions on an IQ test is due to autism, not to innate disability. This is a convenient explanation. It is also a tautology—as intelligence *is* the ability to in some way demonstrate the competencies tapped by an IQ test. There are certainly badly behaved and unmotivated children with autism who will do poorly on IQ testing because of undesired behavior that interferes with doing their best. However, absence of abilities measured by intelligence testing also observed across aspects of daily life can pretty much tell us when intellectual disability is part of a child's picture.

The idea that some children with autism cannot or do not also have intellectual disability probably started with Dr. Leo Kanner, who first described infantile autism in the 1940s. His aim was to make a case that there was a distinct group of children, different from those with intellectual disability (or mental retardation as it was then called) and also different from children with other known psychiatric disorders. Not until the end of his career when he and his younger colleague, Dr. Leon Eisenberg, followed up many of the original sample with infantile autism did it become clear that a number also had a degree of intellectual disability. Many symptoms of autism correlate with deficits that comprise intellectual disability (like lack of language). Professionals diagnosing children with autism must also address whether or not intellectual disability is also likely to be present, as the two so often co-occur.

Which professional is, or should be, responsible for telling parents the truth about the likely adult outcomes that await their autism spectrum child who at age 13 does not remember colors, nor can independently use the toilet reliably? If that pupil's doctor has copped out and has never mentioned intellectual disability, should his teacher do it? Most teachers I know would say it is not their job. A special education teacher will tell you this is what the doctors get the big bucks to do. At the time of diagnosis, when a parent may ask about long-term outcome, it seems nothing but heartless to respond affirmatively to a parent who wants to know whether to save for an adult attendant or college in a way that can dash hopes. Another problem here, as we discussed in Chapter 2, is that most children are diagnosed with autism before beginning treatment, when there are no hard response-to-intervention data yet. For this reason, the American Academy of Pediatrics and other professional organizations recommend soft-peddling on any discussion of intellectual disability and instead point to obvious "developmental delays." But, over time, as response to interventions can be charted, developmental trajectory can be better understood, and treatment planning should be adjusted accordingly. This is why, after all, educators are required to hold annual IEP meetings with quarterly benchmarks for reaching annual goals.

The Passage to Adulthood for More Able Youth With ASDs

WHAT IS THE ALTERNATIVE TO THE ACADEMIC CURRICULUM?

Part of why it may be so hard for both parents and educators to move away from endless years of trying to teach essentially the same things to disabled learners as typical learners is that there is little political will in the United States to formulate and promote an alternative other than the core curriculum. In the United States, unlike in the United Kingdom and European Union, there is virtually no universal educational testing that places pupils into different levels and types of academic or vocational training as they reach early adolescence. Vocational training in the United States, which was once comparable to that in Europe, now lags sadly behind. Even though a German autoworker who attended vocational secondary school can earn much more than an American college-graduated English major working at Starbucks trying to write his or her first novel, America does not support public school vocational education. Perceived nonacademic training in publically funded secondary education in the United States is generally viewed as "below" what we should expect for anyone. This, of course, makes it even harder to establish vocational programs that might be tailored to the expected adult outcomes of special education students without creating the sense of a diagnostic apartheid system.

INTELLECTUALLY DISABLED COLLEGE STUDENT

Is the idea of an "intellectually disabled college student" an oxymoron? No. Many community colleges, junior colleges, small private colleges, and, increasingly, universities have special services for pupils who had IEPs as public school elementary and secondary students. Many pupils who completed public education with IEPs are now further accommodated with high school–level math and remedial language arts classes at community colleges. The emphasis in such classes is seldom the acquisition of specific vocational competencies. It's more of high school, but now enrollment is voluntary. It raises the question of why a student that did not learn ninth-grade math by the end of high school will learn ninth-grade math in community college.

For my money as a taxpayer, I would rather such pupils have access to well-suited vocational preparation. In vocational training, youth with mild disabilities have a chance of success at something they *can* do, rather than a chance to continue to fail at the goals they were not able to achieve for years, even with specialized high school instruction. For some youth with ASDs who have much higher nonlanguage than language IQs (a common profile), vocational work that involves assembling things can give them a chance to use their cognitive strengths in a way school classwork never did—and to earn money to live independently (or buy the video games they are so good at).

HIGHER EDUCATION FOR THE HIGHEST FUNCTIONING WITH ASDS

For pupils with high-functioning ASDs, targeted support, usually to bridge the social chasm that separates them from the student bodies in which they live, can be critical to later success in the workplace. There is a whole tier of higher functioning pupils with ASD who graduate from high school with exceptional grades in one or more areas and exceptional or adequate grades in others. They are rightfully college bound. They may still never have had a friend or blatantly exclaim they don't want one—except maybe a cute girlfriend for those certain sometimes. While we think of college as a very social experience, there are skills in many industrial settings, medical laboratories, and high-technology companies that accommodate competent workers who may not have what others consider a necessary social life beyond the two-dimensional computer screen behind which they sit all day. Supportive cognitive behavioral therapy aimed at getting through difficult social situations in class and in the workplace is increasingly understood as an effective support for helping individuals with ASD and higher intelligence to make it in the mainstream work world.

SUCCESSFUL INCLUSION IN THE WORKPLACE

When a young person who has had an IEP all through his or her school years makes it into the workplace, there will be no IEPs there. There are no parents to argue for accommodations to help the individual. There is ADA, the Americans With Disabilities Act, but it was designed much more with self-advocacy and physical disability in mind. The young person with autism is out from under the IDEA umbrella. There is no teacher to agree that the pupil's special needs will be met through the services provided by a particular IEP. There is just a boss who wants the work done because that is the work he or she is paying to have done.

Yes, under ADA some higher functioning adults with autism have argued for a walled cubicle with a door rather than an open workspace, for a fragrance-free office, the right to wear noise-cancelling headphones, or for natural spectrum lighting. Generally, those who go the distance to achieve these accommodations for themselves still often have more fundamental problems in adjusting to the workplace that have to do with lack of altruism, inability to appreciate the role of teamwork, and a tendency to bristle at any criticism. Most often, there is no system of supports (like a cognitive behavioral therapist) to help the individual hold things together. After a failure or two, many of these potentially productive workers just give up—which is a real shame given all the hard work the individual and those who have helped him or her have put in. Risk for anxiety disorders and depression climbs.

For the higher functioning individual with ASD, years of school accommodations to allow educational inclusion to be successful may be the setup that primes unwillingness to see one's own failures as failures—and not the result of what someone else is not doing to help you. The key to truly successful inclusion in the workplace for young adults with ASDs seems to be that the young person has to want to achieve something, desire it enough that it is worth doing some "social" thing that others want but may not seem intrinsically worthwhile. Let me next give an example and a counterexample.

What Can Go Right, What Can Go Wrong

A beautiful example of success by a high-functioning person with ASD can be found in the life story of Temple Grandin, who has written extensively about her adulthood as a person with autism. A number of years ago, I shared a speaking engagement with her mother, Eustacia Cutler. At lunch, Eustacia and I first talked about a book a colleague and I had written about growing up with a developmentally disabled sibling. Growing up, Temple's siblings resented the extra attention Temple received from Eustacia. One way this resentment was conveyed to their mother was complaining to Eustacia that their sister Temple had extreme body odor, and their laundry would pick up her bad smell. Eustacia asked Temple to use deodorant so her siblings wouldn't complain, but her entreaties were met with Temple's logic: "Just do my laundry separately." Time went on. Temple was interested in cows, and then meatpacking, and she dearly wanted to work in a slaughterhouse. She got her first job in one. Then, after a couple of days, her boss told her that if she wanted to stay in her job, she'd have to use deodorant. As Eustacia told it to me, from that day forward, Temple did.

As a counterexample, a young man with high-functioning ASD had graduated from a very good public university in California and been selected for a 3-month employment trial at a prominent Silicon Valley corporation, having been recruited from his university's job fair. The first weeks at the company were marked by critiques of him not being a "team player" among his cohort of other new employees on trial. He was often being found by his supervisor to be working on something other than the assigned task and, later, found to be responding to helpful peer reviews with nasty e-mails. When I met him, he was accompanied by his concerned mother. She and I agreed that it would be good for him to quit before he was fired, which it seemed would be any day. More important, we needed to unpack what had gone wrong. He muttered *soto voce* to the floor: "No one wants the stupid products this company makes anyway." His mother quickly pointed out to him that this company was in the top 100 of Fortune 500 companies—so there *were* people buying what the company sold.

What are the lessons here? There seem to be some key points for guiding higher functioning young adults with ASD if they are to be successful in joining the mainstream workforce. First, they must pursue something they want to do, which may or may not be what their parents feel they should want to do. Temple's mother was clear to me that Temple was not raised on some sort of farm, but rather in a good Manhattan suburb where a successful student, including Temple's siblings, achieves Ivy League credentials. But, she realized Temple had to be Temple. Eustacia thought there must be opportunities for an able young person with ASD to achieve a sense of independence in plotting her own course in life. Slaughterhouses were by no means Eustacia's idea. Notably, this is not so different from any typically developing young person as he or she goes off into higher education—where parents often hope for one major but get another.

For parents of young adults with autism who still infantilize and overprotect them, accepting what their child can do and wants to do, rather than pushing for what they want the child to do, can be a bit bitter. For parents of young adults with autism, it is very different from letting go of their other children. Parents can trust that their typically developing offspring have developed to the point where they have mental and emotional resources to land them on their feet after a wrong turn. The young adult with ASD is (I think, rightfully) seen as vulnerable, not nearly as able to rebound after a stumble or fall.

Ingredients for More Successful Transition to Adulthood

What should we as a society be doing to create needed supports for talented young people with autism? We do not want them to fall victim to their chain being only as strong as their weakest (social) link. We can pretty much count on the likelihood that these young people with autism may need more support than others their age to prevent them from "going off the rails" as they navigate their early college years or early years of living on their own. Both college completion and moves to independent living tend to take longer than for peers.

This time of life is challenging for all young people. Young people with autism on their own for the first time are less likely than peers to drink too much or to do drugs. That's good. However, they are more likely to stay in their room, not go to most classes, not turn in assignments, or not buy anything to eat except Cheetos for days on end. Often, 4 weeks into their first semester away from home, someone notices one of these things and suddenly the family is in crisis about how to respond.

GO YOUR OWN WAY

Stories about successful transition to adult life have some interesting common elements. One is leeway for the adult to cut his or her own swath. Not having to work full time, not having to earning a living wage, being supported by Supplemental Security Income (SSI), being able to live in a parents' mother-in-law apartment can be bridges. These are not really a plan, of course, but a safety net. Young people with ASDs need a safety net as friendships, social network, and jobs tend to be much more tenuous.

One perspective on the social and emotional lives of higher functioning adults with autism comes from a relatively small, very interesting group of not always specifically employed gadflies on the autism lecture circuit who can provoke others to action through criticism of the difficulties they personally have encountered as persons with autism. If this piques your interest, I'd recommend *Look Me in the Eye* (2007)[4] by John Elder Robison or *Born on a Blue Day* (2006) by the math savant Daniel Tammet.[5] Their traits of autism became the tools of their trade to teach others what it is like to have the core social–communicative difficulties of autism—while being very intelligent in ways that allow success in the mainstream.

INTRINSIC REINFORCEMENT OF JOB CHOICE

A second common element to success for young adults with ASDs is being able to follow one's bliss in a way that leads to functional independence. People with autism do not, by definition, motivate themselves mainly to please others. There has to be something in it for them. Temple Grandin adopted deodorant not to avoid offending others but to keep a job she loved. Success, I would hazard to say, is more likely when parents step back and allow their able young person with ASD to define that success for themselves and then take pride and pleasure in the work they show an ability and motivation to do. Sometimes, that work will lead to more economic independence than at other times.

I can think of one young person with musical talent who has seemed pretty happy working as a grocery clerk—and playing in a band in leisure time. His mother, a special education advocate, realized that as long as her son was happy and found a niche for himself, she would be happy, too. Another young man is an expert in native California evergreens and sells trees for a large nursery, whose tree buyers need to know all about soil, moisture, nutrition, and planting locations for their new trees. He loves to talk trees, and his tree nursery is his niche. I can't imagine that anyone buying a tree from him would know he spent a year at the Lovaas Early Autism Project at the University of California at Los Angeles in the late 1980s. I can think of another who lives at home with his parents, but has no real independent living skills, and mainly rehearses for his career as a pop musician—playing gigs (that his mother arranges) at developmental disability conferences. I think neither this young man nor his parents are un-happy with this arrangement, but it still feels very "special ed" and touches on that problem parents face in letting go of a child who, though an adult chron-ologically, is still vulnerable socially and emotionally.

PARENTS: LETTING GO AS MUCH AS THEY CAN BEAR

A third common element to growing independence in a young person with au-tism is having parents who can let go of their protective custody. For some young people with ASDs, this happens when parents truly move on from au-tism advocacy as their vocation. Other times, it happens involuntarily as a pro-tective parent dies early or is disabled by chronic illness. For other families, this can only be successful if the adult child leaves the parental home and lives in a supported community that can take up where parents left off. Such communities typically can quickly grow further independence where parents would not or could not. I've seen a number of "medium" and lower functioning young adults with autism blossom when they leave their parental home—preparing food, doing laundry, navigating myriad electronic devices. At home, it was often easier and quicker, parents would report, to do things for their young person lest they become frustrated and unhappy.

WHERE TO LIVE?

There are protective environments, and there are overprotective ones. If you are a parent who has caused the writing of 35-page IEPs for 15–18 years of your child's education, fought for a 10th year of speech therapy consisting of a half-hour lunch of conversation with a same-grade typically developing peer, and micromanaged community outings throughout adolescence, you are not going to be "all in" for finding your son (or daughter) a roommate on Craigslist. Besides continuing to live at home, what other choices does your now-adult son have if you want to support his independent living?

Higher functioning people with ASDs will not want, and it is not helpful or even fun, to share a supported living environment with individuals more developmentally disabled than themselves. Group homes such as these with a full-time attendant or two may be a good fit for more cognitively disabled young adults with autism, but not for the cognitively able. The alternative of living alone works well for some if there is structure throughout the day so that aloneness does not breed eccentricity. That can be a big "if."

Semi-independent living models, like congregate dormitory suites with some meals prepared, nearby transit, shopping, laundry and garbage facilities, and a "den mother" who makes sure tasks of daily living get done would be great for many. This is something more than a typical college dorm, but something less than a group home. The best models for this I have seen include group community activities in the evening, ties to places for exercise or arts, or maybe religiously affiliated activities all Sunday. Not surprisingly, like anyone, many young people with autism will talk about wanting a place to come home where they can "chill." Chilling for them may include being in a place where it will be OK to be a bit more autistic. After a full day of living in a world with complex and seemingly unnecessary social details, some look forward to coming home and opting out.

Unfortunately, there is little of what has just been described. I've described the highlights of what I have learned by talking to families, visiting model programs whenever and wherever I can, and speaking with many others in the autism community about places they have worked, and strive to replicate.

The world of adult live–work alternatives that parents usually find is more black and white. The expectation is to enter the mainstream, go to college, and hope things all work out or, for the lower functioning, to opt for a world of special supports for employment and for accomplishing the tasks of daily living. Neither model is well specified in parents' minds, understandably making many parents so anxious they can't stand to think about the future.

What happens by default is that most young adults with higher functioning autism remain unemployed as they trek through years of very part-time community college attendance, even more part-time jobs, mostly hanging around in their parents' homes playing way too many video games while their parents work. These young people, so carefully scaffolded through their school years, now do little except eat too many Doritos—instead of cooking healthy foods, which they never learned to do because that was not considered needed by an education system with a charge to prepare them for the future. Obesity, lack of exercise, and poor health outcomes are common among youth with ASDs in the first 10 years after finishing high school. Beyond that, we have fewer data but none that suggest things get better.

We need more capacity to teach life skills, more alternatives for supporting employment, and more resources to build adult living communities that are places where adults with autism want to live and can thrive. It seems to me that this will not happen as long as we continue with the charade that children diagnosed with autism will somehow acquire a capacity for independence on their own—even though everything else learned had to be carefully taught.

WHAT WE DON'T NEED TO DO

Along with the illusions of inclusion, propelled by the myth that all children with disabilities will benefit from being included with appropriate models, is the idea that the workplace will also embrace inclusion. In recent years, some big technology companies like SAP, Oracle, and Microsoft have announced plans to employ "hundreds" with Asperger's disorder. The media angle has been that these individuals have near-superhuman ability to concentrate on code and identify errors and will work tirelessly because they like narrow repetitive tasks so much. Just leave them with a computer screen and let them debug! These Aspies, it is said, make poor eye contact, but it's all good because geeks are good with instant messages rather than meeting in person—so they won't waste time. How well does this vision for the inclusive workplace play out?

What about virtually everyone's workplace tasks that require executive functions like prioritizing and judgment calls? What about tasks that require you to be aware of what others expect of you? How about the "workability" skill of knowing when you have said the wrong thing, at the wrong time, or to the wrong person? What if you think the software you are working on is point-less, and that there is already something better made by another company? How do you convey that opinion to a supervisor? Should you? What if nobody wants the workstation next to you because you concentrate best if you can rock and hum monotonously while wearing noise-cancelling headphones?

There are real dilemmas to be addressed here. There are employable people among the unemployed and underemployed among the highest functioning adults with autism. Depending on the segment of the autism population examined, un-employment rates for those without significant intellectual disability are often cited as over 50 percent. People with autism often rebound very poorly from being fired, often dwelling on their own grievances, unable and unwilling to take the perspective of the person who fired them or accept the reasons given for being fired as possibly valid. How does an able person with autism decide where to look for a next job after getting laid off from Microsoft or SAP for one of the autistic faux pas I've just enumerated? I've met many who just conclude, "Why bother?"

APPRENTICESHIPS: STARTING LOW AND GOING SLOW

In the nineteenth century, most people acquired employable skills by apprenticing, not going to college and studying things with no direct applica-bility to getting a particular job done. As an apprentice, one started doing the smallest bit of scut work, learning to do it as well as it could be done, and then being supported at moving up from there. The ideal was that you would go as far as you could succeed. Much more work in those days, of course, involved physical exertion or repetitive tasks, with much reward coming from something external—being paid, being valued for your family or community contribution, or conformity to societal expectations of productivity. Some people felt proud of what they produced, such as a good meal, a good crop, or a beautifully made object. While that is still true today, there often is more value placed on service jobs rather than jobs where one produces anything material. However, with fewer jobs to make things, fewer jobs lend themselves as readily to apprenticing and getting satisfaction from incrementally small successes built on each other.

But how could this apprenticeship system work today for the high-functioning people with autism? Rather than years of education involving core curriculum like history, language arts, science, and math, what about vocational training starting in early adolescence when we know that level of cognitive capacity is highly predictive of adult capacity?

Here are some arguments in favor of this: First, educational IEP goals are usually about helping pupils to achieve something that can be called success and that resembles the things that are hardest for them to achieve. If a high-functioning person can't understand the theme of *Moby Dick,* can he or she do a paper of equal length on whale species of the North Atlantic instead? I would argue the answer is only if writing that paper might in some way link to an interest the way Temple Grandin is interested in cows: If whales, environmental protection, or ocean species depopulation is interesting, what about an apprenticeship that readies this individual for working for a state department of fish and game, maybe starting with counting salmon swimming upriver to spawn, maybe starting with hauling the equipment that the person who counts the salmon uses each day? The IEPs should be about laying out tasks at which the individual can be uniquely successful, can gain a sense of mastery and accomplishment in reaching a goal that is personally meaningful, and can have a path to a future employment niche. This should be high school. If this individual gets a job with a fish and game department out of high school and after a few years of counting salmon wants to go to college and study aquaculture, great! After 10 years of counting salmon, though, the individual might be happy to excel at salmon-counting technology.

When do we know, in the broadest terms, where a person with autism can likely "go" educationally or vocationally? In England and elsewhere, O-level exams (*O* for ordinary) at age 14 or 15 are designed to result in a General Certificate of Education, after which a job training path is expected to be followed. In England, age 14 or 15 is considered the age at which a future range of "workability," as we call it in the United States, can be forecast with substantial accuracy. Only a much smaller number of British pupils are qualified to proceed to A-level exams (*A* for advanced)—bound for higher education. Importantly, I am speaking here of a method used with the general education population, not those in special education, whom logic would dictate will mostly have a more attenuated set of outcomes that should certainly be predictable at 14 or 15—or earlier.

By contrast, in the United States under IDEA, special educators are required to broach the idea, only when the pupil is at age 16, that the special education pupil will likely not earn a fully qualified high school diploma, but graduate with a certificate of attendance instead. Even then, a switch to vocational education seldom takes place.

BECOMING MORE BRITISH

What might we be doing between ages 8 and 16 to prepare pupils with autism and their parents for something more like an O-level certification as a first educational milestone? For one thing, many American high schools, including many we consider the "best" American public high schools, would have to rebuild vocational education. They could serve not only students with autism, but also other students with IEPs and provide vocational training as they do in the United Kingdom and Europe for the rest of the (non–special education) high school–aged population who tested into it or opted for it.

What kinds of vocational and apprenticeship opportunities would we need to support in the public sector to make for longer-term employment opportunities based on skills acquired through direct vocational apprenticeship rather than what we do now, which is specious accommodations to the core curriculum? In the context of modern American educational thinking, this idea of returning to vocational education may sound both radical and retrograde. Arguably, it is neither. It could be a step forward to creating employable individuals out of a class of individuals who today are largely unemployable—because they have spent so many years slowly, and only partially, seeking mastery in topics they will never need to know about in their adult world. The arduous pattern of learning things one has no natural proclivity to master, or external motivation to master, fosters an individual with little sense of a self who can be successful. That does not exactly set up the young person with autism to seek new challenges as he or she enters working years. Maybe this is one reason the unemployment rate is so high for those with autism: limited experience with success and limited expectation of success for both higher and lower functioning individuals.

THE GAP BETWEEN INTERESTS AND OCCUPATION

Many parents of youth with higher functioning autism fantasize that the preoccupying, narrow interests of their children will translate into a job. A common hope I hear about often concerns the video game industry. Parents who have teens with autism who play 4 to 6 hours of complex video games each day not surprisingly think their offspring would be great as professional video game "testers" or as video game developers. I've watched families enroll their kids in a major for video game production at a high-tuition local visual arts college; after a semester or two, they meet with a professor to be told that video game players and video game makers are different kinds of people. Video game developers work with others to program, illustrate, plot, and in other ways brainstorm a new product. It takes social engineering and a prodigious ability to incorporate the perspective of the "other" to create a new product.

After dropping out of college classes to become a game developer, what will that young person do next? If video games are really the young person's key interest and area of expertise, how does the person adapt it? The answer may not be that different from what happens to many talented nonautistic youth who early on face not being perfect enough for their dream jobs. Think of how many typical kids dream of being a professional athlete (or astronaut) when they are 10? We encourage those fantasies. It creates an interest and admiration for what it takes to work for excellence. By age 18, an elite few will be recruited for college sports and may go on to become professional athletes. Some may apply to a US military academy and major in a science—if they still want a shot at being an astronaut. Most, though, find other things—and are encouraged to do so because only a select few will make it to that top tier. At college, players of pickup basketball games can still use their love of the sport as a self-reward for a hard study session or as a way to make friends with shared interests.

Parents of youth with autism need a similar model: Video games can be great after work but are not themselves a likely entrée to the work world. Wanting to be a game developer is, for a young person with autism, like the socially immature desire of a 10-year-old to be an astronaut or pro ballplayer: It's a great goal, but somewhere along the line, you need to accept things are not going to work out quite that way. Typically developing children come to compare themselves with others more suited to be astronauts (better at physics, more athletic, more interested in joining the military) and go on to something else. Individuals with autism are unlikely to have a strong capacity to appraise their own strengths and weaknesses relative to others, and so may persist in focusing on unrealistic career goals if alternatives are not presented to them.

Intrinsic reward from a job naturally is one motivator for employment, but let's face it, for many people a job is mostly about earning a living—money for other needs, pleasures, and goals. Even young people who strive for success in arts or music have "day jobs" that fund more pleasurable and creative endeavors where they'd love the chance to succeed full time. More simply, pride at knowing a job is well done, even if the job itself is not particularly challenging or interesting, can be a motivator. One occupational advantage for some youth with autism is the pleasure derived from routine, repetition, predictability, and low novelty—characteristics of repetitive jobs that others may eschew.

Few young adults with autism have well-rounded academic strengths as well as enough social understanding to reach dream jobs they may idealize. While the "broader autism phenotype" (a "shadow" of autism, as described in Chapter 3) is sometimes recognized in parents of kids with autism, offspring fully diagnosable with autism, meaning those with symptoms that hold back adaptation to real-world challenges, will have more difficulty navigating independent living and the world of work compared to their parents. While stories of successes are always interesting and informative, many such stories simply fall short of suggesting what to do to help the rest of the autism population.

THE ALMOST HIGH-FUNCTIONING YOUNG PEOPLE WITH AUTISM

In the posteducation world, young adults with autism who have the cognitive wherewithal to succeed in a way that will allow them an independent or mostly independent lifestyle can face a real fork in the road after high school. I am talking now not of the small number of youth with autism and above-average intelligence, but of the much larger group just below them intellectually. These are the youth who may have average nonlanguage intelligence, but more difficulty communicating thoughts and feelings and borderline intellectual abilities when it comes to cognitive measures of communication. Picture the youth with autism who can have a conversation with someone who knows how to keep the conversation going, but who does not start conversations or chit-chat just to "connect" or even give a monologue about a preferred topic. These are youth who may also have diagnoses of learning disabilities and who may have no friends or just one or two friends who have stuck with them for years. Some lack any discernible achievement motivation. At age 25, such young people have tapered off taking one to two community college courses each semester and lie on the sofa all day while parents work; these young people watch TV and play (sometimes violent or highly sexualized) video games. Parents report problems getting such young people to even shop for dinner, cook preferred meals for themselves, or walk the dog.

This is not a pretty picture. Unintentionally, parents can be enablers—the way a codependent spouse of an alcoholic makes excuses for the spouse's bad behavior and unemployment. Mostly, parents don't know (or try not to think too much about) what goes on when they are away. For example, I asked one single-parent mother, employed full time, what her 24-year-old son, who had graduated from high school, was required to do all day while she's out. He was supposed to walk the dog, go grocery shopping from a list, and make dinner for both of them. She admitted that, on most days, he only walks the dog. (This young man told me he walks the dog because the dog won't leave him alone until he does.) Hearing about young people like this leaves me in despair.

There are few services I can recommend because there simply are few services to develop workability, to support such a young person in a new job, or few jobs designed around young people who need to start by just developing a work ethos. Having struggled in high school with courses that gave IEP accommodations and having failed community college courses leaves little self-efficacy or resilience to try something new. More typically, such young people may do something, like take an art class that meets only a few hours a couple of times per week, and spend time on seemingly insurmountable challenges like getting there and back. When this same young person and others like him or her were 10, we could discuss the merits of different speech and language pathologists for social skills training, how much time in the mainstream versus a resource program might ensure work was understood and completed, enrollment in afterschool challenger sports programs, and so on. Now, there is little out there to talk about to parents of such young people, increasingly concerned about a future they cannot envision.

My position is that these parents waited too long. Their children were not given opportunities to identify potential vocational strengths early enough. High school should have been about job sampling and volunteer internships—not a final period of resource help each day to finish English language arts homework.

SEEKING NIRVANA

When I meet young adults with ASD like the ones I've just described, I think of the lovely narrative in *Exiting Nirvana*,[6] written by my late colleague, Clara Claiborne Park. Clara was a founder of the first American society for parents of children with autism, then called NSAC (National Society for Autistic Children), now ASA (Autism Society of America). In the 1960s, she wrote a book called *The Siege*[7]—about trying to get into her daughter Jessy's "fortress," which she saw as quite the opposite from the *Empty Fortress* psychoanalyst Bruno Bettelheim contemporaneously described. Clara knew there was more inside the fortress than she could see. She just did not know how to reach Jessy.

The book is about Clara's journey as well as Jessy's. Clara's journey as a parent was realizing she would never really get inside Jessy's fortress, but it was OK, because she could tell it was a happy place for Jessy. Jessy's story, told in *Exiting Nirvana*, is that Jessy as an adult essentially had two separate lives. Her "day job" was as the mail room clerk at Williams College in Williamstown, Massachusetts, where her parents then taught. Her autistic "systematizing" mind served her well in this job, sorting incoming mail and weighing and stamping outgoing mail—no one's dream job, but a good stable job where she was alone a lot. Students came for their mail, said "Hi" to her through the tiny mail slots, and then left, so there was not a lot of social demand. After work, Jessy would wander home, observing nearby Victorian homes, then eat a brief dinner with her parents, retreat to her room to draw and paint the houses she had scrutinized in great detail on her walk home, each accompanied by written narratives on the colors used to illustrate each part of the house, as well as a guide to stellar constellations hypothetically viewable behind each house—Jessy's Nirvana.

Clara realized that Jessy did not want to join social groups or have friends—and was self-realized as she was. Jessy earned a decent living and retired after 25 years of service. Clara did not regret her siege of Jessy's childhood but could focus on the happiness Jessy found on her own terms.

How do we discern Nirvana for others with autism, help them prepare for day jobs, and follow their bliss in the leisure hours?

Resetting Priorities

BUILD VOCATIONAL EDUCATION FOR YOUTH WITH ASD (AND TYPICALLY DEVELOPING YOUTH)

Where Is Our Vocational Education?

Americans are obsessed with the idea of their children going to college. No matter how poor, uneducated, inner-city stressed you are, college will be seen as more desirable than not going to college. We have even become obsessed with our special education pupils going to college. This has come to encompass not only higher functioning youth on the autism spectrum, but also many other young people with other learning handicaps educated with IEPs throughout their elementary and secondary school careers.

You may have read things that trade on the belief that half the Physics Department at Cambridge University in England has Asperger's, but in reality, most people with Asperger's don't have jobs. When I chat casually with people I meet who hear what I do for a living, I sometimes find that they believe that most people with Asperger's are physicists, genius computer programmers, and the like. Not only is this wrong, but also reading about special cases like this can set overly high expectations for people with Asperger's themselves and for their parents, so that entertaining many entry-level jobs seems "below" them.

America: The Service Economy

Indeed, not only could many Americans with Asperger's or HFA benefit from the availability of high school vocational education, so could many other American youth with and without learning difficulties. Vocational education at the high school level is not shunned in the rest of the world as it often is in the United States. High school vocational, "polytechnic" training, in Europe as well as in developing economies, is considered not only a path from poverty for residents of third-world nations, but also a legitimate way to learn how to earn a very good living. The trades, and any number of occupations where the sweat of your brow gets traded for cash, are jobs people train to do in non-American secondary education systems. Car mechanics, public works workers, construction workers, electricians, and plumbers do not need what is taught in college, but rather gain sometimes technical expertise at specifically taught tasks sometimes acquired through focused classwork, and often through much on-the-job apprenticeship training. In California where I live, most people, aside from top supervisors, in any building trade, public works project, or maintenance activity are not American born because Americans seldom can learn needed skills to be plumbers or electricians and the like through public education.

Recently, Tim Cook, chief executive officer of Apple, Incorporated, defended making iPhones in China by pointing out that the Chinese have a substantial vocationally trained workforce from which to select workers. America has virtually no comparable vocational training, so there are very few vocationally trained workers for Apple to hire. It's not that Americans are not smart enough to work on precision manufacturing lines like the ones run by Foxconn throughout Asia, it's just that many Americans have an entrenched idea that goods-producing labor is below them. Yes, Foxconn workers would need to spend 3 months of salary to buy an iPhone, but if there were trained workers here, it would be arguably more difficult to ignore available American labor and the social pressure big corporations feel to produce products that allow consumers to "buy American." There are also economic pressures to reduce the offshore earnings American companies accrue when they make and sell their products outside the United States. If more was made inside the United States, because Americans received more training to make iPhones, cars, TVs, or air conditioners, let alone training to build houses, there would be more employment options for our currently least employable youth, both with and without developmental disabilities, who all enjoy playing video games—but need to consider what else they may do for a living other than hope to develop video games. Apprenticeship learning is well suited to the individualized way pupils with ASD are accustomed to learning—task analysis followed by step-by-step teaching, practice, and mastery before moving up.

Rebuilding vocational education in America would require investing less in high school teaching of algebra, geometry, history, and English literature and returning to the model where a pupil of high school age could begin to feel more like an adult by learning how to build an A-frame structure, wire an electrical outlet for that structure, or install its plumbing—all while still in high school. An 18-year-old high school student should be able to feel like a grown-up somewhere other than in the criminal justice system or standing in line to apply for SSI—the first "grown-up experience" for many higher functioning individuals with autism.

Employment and the Chain's Weakest Link

Treating professionals, as well as parents of youth with Asperger's/HFA, can have a hard time facing the limits imposed by lack of social skills. A mature middle-schooler has mastered courtesy, chit-chat, waiting for another to finish what he or she has to say without interjecting, and responding on topic. These language pragmatic social skills often still elude the well-educated person with HFA who is in college. This is the weakest link in the chain of skills needed for employability.

This lack of social skill does not get better and arguably gets worse when such a young person graduates from high school and enrolls in a 2-year associate-level community college where the young person is suddenly much more on his or her own than in high school—no IEP, no classroom aides, no resource rooms—no scaffolding. Special supports such as college "learning assistance centers" may or may not be available. Many with HFA just take what are basically remedial high school classes alongside students for whom English is a second language who are just trying to get their feet on the ground in English and who are reviewing academic content they have already mastered in their native language. Socially, in such classes youth with HFA can grow more isolated as everyone speaks to one another in Spanish or Chinese before the teacher comes in. Instead, what is needed is a learning place where the young person with ASD wants to be.

Identify Potential Vocational "Fits"

A systematic means to identify potential vocational fits through job sampling and on-site support to break down training components and determine whether a particular job is a fit with aptitudes and interests is what is needed. Not only must we generally bring back vocational education in high school—like most Western European nations—but also we must guide pupils with HFA to consider whether the social "load" inherent in a particular job is for them. Unless we help them envision other things and provide choices, this is unlikely, in my experience, to happen on its own. Parents, as much as the young people themselves, need support considering fit into the workplace.

Vocational Fits for Autism

AGRICULTURE

One area where stratified work can fit people with autism is agriculture. With the growth of organic farming, farm-to-table hand harvesting, free-range poultry, handmade cheeses, grass-fed beef, acorn-fed pork, and so on, there is room for workers at many levels to do very simple tasks like picking fruit or vegetables, feeding free-range chickens or livestock out in a field, or preparing batches of bottled and canned goods that carry the artisanal, hand-made, heirloom variety cachet. Interestingly, I find parents objecting less to these agricultural forms of manual labor than other forms of manual labor. Maybe it's because their neighbor's hipster kid who graduated from Dartmouth is doing one of these jobs as a "green," slow foods, locavore.

It's also worth mentioning here that there is a strong social class distinction in parent attitudes about employment after high school: College-educated middle- and upper middle-class parents tend to struggle much more than working-class parents of individuals with autism, for whom working in agriculture, gardening, and other forms of low-skilled manual labor is what many family members do for a living.

HUMAN SERVICES

Another area that offers important job opportunities for individuals with HFA is human services, particularly work in residential care and day treatment programs, where a rich staffing ratio is so important to the quality of life for clients who are much more severely disabled than their attendants with Asperger's or HFA. Providing basic help, care, and guidance to lower functioning people with autism or people with other intellectual or physical disabilities has been a rewarding career for a number of HFA adults I've followed over the years. A nice feature of such jobs is that they can be more understanding of awkward, inappropriate, or missing social interaction skills: Some HFA adults lose their jobs after having "gone off" at work about something they later realize was not appropriate for them to have said or done in a corporate workplace. In a care setting for more severely developmentally disabled people, such behavior can be better understood and be more excusable. Similarly, work as aides in facilities for the elderly, starting with taking an elderly person for a wheelchair ride around the grounds or chatting with an older person who is very hard of hearing or has Alzheimer's disease, can help erase the different difficulties each party has in making chit-chat. Interestingly, these jobs have seemed more available to young women with HFA I have known than to young men, although there should be no real barrier for young men to be a nursing home aide.

SMALL BUSINESSES

Work in small businesses and trades offer people with autism the possibility of working closely with a mentor, which can be key to developing successful accommodation to job responsibilities. In the next section, I talk further about the key role apprenticeship-based training could play in the employability of individuals with autism and consider how to make it work through public programs.

MILITARY

Among a very few HFA adults I have assessed, the military has been one place that can sometimes accommodate an individual with ASD and high technical skills. Training for technical jobs (not combat) can offer careers that go along with a regimented lifestyle dictating exactly where you live, where you eat and when, and what relatively small choices of recreation are available to you and with whom—on a base or on a large ship. Starting with very basic jobs with highly specified responsibilities and working one's way up is what everyone in the military does. The Armed Services Vocational Aptitude Battery (ASVAB) does a great job of identifying competencies needed to match enlistee aptitudes to very specific jobs—with social skill not being heavily weighted.

DEVELOP AN "AAVAB," AN AUTISM APTITUDE VOCATIONAL BATTERY

The type of vocational testing done by the military should be applied to the development of vocational aptitude testing for youth with autism and other disabilities (an Autism Vocational Aptitude Battery [AAVAB]). A federal request for proposals on this topic might yield some very interesting models for testing, job selection, and job training based on autism-specific deficits in social understanding, social motivation, sensory impingements, propensity for repetitive tasks, and the like. It would be fairly straightforward to recruit unemployed young people with autism, test them with the AAVAB, then provide training on jobs selected by the model, monitor a pilot job training program, and successively revise and validate the battery. Right now, unemployed young people with ASD and other disabilities have nowhere to turn for real support in learning what they might be best qualified to do. Existing vocational testing assumes social and communicative competencies that are exactly what sinks job success for people with ASDs.

The goal of an autism vocational aptitude battery would be the same as testing on the ASVAB, civil service exams, or other vocational tests but would need to also emphasize the motivational, communication, and social competencies that pose particular difficulty for the individual with autism. The basic jobs on such a vocational aptitude measure would need to include tasks for individuals with mild and moderate disabilities, as well as jobs for more able people with ASDs. Some sort of ancillary coding that indicated the type and amount of training that would be needed to get to job success for each job would be a good way to factor in the settings, number of hours, direct teaching, coaching, or task analysis that might be needed for success.

CREATE OPPORTUNITIES FOR APPRENTICESHIP LEARNING IN AUTISM

Apprenticeship learning in small workplaces offers a great potential opportunity for individuals with HFA. For individuals with ASDs, on-the-job coaching programs that could be available to small businesses through a training stipend would be beneficial for employers with small personnel budgets who are willing to hire individuals with autism for "back-of-the-house" work. Stock work, data entry, and janitorial work can be done in a highly routine manner or in the evening when workplaces are emptier. A workplace with "less" can be "more" appropriate for young people with ASD easily overwhelmed in a more social workplace environment. Jobs on the "floor" in big-box stores, chain stores, and supermarkets almost always are a poor fit for the relative strengths and weaknesses of a person with HFA. Some young people I have met struggle on the floor in Walgreens, helpfully giving way too much information about toothpaste to one customer (who develops a look of "how do I escape politely") while other customers wait.

There are many public institutions that could be incentivized to hire people with ASDs, starting with entry-level positions doing janitorial, grounds, or cafeteria work in public schools or government offices. The satisfaction of having a routine and sticking to it for many with ASDs is more reinforcing than every day having something different to do. Routine jobs are often some of the hardest to fill as repetition is more likely to be seen as "boring" by people who are not autistic.

Jobs that require a little social chit-chat and a little on-the-spot flexibility, like bagging groceries, are likely to be a poorer fit. Chit-chat with the person getting groceries, packing bags quickly (with every bag having different contents), and being alert to nonverbal signals from the customer or clerk if things are not going quite as expected make such a seemingly easy entry-level job relatively more demanding for people with ASDs. On the other hand, a job that involves taking grocery boxes off a large delivery truck at 9:30 p.m. as a starting job, working up to unboxing and shelving the contents, and with even further time and experience, logging inventory into a computer is a potentially better fit.

INCENTIVIZE EMPLOYERS TO TRAIN AND HIRE INDIVIDUALS WITH ASD

Apprenticeship opportunities, especially if they can be incentivized in a way that (a) employers receive less costly labor during the trial/ training period and (b) trains employers to provide the training themselves may be the most cost-efficient way to seed employment practices in businesses that can then hire successive people with autism. This could involve something as simple as potential employers attending a daylong training on what kinds of accommodations a person with an ASD may need, such as very explicit step-by-step written or pictorial directions, the expectation for reduced hours, or designation of an "alone" time break space. Employers need to understand how to give very explicit feedback to employees with autism ("Thank you, I understand, do not explain further"), how to reward on-the-job success with things like task choices rather than social praise alone, and how to be direct in expressing what needs to be done—rather than surmising the individual with an ASD can look around and intuit what needs to be done next.

Employer training course attendance could result in qualification for placement of an employee who could be subsidized during the time the worker with ASD was still training or working at a slower pace than comparable employees. The subsidy could be accomplished by tax rebates to the employers or direct payments from a public program. This would have advantages over the current "supported employment" model, where a job coach essentially must learn the job alongside the person he or she is supervising and then help the supervisee develop mastery. The employer is more likely to be knowledgeable about how best to master a job and to use the training as an opportunity to set up a mentoring relationship. Not coming to work with what is essentially a one-to-one aide, which is what a supported employment coach is, would also decrease stigma with new coworkers.

LET'S GET OVER FEAR OF LOWBALLING

The expectation on the part of parents and conveyed to their young person that he or she should be thinking about a "career," rather than just a job, is one of the biggest barriers to steady employment I see in the young people with ASD that I know. Starting low, a plan to go "slow," and emphasizing that success is being good at your job, whatever it is, is more important than what the job "sounds like."

Not all jobs are careers. This can be hard for parents who have careers to even conceptualize. This is, of course, particularly hard for more upper middle-class families, who understandably want a life as much like their own as possible for all their children. It is much easier to tell a father who runs a landscaping business that his son should be able to grow up and work in his business with him than it is to suggest to a father who is an attorney that his son might do well mowing lawns as an adult. Arguably, a major cause of unemployment among adults with HFA is the perception that an entry-level job is below what others at the same level of education might expect to obtain. No one with a bachelor's degree will feel he or she might like mowing lawns, and his or her parents are not likely to suggest it. (How about harvesting organically raised heirloom grains? Well, that is another story completely—or not.) One problem, I believe, for parents of young adults with HFA is that they have derived comfort from the fact that their young person is superior in many ways—to others with autism. Entry to the workforce where benchmarks for success now are calibrated not to others with autism, but to everyone else, can be a difficult shift in thinking both for parents guiding the young person's transition to adulthood and for the young person him- or herself. Another way in which parents need to be educated to think about supporting transition to adult employment is focusing on the realization that their young person will always be able to "trade up" to a more complex job once having made a success of one or more simpler entry-level jobs. Parents also need to realize that saying their young person is "in college," when he has in fact dropped most of his courses, is taking only remedial ones, or is even in a special education–funded transition-to-adult-living program for 18- to 22-year-olds on a community college campus is really not helpful to planning a real future for that young person.

The early twentieth century in the United States was replete with many "rags-to-riches" tales of poor immigrants arriving in the United States starting out as street vendors and ending up as store owners or starting out delivering newspapers and ending up running a newspaper. There is nothing wrong with starting out low and going slow with mastery and success tied to advancement.

DEVELOP ADULT COMMUNITIES

What Are the Alternatives?

Parents of children with autism aging out of the education system (which provides a daily lifestyle through age 18 for high school graduates and until age 22 for those with moderate to more severe disability) usually start to worry, even before that, about where their adult children will reside for the long term. For almost none are the choices satisfactory.

Some parents state unwaveringly that their child "will live with me forever"—then acknowledge there will need to be a plan if one or both parents become disabled or after they die. The solution then for most such families is that the individual will "go live with his [or her] sister." In work I've done on unaffected siblings, I can tell you that there are more parents who say this than siblings who agree with their parents, though they may never vocalize disagreement to them. Some siblings promise parents that they will always care for a brother or sister—until the siblings marry someone who doesn't see that in *his or her* future or until they are married with children of their own who need them.

Valuing Independence

Many would like their young person to learn to live outside the family home but believe all the choices out there are tantamount to institutionalization. This is not the case. There are decent, caring group homes in many locales and a small number of model communities throughout the United States, but nothing even near the number of options or the number of placements there need to be. Some young people with autism have a good potential to live on their own, or with a roommate, but may need some training and support to become fully independent. Others may need a more supported community that is coordinated with work or, for lower functioning adults, day treatment. Complicating the development of programs of any sort is a debate about whether adult living arrangements for adults with ASDs should be inclusive of nonhandicapped peers or integrated with other comparably disabled nonautistic peers. Live–work communities such as agricultural or crafts communities are still on the books with many public agencies as meeting criteria as "institutions" because the individual lives and works on the same property, a ridiculous position.

"Far From the Tree": Argument for Autism Communities

Andrew Solomon, a sociological commentator, urban anthropologist, journalist, and all-around Renaissance man, wrote a wonderful book, *Far From the Tree*,[8] detailing communities of individuals who had far more in common with one another than with their families of origin. He detailed life inside several distinct subgroups with their own cultures that defined how their members could interact, and preferred to interact, with one another, sometimes with strong preference to remain outside the mainstream. Included in his analyses were the culture of deafness, the culture of dwarves, gay culture, and several others. One chapter was on the culture of autism.

I would agree that there is a culture of autism. People with autism follow distinct social rules, not our rules, not any intuitive social rules, but rules that emerge from how they can most readily understand the world around them without being overwhelmed by it. For example, when I first meet a toddler with autism, I don't try to smile or make eye contact. I get down, get right in front of him (or her), call his name, and immediately cover my face with my hands and wait for him to notice I've covered my face. (I surreptitiously peek.) If he looks my way (which he usually does), I do a very quick "peekaboo" and instantly cover my face again. I do this maybe 5 or 10 times to show I am not going to impinge on any needed social space, to diffuse the newness of my arrival, and for me, to gauge how autistic he may be.

The culture of autism is what this child is born to, just as he might have been born to one of the many of Andrew Solomon's other "cultural" groups. We can do as much as we can so that being autistic does not get in his way as he learns, as he navigates nonautistic culture, but that autism, to some extent, most often remains that person's culture of strongest reference. The individual may learn to be "not autistic," but often it appears and feels to be more an element of learned behavior rather than "second nature."

How can I describe this? I was recently discussing lifestyle for adults with Asperger's with an anesthesiologist, originally from mainland China but living and practicing in the United States for 40 years; she had attended a grand rounds I had just given. I asked if after speaking and interacting in English all day, she went home and spoke Chinese. She said she did; it was her way of unwinding. She and her husband not only got the *Wall Street Journal*, but also got a Chinese newspaper, and she liked to read the Chinese newspaper and watch Chinese movies. She affirmed that her main cultural reference group had remained Chinese, though she could do "American anesthesiologist" during the day.

Similarly, I have met many adults with autism, especially single young men who have grown up with their HFA or Asperger's diagnosis as part of who they are, how they see themselves, how they explain themselves to the outside world. In keeping with Andrew Solomon's hypothesis, when they go home at night from a day of work in the "mainstream," many prefer life in an ASD community. They troll Aspie websites for conversation, social validation, and camaraderie and blog with others who self-identify as having Asperger's disorder. They play Dungeons and Dragons on the Internet and follow *Star Trek* conventions (but usually don't want to attend). They find ASD support groups and conferences on HFA to meet up and voice their perspectives on how they "translate" autism into their daily nonautistic lives.

A Culture of Autism?

In America today, the group most advanced in its thinking about a culture of autism is Project TEACCH, in North Carolina. TEACCH[9] is the legacy of Dr. Eric Schopler, also founder of the *Journal of Autism and Developmental Disorders,* the long-established and most prominent journal for scientific research on clinical aspects of autism. TEACCH embraces the life of the person with autism and his or her family from, as Dr. Schopler used to say, "cradle to grave." The TEACCH philosophy promotes visually supported, very structured teaching for the youngest children and continues supporting a highly routinized life through adulthood. In my book, *Helping Children With Autism Learn,*[10] I detail a TEAACH autism adult community I visited some years back. There are now others that have incorporated its principles and added to them as we have learned more about autism.

A key TEACCH idea is that home, and the definition of one's social group as an adult, is an autism home. In such a model, adults live in congregate housing with two- or more bedroom apartments, townhouses, or homes in close proximity to others in their community (think of apartments with shared and adjoining outside and maybe inside space). Residents may attend school, job training, or work or go to day treatment during the day. In the evening, with the TEACCH model, life may be structured—one night, movies; another, pizza; a third, bowling or miniature golf, barbecues, grocery shopping, a gym session, and so on. Group participation is geared to allow for meaningfully constructed leisure interests and to prevent self-isolation and diversion into excessive time spent in odd or repetitive routines or interests. The autistic preference for routine becomes a natural motivator for following routines embedded in the group's culture. Routines that confer rich experiences importantly keep the individual active and away from a solipsistic existence that can envelop adults with autism without fixed expectations for how to spend time.

Individuals learn to be responsible for themselves and their space. Personal hygiene, cooking, taking transport, and managing money can all be both taught and supervised as needed. Interestingly, in the TEACCH model, many of the highest functioning adults did not wish to move elsewhere after their participation in all the training aspects of the program was completed, and they were independently doing all their own tasks of daily living. The community TEACCH was formed intentionally at first and then grew and was sustained organically. The idea has been to create a home where you don't have to worry about whether what you do or say is going to be misperceived and where you are accepted for who you are.

We Need More Adult Autism Residential Communities

Funding to start such a community, perhaps tax breaks to build housing, development of curriculum to train staff, programs within the autism community to develop peer mentoring, links to apprenticeship on-the-job-training, and maybe on-site workplaces could help make such communities self-sustaining. Autism communities should not necessarily be a clinical endeavor but perhaps sponsored by a sectarian organization or by an employer. Just as people with ASD may not enjoy the constant company of those they call "neurotypicals," they similarly don't do well in Section 8 (publically subsidized) housing, where they are mixed with the mentally ill and drug users—who tend to exploit them if they relate to them at all.

Communities for the More Disabled Adults With Autism

A community for more seriously disabled adults with autism needs higher staffing. Such communities are rare, but shouldn't be. While developmental service agencies fund group homes, they are often not more than ambulatory nursing homes. When parents of young adults with LFA hear of these, they are saddened. It is not what anyone wants for their young adult, even if these young adults have limited self-help, low independence, and few aptitudes that seem applicable to developing vocational skills or even leisure interests.

What would be a better quality of life? My criteria delineate a place where people with LFA can have personal space (like a private bedroom); can live with others, not alone; can live with other developmentally similar individuals with respect to language and overall cognitive level (their "culture"); and can be supported through routines and natural environment supports to become as independent as possible at carrying out needed health-related behaviors like nutrition, exercise, and hygiene to establish meaningful self-sufficiency.

The first need for those with LFA is to inculcate work and living habits that support following routines that can help individuals achieve competence in each needed activity of daily living. Many with LFA leave schooling at age 22, still not able to fully dress or bathe themselves, care for teeth and hair, or prepare simple versions of preferred foods—because that was never taught, even in their transition to adult living school services.

Development of Leisure Skills for Individuals With LFA

Another need is to support development of an individual's repertoire for leisure activity and health-related behavior: supports for staying physically active and healthy; making art, music, or crafts; becoming a specialist in an aspect of daily living like cooking, gardening, housekeeping; or learning how to self-engage without perseveration on electronic media (Internet, computer games, TV, videos). Where do my criteria for what an adult life for a lower functioning individual with autism come from?

In 30 years of watching people with autism grow up, there are several universal themes: Many parents reflexively declare their child with LFA will live with them "forever." Unpacked, that often yields a perspective based purely on emotion and the instinct to protect their beloved and vulnerable child. There is nothing wrong with this impulse and everything good about it—except for one thing. Many adults with LFA who stay home, as well as many who actually can function fairly well, are infantilized by parents if they stay in the family home after siblings grow up and move on. This is not good for them. It is not good for parents who take care of them. The autistic adult with few requirements to engage in self-help tends to become increasingly helpless and often unmanageably demanding (like eating an increasingly narrow range of unhealthy food or insisting on hours and hours on repetitive YouTube viewing). The parent who is growing older faces a higher morbidity of stress-related illness after years of caring for that child with autism. In any case, a parental illness or loss can change plans for perpetual care of their adult with autism. An infantilized adult suddenly thrust into a care setting he or she has never been prepared for may have a rougher entry than if parents had tried independent living years before. On the other hand, I have met parents who never planned on any type of residential care deciding to try it after one was diagnosed with limited time left and wanting to travel or spend more time with grandchildren. Sometimes while feeling they "had" to put their adult with autism into a group home, they have been surprised to see it work well. I don't think a parent should have to wait until given a terminal diagnosis to feel it is okay to make such a decision. Instead, such a decision should be planned and considered, and the adult prepared—just the way things were done throughout school years.

After schooling ends at age 22, far too many more severely disabled individuals with autism stay home, eat all day, and gain a lot of weight. Agitated behavior, which was manageable when it was a hungry, preverbal 3-year-old kicking the refrigerator, is not manageable when it is a hungry, nonverbal 23-year-old, made hungrier by a regime of atypical antipsychotics, and who with one sweep of an arm clears the shelf of the fridge not containing preferred food. Just to be clear, such young people are more often than not ones who received many services when younger, including early ABA, years of one-to-one aides in school—not young people who more successfully accrued the benefit from their FAPE through their educational histories.

Other adults with LFA who stay home are quite passive, spending hours each day playing the same video game or watching the same movie—not good for cognition at all. Rare are those with parents who can demand and get help washing dishes, cleaning house, or taking care of personal hygiene independently and effectively. Mostly the scenario of the adult with LFA remaining in a parental home is of an individual who lacks purpose, lacks a meaningful quality of life, and is taken care of, with nothing expected in return. It is heartbreaking to see this.

What's the alternative? There is not much, unfortunately. At one time, these individuals were warehoused in state hospitals. Some state hospitals were fine; some were bad, and some pretty horrible. Largely because of the horrible ones, these places are largely closed down or greatly reduced in census in many states, replaced most often with intermediate care developmental disabilities facilities (ICDDFs)—group homes, often run, as described previously, as nursing homes for low-functioning people with autism (and other developmental disabilities).

There is no substantial body of research on alternative life care models for such handicapped adults. Very few federal or state agencies for health, mental health, developmental disabilities, or special education issue requests for proposals for model programs. There can be little meaningful needs assessment because it is hard to gauge how many families would utilize aggregate life care settings for their adult family members with LFA if (a big if) there were good ones to be accessed in the individual's community.

A Couple of Models: We Need Many More

One set of parents I have been involved with has developed a community in Sonoma, California, called Sweetwater Spectrum; I serve on its professional advisory board. It has been built as a lifelong home for their young adults with autism—with the mission of enabling a "life with purpose." Some, but not all, are lower functioning. I think this mix is mutually beneficial for the higher and lower functioning residents as some of the more able adults help create a culture of activity and conversation that might be harder to achieve if everyone were nonverbal or if populated only by adults with autism who mainly speak when asked direct questions about their own preferences. The community consists of four 4-bedroom houses and a community center building, a swimming pool, a greenhouse, and a small orchard. In each home, residents each have a bedroom, a living room, and a shared kitchen. Resident assistants are there to help residents acquire and maintain self-help skills in their homes, as well as serve as companions for leisure activities.

One brilliant idea the Sweetwater founders had was for parents of its residents to take out a very high-value life insurance policy, with Sweetwater as beneficiary and as the guardian of their adult with autism after parents pass away. More innovative economics around such communities will be needed if they are to become available for more than a fraction of the ASD population. One way to create autism communities is for parents to band with others with whom they share cultural practices and affinities that can be reflected in the congregate homes they make for their adult children.

Another idea that potentially could suit some adults with HFA is to live and work in communities for adults with LFA acting as residential assistants. Because of even very rare outbursts, some adults with HFA have been unsuccessful in workplaces that don't tolerate, or know how to handle, the individual with HFA on a "bad day." Working in an adult facility for adults with LFA can be much easier if the worker with HFA's own social liabilities are understood and accommodated as much as possible. In such a safe setting, a "meltdown" will be seen for what it is and not necessarily a clear indication that the individual should be fired.

For some nonverbal or low-verbal adults with good nonverbal skills, highly coached, routine jobs can be a fit. There are programs in Texas that make jams and one where participants write computer code for games; there is another in Vermont that makes cheese. I visited a community for young women with autism in Phnom Penh, Cambodia, where the women were supervised as each methodically brushed black lacquer on serving trays, made silk rose corsages, and sewed on buttons for clothes made in another workshop on the campus. In Cambodia, a large proportion of the population is mentally traumatized by the reign of Pol Pot or physically disabled by land mines, and the attitude is that all must work, despite mental or physical handicap. Interestingly, people with disabilities like autism seem to have simply been included in this "rehabilitation-through-work" philosophy.

In the United States today, creating communities that allow residents to live and work on the same campus has the potential to give more, rather than less, autonomy by making independent navigation of "home" as viable as for someone much less disabled. An impetus for such self-contained and safe places need not be construed as institutionalization if places for living, recreating, and working are integrated in a way that promotes more hours of self-determination in an individual's day.

Better Schools, Better Homes

The aim of this chapter has been to raise more questions than provide answers about the future of all adults with autism. This group does not do well now. First, we need to change secondary education so that we teach meaningful things. Secondary education must also include experiences that build good work habits and provide access to job sampling, mentorships, and job apprenticeships.

After our young adults with autism leave their school years, we absolutely need to create more evidence-based alternatives for teaching daily living skills and work skills and creating viable adult homes. We need research on model communities, needs assessments, autism-specific vocational testing, pilot projects, and longitudinal outcome studies so both the individuals and their families have choices—and can set goals during the school years to be prepared for a life with meaning as they reach the threshold of adulthood.

What's Next?

In the next chapter, I tackle some difficult questions about who should pay to make life better for individuals with autism. Throughout a child's life, the "hot potato" of autism health economics is passed from developmental service agencies to schools to medical insurers back to developmental service agencies, depending on the state, the individual's age, and needs: When is learning readiness "behavioral," and when is it "educational?" Is it a distinction without a difference? Should what is being taught determine who pays? How should special education choice be funded? Is autism intervention really "medically necessary"? By what definition can autism treatment be construed as medical? Should medical insurers be paying, or are they being targeted as a deep pocket? How do parents navigate this? When does the "squeaky wheel" get greased, and when do dollars go to those most likely to benefit? Basically, what are the politics of autism health economics?

Notes

1. Shattuck, P. (2015). *National autism indicators report: Transition into young adulthood.* Philadelphia, PA: Life Course Outcomes Research Program, A. J. Drexel Autism Institute, Drexel University.

2. Roux, A. M., Rast, J. E., Anderson, K. A., & Shattuck, P. T. (2016). *National autism indicators report: Vocational rehabilitation.* Philadelphia: Life Course Outcomes Research Program, A. J. Drexel Autism Institute, Drexel University.

3. Creamer, J. (2015). *Programming hope: Changing the face of autism* [film]. P. Hollingswood & J. Craemer, producers; J. Craemer, writer/director (Kickstarter).

4. Robison, J. E. (2007). *Look me in the eye*. Pittsburgh, PA: Three Rivers Press.

5. Tammet, Daniel (2006). *Born on a blue day*. New York, NY: Free Press, Simon & Schuster.

6. Park, C. C. (2002). *Exiting Nirvana: A daughter's life with autism*. Boston, MA: Little Brown.

7. Park, C. C. (1982). *The siege: A family's journey into the world of a child with autism*. Boston, MA: Little Brown.

8. Solomon, A. (2012). *Far from the tree: Parents, children and the search for identity*. New York, NY: Scribner/Simon & Schuster.

9. UNC School of Medicine. (n.d.). TEACCH autism program home page. https://www.teacch.com/

10. Siegel, B. (2003). *Helping children with autism learn: Treatment approaches for parents and professionals*. New York, NY: Oxford University Press.

6}

Autism Health Economics

Cost savings from EIBI [early intensive behavioral intervention]
range from $187,000 to $203,000 per child for ages 3–22 years,
and from $656,000 to $1,082,000 per child for ages 23–55 years.
Differences in initial costs of $33,000 and $50,000 per year for
EIBI have a modest impact on cost–benefit balance, but are
greatly outweighed by estimated savings.

—J. W. Jacobson, J. W. Mulick, & G. Green, *Behavioral
Interventions, 1998*

The Issues

This cost of early autism services referred to in the quotation, plus additional
costs accrued by families living with autism (such as forfeiting one parental
income to provide extra care and care coordination, plus cost of uncovered
speech and other therapies), is high. Early intensive behavioral intervention
(EIBI) for autism (what we have talked about so far as applied behavior analysis [ABA] or discrete trial training [DTT]) went from being considered an
experimental treatment in the late 1980s to being considered the standard of
treatment for autism by the late 1990s. The cost cited by Jacobson, Mulick,
and Green[1] as $33,000 to $55,000 annually 20 years ago is now even higher
and continues to mark autism as the most expensive childhood developmental
disorder to treat. In this chapter, I explore how autism treatment became so
costly, if it is justified as argued in 1998, and how we might do things more
cost-effectively.

THE COST OF AUTISM AND FAMILY BURDEN

The Family Experiences With Autism Survey[2] found that many families forfeited
future financial security and even experienced bankruptcy to provide what was
judged possibly helpful therapy for their child with autism. Further, it seemed
that less educated, lower earning families were most vulnerable to pursuing

therapies not reimbursed by insurance (more likely, non–evidence based) than higher income families, who also made unreimbursed expenditures, but more often on evidence-based therapies, like speech therapy. Any way you cut it, the overall cost of autism is high, and the direct financial burden to families often is high. In this chapter, I explore who pays, who should pay, and models for making treatment cost-effective and more widely available.

Studies showed the cost of supporting an individual with autism spectrum disorder (ASD) and intellectual disability (ID) during his or her expected life span is $2.4 million dollars, $1.4 million when the individual does not also have ID. The largest components of this cost were special education and parental productivity loss.[3,4]

While these costs are significant, autism health economics is a taboo topic in the autism advocacy community. Nobody dares ask whether an autism treatment program offers good treatment for a good value. Autism accrues the highest per pupil expenditure for schools, and EIBI programs cost the entities that fund them far more than any other kind of early intervention. How did this happen? Should this be happening if such treatment is not cost-effective? What could happen instead?

Early intensive ABA programs, also called EIBI programs, for young children with autism became widespread in the 1990s. This was driven by two closely related factors: (a) the claim of Dr. Ivar Lovaas, the originator of this treatment method, that almost half of treated children would recover from autism and (b) a 1998 paper,[1] previously mentioned, that asserted that, based on Lovaas's data, it was cost-effective to spend $33,000 to $50,000 per year (in 1998 dollars) because of the long-term savings that would accrue due to the number of cases who would have recovered from autism and not need any level of lifelong care. We now know that EIBI outcomes are not as robust as estimated in those years, though EIBI remains a key evidence-based tool for early intervention in autism.

WHO SHOULD PAY?

The main topic in this chapter is *who* should pay for the costly standard for autism treatment now in place: Medical insurance companies think schools should pay, saying autism treatment is mainly (special) educational. In the 1990s and 2000s, parents too would argue that schools should pay, saying that developing compliance and attention, behavior management, and social skills are all the school's responsibility (in addition to curriculum) because children need to comply, attend, behave, and know how to be part of a classroom before they can access curriculum. In the 2010s, national grassroots state-level legislation in a majority of states has now made it so that medical insurance companies must pay for autism treatment, based on the argument that because autism is a neurobiological disorder, evidence-based treatment for it can therefore be considered "medically necessary" *habilitation* of the brain in the same way that recovery from a stroke is *rehabilitation* of the brain.

In this chapter, I examine the assertions behind whether public health authorities, developmental disabilities agencies, educational institutions, or medical insurance should pay for autism treatment, and I develop some rational guidelines for apportioning responsibility for different aspects of care. To date, such discussions among these stakeholders are often emotionally fraught and results based more on advocacy efforts than on a sound consideration of either treatment outcome research or health economics.

Presently, EIBI is a juggernaut for autism health economics, with a rather low correlation between costs and outcomes. As in the health economics of cancer treatment or end-of-life care, there is an oddly American confluence of a "can-do" attitude and unfettered optimism that propels the adoption of treatment plans that can fly in the face of data that predict lack of treatment efficacy. How about for autism treatment: Can the correlation between costs and outcomes be increased? It is well known that the United States spends more on health care overall than European nations, and that more spending has not been shown to correlate to better outcomes.

How did things get this way? Can we do a better job distributing autism treatment dollars? Rather than ignore that cost is a factor, that realistically limits availability of service, can we develop more down-to-earth guidelines so that ongoing treatment funding is tied to substantive and demonstrable benefit rather than to the squeakiest wheel? What about studies that compare efficacy of EIBI and not-so-costly intervention methods? If EIBI or another treatment yields much less benefit for a given child than most others, who should be responsible for deciding a less costly treatment can be equally effective?

MORE IF IT WORKS, MORE IF IT DOESN'T

The way things stand now in the health economics of autism, there is almost complete abdication of any responsibility on the part of diagnosing clinicians when costly treatments yield little gain. A clinician is rightfully understood to be committed to a child's progress if he or she recommends costly treatment like a home ABA program. A majority of clinics providing early autism diagnosis and initial EIBI/ABA treatment recommendations engage in a practice of what can be called "diagnose and adios," meaning there is no plan for revisits for the clinician to learn if what has been recommended is working or to modify recommendations based on progress. In diagnosis of virtually any other chronic medical disorder, this would not be considered good practice. Arguably, it happens to families living with autism because most treatment following diagnosis is educational and behavioral, not medical. The medical settings where most autism diagnosis take place offer few, if any, educational or behavioral services for autism, so there is no responsibility on the part of diagnosing doctors to continue to care for the patient that has been diagnosed with autism. This leaves parents of children with autism without professional guidance as they advocate either for what was initially recommended or for whatever is felt to be helping their individual child. Typically, parents feel whatever they are doing is helping, but they might feel more would be better.

This leads to the perennial autism treatment conundrum: If this costly treatment is doing little, the individual may not be getting enough of it; let's try even more. If this individual is doing well with this costly treatment, he or she might do even better with more. Is he or she really succeeding? How do we define success? Is any progress success? Children in special education seldom get letter grades. But a school producing only C or D students would not be considered adequate by anyone. How do we know when an autism treatment program is producing only C or D students? How do we calibrate expectations for success so we can have a sense of whether a student's lack of progress is due to the student's degree of handicap or being in an inadequate treatment program?

I have talked in previous chapters about revising the individualized education program (IEP) (annual educational) goals so they are more closely tied to a student's developmental trajectory based on assessment, rather than to things like diluted versions of age and grade core curriculum. I believe this is one step in the right direction, but such effort must also be tied to teaching methodologies that are evidence based and have been proven effective for children with autism. We have research that defines a small body of evidence-based autism treatments. However, even in a successful treatment trial, not everyone will be a responder. A successful treatment research outcome is based on a significant number of subjects benefitting more than whatever the control group got. This means it is not enough to give an individual an evidence-based treatment. It is also necessary to monitor treatment responses to see if a particular individual is indeed a responder. If not, logically, a treatment plan should be modified. This goes back to the idea that if an evidence-based treatment is not working, an individual may just need a higher "dose" of it. This is possibly the case, but it is also possible that this individual is a nonresponder (or poorer responder) than most receiving this particular (albeit) evidence-based treatment.

HOW DID AUTISM TREATMENT GET SO EXPENSIVE?

In the late 1980s, methods of behaviorism—basically, Skinnerian principles of behavior change—were adopted wholesale for training children with autism. This happened very quickly after publication of a single paper reporting on about 40 subjects and showing strong support for "curing" half of the cases of autism. This was work that I have referred to already, by a University of California at Los Angeles (UCLA) psychology professor, Dr. Ivar Lovaas. Overnight (and this was before the Internet), every parent wanted what popularly came to be referred to as *applied behavior analysis* for their child with autism. (Confusingly, outside the field of autism treatment, the term *ABA* is understood more broadly to refer to a whole field of intervention for both typical and developmentally disabled individuals.) Today, home-based, intensive, behavior-changing therapies for autism growing out of Lovaas's original work cost up to $90,000 per year for a single child. These therapies can involve up to 40 hours per week of trainers and tutors drilling the child with autism in one-to-one sessions, starting with a method of ABA called "discrete trials" or DTT simply to teach one word or one concept at a time by "shaping" it as a "behavior."

Lovaas's work started a movement that made autism treatment more costly than any other developmental disability because obviously it was very labor intensive—at least one trainer at all times for each child. Lovaas's autism treatment curriculum manual to use these methods to teach basic concepts to very young children with autism, *The Me Book,* first published in 1981, went viral in the early 1990s.[5] It presented the methods that had been heralded in Lovaas's paper to "cure" half of all autism cases in his study. For many years, the "half-will-be-cured" mantra was repeated in every advocacy effort to obtain ABA treatment for autism. The use of terms such as *cure, recovered, indistinguishable from normal,* or *optimal outcome* have been bandied about in the last 25 years. It is generally agreed today that nowhere near 50 percent of all children with autism end up "cured," as further research has not supported that. However, there is still substantial pressure in the autism community to endorse the position that nothing has the unique efficacy of early use of ABA. In fact, today, even the Lovaas Institute, the nonprofit organization that continued Lovaas's UCLA work, has dropped the 50 percent claim, though they note 90 percent show some improvement.

There has, of course, been much more related research on Lovaas's early form of ABA since then. Efficacy has only improved as programs have introduced further methods that imbed natural consequences for newly learned behavior and provide supports to use newly emerging skills across various places the child learns and socializes. Nevertheless, many programs using "old school" ABA persist, and whether using original or more modern ABA technologies, there is still little accountability for their cost relative to a child's progress. We still don't know how much progress a child could have likely made just as the result of development or from another less intensive, less costly treatment. There still are few studies of "individual differences"—meaning tracking of traits that might tell us who does best with ABA. There still are few studies that tell us how ABA as an only treatment or as a treatment combined with other things—like targeted parent training, social skills groups, or an autism-specialized developmental preschool—compares in effectiveness. There are still few studies that tell us if there is more differential effectiveness for the youngest learners (2- and 3-year-olds) compared to older learners (4- and 5-year-olds).

ABA Justified by Saving Lifetime Care Costs for 50 Percent: False

In the early 1990s, it was argued such costly programs were in fact cost-effective because a lifetime of care costs were to be made unnecessary for half of the population with autism, who would be cured or recovered from autism. This was the first grand miscalculation in autism health economics, as I stated at the beginning of this chapter. This argument is seldom voiced anymore, but the spirit of this argument, that ABA programs have greater value with respect to adult outcomes compared to anything else, persists despite absence of supporting evidence. Some of my own data, contrary to the assertion that nothing helps like early ABA, have been reviewed as a dangerous thing to say. (We followed a small group of individuals from time of diagnosis and before ABA until early adulthood. ABA certainly helped many who did exceedingly well, but not everyone who did exceedingly well had received early ABA. Consistent with existing research, lower functioning individuals with autism had similar outcomes, whether or not they had received early ABA.[6])

How ABA Programs Took Over

Today, we know that only a handful of children "lose" their diagnosis with use of early ABA programs, but such programs are still seen as a singularly effective treatment. There still is great debate about what percentage this is. The number who "lose" their diagnosis is affected by just who is counted (i.e., how marked autism signs were at initiation of treatment) and what the definition of "cured" is. Again, in my own experience, if counting early diagnosed, early treated children with mild signs, perhaps 25 percent "lose" their autism diagnosis, though half may still have slight learning, communication, and social problems. These problems no longer add up to autism, so maybe 5 percent will have no developmental diagnosis.

What is true is that these early ABA programs were, and still are today, typically the first substantial help families received for their children and the first time a mother and father saw any improvement. How can a parent not feel committed to the first thing that really helped their child? On the day of diagnosis, many parents recall feeling that their child's diagnosis meant he or she was a lost cause, that nothing would ever get any better, and that it was frightening and depressing to think about how things might get even worse—developing further symptoms their child did not have, but that they had read about in other children with autism. Loyalty to early ABA programs for autism has naturally accrued through its role as the first intervention to give back hope.

No Placebo Control Support

The excitement, then, around the introduction of early ABA programs was totally understandable. However, the excitement was so great that no placebo-control, randomized controlled trials of the comparative effectiveness of ABA were ever possible. There was so much fervor around ABA as it came to be seen as a new treatment "discovery" that it was impossible to do the kind of study the Food and Drug Administration (FDA) requires for any new drug—randomly giving it to half the subjects, giving a placebo to the other half, and seeing if a double-blind study could tell the difference.

Why didn't it happen? No parent wanted their child to be randomized to the placebo arm (the condition of no treatment for now) and risk missing out on something believed to be their one best hope. If a "wait-list control" design were to have been used, there was real concern that placebo-group children (those "waiting" for treatment) might receive elements of an ABA program if, for example, parents bought a copy of *The Me Book* and initiated a DIY (do-it-yourself) ABA program while they waited. Studies that compared ABA to various forms of "treatment as usual" (including one of my own) did not begin to appear in the literature for a good 5 years after Lovaas's study, by which time ABA had spread from UCLA to everywhere, and ABA providers had gained a very solid foothold for these costly home-based programs.

The Die Was Cast

Very costly early programs certainly can claim to be effective evidence-based early treatment for autism. Early ABA programs for children with autism are clearly a powerful tool in our autism treatment toolbox. I often recommend such treatment. However, I have been accused of being "against" ABA because I do not *always* and *only* recommend ABA as a first early autism treatment.

Why is the issue of early ABA treatment for autism so polarizing? How does viewing the ABA therapy issue as a "for" or "against" issue mute rational discussion of when and how much ABA may be appropriate and when another less costly program may be comparably effective?

At the time ABA programs began to proliferate in the early 1990s, I was seeing some of the first children who went through the actual ABA programs at UCLA in Dr. Lovaas's clinic. Parents with children from all over the place temporarily moved to Los Angeles for a year to access treatment offered through his university clinic.

ABA: Seeing Was Believing

The first couple of 2- to 3-year-old children with autism that I had seen and who had then gone to Dr. Lovaas's UCLA ABA treatment were quite improved over what I had ever seen before. I was particularly impressed with the improvement of the first two such children I saw. One stopped screaming all the time and now spoke well in sentences when spoken to. He seemed "within normal limits" of any 3-year-old boy, though he still spoke somewhat less well than others his age. The other, in just 6 months, had developed language understanding, some expressive language, some imagination, and a bit of eye contact. As I discussed in Chapter 4, these early cases were eventually funded by school authorities, the flood gates opened, and more school districts in more states were compelled to pay for ABA. In many ways, this was fantastic. Parents who had no hope of funding such programs themselves now had access to something that could significantly push their child's development forward because schools would have to pay.

Not All a Bed of Roses

But, something happened. My view of the data on benefits of EIBI grew more nuanced as I saw more and more children receiving early ABA in my clinic and all over the United States. I realized not all children improved comparably. I closely reread Lovaas's original research report and talked with him about it. In his seminal published research study, subjects that hadn't developed spoken language in the first few months of his ABA therapy had been "deselected." This meant that nearly half of cases that had been reported as "recovered" or "cured" were from an upper tier of the population of young autistic children who displayed less severe language difficulties.

Language, of course, is pretty key to understanding and interacting and for the potential for across-the-board improvements in a wide range of areas of development. However, parents of the children showing more minimal gains now felt as entitled to costly ABA services as parents who were lucky enough to have their children begin to speak within 3 months of using ABA methods and were part of this upper tier.

Nobody wanted to tell a parent 3 months into an ABA program they had spent 9 months litigating to get that their child was not the kind of "responder" described in Dr. Lovaas's research; that Dr. Lovaas himself would have deselected their child. Further, deselecting was certainly not good marketing for the rapidly growing companies providing ABA—though many heading the first ABA companies were doctoral, master's, and undergraduate students of Dr. Lovaas from UCLA who had definitely studied at his feet and knew these data.

Chinks in the Armor

Five years on from Lovaas's first pronouncements about ABA treatment for autism, comparative research, longitudinal studies, and studies looking at which children were most likely to be helped began to appear. However, ABA had already taken on the luster of a "gold standard" for early autism treatment to "beat." Indeed, there *was* no singularly better treatment out there that had been tested on a significant number of children.

It was, however, becoming understood that the most intellectually disabled children did not respond as robustly to ABA.[5] One question addressed by Dr. Tris Smith, at one time Dr. Lovaas's lab director and now a highly respected scientist, was that children with autism and severe ID also did no better with ABA than with less intensive treatments. However, it was less clear what kind of less costly, less intensive program would produce comparable results for such slower-progressing children. Additionally, there were other questions, like whether fewer hours per week—like 25 to 35—might provide comparable gains. This suggestion first came from a study I published with one of my graduate students, Dr. Stephen Sheinkopf, also now a senior autism scientist.

The "less-than-40-hours-per-week" suggestion as a topic for further research produced an enormous backlash. It was a message advocates of ABA did not want to hear, did not want to "get out there," fervently believing that if any chinks in the 40-hours-per-week armor appeared, all might be lost. Many did not see early ABA as a treatment tool to be tested, elaborated, and even possibly improved—beyond the original Lovaas catechism, well guarded by his apostles. When I would speak on the need for further studies comparing the effectiveness of 25 versus 40 hours per week of ABA/EIBI, I would be leafleted and heckled by true believers. Fellow speakers would sympathize as we would leave the speakers' dais. Passions on the topic were running very high.

Interestingly, many children who are authorized for early ABA programs these days get 15 to 25 hours of treatment per week, seldom more. Today, most parents can't imagine fitting more ABA hours into their lives with such young children who nap, go to speech therapy, and maybe also attend a social skills group.

Autism Treatment as Medically Necessary

THE STAGE IS SET

By the early 2000s, using intensive one-to-one therapy to treat young children with autism was well accepted as first-line treatment—not only because of Lovaas's original work, but also because of accumulating studies of other excellent behavioral scientists. There was still no significant impact of comparative studies that would confirm or refute that early ABA was more effective than other early intervention methods—though some good data existed for approaches such as the Denver Early Start model. A year of home-based ABA for 25–30 hours per week was costing about $65,000 per year. Educational authorities were increasingly accepting that they would have to pay for ABA—at least for part of the day—and began to train their own interventionists from the education sector rather than contracting with the cottage industry of ABA providers that had become established and had self-designated certification (like board-certified behavior analyst, or BCBA). Educators often felt BCBAs lacked a broader understanding of child development and of educational methods compared to their own credentialed early childhood educators. Educators sometimes still have ambivalent relationships with BCBAs as a school district might have been court ordered to work with a BCBA to develop a child's ABA program. Educators sometimes saw BCBAs as having a limited understanding, and often outright diffidence, about well-established classroom curriculum for children with autism. Nevertheless, educators found themselves developing or funding early ABA programs for 3- to 5-year-olds and sometimes hiring BCBAs to develop behavior plans that in the past had been covered mainly by school psychologists.

IDEA PART C

Early Intervention for Infants and Toddlers With Disabilities, known as IDEA Part C, covers services for children diagnosed with autism under age 3 (until IDEA Part B, school-based services, kicks in). Many families therefore had first gotten access to early ABA programs under Part C. These families were not about to give up their child's early ABA program as their child transitioned to Part B services because they would feel they were just getting started, seeing nice early improvements often associated with early stages of ABA as their children developed compliance, attention, and learning readiness for the first time.

Generally, there has been much less resistance to funding early ABA by public agencies (public health and developmental service agencies in most states) who were administering Part C services for children under 3, partly because they had a time-limited responsibility to pay for them, sometimes only a few months from the time of diagnosis until the third birthday, if even that. These agencies knew they would be able to end their responsibility for the cost of serving a young child with autism who was receiving early ABA the day the child turned 3. The problem was that a positive response to one-to-one teaching raised parent awareness that EIBI was an effective way for their child to learn. They wanted more. They wanted *someone* to pay for it.

THE THIRD-BIRTHDAY WATERSHED

Let's take a step back: Imagine being a parent of a young child with autism—you have just gotten his diagnosis of autism at, say, 2½ years old. Three months later, at age 2¾, your child begins to receive early ABA. You have spent the past 3 months—*at least*—getting more assessments to learn if the diagnosis is really correct, getting a BCBA to determine whether early ABA will be appropriate, and then waiting for your child's program actually to begin. Then, 2 months into your child's early ABA program, in which you are really seeing your child doing things he has heretofore failed to be able to do, you receive a letter from the public agency funding his services saying the program will be defunded in 30 days—on your child's third birthday. Talk about stress!

What I have just detailed is almost a best case scenario. Many families receive nothing before their child turns 3. They never get near IDEA Part C for early intervention, usually because diagnostic assessment for autism has not been completed. After age 3, it is up to public education to serve the child with autism (IDEA Part B). As a new funding source, the schools start over again, using their own kind of assessments for eligibility, scheduling and then holding IEP meetings to determine what services can be accessed, and discussing what the child will be taught. For many families living with autism, their child's third birthday and the changeover in services can be almost as stressful as getting the diagnosis itself. With a school's preschool program on offer, hours of continued ABA, if agreed to be continued at all, are usually reduced, at least by the number of hours the child will be attending preschool. Parents, on the other hand, are out there on the Internet, reading that their child can now handle more intensive intervention as he turns 3, has given up his nap, and is really just starting to learn. The schools push back with the assertion that preschool *is* more, but it is not one-to-one, and parents tend to be unhappy realizing that even a class they saw, and thought was terrific, is just not going to provide as intensive a learning experience as good-quality one-to-one tutoring (that is, the home ABA program).

Generally, service provision has been a patchwork of state and federal funds supporting different kinds of services through public health, developmental disabilities, and educational authorities. By no means has everyone received what they wanted. Not everyone got as much as they felt their child might need to fully benefit. Here enters the demand that third-party medical insurers play a role.

THE PROBLEMS

The identified problems are several: Some states lack public health or developmental service agencies with the will or funding to provide much early intervention. Some educational authorities also do. A "good" strategy for public agencies hoping to avoid providing evidence-based costly programs is not to identify a child as having autism in the first place, then the agency will not be encumbered by having to serve that child's autism. Some states have tried to accomplish this by claiming autism can't be diagnosed until age 5!

But, the preschooler with autism absolutely needs daylong support to learn best, to not regress into patterns of undesired behavior. This means parents rightfully still want 2 to 3 hours of ABA services after school also, sometimes even successfully arguing for weekend sessions. In this sort of scenario, a child might receive 15 to 20 hours of school plus an additional 8 to 15 hours of intervention—a total of 20 to 35 hours per week, all told. Who can pay for this?

Educational Necessity and Medical Necessity

The question of financial responsibility for this much autism service sets up a framework for discussing the ways in which evidence-based autism treatments could be construed as either "medically necessary" or "educationally necessary."

From the beginning, medical necessity for autism treatment required some fancy footwork. We weren't talking about a child needing a wheelchair ramp to get to his first-grade class. We were not talking about needing a school nurse to administer anticonvulsants to a child with epilepsy, or even Ritalin to a child with attention deficit hyperactivity disorder (ADHD) so that child could pay attention in class. The tactic was talking about autism as a biologically based disorder, so treatment was obviously assumed to be treating the biology that was amiss—trying to change it and make it more normal.

This assertion that intervention might be changing biology can be unpacked a bit more: Indeed, many children with autism are considered to have a biological basis for their symptoms in the form of genetic abnormalities—too many or too few copies of a gene, either inherited or a new mutation. Well, children with Down syndrome have a well-described genetic basis (three copies of chromosome 21 instead of the usual two copies) that leads to their learning difficulties, but we don't pretend that education is influencing the biological cause of their difficulties. How is that different from autism then?

Well, genes do things that make the biology different. In Down syndrome, it makes the children look different, and it makes their brains different. In autism, the genetic differences (or "phenotype"), what we see clinically, are more varied and more poorly described than in Down syndrome and do not produce stigmata of physiognomy as they do in Down syndrome, but they presumably also make the brain different.

HOW DO WE CHANGE DIFFERENT BRAINS?

We teach the brain to create new neural connections, new pathways through education. As for all children, autistic or not, with Down syndrome or not, engagement in the learning process and mastery of new knowledge promotes neuronal activation, new neural connections, new pathways that reorganize the brain and expand capacity. While we largely cannot directly image these new pathways in humans as they appear, we know these develop by cross-sectionally studying developing brains, mainly in mice via looking at the mouse's brain, which is "harvested" after teaching a new skill.

So, if a brain changes, that is a biological change. Right? A positive biological change in an organ as the result of treatment can be argued to be a medical change, a medical improvement. Therapy that presumptively changes brains in children with autism can therefore be construed as medically necessary treatment.

The problem with this argument is that all effective education is presumptively going to change the brain. If you look at activation of a typically developing 5-year-old's brain as you read to her, pointing to the words before she learns to read them for herself, after she learns to read them new neural pathways will be active for the reader that were not yet active when the child only listened but did not read. In fact, there is no bright line between treatment for autism that is "educational" and "medical." So, can there be such a thing as medically necessary autism treatment? If there is such a thing, should third-party payers (medical insurance) then be the ones paying for it?

DEFINING MEDICALLY NECESSARY AUTISM TREATMENT

I mentioned in Chapter 3 that I served for a year on a California State Senate commission, the SB946 Autism Advisory Task Force. We met monthly for a year in daylong sessions to decide on what could be considered medically necessary autism treatment. The goal was to delineate what the California Department of Managed Health Care would require medical insurance companies to fund. California was neither the first nor the last to legislate this new kind of entitlement. Presently, the majority of states have autism medical health insurance coverage mandates. The authors of SB946 had sidestepped defining medically necessary autism treatment, saying a panel of experts (us) could address that.

Whenever the panel met, there was a lot of excited talk about third-party payers opening their deep pockets for autism treatment. The stakeholder community was varied, to say the least: parent advocates ("It's all medical"), ABA advocates ("It's all behavioral, but everything is"), and the voices for the insurance companies ("It's never been medical before!"). We sorted through the literature on evidence-based autism treatment to at least make sure nobody paid for treatments that lacked efficacy data.

We skirted defining medical necessity for a few meetings, then tabled it, as though it would be easier to define as more of our work was done. We *could* reach consensus on a few things, like agreeing that teaching math was "educational." But what about teaching colors or shapes? What if teaching colors and shapes was the curriculum in place in order to shift the child from doing something just to receive a food reward to being willing to do it for social praise? But wasn't *that* educational? Children learn colors and shapes in school. Because learning to respond to social praise addressed a core deficit in autism, was that also medically necessary?

The truth of the matter was that our task force, like similar commissions in other states, simply vacated our responsibility to delineate what was educational and what was medical. It basically ended up that any empirically effective autism treatment could be classified as medically necessary under the law, simply because the law guided us to declare that effective autism treatment was medically necessary. Does this sound a bit circular to you? It sounds circular to me (and I sat through about 80 hours of committee meetings trying to contribute to a tighter definition)!

In our task force work, we envisioned (and recommended) that insurance companies be allowed (in fact encouraged) to reevaluate progress from autism treatments they funded to ensure efficacy. From a medical underwriting perspective, it wouldn't make sense to do otherwise. It is one thing for there to be research validating a treatment approach. To be effective, an individual must also demonstrate being a responder to that treatment. Since implementation of this legislation, I seldom hear of children being exited from medically necessary behavioral programs when either habilitative criteria are met or, conversely, when there are few clinically significant gains.

In California, SB946 has become a carte blanche, mainly for ABA providers. The ABA providers have a strong, well-organized lobby that has done a good job of excluding other evidenced-based treatments for autism, like parent training, speech therapy, or social skills training, offered by anyone but a BCBA to get a slice of the "medically necessary" pie. Many children stop or taper ABA treatment as more special education services become available. This transfer of responsibility for intervention for the same goals from medical insurance companies to special education exposes the hypocrisy of insisting ABA therapy be called medically necessary in the first place.

Cost Shifting in Autism Health Economics

What declaring ABA as medically necessary accomplished was to open the door for a new kind of cost shifting in autism health economics. *Cost shifting* can be defined as an economic situation where one individual, group, or government underpays for a service, resulting in another individual, group, or government overpaying for a service. Until 2005–2010, public health and developmental disabilities agencies and educational authorities had been paying a great deal for autism treatment, paying for almost everything. Prior to the first state mandating that medical insurers pay for ABA, medical insurers paid for virtually no treatment for children with autism. Insurers would most often pay only for diagnostic assessment. Once the diagnosis of autism was in place, they bowed out. On rare occasions, some medical insurer had paid for speech therapy and, even more rarely, an ABA program. (The individual cases of such payments that I knew about had occurred where there was a parent who was a squeaky wheel virtuoso.)

Until the medical necessity determination about autism, the medical establishment did acknowledge that autism was a biologically based disorder, but spent virtually nothing to remediate the symptoms of the condition. Some insurers were paying for genetic testing or brain imaging, though such testing can cost thousands and has virtually no likelihood of findings that might direct treatment.

Medicine as a field was happily doing research on better describing autism (psychiatry), looking for genes that caused autism (genetics), and doing brain scans to see if it was possible to figure out how brains with autism were different (neurology). In medicine, nothing was happening to *treat* autism except the occasional prescription of an atypical antipsychotic, anxiolytic, or psychostimulant drug.

Interestingly, the impetus to shift the cost of autism care to medicine came not from the education arena, already staggering under the cost of children with autism as their highest per-pupil expenditure student, but from parents—who saw medicine as a deeper pocket than education was. They were right.

NO FREE LUNCH

Of course, there is no free lunch. There is the cost to us all of education funded by tax dollars. There is the cost to us all of medical care funded by insurance premiums. It's one thing to find a way to pay for intensive treatments, but shouldn't we be asking: Are we sure this works as well as we hope? With increasing resources to pay for autism treatment, how do we develop ethical guidelines that do the best job of getting children treatment that benefits them?

WHAT IS A CHILD'S IMPROVEMENT WORTH?

When a child with autism shows meaningful benefit from evidence-based treatment, I will help in any way I can to make sure access to that treatment continues. For me, as a developmentalist, a meaningful gain is one where, over a given period of time, the child progresses as much or more than would be expected from his or her previously measured rate of development. As I described in Chapters 4 and 5, this means that if a 2-year-old's receptive language is at the 1-year level (50 percent of expected) when the child begins early ABA, and a year later, when the child turns 3, it is at the 2-year-old level, the child is now only 33 percent delayed. This is great progress! We are closing the gap! Whatever is being done is producing more improvement than would have been expected with development alone, which would have been 50% of expected growth. A strong argument can be made that such treatment should continue.

If that does *not* happen, and at age 3 the child has made only 3 months of progress instead of 6 (and so now is at the 15-month level), the child is now 75 percent below age expectations, not just 50 percent. I would argue that we should be obliged then to consider what other treatment might work better *and* whether a less costly treatment might be just as effective.

My developmental standard is not one that I find many really want to discuss explicitly with me. There is, though, among professionals in the field of autism, plenty of quiet recognition of the point at which a given child is unlikely to do better with continued intensive services. It certainly should not be automatic to cut services if a child is a slower learner. However, the child's innate level of capacity or disability should be recognized as the powerful prognostic factor it is. Maybe it will be the most powerful prognostic factor, more powerful than which treatments are used or how much treatment is received.

BEARER OF BAD TIDINGS QUANDARY

Nobody I know is interested in meeting with parents to tell them that their child's minimally effective and costly autism treatment could be replaced by a less costly one because he or she believes the less intensive, less costly treatment is likely to be equally effective/ineffective. I often hear from parents: "Well what about just another quarter of ABA?" "What about if we *increase* the number of treatment hours?" Or, "I can't believe he won't regress if we stop this and try something less intensive." Or, "It helps *me* to keep doing this, but really I agree, there hasn't been as much improvement as I had hoped." As someone who talks to parents about treatment planning, telling parents that their child very likely will not do more poorly with less treatment is the worst kind of day to go to work. There is no comfort in knowing it is an even worse day for the parents.

Some professionals steer clear of such situations. It is easier professionally to exude an optimistic bias. My personal ethical standard for this is that I should not stand in one room training child psychiatry residents, telling them this child will progress very slowly, and then meet with parents and be optimistic or noncommittal about their child's likely rate of progress. It is *their* child. They need to plan for his or her future. Very importantly, they need to know that their child's lack of progress may be due to his or her lack of endowment—and not because they have not been doing everything possible for their child. It is really hard for parents of more significantly impaired children with autism to feel good about anything having to do with their child's learning when that child's rate of learning is very minimal. From my perspective, acknowledging how hard a child's parents have worked, and that they deserve a pat on the back is more truthful *and helpful* than punting the truth. The economics of autism treatment come into play here when costly treatments are then recommended to a family more as a palliative for the parents than as an actual treatment for the child.

GATEKEEPERS

A treatment's gatekeeper, by definition, both opens and closes the door on a treatment. The treatment resources not assigned to one child are then, hypothetically, available for someone else. The gatekeeper is there at the beginning to approve services and to step in again when it is time to terminate services. In reality, in any community, the treatment resources can only serve a given number of children—whether the resources are ABA programs, special education classes designed for children with autism, speech and language therapy, and so on. Gatekeepers are resource allocators, a necessary function to keep the economy of autism treatment chugging along.

The gatekeeper may adopt one of two strategies. The first is to not open the gate in the first place. The second is to point out that the gate closure is due to the child "aging out" of a service (like early ABA). The third is that the family must look for a different gate to go through—the service isn't educationally necessary (like social skills training) if the gatekeeper is an educator or isn't medically necessary (like after-school behavioral support) if the gatekeeper works for a medical insurance company.

The clinician, the autism expert, the professional who knows the child and is most knowledgeable about what may benefit the child, is virtually never the one holding the gatekeeper purse strings. Clinicians recommend treatments based on their understanding of the research evidence, but they also strive to maintain a positive and therapeutic alliance with the family. It is hard for a clinician who may objectively want to say "No," because he or she really doesn't see how a given service will be effective, to say that to the face of a mother going through her tissue box. This is why clinicians have been largely passed over as gatekeepers. What would work better?

ALLOCATING RESOURCES

I have struggled with the ethics of recommending treatment I don't see as supported by outcome research. The clearest parallels I can identify come from examining the ethics of cancer treatment. In cancer treatments, we often hear that any treatment that might reduce the number and size of tumors is good. However, there is also agreement that it is not always easy to say when reduction in size or number of tumors is a meaningful indicator of the hoped-for longer-term outcome of cancer remission. For oncologists, it is hard to tell that to a cancer patient sitting right in front of you, hoping for some good news that indicators are not all that positive. In the United States, we have a philosophical impasse among oncologists who consistently lobby for more chemotherapy or radiation in a cancer patient until the end and those who argue for end-of-life hospice care that allows the patient to die comfortably and say goodbye to loved ones while conscious, clear-minded, and suffering as little physical pain as possible. At the inception of Obamacare, the Affordable Health Care Act, legislative opponents raised the prospect of "death panels"—shadowy functionaries who might make a decision for you that was different from what you might make for yourself. Americans love their personal liberties, so the idea of death panels tugged at Tea Party/Freedom Caucus heartstrings. What is the societal benefit of equitable resource allocation? "Socialized medicine" is the not infrequent American interpretation of any attempt to allocate on the basis of treatment response.

As in cancer treatment, in autism treatment the standard can be to treat more if there is improvement *and* to treat more if there is no/minimal improvement. The standards for both conditions present identical tautologies. Both standards can say to treat whether there is improvement or not. What other standards might guide changing, reducing, or discontinuing ineffective or minimally effective treatment?

Reducing Treatment to Reduce Side Effects

Let's look first at possible side effects of autism treatment. When we speak of behavioral interventions, be it an ABA program or any special education designed to change behavior or knowledge, the possible side effects are similarly behavioral. In the case of autism, the side effects are manifested in how the child acts. Most often, we speak about these "side effects" as increases in behavior incompatible with instruction. Simply put, you try to teach the child that this thing is a "circle" and the other a "square," and the child screams as you say it. Screaming is incompatible with instruction. You can't listen well while screaming, so as an interventionist, you want to figure out how to stop the screaming. But, screaming may be a side effect of too much instruction. Maybe you can stop the screaming simply by stopping the task demand. The child being asked to recall "circle" and "square" may not understand, not remember, or not give a damn which is a circle and which is a square.

There are two ways forward to manage side effects of instruction: Solution 1 (stop teaching) is to agree that the child does not need to know a circle from a square. For Solution 2 (revise teaching), figure a new way to teach shapes that is more understandable or meaningful to this child. Mostly in behavioral intervention and education, we never really consider Solution 1, dropping the selected goal. Instead, we almost always go for Solution 2, deciding there must be another way to reach the teaching goal. With this attitude, you can buy into the idea that just about anything can be taught to anyone; it is just a matter of finding the right way. Revised teaching can be an endless road and may not result in a good allocation of resources if (a) the child never masters what is taught, and (b) the persistent teaching generates side effects—maladaptive behavior that then also must be treated. Solution 2 also can be insensitive to and disrespectful of a child's relative strengths and weaknesses, battering the child with repeated attempts to compensate for weaknesses, reducing time to develop his or her strengths. Sometimes, we end up spending more time treating the side effects caused by unnecessarily persistent teaching.

Could solution 1, simply moving beyond the teaching goal, be justified as cost-effective if we had a crystal ball and could know the child would never learn the difference between a circle and a square, green and blue, or an anxious face and a sad face? Yes, but these are simplistic examples. We could be talking about a more profound goal—like acquisition of oral communication—or not. So, there is always a complex cost-to-benefit analysis that needs to be considered before designing curriculum. It involves not only the cost of teaching something, but also the likelihood of success, and finally how critical mastery of the taught material will be.

Can One Know a Child Is Highly Unlikely to Learn Something?

Can one know if a child is highly unlikely to learn something? In fact, we do have some data, some empirical, some more clinical or experiential: A good example is that there is long-standing research that a child with an ASD who is nonverbal at 8 years old (and who already has had reasonable speech and language therapy for 4 to 6 years) is very unlikely to develop spoken language that can be used beyond speaking a few sounds or words that can be meaningful communication to familiar people around him or her. Such limited vocal output is likely to be quite meaningful to this child's parents or to those who care for him—but it is not the hoped-for development of true language with flexible vocabulary, grammar, and syntax. Should this child still receive speech therapy aimed at a goal he or she is unlikely to reach (oral communication), or should efforts be shifted to teaching nonoral communication (with pictures, gestures, or an electronic device) that has a reasonable chance of broadening the child's universal vocabulary and ability to have needs met by those who know this "system"?

Nobody wants to tell a parent it "isn't worth it" (cost containment implied) to continue to give speech therapy aimed at developing oral communication. When the advising clinician makes a recommendation that sounds like gatekeeping, any suggestion to reduce or cut off service, it can come out sounding like that clinician has "given up" on that child. Again, this is analogous to chemotherapy: The doctor is hesitant to give up on more chemotherapy if the patient wants to go forward, even if the data strongly indicate only a very small chance of further benefit.

Foxes and Henhouses

Fortunately, the way oncology care is set up, the one thing we don't worry about much is that the doctor is only recommending more chemotherapy because the doctor will make more money. The same is not quite true in autism treatment. Let's take the case of early ABA programs. Now that medical insurers are paying for them, many of them employ BCBAs (credentialed behavioralists) to "assess" the newly diagnosed child with autism and decide whether the child needs an early ABA program. A BCBA's training typically has included working in an early ABA program and coursework about principles of behaviorism. Only rarely has a behavioralist's training also included training as an educator and regarding educational models for autism treatment (like the TEACCH model described in the last chapter) or psychosocial models (like the Early Start Denver model). There is evidence for the effectiveness of both of these models. What do you think the average BCBA will recommend: the treatment he or she has firsthand knowledge of (i.e., ABA) or a treatment with which he or she has no direct experience?

I have never seen a report assessing a child for the appropriateness of an early ABA program where the BCBA did not conclude that an ABA program was exactly what the child needed (and that, in fact, could be provided by his or her agency). Yes, early ABA programs very often are appropriate, but if the child is very young (say under 14 months old), is significantly developmentally disabled, has a sensory handicap like being deaf or blind, or is considered autistic but is coming out of a home where there has been neglect, abuse, or trauma—maybe ABA is *not* where you would want to start, that is, *if* you knew about anything else besides ABA.

A Better System to Allocate Autism Treatment Resources

In developing ethical criteria for providing autism treatment, it is time to not just pass the hot potato of who should pay for autism treatment, but to shift focus to developing a system that provides assurance that each child with autism gets what we have good reason to understand should be effective. We need a system of care reflective of the fact that quality treatment resources for autism are not elastic and will simply expand as demand expands, but instead are limited and need to be somehow fairly allocated to those who will reasonably achieve demonstrable benefit.

So far, I have examined how things are now: No one wants to be the bearer of bad tidings, saying a treatment isn't working or isn't delivering the promised benefits, or be the one to opine that something less costly might be equally effective. No one really wants to be a gatekeeper either—administratively making life-changing decisions just because a child is still 2 years old and not yet 3 years old; has private versus public medical insurance; or lives in a well-funded school district or not.

By passing the obligation of providing a particular treatment to another autism treatment stakeholder, the hot potato of autism treatment funding *can* be passed from public health agency to schools to medical insurers, but should it be? My perspective has been shaped by 25 years of heading an autism clinic in a top research university, and now heading a nonprofit organization that can focus on serving families with public medical insurance. There are families who want their child assessed at a top research university like University of California at San Francisco. There are families of new immigrants who do not speak English (may not be documented) but are funded for assessment by public agencies charged with seeing they get timely diagnostic assessment for autism, too, even though those families may struggle to understand what the diagnosis may mean for their child and what they can or should do about it.

My starting point in proposing revisions to autism health economics is grounded in the belief that every family deserves what may best help develop their child's full potential, irrespective of a parent's level of education, income, knowledge of "the system," or any other socioeconomic indicator. Demonstrable, developmentally meaningful, functional change should be the paramount goal. If therapy is working, if education isn't working, teach something different and perhaps developmentally more meaningful. If a parent is distraught at coming to terms with a child's limits, make therapy available to that parent, not further child treatments that torture the child by hammering on the child's disability and ignoring what he or she may actually be able to learn to do for him- or herself.

Resetting Priorities

In the final section of this chapter, I speculate on how things might change to create a more ideal model of resource allocation for autism treatment that is fair both to stakeholders who bear the costs of providing treatment for autism and to the families hoping to receive it. The first big issue is defining clinically significant gains—simply meaning it should be agreed it is more worthwhile to devote resources to behavioral or educational change that research predicts is likely to be achieved. If a child reaches a point where a treatment like ABA no longer results in developmentally meaningful change, it should be discontinued—and replaced with something else. The second issue is the foxes-minding-the-henhouse predicament: private providers who get to decide if the child needs what they happen to sell. These first two issues have been discussed. The third issue has to do with navigating the systems where autism treatment resources exist. Some families do this better than others, and it would be worthwhile to level the playing field.

Much of what has been established today as entitlements to autism treatment has come from litigating for evidence-based treatment when it hasn't been offered. Tort cases have forged precedent for widespread creation and funding of more intensive services for children with autism. In many respects, this is great, but in another, it is clear such litigation has led to a willy-nilly pattern of lawsuits that has formed a landscape of great inequality for many children with parents lacking the wherewithal to sue for their child's special education entitlements. Presently, not an insignificant amount of special education budgets is reserved for litigation costs. Numbers vary from state to state. For example, in Scranton, Pennsylvania, the largest district in Lackawanna County, serving 10,000 pupils, one recent year's special education litigation costs were $260,000. In a small nearby district of Uniondale serving 1,680 pupils, litigation costs that same year were $205,000.[7]

Even the US Supreme court has weighed in on the need for criteria to de-limit what should be paid for in the education sector under IDEA, as litigation has become such a substantial part of ascertaining appropriate autism treat-ment.[8] Medical insurers have begun to pay for ABA, but little has been done to establish how much and for how long such treatments should be funded.

THE COUNTERPRODUCTIVITY OF THE ADVERSARIAL PROCESS

In Chapter 4, I talked about alternatives to litigation in determining special ed-ucation access. Litigation under IDEA is driven by "squeaky wheels." What we didn't cover in the last chapter, but I cover here, is just how much litigation costs and what this takes away from the children who are not direct beneficiaries of litigation. Those who complain the loudest and hire the most persistent legal representation tend to get more services for their children. There are lawyers who only represent parents in such complaints. By the nature of their work, these attorneys must become strong advocates for their clients. A number of prominent special education lawyers in the United States who specialize in autism litigation have children of their own with autism. Some work diligently to understand the individual issues each client's case represents, realizing many of their clients are very different from their own child. But some attorneys and advocates endlessly reenact the trauma first experienced as the plaintiff parent of a child with autism, convinced that anyone involved in their child's treatment was probably holding back on the best their child might receive. Such litigators have created a narrative that villainizes the same autism treatment authorities from which they then seek remedy. It can undermine the counsel's objectivity and, ultimately, trust in the al-truism of the public health or education authority to do a good job.

To speak truth to power about how litigation for special educational serv-ices has served the autism community is to say two opposing things: On the one hand, we would not be where we are today with respect to comprehen-sive autism services if it were not for hundreds of administrative due process hearings within state departments of education over access to appropriate programs. There are amazing parents who have put a great deal on the line emotionally and financially to do well for their own child while knowing they are also doing right for countless other families who will follow them. On the other hand, there have been numerous lawsuits in pursuit of non–evidence-based treatments sometimes pushed by acting-out parents unable to accept that no one but them will ultimately be responsible for their child. There are opportunistic civil lawsuits—like alleging that two lower functioning teens with autism in the restroom at the same time with pants down must mean there was sex abuse, that a teacher physically restraining one child from injuring an-other must be committing child abuse, or that a preschool teacher using sign language to signal "stop" on a child's own hand was actually slapping him. The legal standard for frivolous lawsuits is high, but it would be great if plaintiffs (or their contingency fee lawyers) in such civil actions had to risk bearing some costs of their litigation if their actions were deemed "ill-considered," dismissable on summary judgment.

These days, I can find autism education litigation disillusioning: Many fine teachers are incredibly stressed at the idea of being deposed or having to testify in court—even if they use well-accepted curriculum approaches or in abuse allegations are not the accused, but the teacher in the room next door. It has driven some from special education and caused additional "cost" to a school district that must then find a new teacher. We need a revised system of ensuring access to a pupil's free and appropriate public education (FAPE) that does not direct so much money to litigation and directs more money to children.

Parents advocating for their children have paved a valuable road for driving new evidence-based autism treatments into wider use. Evidence-based research can guide a clinician or teacher to select a treatment, but whether the treatment proves effective for a particular pupil is another thing. Again, this is like cancer and chemotherapy: An oncologist reads the research, then also considers a patient's treatment responses to determine future treatment. We need something more like this for autism treatment, meaning if a selected treatment is not as effective for a given child as research says it should be for some, alternatives (maybe less costly, less intensive alternatives) should be considered. The use of intensive one-to-one ABA programs has gained such an outsized presence in autism treatment that it is often seen as the only remedy that will address earlier inadequacies in the child's education. When lawyers and judges become involved in deciding FAPE, the decision that is handed down in favor of a prevailing parent more often looks like a blank check, not a treatment plan that should be subject to modification as treatment response data are accrued.

The "punitive damages" concept in civil litigation does not map particularly well onto "compensatory education," often ordered in educational due process hearings. The assumption that a child who has been deemed not to have received FAPE can "make it up" with compensatory education may or may not be true and will likely hinge on the child's severity of autism and ID, as well as the need to "undo" maladaptive behaviors that may have emerged as functional communication during the time the child had been poorly educated. This means that a child with a lot of tantrums, aggression, and even self-injury may have learned this is a way to get others to give him what he wants—instead of learning to ask with words, gestures, or pictures. Being awarded a good-quality program as compensatory education may or may not be adequate to target the replacement bad behaviors with the desired ones, as well as teach targeted curriculum goals. On the other hand, a child with significant ID and autism may be such a slow learner that, actually, he or she may have not learned that much during some period in which education standards or methods were inadequate and so is less far behind as a result of inadequate teaching than a more able pupil deprived of FAPE for a comparable period. I have tried to explain these factors potentially limiting efficacy of a compensatory education award to administrative law judges and am not sure I've hit the mark.

In litigating for access for autism treatment, it most often feels like someone "wins" and someone "loses." The corollary of this is that the winner is the good guy, the loser is the bad guy. Over time, the very court decisions that have opened the door for new evidence-based treatments to be available to children with autism have too often cast educators as bad guys because they "lost." This has caused special education teachers who are good teachers to flee their chosen profession because they didn't happen to be using the methods the judge decided were better, "proving" the teacher was "wrong."

In Chapter 3, as I laid out some of the legal problems attendant to the right to full inclusion, I said I would cover more about how we might rethink the role of litigation in access to special education for autism in this chapter. Litigation, as essentially a method of special education program development, is inefficient and very costly economically. Any superintendent of special education would be foolish to forgo sufficient liability insurance in favor of increased expenditure on two more high-quality special education classrooms each year. How does *that* benefit children with ASD in need of high-quality, tailored programs? How does a school district that may spend 3 percent of its special education budget on one pupil with a successfully litigious parent (as described in Chapter 5) not be seen as robbing Peter to pay Paul by the rest of the parents of children with autism in the district who hear about the litigation?

Parents read on the Internet that they must "fight" for their child's IEP. They read this will be the only way to get the best for their child. I always try to disrupt this sort of narrative by parents spoiling for a fight: I usually start with, "Nobody goes into special education to get rich or famous." Then, I move on to "You will attract more bees with honey than vinegar." To strive to be a quality provider of help to children with autism, I really believe you have to be a good person, as well as well trained—and deserve to be treated respectfully. The hard part is that parents don't know what they are looking for when they see a special education class. They only know they want their child not to need a special education class, and classes they are shown seem populated with children who *do* seem to need special education. It can be hard to think of your own child as one of them.

A (Fairly) Radical Proposal

We need a system of resource allocation that is more cost-effective as well as efficient than hearings in front of administrative judges (or higher courts) who are not autism experts, listening to lawyers and advocates who are not autism experts present witnesses who may be "hired guns" for one side or the other. Yes, the legal venue has been a productive place for our autism community in terms of gains in treatment access through tort complaints. It has also been costly in terms of autism resources that could have been spent on treatment or treatment research, especially with complaints that really are more nuisance than groundbreaking. In Chapter 4, I talked a little about the idea of replacing educational due process judges with expert panels with an eye to adjudication that could result in more appropriate and evidence-based treatments. This model may also have a role in reducing the cost of such legal actions.

Expert Arbitration

Instead of hearings in front of nonexpert administrative judges who do strive for fairness under the law, we should consider panels of experts in autism development and treatment who are charged with producing decisions that support evidence-based treatment standards. Such panels could draw on a growing number of autism experts: In the early 2000s when the International Society for Autism Research (INSAR) was in its infancy, about 200 autism experts attended its first meeting. Today, that number has increased 10-fold. In addition to INSAR members, there are credentialed autism educators, an additional group of professionals with autism treatment expertise that largely does not overlap INSAR membership. A third group has autism experts who are behaviorists represented by the Applied Behavior Analysis Association, relatively few of whom are either autism educators or INSAR members. An expert arbitration panel consisting of representatives from these sectors of autism expertise could replace administrative judges at educational due process hearings. Something similar has been proposed by AASA (American Association of School Administrators), the School Superintendents Association, in a response to costs, budget, and staffing disruptions brought on by the doubling of due process hearings when comparing the 1990s to the 2000s.[9]

Panelists would need to be schooled in rights of appeal and perhaps complete a course taught by administrative law judges. Lengths of hearings could be better managed because there would be much less need to present background research or relative importance of different kinds of research and clinical studies. Experts could more readily ascertain the appropriateness of current treatment given prior data or more readily ascertain whether data appropriate for making treatment decisions had, in fact, been considered. Such a system could be designed to be time limited with respect to evidence with graduate student–level "clerks" used to efficiently cull and summarize ahead of a hearing exhibits that plaintiff's counsel or defense's counsel wished to present.

Presently, administrative hearing officers and administrative judges virtually always "fly blind"—never actually meeting the plaintiff. As they are not clinicians, this is understandable. From the point of greater justice, this is a little like a civil or criminal trial where the judge or jury would be barred from even laying eyes on the defendant. While defendants are protected from self-incrimination by not having to testify, there is no reason an expert clinician on an arbitration panel could not carry out additional investigation of a plaintiff in consultation with his or her panel members as part of evidence to be considered.

CURTAILMENT OF TREATMENTS THAT DON'T WORK
AS WELL AS HOPED

In Chapters 4 and 5, I talked about how special education and ABA programs that are evidence based will be differentially effective, depending on the child's underlying disability. I argued that response to intervention (RTI) measurements should be more important in selecting, and in evaluating, the effectiveness of selected treatments. Then, I focused on how moving away from the core curriculum, and considering longer-term prognosis, as early as age 8 or 10, should be more influential in determining what is taught. Presently, the practice of trying to teach many middle- and low-functioning children with autism things they will not likely ever learn, given level and type of disability, results mainly in going for limited results (changing the goal from learning 10 new receptive nouns to 5 nouns) or simply changing methods to teach the perennially unmastered content (continuing to try for 10 nouns, but with an iPad). A key example of this is the continued teaching of oral language skills to children with minimal oral language progress—which avoids switching emphasis to other augmentative methods for learning designed for children, like this child, who will never develop significant oral language.

Most important, these practices hammer a child's disabilities, leaving the more disabled child frustrated and often acting out with inattention, agitation, or aggression. These methods do not respect who this child can be, the child's need for independence as best he or she can achieve it, or look forward to preparing the child for the adulthood he or she will reach. On another level, it wastes resources that should be redirected to creating programs geared to helping this child to achieve realistically set goals.

The Cost of Autism

Yes, we have many more economic resources to access for autism treatment than we did 30 years ago when it was not yet widely recognized that children with autism learn differently and can grow up to have their own "culture"—as Andrew Solomon, among others, has defined it.

The real issue is that much of autism education is not calibrated for a path to likely successful adult outcomes. This results in most with a diagnosis of autism "falling off the cliff" between 18 and 22 years of age (as Dr. Paul Shattuck was quoted as saying in Chapter 5) when treatment and training access declines precipitously. The damage from this fall, I am arguing, is essentially a self-inflicted wound. Those who guide youth with autism through the school years ignore their mandate to prepare these young people for adulthood by focusing on domains where they can develop their best skills. Instead, the mandate has been subverted into attempts to make "them" as much like "us" as possible.

There is a crying need for a sea change: An earlier educational focus on developing skills to allow independence, as well as becoming prepared for viable employment, is critical. We need treatment and education that support realistic adult outcomes, acknowledging that whatever we are doing now leads to over 90 percent unemployment and underemployment in adults with autism, irrespective of whether they are higher or lower functioning.

Autism experts must take back the course of autism education not only by setting goals based on research from treatment controlled trials and from work on the developmental course of autism, but also by being realistic with parents about what they need to do to plan for their children's futures and what kinds of curricula they should seek for their children. Our current state of affairs is emblematic of the fact that we have not yet developed sufficient strategies for cost-effective paths to adult success.

What's Next?

So far, the "autism treatment" I've talked about has been educational and behavioral. However, parents are well aware that autism has a biological basis. To that end, many seek biological interventions, too. I talked about autism psychopharmacology treatment in Chapter 3 and how the field of psychiatry and Big Pharma have cleaved it from the rest of autism treatment as its own as drug companies seek to do trials that will lead to approval of an agent to treat autism. Medications do have a role. Medication that can work in conjunction with other supports for learning readiness can play a key role for many individuals in an overall autism treatment plan.

Many families, though, turn to the Internet and find a whole world beyond evidence-based medicine and evidence-based behavioral or educational treatments. How do we understand these sociologically? How do we address complementary and alternative medicine for autism in general? When might it be helpful? When might it be benign? When might it be dangerous? In Chapter 7, I'll address how autism treatment in the age of the Internet presents doctors with never-before challenges in managing care. It's another aspect of the politics of autism—and what it means for America.

Notes

1. Jacobson, J. W., Mulick, J. A., & Green, G. (1998). Cost–benefit estimates for early intensive behavioral intervention for young children with autism—General model and single state case. *Behavioral Interventions, 13*(4), 201–226. doi:10.1002/(SICI)1099-078X(199811)13:4<201::AID-BIN17>3.0.CO;2-R

2. Harpe, D. L., & Baker, D. L. (2007). Financial issues associated with having a child with autism. *Journal of Family and Economic Issues, 28*(2), 247–264. http://doi.org/10.1007/s10834-007-9059-6

3. Buescher, A. V. S., Cidav, Z., Knapp, M., & Mandell, D. S. (2014). Costs of autism spectrum disorders in the United Kingdom and the United States. *JAMA Pediatrics, 168*(8), 721–728. doi:10.1001/jamapediatrics.2014.210

4. Leigh, J. P., & Du, J. (2015). Brief report: Forecasting the economic burden of autism in 2015 and 2025 in the United States. *Journal of Autism and Developmental Disorders, 45*(12), 4135–4139. https://doi.org/10.1007/s10803-015-2521-7

5. Lovaas, O. I. (1981). *Teaching developmentally disabled children: The me book*. Austin, TX: University Park Press.

6. Smith, T., Groen, A., & Wynn, J. (2000). Randomized trial of intensive early intervention for children with pervasive developmental disorder. *American Journal on Mental Retardation. 105*(4), 269–285. Retrieved from http://analisicomportamentale.com/media/Smith%20Groen%20and%20Wynn%202000.pdf

7. Morgan-Besecker, T. (2015, December 20). Special education legal fees major hit to local schools. *The Times-Tribune*. Retrieved from http://thetimes-tribune.com/news/special-education-legal-fees-major-hit-to-local-schools-1.1985439

8. Feldman, N. (2017, January 16). US Supreme Court attempts to delimit special education costs. *Hartford Courant*. Retrieved from http://www.courant.com/opinion/op-ed/hc-op-feldman-supreme-court-special-education-0115-20170113-story.html

9. Pudelski, S. (2016). *Rethinking special education due process*. Alexandria, VA: AASA, School Superintendents Association.

The Allure of Complementary and Alternative Medicine

There are in fact two things, science and opinion; the former
begets knowledge, the latter ignorance.

> —Hippocrates (ca. 460–400 BC)

Introduction

Parents of children with autism spend millions of dollars annually on noninsured
"biomedical" tests that are not offered at any major medical center. Alleged
"positive" results from these pricey tests may result in costly prescriptions for
medicines not approved by the Food and Drug Administration (FDA), as well
as for "prescriptions" for supplements and serums that lack any peer-reviewed
scientific support. One 2006 study in the *Journal of Autism and Developmental
Disorders* reported that 74 percent of parents surveyed had used nonconventional
autism treatment, noting that this incidence was higher than clinicians suspected.
The effects of receiving such *complementary and alternative medicine* (CAM) may
range from mostly harmless to occasionally deadly. Nowhere in the field of autism
treatment is the truth more vulnerable than when it comes to the use of CAM.

For a little history, the late Dr. Bernard Rimland, a San Diego psychologist (for the US Department of the Navy) had a son with autism and in 1964
led the charge to kill the "refrigerator mother theory" of autism etiology in
a groundbreaking book, *Infantile Autism: The Syndrome and Its Implications
for a Neural Theory of Behavior*.[1] After the book's publication, he cofounded
the National Society for Autistic Children, the first US parent advocacy organization for autism. In 1967, Bernie Rimland founded the Autism Research
Institute (ARI) and began his search for neuroactive agents to treat autism.
I knew Dr. Rimland, and his heart was in the right place, but as time went
on, his ideas became less well supported by research. In the mid-1990s, ARI
sponsored the founding of DAN! (Defeat Autism Now), whose affiliated
doctors spearheaded practice of a number of empirically unsupported autism
treatments. DAN! promoted the idea that autism happened in those with a

somehow lowered immune response exposed to environmental "toxins" (including vaccines) and certain foods (like those containing gluten or casein). I call this an "idea" and not a "hypothesis" as in the last 20 years there has been virtually no confirmatory testing that supports this.

DAN! protocol training was offered only until 2011. At that point, ARI let visitors to their website know that they were discontinuing DAN! training because, as they put it, completing the DAN! seminar, signing a pledge to engage in DAN!-consistent practices, and requesting to be on the ARI list of DAN! practitioners was not a guarantee that such individuals could do things as they had been taught. However, there are still lists of DAN! doctors online, as well as Generation Rescue doctors who continue to assert that vaccine-caused autism can successfully be treated biomedically, despite lack of published research on either cause or treatment. Bernie Rimland's founding of DAN! lit a fire that is still burning.

I have never been sure how Bernie Rimland went from exceptional scientific thinker to something more like a huckster: When I first met Rimland around 1983, he was, in my mind, a towering figure in what was then a small, fascinating field of developmental psychopathology—the study of autism. In 1974, I'd written my senior thesis in college on the etiology of autism, and his work was what had helped me realize that Bruno Bettelheim and other psychoanalysts were wrong about what caused autism—at the time believed to be the result of a cold and rejecting mother. In the 10 years after I first met Rimland, he started to promote non–evidence-based treatments, even though he himself was a research-trained psychologist who knew what a good study leading to a valid conclusion should look like. I still clearly remember one of my lowest moment as an assistant professor was when I invited him to give a grand rounds at the University of California at San Francisco (UCSF) on the history of autism; instead, he talked about CAM in autism, taking a dimethylglycine (DMG) tablet (the autism treatment he then was promoting) while at the lectern. He told the assembled audience of child psychiatry faculty he was doing this to demonstrate its safety despite lack of FDA trials.

"IF IT SOUNDS TOO GOOD TO BE TRUE, IT PROBABLY IS"

Rimland promoted the DAN! Protocol, which in its heyday introduced and endorsed many non–evidence-based CAM treatments for autism (like the gluten-free, casein-free [GFCF] diet) that live on despite no accumulation of efficacy data after 20 or more years. Rimland put autism on the map for CAM practitioners looking to "help" another group of susceptible folks—the parents of children with autism.

What kind of people make up this confederation of DAN! doctors who, along with naturopaths, homeopaths, and others, are ready to turn a profit on these vulnerable parents? Many parents drowning in their child's diagnosis of autism only need to hear that some treatment has been the pot of gold at the end of the rainbow for some other family—and also can be theirs. The Internet, of course, to mix metaphors, is the Yellow Brick Road to the pot of gold.

Psychologically, how and who are the parents lured into this? How can professionals and friends help shield parents from hucksters while not quashing hope by pooh-poohing everything that doesn't have a randomized clinical trial standing behind it? There are many CAM practitioners who mean well and realistically understand that what they do may not help everyone, but optimistically hope that what they can do will indeed help most who ask about the treatment he or she proffers. Many of these CAM treatment protocols are benign.

Then there are the doctors and "doctors" that profit from selling false hope through expensive and incredible treatments—like bone marrow transplants or chelation. Does every provider of such a nonempirical, costly, potentially dangerous autism treatment deserve a *60 Minutes* exposé? As we explore the world of autism CAM, *complementary* or even *alternative* can be too kind a term when the most likely outcome of a particular treatment is very likely to be dashed hopes.

There *is* much good complementary medicine practice in autism; there are also benign alternative medicine regimes. What I find fascinating is the cultural anthropology of all this: Which parents (and doctors) delve into autism CAM a lot or just a little? What influences the selection of the most far afield treatments? Who is most likely to select them? What do parents who undertake CAM treatments that impose known risks on their children really expect? How do they weigh risk when they know there may be harm? If the risk is death (like with chelation), are such parents child abusers? If the risk is nutritional insufficiency (like a GFCF diet), is that child abuse? How does the pernicious interpretation of placebo effects get exploited to maintain ineffective treatment regimes?

DEFINING CAM

I begin with definitions of complementary and alternative medicine because I don't want to give the impression CAM is necessarily a bad thing. But, there is much room for abuse when consumers, especially consumers who are parents of young children, face a serious difficulty where they cannot understand the cause or causes. This is the case with autism.

I have no way of being sure, but I think that an unresolved and preoccupying need to know, "Why did this happen to me?" when their child is diagnosed with autism is one factor that will predispose parents to pursuing bad CAM. There are bad CAM purveyors, and there are ones who actually think that what they offer is legitimate therapy. Further, when parents are spending their time and resources on CAM therapy, they may be missing out on evidence-based treatments. What would lead someone to take this sort of risk for their child? Key to motivation for some of these parents may be that evidence-based treatments are usually held out as palliative, bad CAM treatments as curative.

Indeed, all clinicians are challenged to walk a line between wanting to offer hope and not offering false hope. Some parents are more vulnerable to false hope than others. How can we understand the gravitational pull of the world of CAM so that we can catch ourselves when unwittingly drawn in? Is there something about our American character that makes us feel so entitled to a good life that we have a preternatural certainty that cures for our woes must be out there?

Some of the CAM issues I consider here will, in obvious ways, resonate beyond treatments for autism. After laying out the broader issues around who gives and who utilizes CAM and when, I delve into the checkered history CAM has had in treatment for autism. We explore what it is that has drawn so many quacks to the treatment of autism. We will try to understand how optimism and trust, when abused, promulgate illogical decision-making in otherwise pretty rational parents. We examine how the Internet, that electronic information highway, has played a role in leading parents, who generally don't have an advanced degree in biochemistry, off the wrong exits, and eventually into the back alleyways where "fake" autism potions are sold.

THE ROAD TO FALSE HOPE

It is said that the road to hell is paved with good intentions. It may be that false hope is the lure. From where I sit, many outré and unconventional autism treatments pave this road. I have met some of the peddlers who travel this route. Some will look you right in the eye and tell you they are doing good. Some market by allying with parents who evangelize for them, much like the TV ads of folks before and after losing 250 pounds on some diet. There are a lot of motivated but demoralized parents out there, who believe in the treatments they have been sold by someone they consider more knowledgeable than themselves. Sometimes, this "someone" is not knowledgeable at all. Once parents feel that what they hoped was the truth about autism treatment is a moving target (applied behavior analysis [ABA] does not work as well as expected; speech therapy has not taught the child to talk), anything else held out as autism treatment may seem comparably suspect.

In terms of biomedical treatments, child psychiatrists and neurologists are the medical practitioners most able to judge and prescribe valid treatments, with pediatricians coming in close behind. Interestingly, physicians engaged in biomedical treatment for autism seldom are child psychiatrists or pediatricians, but more often include family practice doctors, allergists, and gastroenterologists—physicians who in the normal course of their practice are not diagnosing or caring for signs and symptoms of autism.

The worst of the worst CAM purveyors hawk stem cell therapy, chelation, hyperbaric oxygen chambers, spinal manipulations, a special brain scan that reveals problems that scans paid for by insurance can't reveal. Honestly, it makes my blood boil to be preached to by one of these illegitimate peddlers as if they also are scientists. Importantly, while some of these treatments can sound far-fetched, none is a singular example of a treatment offered by only one person or clinic. With the Internet, chat drives demand; false hope drives demand and an almost instantaneous market for more of what any one person offers and anything another person claims has helped.

While non–evidence-based biomedical CAM for autism may attract the most dollars, there also are a few occupational therapists (OTs) and speech and language pathologists (SLPs) who have dabbled in getting a slice of the CAM pie. In this chapter, we also talk about the "sensory integration training" that many OTs now offer for autism and techniques like "rapid prompting" or "facilitated communication" (F/C) that a small number of SLPs have supported. Interestingly, among OTs and SLPs I have known who offer these treatments, many know so little about scientific method that they can't discern a placebo effect and can most successfully promote their methods with hopeful parents who can't see placebo effects either.

NO STONE UNTURNED

I do not see parents getting pulled into a treatment with little or no evidence for efficacy as inherently a sign of moral or ethical weakness. Rather, I often understand trying out a non–evidence-based treatment as leaving no stone unturned in a quest to discover any possible help. There is no glory (or clinical value) in condemning someone who has been snookered by a snake oil salesman. In fact, it may be argued that the school of hard knocks is a pretty good place for parents to become attuned to what is a sales pitch and what is science. Nevertheless, time and financial and emotional resources spent pursuing too-good-to-be-true panaceas might be better spent on treatments that offer some help and are backed by data, or at least solid reasoning.

AMERICAN POSITIVISM

I suspect some readers of this chapter may be pulled in by the weird sociology behind attraction to CAM. But, if you are the parent of a child with autism, a friend or relative of such a child, or a teacher or therapist of children with autism, I hope this chapter leaves you feeling you have downloaded a better "app" to act as a "GPS" as you cruise the Internet for information on autism treatment. But if you are approaching things you have read and heard about autism more as a sociologist, you might ask what happened to all the miracle cures for autism that have come and gone from the front pages of the *Wall Street Journal, New York Times, Time,* and *Newsweek*? To better understand how things that turn out to be "fake news" make such an initial splash in the world of autism, you really need to try to understand what it is like to be the parent living with a child with this diagnosis and how moments of marked distress at some action attributable to the child's autism provide fertile ground for charlatans.

One thing that may cause parents of children with autism to struggle more than you might think is that they "look" so normal most of the time. If the child is eating, sleeping, or watching TV, he or she is likely to look like others of the same age. A child with autism looks normal (unlike a child with Down syndrome) and isn't physically handicapped (like a child with cerebral palsy might be). For a parent of a child with autism, until a friendly stranger in a grocery store says "Hello," or until your child pushes another child from "his" swing he prefers at the park, things may be looking just fine. You, the parent, may even be hoping that as your child approaches the swinging peer, this is finally the moment your child is going to be interested in doing something with that other child. The next thing you know, you're apologizing for your child having pushed this child off the swing. That may be the moment a parent feels desperate enough to reach for something, anything, that he or she has heard or read about that promises to make these untoward experiences stop.

OF TIGER MOMS AND LION DADS

As someone who has ushered families into the world of autism thousands of times, I can tell you it is one of those awesome, humbling life experiences as parents involuntarily take on the mantle of caregiver for a child with seemingly all-consuming needs. As you, the parent, grasp the problems, you fear that probably you will never be doing too much to help your child improve. You know you must be strong, but getting the diagnosis leaves you feeling very vulnerable. The diagnosis can be a psychic attack. Despite your own emotional feelings of weakness, more than anything, you want to protect your child, and more than that, you want to rally yourself to do whatever your child will need to thrive. You are going to do whatever it takes to find out what might help him or her. As a parent, you are in a place you want to leave as soon as possible. As soon as you feel a treatment may have helped someone, even if it was a small dietary change, a vitamin, or swinging on a carpet-covered log at OT, you can feel yourself standing up from that rock-bottom place where you were left by getting the diagnosis and rising up with renewed energy. The risk of placebo effect is high: If at such a moment you try something new for your child, whatever it was that you feel may have helped him or her, you've imprinted on it—and you want more.

Maybe even before the diagnosis, you began to do things you now feel were helpful. Maybe you changed your child's diet, you gave the child megavitamins, or you held off on a vaccine. Maybe that was it. Maybe things would be worse now if you hadn't. How can you know for sure?

At the diagnostic visit, you tell the doctor about these things you feel have already helped. The doctor might seem a bit skeptical, pointing out the lack of data to expect improvements from these treatments. Instead, he or she praises your mindfulness of your child's struggles to communicate, your intuitive ability to "scaffold" your child, and having already started speech therapy as more powerful reasons for the improvements so far. You agree, but maybe it also *was* the diet or vitamins. You are more than willing to just keep doing it all.

Why Do We Call It Complementary and Alternative Medicine?

ORIGINS OF CAM

A formal definition is that *complementary medicine* refers to healing practices and products that work in conjunction with conventional, evidence-based medicine. The term *alternative medicine*, a close relative of complementary medicine, encompasses medical therapies that are not regarded as clinically orthodox or necessarily evidence based, such as homeopathy or naturopathy, acupuncture and acupressure, chiropractic medicine, or Ayurvedic medicine. They might be working, but if they are, we can't prove why in terms of Western medical knowledge.

CAM treatment protocols first gained acceptance in the mainstream medical community as adjunctive therapy in cancer treatment. A clear example of CAM is when a cancer patient receiving chemotherapy may also undergo acupuncture or use medical marijuana to help manage chemotherapy side effects like nausea and vomiting. If the patient says it's helping, that's all the proof needed. A cancer patient in chemotherapy does not yet know if the chemotherapy will "work" but feels it is his or her best chance. Nevertheless, complementary therapies that build overall wellness such as a special diet, exercise, or meditation regimes are common—generally seen by treating physicians as having no or low downside risk and giving back to the patient some sense of agency over the outcome (cure) he or she seeks.

Parents of a child with autism do not yet know if their child's home ABA therapy program will be as effective as it has been for some, but would like to complement it with something the mother or father can do by him- or herself— such as a special diet or nutritional supplements. Generally, treating clinicians see little or no downside risk, and parents feel more active in the overall treatment efforts. CAM can allow the patient or parents to feel that no stone is being left unturned. On the face of it, this is fine.

CAM VERSUS QUACKERY

But CAM gives cover to quacks. We all would like to think we will know a quack from a legitimate, or at least an earnest, practitioner when we meet one. But would we? Think about your own most refractory medical issue of the moment: It could be back pain, migraines, lactose intolerance, whatever. Do you think you would be a bit more "experimental" in undertaking further treatments for that issue than if you had not already tried many things that you had hoped would work better than they did? That's the Achilles heel where the quack's arrow is aimed.

A great website for specifics on autism quackery can be found at http://www.autism-watch.org, put together by Dr. Stephen Barrett, a physician who has devoted his "retirement" years, his encore career, to sleuthing and exposing medical quackery. Interestingly, autism has become a particular focus of his work. What is a good way to sniff out a quackery website? Look for ones for a particular biological or treatment method that list alphabetically all the problems it can address: If autism is listed alongside other *A* disorders—such as Alzheimer's, attention deficit hyperactivity disorder (ADHD), addiction, and allergies—well, my guess is that it helps none of these, and that there is no real reason to suspect it should. To quote the pundit Jon Stewart of *The Daily Show* (August 6, 2015): "If you smell something, say something."

INHABITANTS OF THE WORLD OF CAM

There are different kinds of people who undertake CAM for their child with autism. At one end, some people start with little confidence in what may be achieved by an out-of-the-mainstream approach, but feel they just need to try more things. At the other end, some are more comfortable with CAM than anything understood to be conventional medicine. (I'm in California; I meet many such folks.)

All along this continuum will be individuals with varying abilities to judge clinically significant change. For example, some parents may try an "autism diet" to help autism symptoms, but find it "only" helps reduce their child's diarrhea. Others may conclude the same diet is an invaluable autism diet. Some of the ones for whom the "autism diet" didn't help with autism symptoms, but are glad it helped the diarrhea, may keep looking for more CAM autism treatments—because the diet *did* help their child's diarrhea, and the naysayers had said it would not help at all.

When a CAM treatment appears to work, those who think it works may have wildly different explanations for why it did work: With Internet access, blogs fill with theories. The very fact that no one can explain why a given treatment might work and that, over time, there are almost as many causal explanations as blog posts speaks for itself. The best explanation may be that it's a transitory or placebo effect. My guess is that when a CAM treatment is no longer seen as effective, fewer people are motivated to post about that.

WHEN CLINICIANS SUPPORT CAM

Mainstream clinicians can be described as having different tiers of support for CAM: First are those practitioners helping patients with severe and likely intractable diseases who encourage CAM as an adjunctive treatment, as in the case for cancer. Second are "lukewarm" clinicians managing conditions seen as intractable, but not necessarily life threatening, and that can be well managed with conventional treatments (for example, insulin to treat diabetes) and see little reason to discourage CAM, but also believe that nothing but the mainstream treatment is what will help. Third are clinicians who at times can be hostile to CAM, especially if it means forgoing a conventional and effective treatment (for example, refusing a blood transfusion following blood loss and opting instead for prayer) and which can bring a doctor up against his or her Hippocratic standard to "do no harm."

Then there are the practitioners of CAM themselves. Some are trained in evidence-based practice, such as physicians who embrace "integrative" medicine, where CAM that passes the "do no harm" test may be more proactively recommended than by more conventional physicians. I'd argue that there is not much to worry about in these cases.

There are also nontraditional practitioners, such as acupuncturists, naturopaths, and massage therapists, who are essentially unregulated with respect to whether the complementary and alternative regimes they offer may be effective, placebos, ineffective, or harmful. Many such practitioners tend to be less well educated in the causes and processes of diseases but may not present themselves to patients that way. Some CAM practitioners are interested to observe, and test hypotheses, and will disclaim any guarantee of success from the outset of a treatment. The ones I worry about more are self-satisfied that they already know what they need to know about the goods they sell. These are the ones who arguably just want to make money.

Deconstructing Complementary and Alternative Medicine

We hear most about CAM at the two extremes of medicine—preserving wellness and surviving cancer. But most Americans have personal experience with complementary medicine through the wellness industry. Most of us take daily vitamins and minerals in hope of raising good cholesterol, lowering bad cholesterol, keeping our bones strong, or for San Franciscans like myself, taking vitamin D because we don't get enough sunshine. We seldom worry that too much of one of these daily supplements might do harm, perhaps desensitizing us to the more alternative regimes a CAM practitioner might suggest.

There are at least two entry points for parents of children with autism for using alternative methods: The first is when treatment guided by best practice medical science does not seem headed to the hoped-for outcomes. The second is when lack of trust that best practice treatment really should be the first-line treatment or be the treatment at all.

How does each of these play out in the treatment of autism spectrum disorders? For one thing, lower functioning, more disabled children respond more slowly to any kind of (evidence-based) treatment. This can be really disheartening for parents who hear about higher functioning children having more robust responses to the same treatment—like early ABA. Another type of family may reject the strict, arguably somewhat authoritarian, methods of ABA. When some parents see that ABA can make their child cry, they just don't want any part of it. They call it "dog training." Generally, families that already are wary of the values of mainstream culture, seek alternative child-centered education for their nondisabled children, and are antivaccination (more on that in Chapter 8) are the ones I find most interested to pursue CAM offered for autism. Once on the Internet, with help of affinity search results, such parents may come to believe in a CAM approach they have researched.

PARENTAL ATTITUDES TO PRESCRIBED AND NONPRESCRIBED DRUGS

Interestingly, because the diagnosis of autism is usually made in fairly young children, parents are often wary when prescribed medication is suggested as a first-line treatment. This is a good reaction because, in fact, best practice would indicate that behavioral interventions (e.g., behavior therapy, communication therapy, training in social skills and play) should indeed be first-line treatment. Most parents are understandably reluctant to give prescribed psychoactive substances to their children (with autism, ADHD, whatever) unless they feel they *have* to. "Have to" usually means the child has done something to endanger him- or herself or others, and that using behavior management or education alone to prevent the dangerous behavior hasn't worked.

But many, if not most parents faced with the suggestion they try a prescribed psychoactive medication for their child for the first time will ask what *nonprescribed* agent might achieve the same results for their 3-, 4-, or 5-year-old. This is a question parents should definitely be asking. However, what is less often asked is how an over-the-counter psychoactive medication compares in effectiveness and safety to a prescribed psychoactive medication. The fact that you can buy something at a "natural foods" or Whole Foods grocery store or order it on Amazon, amazingly, can go a long way in quelling inquiry about possible side effects or high-dose toxicity. Often, the main consideration is that, maybe, the "natural" alternative will not prove as effective.

What exactly do I mean by an over-the-counter psychoactive? Well, coffee and tea are psychoactive (stimulants). A shot of brandy or some St. John's wort might calm you down. Melatonin might help you sleep. Should a parent be giving melatonin to a 3-year-old with autism? A 2-year-old? Melatonin, for example, may be helpful, but how much? How young is too young to give it a try? What about behavior management by Benadryl?

A duality presented by over-the-counter CAM regimes is promoting efficacy on the one hand and harmlessness on the other. A homeopathic agent bought over the Internet may lack specifics on dosing (especially for children), possible side effects, or signs of overdose. Given that you can make yourself sick with too much ice cream, why would anyone think you can't get sick from too much of a megavitamin?

In reality, many psychoactive substances, from tobacco to alcohol, are available without prescription. Even among over-the-counter medicines designed especially for children, like cold or allergy remedies, too much will not be good. For every drug the FDA *does* approves, detailed statements about dosing, side effects, and contraindications guide safe use. Many parents are unaware that unprescribed agents are not FDA regulated and so will lack FDA dosing and side effects information.

HOW NEW CAM TREATMENTS GAIN ACCEPTANCE

Sometimes, I meet a parent who enthusiastically asks if I have been to a new autism treatment website for some new alternative treatment I haven't heard about yet. Often, there is an assumption I must know all about this new autism treatment because it is, I am told, *everywhere* on the web. Maybe a Hollywood celebrity also has been blogging about it. I'm always interested to hear what's new on the autism CAM front, so I ask what it is, what it targets, how it is supposed to work, and about potential side effects. Not infrequently, I hear the treatment helps "autism." "Yes, but what aspect(s) of autism? Sociability? Communication? Repetitive motor movements? Sleep, maybe?" Often, testimonials link the new treatment improvements to whatever the user hoped might improve.

Would this bother you? It bothers me. When I hear that a new treatment just happened to help the child's most marked difficulty, I smell a placebo effect. I consider myself broad-minded: I believe there are criteria to estimate the value of things, even before a randomized clinical trial. But there is a wide-open field between testimonials of hopeful respondents to a treatment and a controlled, hypothesis-testing study. What if the reported improvements were due to a conventional, evidence-based treatment going on at the same time? Do Americans just want to be the first to discover new things? Is it a drive to be the first on your block (or in your autism parent support group) to benefit from this new thing before anyone else? Is there a love for being an "early adopter?" Do Americans have an optimistic bias? Are Americans too eager to believe that what they read on the web must be true?

CAM AND LIMITS TO EVIDENCE-BASED PRACTICE

Evidence-based treatment or medical practices are those based on clinical trials that convincingly demonstrate significant benefit for the treated over the untreated, a placebo group, or a "treatment-as-usual" group. Being able to rely on clinical trials is great, but most interventions for autism, be they clinical, behavioral, or psychopharmacological, either lack clinical trials entirely or lack sufficient study of responder characteristics. Even with a clinical trial, we often can't be sure exactly *who* will be helped, how much is a low but therapeutic dose, of likely response as a function of age or body size, or how long the agent can be used safely, among many other things. If the child to be treated is very similar to those on whom the treatment has been validated, terrific. Often, however, we don't really know key responder characteristics (like high- or low-functioning autism) or what the "active ingredients" of the treatment were (one-to-one teaching or the use of discrete trial methodology). This leaves a lot of wiggle room.

As optimism in what can be accomplished through evidence-based treatment diminishes, parents naturally will become discouraged. This is when many parents, just like anyone facing any life stressor, can be expected to turn to their social network for support. Social media provide a ready social network of others with very much the same interests and questions. It is also often a place where people tend to be pretty opinionated. Should you do what a Facebook "friend" suggests and try a complementary treatment your child's doctor never even mentioned? What about a treatment your child's grandmother, with no postsecondary education, was impressed with because it had a well-put-together website for a treatment you never heard of before, like cranial-sacral massage. Could massage hurt? Grandma says she'll pay for it.

I've even seen physician–scientist parents, looking hard for something new, be impressed by a well-put-together website if there are claims of yet-to-be-published clinical trials, proposed biomarkers, and mechanistic hypotheses that seem remotely plausible. They come in telling me that there is new work on glutamate receptors, and that they understand that regulating excitatory neurons is where treatment trials are going. They want to try something that moves away from the only partial successes of treatment with other neurotransmitters like norepinephrine. What do I think? What about intranasal oxytocin? D-Cycloserine? Both are reported to be helping in trials with schizophrenics.

Most parents are in between these two extremes of believing anything that someone says might help versus staying up all night scouring PubMed (the National Institutes of Health [NIH] database for peer-reviewed medical journals), but everyone is seeking a new truth that might help their child.

A TRUTH IN SEARCH OF A HYPOTHESIS

As I stated previously, a child's limited response to initial treatment is what, in my experience, is most likely to open the first lacuna into which rationale parents use to slip from needing data to not necessarily needing data. This is so understandable: Imagine the feeling of sadness (and desperation) when you, the parents of a 2½-year-old child 4 weeks into a home ABA program, learn that another child of similar age now has 50 words, and your child still has none and isn't even copying sounds yet. Imagine a minimally verbal 5-year-old who has had 3 years of one-to-one ABA and the parents have just learned their medical insurance is denying more treatment because of the child's minimal progress. You begin to lose faith in what you have been told is "right" to help your child. You may also lose faith in the expertise of the people who told you to do what you have been doing. You feel you've got to turn somewhere else.

When that turn is made, proven science (proven ineffective as you now see it) can take a back seat to new treatments said to work, even if they are based on shaky hypotheses. This is what I call a truth in search of a hypothesis.

Take "leaky guts." Doesn't sound good, does it? I think it would be safe to say that 99.9 percent of the lay public has no idea what it takes for guts to leak (for increased intestinal permeability). Nevertheless, it sounds revolting. It sounds like something you don't want for yourself, let alone your child with autism who can't talk and can't tell you if his or her leaky gut is hurting. A parent reads on the Internet that leaky guts in autism cause certain neuropeptides to leak out of the gut and cross the blood–brain barrier, attacking the child's brain. The parent also learns that removing gluten and casein, something called a GFCF diet, can stop those neuropeptides by preventing their formation inside that leaky gut in the first place. Exactly how does gluten or casein produce these neuropeptides in the gut? The reader doesn't know, the reader doesn't even know what a neuropetide is or is supposed to do, but can tell he or she is already over his or her head medically. Why not just take what you have read at face value and give it a try? Whole Foods, you have noticed, boasts quite a number of foods labeled as "gluten free," "casein free," or both. Maybe you are late to the game.

In fact, the GFCF diet is one CAM treatment for autism that has been well studied: Not only are there no observable benefits to behavior or cognition from going gluten or casein free, such diets increase the likelihood of certain nutritional deficiencies in young children.[2]

DO NO HARM

Autism treatment professionals always hope that when a new autism treatment hits the airwaves, newspapers, or Internet that it at least does no harm. Professionals do not always know if parents are trying CAM treatments, often a sort of "don't ask, don't tell" the doctor does to avoid "mixing it up" about CAM unless he or she "has" to. Here's one scenario based on the GFCF diet: Parents start coming in, some asking whether they should go gluten and casein free. Other parents come in and announce they are doing it, and the results are tremendous. Other parents don't mention it until you ask.

The GFCF diet scenario allows me to differentiate three groups of adopters of complementary and alternative treatments for autism. The first group is made up of parents who understand that what they have read about GFCF diets is hypothetical and feel a professional may be able to help them understand more. The second group is looking for benefit, but somehow they are not sure they want to tell the doctor. The third group has made the decision to "go for it"; these individuals have their child on the diet, are fanatically strict about it, and are sure all positive growth, irrespective of other therapies, would not be going as well if not for the GFCF diet.

If you are a clinician reading this, you know the first two groups can be engaged in a rational discussion. The third group is more narrow-minded. You realize that if you dismiss the GFCF diet, they likely will never bring their child back to you again. What would *you* do?

SECRETIN AND THE LEMMING EFFECT

A special set of issues for CAM in autism arise when a new biomedical treatment is widely adopted before there are data to support efficacy. Some single-case reports, especially appearing in first-tier mainstream media, can engender so much interest that rapid adoption ends up standing in for needed clinical trials. There was an interesting case like this with a hormone called secretin. Remember how the *Wall Street Journal* used to do those heart-warming stories of individual perspicacity on the front page, left-side column, before Rupert Murdoch took over? In one report, a mother had stumbled on secretin as a cure for autism while having her child tested to rule out a problem with his pancreas. An injection of secretin, a peptide hormone to challenge pancreatic function, happened to have cured her son's autism—this mother told the paper's reporter. (Later, it turned out the child had begun a home-based intensive behavioral treatment program around the same time as the pancreas test—but no matter.)

The genie was out of the bottle; everyone wanted to try secretin infusions for *their* child with autism. The NIH Autism Centers of Excellence at the time were asked to begin trials despite the lack of any hypothesis of why secretin should "work" or what aspect of autism it might work best on. The secretin supply, usually only drawn on for occasional pancreatic diagnostic testing, quickly dried up. Unsurprisingly, the *Wall Street Journal* had given the New York Stock Exchange call letters for the company that sold a formulation of secretin at the end of its front-page article on this mom and her boy. Whether the company experienced an uptick in profitability, I do not know. I'm guessing the answer is yes.

The secretin brouhaha continued for more than a few years. I was part of one early secretin study, not out of enthusiasm or conviction, but motivated by an opportunity to collaborate with a pediatric gastroenterology colleague with an office eager to take calls from my clinic's patients, who were inundating our voice mail in the days after the *Wall Street Journal* story broke. We tested language development pre- and postsecretin infusion and found nothing exciting. Eventually, a very well-done double-blind, placebo-controlled, randomized clinical trial (the best kind of drug efficacy study) of secretin appeared in the *New England Journal of Medicine*—and it also found nothing.[3]

The *New England Journal of Medicine* study, though, was fascinating with respect to what it taught us about the allure of CAM: At the end of the study but before unblinding, all parents were ask to rate possible gains. It turned out placebo cases reported positive gains just as parents of secretin-receiving children did. When placebo-group parents learned their child had received a placebo, not secretin—and it was made clear to them that all their reported gains therefore were illusory—most *still* wanted a chance to try secretin. In blind drug–placebo trials, it is common to offer an open-label extension of the agent studied so those who receive placebo first (and might suspect it is the placebo) will be motivated to stick it out for a chance to receive the drug when the "real" study is over. These were not stupid people in the secretin trial placebo group, and not bad parents, but good parents, already down a road they had decided was worth traveling, just trying to reach their destination.

HOPE SPRINGS ETERNAL

A secretin-like story has been repeated with other biologics, some over the counter, some prescribed agents: These range from an early entrant, Super Nu-Thera, which was heavily promoted by Dr. Bernie Rimland's ARI; to injectable B vitamins; to the more current interest in *N*-acetyl-cysteine (NAC), heretofore mainly an antidote for liver poisoning after overdose on acetaminophen (Tylenol); or sulforaphane (an extract of broccoli root). Antiviral drugs like acyclovir or valcyclovir, antibiotics like nystatin, enzymes like DMG, or even hormone treatments like Lupron have all had their moments in the autism sun. These agents are prescribed with little in the way of proposed mechanisms of action and no empirical confirmatory studies emerging even after some, like nystatin, B vitamins, and DMG, have circled the autism "block" for decades, with reemerging interest for each new generation of parents.

Nonmedical Complementary and Alternative Treatments for Autism

ALTERNATIVES FROM NONMEDICAL PRACTITIONERS

Though CAM with biologics has a certain savoir faire from the seeming imprimatur of being "medicine," the same story has been written by less-than-worthy chiropractors, slightly out of the mainstream OTs, and way out of the mainstream communication specialists. In my experience, not having gone to medical school results in a group of individuals who know and care even less about scientific method. Maybe that's what makes them better at using their imaginations to come up with some of the most exotic and costly quackery for autism. To be fair, there are two very different kinds of treatment providers in this group: the would-be miracle workers who naïvely think they are helping and the bona fide scammers.

AUTISM HOMUNCULI AND A SPECIAL KIND OF PLACEBO EFFECT

Certain clinicians treating children with autism promote treatments where they themselves, as particularly gifted clinicians, saw something, broke through, and they talk about having discovered a new "way" into autism never before seen by others. These purported cures draw on what I refer to as the homunculus theory of autism. Homunculus theory holds that inside each intellectually disabled child with autism there is a normally developed being, capable of the same expressive language and academic skills as others the same age, despite not having been through the trial-and-error practice and learning typical learners need. Believers in autism homunculus theory will tell you that with just the right supports, the right key, the homunculus's mental prison will be unlocked and a fully developed, fully intelligent person will express him- or herself. I see this belief adopted by parents of 3-year-olds with autism who test with a receptive language age of a 6-month-old, with the parents claiming "I know he understands every word I say—he just doesn't act like it." I see it in the mother of a nonverbal 13-year-old (with language understanding of a 1-year-old) who uses a dubious communication device with her son to show me that he has spelled out that "I am normally intelligent, and you should not violate my rights by underestimating my capacities." That's the autism homunculus talking, and it's a very peculiar placebo effect.

In Chapter 2, I talked about Dr. Alan Frances, who worried about "saving normal." I also worry about *fabricating* normal—a not uncommon fantasy about severely impacted children with autism. As we say in my business, "Denial is not just a river in Egypt." Denial, as the early psychoanalysts first pointed out, is a coping mechanism to titrate painful reality—when a painful reality is what you have to face.

However, there is a happy ending of sorts to a parent's denial of their child's severe problems when the homunculus is "found." The parent goes from one day being told their child will never learn to speak (among many things) to being greatly relieved to learn that was all wrong, that there *is* a normal child "in there." This is a variation on the Horatio Alger rags-to-riches myth: This Horatio Alger–like child has gone from "rags" (intellectual disability) to seemingly being quite able. Despite being in special education classes where the homunculus child's capacities were assumed not to exist, it turns out that the child can expound as well as any adult on topics he or she is queried about, from the Common Core curriculum to whether ISIS is a menace to America. This peculiar placebo effect has been seen when parents try certain bogus methods for augmenting the child's communication that I describe next. But, first, one more word on the psychology of all this.

In 2013, *The Reason I Jump,* ostensibly written by Naoki Higashida, a 13-year-old nonverbal Japanese boy with autism, was reviewed by Sallie Tisdale, not only a well-published author herself, but also the mother of an adult with autism. She resonated emotionally with the book, but found Naoki's author-ship improbable. She talked about how the English edition of this book "is being treated more as a fragile objet de consciousness than a book, as though criticism or analysis would be vulgar."[4] She hit the nail on the head: Many of us *want* to believe, but most vulnerable are parents who understandably need to feel all the hard work that has been done to help their child has been helpful indeed.

FACILITATED COMMUNICATION AND RAPID PROMPTING METHOD

Most notable autism treatments that have brought forth the homunculus specter are facilitated communication (F/C) and its kin, the rapid prompting method (RPM). F/C landed in the United States via Australia in the mid-1990s at Syracuse University, where an active center for its dissemination mushroomed. F/C involved a strict protocol where a "facilitator" held a child's wrist just so, above a computer keyboard or a laminated paper with the alphabet printed on it. The idea was that the child would move his or her supported hand to spell out answers, thoughts, and feelings—once the child could sense a certain something in the facilitator's touch that conveyed that it was safe to let his or her true self be known for the first time. This might sound like a Ouija board to you. (I said so in a study I wrote up for the *Journal of Autism and Developmental Disorders.*[5]) A facilitator would say that he or she was fortunate enough to have a special gift, a special understanding of people with autism that enabled him or her to do this facilitating.

All kinds of people believed in this: I remember a well-educated mother with a 3-year-old child diagnosed at our UCSF clinic the prior year telling me that with F/C she had learned her son (now 4) was actually a genius—and liked reading the *Wall Street Journal* in the morning. Another showed me essays written by her nonverbal teen son where he explained he was not mentally re-tarded, but simply unable to communicate as others did—though to express such things, he didn't even need to look at the keyboard as his hand was held over it: He could look away and "touch-type" one-handed, with his wrist suspended over the keyboard by his facilitator.

My basis for calling F/C a Ouija board came from a "natural experiment" I was able to carry out in 1994 when F/C was in its (first) heyday. As director of the UCSF Autism Clinic, I was contacted by social workers from two different county Child Protective Services (CPS) agencies, each saying they had taken custody of young people with autism who, through F/C, had alleged they had been sexually molested by their fathers. About the same time, I was contacted by two facilitators from yet another county asking that I write a letter supporting their F/C work so they could apply to obtain Medicaid reimbursement for it. I agreed to write a letter if I could check out their work first. They agreed to come to my clinic and facilitate with a couple of children I would have there for them to meet for the first time. I arranged for each facilitator to meet each child in CPS custody and be given as much "getting to know you time" as wanted, and then each child in turn would be asked a standard series of questions—like "Who do you live with?" "How many brothers and sisters do you have?" "What is you favorite thing to eat?" We would videotape and compare the response to the answers provided by parents ahead of the sessions. The facilitators knew nothing of the alleged sexual abuse. In addition to answering our questions, we thought if there had been abuse, the children might mention something.

The results? One facilitator had each child type short telegraphic statements with errors in grammar and spelling; the other facilitator received consistently literate responses from both. One facilitator established rapport by offering the 13-year-old African American male subject a Grateful Dead bootleg concert recording, asking if he liked rock and roll. He stood, looked at himself in our one-way mirror, said "Motown!" and began to dance—a bittersweet moment. (We had been told he was nonverbal, and that's why he had a facilitator.) The other facilitator, working with a 14-year-old second-generation, California-born Latina, had her writing that tacos and burritos were her favorite food, while the girl, not looking at the keyboard where she was "writing," repeatedly tapped a picture of "granola bar" on her choice board and which her mother had listed as her favorite food. The whole thing was embarrassingly bad.

Needless to say, predetermined questions and answers did not line up, the facilitators were debriefed and were told I had no basis to write a letter supporting their Medicaid claims for service. They left calling me a nasty ivory tower something or other, followed up by a letter saying the same thing.

Today, I have only occasionally got into F/C discussions with parents, even less often with practitioners. But, to my surprise and dismay, recently there was a *New York Times* story about a lawsuit where a female F/C therapist had what she described as "consensual" sexual relations with her patient, a severely handicapped adult man who, she asserted, had "told her" that was what he wanted.[6]

But, F/C fever was "replaced" in the mid-1990s by RPM. Just when I thought we had really hammered that wooden stake into the F/C vampire's heart, there arose the RPM. The developer of RPM, Soma Mukhopadhyay, a mother of a son with autism, Tito, was brought to the United States from India after being discovered there by a Hollywood celebrity mom, Portia Iverson. Portia recruited Soma to Los Angeles to teach Portia's son with autism through RPM. Like F/C, RPM also involved an alphabetic template or keyboard, but there was a lot of shouting at the child to pay attention and do his best. There was no wrist holding as in F/C, but a claim, basically, that with enough shouting, the child would learn to use this method independently. Soma toured the United States with her son demonstrating RPM, and I even had a chance to meet him and his mother when he came to UCSF because a colleague of mine, Dr. Michael Merzenich, did a brain scan of him. (I never heard what he had learned.)

Present-day RPM involves a template that looks like a black, hard rubber alphabet stencil about 8.5 by 11 inches. The child is handed a pencil to poke at sequences of cutout letters to spell things out. The adult might have to rapidly shake the template back and forth to keep the child focused rather than shouting (not to help the pencil land on the right letter, mind you). Here are two examples of RPM: First, a nonverbal teen moderately to severely handicapped with autism who has "written" that he is not a disabled person at all, but is quite able and trapped in a sensory cage that leaves others feeling he is not as intelligent as they are. The second example is rather different: He is a teen boy with autism, formerly verbal and of normal IQ, who has been mute since severe hypoxia during surgery. He now works off a stationary RPM template, typing things more like one would expect—like "I want mom's TV in my bedroom." No, I can't say RPM is completely bogus, but for 99.9 percent maybe?

AUDITORY INTEGRATION TRAINING

Auditory integration training (AIT), also sometimes referred to as the Tomatis listening method, has taken many forms over the last 30 years. It has been heavily promoted by the late Dr. Rimland's ARI in San Diego, California, which, as already described, brought us DAN!, B-vitamin therapy, Super Nu-Thera multivitamins, DMG, and nystatin (reportedly for autism-causing maternal yeast infections).

Despite the fact that I had already become wary of anything sponsored by Bernie Rimland long before he got behind AIT, the idea of AIT was intriguing and had some interesting potential explanatory theories that could be tested. The idea was that if a child is hyper- or hyposensitive to sound, the child's audiogram could guide you in remastered music recordings—amping up frequencies that are "low" on an audiogram (and presumably insufficiently attended to and processed) and tuning down frequencies perceived as "too loud." Listening to these rerecorded works, which sound pretty similar to the original recordings, it was hypothesized to retrain hearing—with improved attention to the former lows and less overattention to the former highs. This was an interesting idea, but after all these years it has not managed to cross that threshold into being an evidence-based treatment supported by any double-blind work, though such work would be easy to do—if there were even preliminary data to justify such a study.

Nevertheless, parents will describe how their child loves going to AIT. The music is chosen to be something their child prefers, and the child sits in a comfy chair with headphones on and listens. Aside from kids tolerating AIT well, some parents will swear by it (as will the therapists who administer it). Published data (e.g., pre-to-post changes in audiogram), even using a single-case design and single-case data, are sparse.

SENSORY INTEGRATION THERAPY

In the "nothing-to-lose" category are CAM therapies for sensory difficulties associated with autism. Sensory integration therapy (SIT) is experiencing a renaissance now, although it has been around since the 1970s, based on the 1975 book *Sensory Integration and the Child* by Jane Ayres.[7] A child's sensory over- or underresponding is sometimes referred to as sensory processing disorder (SPD), and though not a validated diagnosis, it overlaps with signs of autism. Children with presumed SPD do things like cover their ears in response to certain sounds (like blenders, vacuums, garbage disposals, and restroom hand dryers); show tactile overresponding (to long sleeves, long pants, or shirt tags); and show proprioceptive sensory seeking (swings, hammocks, escalators, elevators). Children with autism may do all these things, too, with the difference being that the SPD cases lack the social and communication difficulties associated with autism. OTs following Ayres's work initially treated children with SPD symptoms using methods they called SIT. When OTs discovered many children with autism also had sensory processing problems, they began to treat them. Sensory differences make children with autism stand out from others in public as they scream and cover their ears at fireworks, dart across the mall to ride the escalator alone, and refuse to relinquish a certain swing at the playground without a meltdown. These are certainly behaviors parents wish to decrease or eliminate—so there is a market for SIT treatments among parents of children with autism.

The market for treating SPD symptoms consists of activities supposed to ramp up or tune down perceptions that are too intense or too low. There are no pre-to-post, let alone double-blind, clinical trials that show any SIT treatments achieve "sensory integration," implied to be some sort of positive neural processing change. SIT treatments include weighted vests, carrying heavy boxes, and sitting on bumpy cushions or exercise balls in class. Stroking children's arms with soft surgical brushes and compressing joints are used to deter tantrums and are described as "helping the child regulate." *Regulate* has become a buzzword among SIT proponents: If a child behaves badly, he is said to be "dysregulated" and needs a "sensory diet" to stay "regulated." Interestingly, this implies some sort of physiological change will result in improved behavior. But there are no studies that operationalize "regulation," like studies of change in heart rate, movement, respiration, or galvanic skin response (GSR), and so on when SIT is used to regulate a child. If I point this out to an OT who does SIT, the OT will point out to me that he or she is a clinician, not a researcher, which is fair enough for the OT to say, I guess.

The SIT catalogs sell a miscellany of objects—hard chewy things, body socks, tight Lycra suits, gym mats, hammocks, and swinging carpeted logs to provide deep pressure and other enhancements (most recently, finger spinners) to alter proprioception and promote "neural reorganization." Because there is no proof that SIT evokes physiological changes and that any such change correlates to behavior change, prescribing which SIT apparatus might help is simply not empirically supported.

A downside to SIT is that if a child has a tantrum in class and you reorganize the child by giving him or her a "sensory break" like a swing in a hammock or a backrub in a beanbag chair (instead of having to stay in circle time), you may well be reinforcing tantrums. Providers of SIT talk about "sensory diets"—meaning SIT to proactively deter undesired behavior. This has resulted in kids going to school with a necklace of "chewies" or individual education programs (IEPs) with 10 minutes of brushing and joint compression before instruction. Not surprisingly, sensory diets also lack validation through any clinical trials—though, again, it would be easy to design one.

Despite the lack of data for interventions like AIT or SIT, they continue to be used, and certain therapists and some parents continue to point to perceived benefit, though I seldom see pre-to-post data to support effectiveness, even for a specific child. Fortunately, medical insurance does not typically pay for these treatments because of the lack of data. Unfortunately, it means parents are more likely to pay out of pocket for them.

SEEING THE WORLD THROUGH ROSE-COLORED GLASSES

"Rose-colored glasses" is an endearing metaphor. In treating autism, vision therapy with prisms, microprisms, colored lenses, or filters is sometimes prescribed to correct presumptively "faulty wiring." This is another non–evidence-based autism treatment bandwagon that some optometrists have climbed aboard.[8] Much of this started when an Australian woman, Donna Williams, wrote a memoir discovering that her lifetime of difficulties was due to autism. She reported that with vision therapy, rooms felt less crowded and overwhelming, and that auditory hypersensitivity also decreased. At some autism meetings, it is easy to spot the adults with autism who are into this as they walk around in their weird prismatic, deep purple or deep red lenses. If they feel it is helping them, fine. Exhorting others to do the same in the absence of data, or even a good hypothesis why it should be helpful, is another thing.

Dietary Treatment for Autism

We all eat food. It is the one thing that parents can control as they deal with what feels like the out-of-control implications of their child's diagnosis. Every parent whose child receives a diagnosis of autism asks, "What caused this? Was it anything I did?" The diagnostician can recite some data from genetic and epidemiological studies. Unless there is already an older autistic sibling, which speaks most convincingly to a genetic cause, most parents wrack their brains trying to identify if it was anything *they did* to trigger autism or make it worse. This free-floating guilt looking for a place to land may land on something the parent may feel will "undo" something inadvertently done wrong.

"Was it the vaccines?" "Do I live too close to a big freeway?" "Was it the daily glass of wine I drank till I learned I was 6 weeks pregnant?" Increasingly, parents ask about their child's diet as a possible causative factor, although there is no strong research evidence for this, and there is research evidence to the contrary, implicating a complex of genetic and other epigenetic factors.

THE GLUTEN-FREE, CASEIN-FREE DIET

Interestingly, I don't think any parent I have met really thinks food containing gluten or casein caused their child to have autism, but a great number have read on the Internet that gluten or casein elimination diets are an absolute necessity for a child with autism, much as a sugar-free diet is for diabetes. The GFCF diet is amazingly popular. Like many classic CAM interventions, the GFCF diet is promoted not only for autism, but also for a whole alphabet of ills (in addition to celiac disease, for which it is medically indicated). Why do people try this diet so readily? It is not easy to follow rigorously. Major proponents will link one little slip of the lip (for example, a bite of "gluten" cupcake at a classroom birthday party) to all undesired behavior for the next week. Once, I was told by a parent that McDonald's was the safest place for a GFCF lunch because McDonald's does not cook any other foods in its French fries fryer.

In studies I described previously in the context of secretin research, not only is there no evidence for any benefit from the GFCF diet for children with autism, but also there is a great study showing it does *not* work: In 2015, a colleague with a long-standing interest in encouraging families to preferentially adopt evidence-based treatments, Dr. Susan Hyman at the University of Rochester in New York, was actually able to give two groups of families "blind" diets. One set of families got a complete family diet with gluten and casein; the other group received a diet without gluten and casein. Parents in both groups frequently rated changes in their child with autism; there was no difference. We need more research like this that matter-of-factly addresses ineffective treatments.

Nevertheless, I find many parents put their child on a GFCF diet even while wait-listed for an appointment to see if their child actually has autism. I struggle to remain sanguine when I then hear about the child on a GFCF diet, who eats very few foods, his or her choices made more limited by the parents' choice of the GFCF diet. When a parent with their child on a GFCF diet wants advice on how to expand narrow food choices, I can't help but talk about the absence of evidence to support such dieting. In addition, GFCF-dieted children run the risk of deficiency in calcium, which is needed for growing bones. I have even met parents who wonder if their GFCF-dieted child's "craving" for ice cream is like craving a narcotic and all the more reason to stick to being GFCF.[9]

DAN!, GENERATION RESCUE, TACA, AND THE LIKE

A number of websites have come and gone as hubs for autism CAM. While those identifying themselves as DAN! doctors are no longer formally linked to the ARI in San Diego, ARI remains a hub for DAN!-trained doctors and parents seeking them out. Generation Rescue has its roots as an anti-vaxxer group, fueled by Hollywood celebrity parents and their celebrity friends, who are presumably, it is hoped, only lending their name to be supportive (and can't be faulted for not reading Centers for Disease Control and Prevention [CDC] studies on vaccines rather than reading scripts for their next movie). Many parent-initiated sites host discussions where an evidence basis or even solid medical theory is neither required nor present and, not infrequently, not particularly welcomed. Some organizations like TACA (Talk About Curing Autism) and the Autism Society of America (the oldest parent-founded autism group in the United States) try to focus on supporting parents and families as much as "curing" children, but threads about "cures" draw readers like moths to flame.

Interestingly, among physicians, DAN! doctors continue to be active. DAN! doctors are a miscellany of clinicians who can charge about $300–$400 per month for services that are not covered by insurance and do not include the cost of the biomedical supplements they "prescribe." DAN! doctors are most often naturopaths, osteopathic doctors, allergists, chiropractors, or general practitioners with no explicit training in autism who apparently see a market opportunity. I am always fascinated to learn of new DAN! doctors who have none of the training of child psychiatrists or child psychologists in diagnosis or the evidence-based treatment literature. How do they even know that the child who has turned up is autistic? While parents understand that children with autism can be quite different from one another, these non–autism-specialist practitioners may promote treatments with little attention to these differences, gloss over details about who is most likely to benefit, and animate false hope for benefit from any treatment that hasn't been tried yet.

To view DAN! doctors, Generation Rescue promoters, and the like with a different lens is to note they are absent as presenters at scientific meetings like the International Meetings for Autism Research or at national meetings of pediatricians or child psychiatrists supported by the American Medical Association. On an emotional level, these autism CAM purveyors certainly provide at least brief solace, hope, and a feeling of affiliation to desperate, exhausted parents trolling websites on their computers, alone late at night after their child with autism is finally asleep. But they breed frantic desperation, especially in those most vulnerable to what is being sold, which, ideally, in the reader's case will turn out to be a needle-in-the-haystack cure for his or her particular child's autism.

Therapeutic Animals and Autism

Another branch of alternative therapies for autism involves animals. There is a line of thought that a connection between a child with autism to an animal is therapeutic. It would be difficult to argue that there is any downside to allowing a child to enjoy a swim with dolphins, the companionship of a dog, or development of horsemanship. However, calling these activities therapies should get us questioning just how we should be defining "therapy."

DOLPHINS

Let's take dolphins first—they are fun, but in no way therapy. Swimming with dolphins is, at best, a free vacation for a stressed family with a child with autism, courtesy of altruistic friends and neighbors who help raise funds so the family can spend a little time at a resort that harbors tame dolphins. Undoubtedly, it could be more profitable for the resort to call it "dolphin therapy" versus just having hotel guests who pay to swim around in a lagoon of dolphins because it sounds like fun. (I once appeared in a CNN piece on dolphin therapy for autism as the academic party pooper, naysaying the relaxed guy in the aloha shirt standing on the dock of the dolphin lagoon in Florida advocating dolphin therapy.)

DOGS

I know a number of children with autism who have obtained Canine Companions. This is a wonderful program that has gone beyond Guide Dogs for the Blind to offer highly trained dogs (usually Labrador retrievers) to people with many other disabilities. The therapy dog may be able to make a social connection with a child who shows little interest in making a connection with most people. For a school-aged child, the dog can draw in peers who are curious to meet the dog, and in doing so, meet the child with autism as well. This is a fine thing. But I am less certain whether such a dog needs the level of training a Canine Companion has. It would be great for a therapy dog trainer to study just what skills a dog needs to provide companionship to a child with autism. The dog doesn't need to pull a wheelchair, turn on light switches, or bark when the doorbell rings. Maybe if dogs with less or different training were trained just in enough ways to be suitable companions for children with autism, more children with autism could have them.

Dogs as "therapy dogs" raises the question of just what is therapy, and asks what a "therapeutic effect" *is*. I'd argue that even if it wasn't possible to show that a therapy dog changed the rate of social initiation, sustained social contact, or any measurable child outcome, the simple reality of a relationship between a child with autism and his or her dog is probably enough for it to be a good thing for that child to have one. What we come to here is the line between therapy and leisure. Developing ways for a child with autism to spend leisure time is a valid aspect of life skills training, even if it does not explicitly reduce autism symptoms.

HORSES

Equine therapy or hippotherapy (horses, not hippopotamuses), as it is called, has been around for a while. The potential therapeutic effects of hippotherapy raise many of the same questions as for therapy dogs. Hippotherapy for children really started with getting little kids with cerebral palsy or paraplegias up on a horse. For a child with a physical disability, the idea was that being up on a horse would be a more fun and empowering way to see the world than from an electric wheelchair or a walker—wonderful.

Kids with autism followed. Though children with autism have independent locomotion, too much some parents would say, it has been argued to help a child with autism develop sustained attention and push him or her into a reciprocal social relationship via guiding the horse. Hippotherapy for autism got a boost in the 2009 book (and movie that followed), *The Horse Boy: A Father's Quest to Heal His Son*,[10,11] the story of a Texas dad who traveled to Mongolia to see if a combination of shamanism and Mongolian horses would "recover" his son from autism. It was a great adventure. The father felt there were improvements. Not unexpectedly, the boy's father collected no empirical single-case data to illustrate the improvements in his son that he perceived. How do we separate claimed benefit from expected maturation? What would we need to know to deem something like hippotherapy to be therapeutic rather than "just" an opportunity to expand leisure skills?

Hippotherapy, like therapy with dogs, raises the same questions regarding what we should be calling therapy. If a child with autism can express that he or she likes riding horses, is that then a therapeutic effect? Many of us love the activities we choose for recreation (including horseback riding). If we delimit a therapeutic effect to being something that lessens a symptom seen as functionally impairing, can having a therapy dog or hippotherapy pass the test for being therapeutic? There are no studies of whether either is therapeutic by this definition. What would we look for as therapeutic effects if we were to design a study? Sustained attention? Social initiative as measured by physical and verbal commands to guide the horse? To be therapy, would any such gains, measurable while horse riding, need to generalize to other aspects of life where improved attention and social initiative were expected?

I think you see where I am going: Even if such generalized benefits can't be proved, just having a therapy dog or horse riding may be something that is good for the child's overall quality of life—but may not be fairly designated as therapy.

INDIVIDUAL DIFFERENCES IN TREATMENT RESPONSES

The term *individual differences*, with respect to research, refers to the fact that in any treatment study where the study group as a whole is deemed to have benefitted, there will be some in the study group who did not benefit, some who benefitted much less than average, and some who benefitted more than average. Conversely, in a treatment outcome study where there was lack of significant benefit for the study group, there are likely some who actually showed benefit. Such apparent benefit might be real, but statistically is more likely a placebo effect (temporary), accrued from something other than the treatment (like hope). The fact that a single treatment outcome study can tell us everything about responder characteristics (i.e., exactly who will benefit in the expected way) creates a fertile field for interest in treatments where there is a single compelling story of benefit. So, the challenge we face as evidence-based clinicians in recommending a non–evidence-based treatment can be rejecting an alternative treatment approach just because it has not been subjected to systematic study. Conversely, clinicians face a press to accept unproven treatment simply because a single-case report of benefit has been appealing and convincing. This is all well and good, but parents will not want to wait for science to catch up with what they may feel they already know.

SIFTING THROUGH SHAM MEDICAL TREATMENTS FOR AUTISM

To be fair, I really believe that most nonmedical practitioners of largely bogus treatments (like F/C or RPM providers), just like almost all qualified special education teachers, SLPs, and OTs, have good intentions. Nobody I have ever met who has chosen to take care of children with autism is doing it to get rich or famous.

But, how about folks who claim therapeutic benefit from costly interventions that medical insurance is very unlikely to cover and for which those making the claim are the direct financial beneficiaries? Many autism

CAM quacks are generalist doctors who will admit that they have never diagnosed autism and really don't know how. A variety of immunologists and allergists have been drawn to autism, proffering various arguments about inflammation and autoimmune responses—in the gut, in brain fluid, and in nerve cells in the brain.

Here are some of the most outré: New ones have certainly arisen since I've written this paragraph, some in this paragraph may already be on their way out or gone—though on the Internet, it can be hard to ever be completely gone. On the Internet, much of this is market driven, and there has never stopped being a market for autism cures. There are chiropractors who do spinal manipulation and, in the case of autism, offer cranial manipulation to decrease the amount of spinal fluid in the brain. This treatment depends on convincing parents that their child must have too much spinal fluid, that too much spinal fluid is bad, and that spinal manipulation, or other cranial-sacral manipulation, can make it better. Sonar depuration to "regenerate" supposedly damaged brain cells is another peculiar alternative autism treatment. Are damaged brain cells involved at all? What can "fix" damaged cells? Echolocation? That's what sonar is. Other parents have paid big bucks for RNA drops to replace allegedly "bad" RNA in the child's cells. These break down on swallowing. What cranial manipulation, depuration, and RNA drops have in common is that they are offered by sellers who probably know better than their buyers what chiropractic, sonar, and RNA does and doesn't do. Nevertheless, some sell whatever they know, as treatment for autism. You can google any of the terms I've introduced here, adding "and autism" and all sorts of stuff will come up. Jumping down the rabbit hole is your choice.

Then there are the treatments that go beyond outré to outrageous: A couple of doctors have had malpractice suits filed against them for injecting urine or hydrogen peroxide, not to mention EDTA (ethylene diamine tetra-acetic acid), a chelating agent that killed at least one boy with autism (as mentioned in the next chapter). I am not sure why any practitioner would have done any of this, except, I guess, if you are going to inject something ineffective, it might as well be cheap for you to obtain, but at least, it also should be harmless.

What about something expensive? Doesn't that sound inherently more promising? What about stem cell transplants? I know families who have traveled to South America and Asia for them. One such parent is a nurse, the other a highly trained engineer. Such parents are not dumb, but arguably are naïve and certainly susceptible. There is no evidence that such costly and potentially dangerous intervention can even hypothetically be helpful to a child with autism.

In the category of expensive and uncomfortable for the child (but probably harmless) is hyperbaric oxygen chamber therapy (HBOT). HBOT is a well-proven and effective method used after a too-rapid ascent from a prolonged, deep scuba dive to reoxygenate blood and alleviate narcosis (decompression sickness). Some have postulated that more oxygen will help the brain of a child with autism do things a bit better. You can even go to YouTube for a video to build your own HBOT chamber.

If HBOT and stem cell transplants didn't sound costly enough for a shot-in-the-dark treatment, there's intravenous immunoglobulin (IVIG) infusions to treat presumed antibody deficiencies with a blood product that requires 1,000–15,000 blood donations per batch. If a parent has a lot of money and becomes convinced autism is an immune or inflammatory disease, the parent just might seek out IVIG infusions for a child with autism and find a doctor who will provide them. How much does it cost? For how long? What kind of changes are expected? The answers to these questions are unknown.

In my opinion, the most dangerous autism snake oil salespeople are folks offering chelation, biologics that are aimed at removing metals from the blood and tissue. These quacks got a big boost from the vaccine scare that I cover in the next chapter along with details on how chelation may be medically harmful.

Explaining the Durability of CAM in Autism Treatment

I've talked about many CAM approaches that have been undertaken by parents of children with autism. Some try many. Some try a few. Some try ones where there appears to be only their own effort as the "cost" (e.g., paying for hippotherapy); some try ones with possible deleterious effects to their children that are ignored or considered "worth it"—like becoming calcium deficient because of a GFCF diet. Some try things—like chelation—that kill the occasional child with autism.

Is there something about parents of children with autism that disproportionately draws them to ideas that others more readily eschew? I believe yes, there is. First, I need to describe what is sometimes called the "broader autism phenotype" (BAP)—having a "shadow syndrome" of some of the social and cognitive symptoms affecting their children. (This was mentioned a bit in Chapter 3.) Second, I'll talk about getting the diagnosis of autism for one's child as a major life stressor that provokes a process of mourning for the lost (hoped-for) child and sometimes provokes a more complicated, unresolved mourning and coping process that can be expressed as passive aggression to the child and as active hostility to those seen as responsible for the child's condition (like a vaccine manufacturer).

ARE SOME PARENTS OF CHILDREN WITH AUTISM ALSO A BIT AUTISTIC?

When I speak with special educators who deal with children with a range of physical, cognitive, and mental disabilities, I am often asked why are the parents of the children with autism the most difficult to deal with. "What do you mean," I ask? They respond, "Three IEPs each year, not one." "A 35-page IEP; not 12 pages." "Saying they plan to bring their advocate to our first face-to-face meeting." My colleagues in pediatrics and neurology say similar things about the parents of the children I see: "I feel badly; this mom clearly wanted and needed more time (so I'm sending her to you)." "I had a really hard time explaining the benefits of vaccines—even though he was the one who raised it." I also hear similar things from lawyers and advocates who work with families with children with autism. "You think I'm obsessive; this dad sent me all his boy's records in an e-mail with 10 attached PDFs, and then the next day, I got a FedEx with printed out hard copies of the same PDFs, plus the same records on a CD." From autism clinicians: "When I started to take a history, I heard so much about what happened when he was 22 months old in the hour we had, that I never really got the big picture about why they had come in." "What's up with this, Dr. Siegel?" I have two answers: BAP and autism as the death of the hoped-for child.

The Broader Autism Phenotype

Some, certainly not all or even most, parents of children with autism really display signs of that BAP, a shadow syndrome of autism. Not all families will have one BAP parent, but it seems as though a number do, much more often fathers than mothers. These parents almost always seem to have a very much smaller "dose" of autism than their children, as well as numerous strengths their children lack, but have it they do. BAP parents have difficulties seeing the forest from the trees. For the parent with a BAP, important and extraneous detail flow together until the listener can become a bit confused whether the important point *is* the important point or just a detail. With the BAP-type parent, key points the parent wants to make are repeated and repeated, seemingly irrespective of giving a "Got it!" "Yes, OK," or other verbal or nonverbal cues. On the other hand, for such a parent, a belief, once adopted, can verge on becoming an idée fixe, and overused, with bias against entertaining other hypotheses that may come along providing data that contradict the existing belief. It is fairly easy to draw a straight line from the point at which a BAP parent adopts a personal theory about his or her child's autism and tenacious pursuit of any treatment that fits with his or her personal theory of his or her child's autism.

As I noted, not all parents fit this BAP mold. In fact, we now know many cases of autism probably arise from noninherited genetic factors, such as de novo mutations and epigenetic triggers (more about that in Chapter 9).

Autism as the Death of the Hoped-For Child

The second factor that may drive an interest in CAM for autism is parental struggle to accept that their very normal-looking, and in some ways normal-acting, child is deemed to have autism just because he doesn't talk much or interact with others much. For many years, I have been interested in better understanding what I see as a complicated, unresolved sense of mourning for the hoped-for child in some parents of some children with autism. I am interested in this because this emotional state, which can be thought of as complicated grieving, can become a barrier for a parent to move ahead with helping their child with autism, being close to other family members, and enjoying life. I want to help people like this, just as I want to help anybody with a child with autism who seeks advice about his or her development. These people, however, may not want the help of someone like me—who believes more in making each child the best he or she can be—but does not believe in either sudden or inexplicable recoveries from autism. It seems obvious that these parents might be helped with psychotherapy, but few clinicians or grief counselors focus on this unique kind of loss—that of the hoped-for child.

In my experience, and in work using a measure I developed several years ago called *Adjustment to the Diagnosis of Autism* (ADA), in the first year after diagnosis, parents bifurcate into one of two groups.[12] For the first, the hoped-for child indeed appears to be gone, and there is substantial acceptance of the diagnosis according to the ADA. The parents still dream about this child. They still imagine the child as a future loving big brother or big sister, and even as a normal adult, but also *do* see the child before them is quite different from others his or her age. Parents in this first group want to be practical and do everything that it makes sense to do. They set out to master the rules of the medical insurance industry and the special education system. These parents do act in a way they feel is in the best interest of their child and, in their commitment to do so, may take a detour down some alleys—spending a few months trying the GFCF diet or separating subsequent vaccines. A couple of years after the diagnosis, these parents are less depressed and less stressed than the second group of parents. They sail along fairly smoothly.

This second group of grieving parents experiences higher levels of self-blame and reports frantic feelings, the need to eschew old social supports and instead go "all in," joining autism support groups, following autism blogs, and getting lots of online support for trying everything and anything that might help their child. They struggle to prioritize. Many are very angry this has happened to them. (I often see and hear the anger more in fathers than in mothers.) In this frenzy of sadness, anger, and the need to act urgently on behalf of one's child, it becomes hard to tell when talking to such parents, what really makes sense and what doesn't. These parents, I believe, are the ones who become most vulnerable to CAM scams. These parents experience more despair and as a result perceive more caregiver burden, lack self-acceptance, and have low life satisfaction according to the ADA and other stress measures.

The stages of adjustment to a diagnosis of autism can follow well-described stages of grief that one might experience at the loss of any loved family member. I have, over the years, written about this several times and summarize this work here to show how mental life can be so disorganized by receiving a diagnosis of autism for one's child that appreciation of mainstream treatments is restrained. Instead, there can be a vulnerability to treatments that promise resolution of grief by restoring the hoped-for child.[13]

Outcry

The initial outcry in response to getting a diagnosis of autism virtually always includes "Why me?" Maybe risk factors like family history, parental age, or the BAP of the other parent provide some explanation, if not solace. More often than not, there is not even that to hold. Many parents spend some time lost in the forest of grief and can't see the road out—the things we know are likely to be effective treatment. In fact, in response to treatment suggestions, I might hear, "If I just do what everyone else does, there is no way my child will get cured." In this outcry stage, I hear stories about a post on the Internet of a child cured this way, another cured that way. Hope, pinned on random "finds" on the Internet, alerts me to a parent having an especially hard time working past that outcry stage to acknowledging the new reality for family life—even if we can't yet be sure what that new reality will look like in 5, 10, or 20 years.

Denial

The next stage of complicated, unresolved grieving is denial. Some become more stuck than others in coming to terms with their child's disability. It is here that a parent might invest in the belief that the hoped-for child still lives—but is locked away. If the parent can't believe that F/C or RPM can unlock the child, maybe chelation could work. Imagine the desperation a parent might feel, believing his or her child is "in there," locked away, and not knowing how to rescue the child.

Intrusion

Most parents of older children with autism look back and see the first couple of years after their child's diagnosis as a blur. They ran around getting assessment after assessment. They fought for and got ABA services, a preschool, and their first IEP. They dealt with numerous agencies, therapists, tutors, and trainers who came and went. When the child is around age 6, many families take a deep breath for the first time in years. For one thing, the pace of the effort since the diagnosis is unsustainable.

The early intervention "window of opportunity" has more or less "closed." At this point, a small number of children with early diagnoses of autism will be doing quite well indeed. For them, the sprint will be seen as having paid off. For other families at this point, the child may be doing much better compared to what was feared in those most despairing moments of early sorrow just after the diagnosis. Even if the child is not "recovered," it is possible to see what the way forward may be.

But, for some families, those still struggling with complicated unresolved grief, the anger boils over. "This is not my fault! Whose fault is it?" Lawsuits for compensatory education are filed. A paranoid sense of the world as somehow selecting them out for punishment can gain traction.

Acceptance and Chronic Sorrow

Not unexpectedly, even those with the healthiest coping may not achieve full acceptance of their child, even after years of treatment, and even with diminished signs of autism. By comparison, one may lose a beloved family member to cancer after a long struggle and heroic interventions. There will be moments when one choice or another along the cancer treatment journey will be rehashed and reevaluated, but the bell cannot be unrung. In families who have lost a child to cancer, there can be a chronic sorrow, reawakened when imagined milestones would have been passed—"He would have been 21 today." "He would have graduated from college this year." The same is true with autism, but with a poignant twist because the son or daughter is there to witness the graduation of a same-age cousin or marriage of a sibling. These are milestones that families living with autism may navigate with unease, but they do get through it. Not all families get to this place, and I wonder if the families who have spent years pursuing non–evidence-based treatments in hope of a cure are the ones more likely to cling to their hate and anger. When I read the Prologue of Dr. Paul Offit's book, *Autism's False Prophets*,[14] his comprehensive view of non–evidence-based treatment for autism, he spoke of the hate mail he still receives. In the terms I am using here, these are the families with complicated grief marked by a failure to achieve acceptance, trapped in unresolved chronic sorrow.

REROUTING DETOURS INTO NON–EVIDENCE-BASED TREATMENT

We, as a mental health community, have long since turned away from blaming parents for their child's autism—which came with insisting on almost-daily psychotherapy for the child, for the mother, for the father, for the couple, and for the family. Instead, today, we offer families basically nothing. We offer almost no family-oriented therapeutic support despite awareness of the rocky road traveled with a child with a disability, particularly a child with autism who gives so much less back socially and looks so normal compared to children with other developmental and physical disabilities. One study of mother-caregivers of children with autism from my UCSF Autism Clinic population found that mothers of children with autism were more stressed as caregivers than older women caring for husbands with Alzheimer's.[7] The older women could emotionally feel rewarded for caring for these seeming strangers by remembering the husband he once had been. The mothers of children with autism have only an old and faded image of their long-ago, hoped-for child that had never emerged if they do not come to feel that Holland can be as nice a place as Paris (the parable used in Chapter 5).

CAM and the Politics of Autism

It is a good thing to have hope. It is a bad thing to feel snookered. One of the things we face with CAM in autism is everyone's feeling of entitlement to a cure. This comes from a belief in a cure being possible *and* within ones' own agency.

This is peculiarly American. Several years ago, my book *The World of the Autistic Child,* was translated into Portuguese by a Portuguese professor of special education, Dr. Luis Miranda-Correia,[15] who then arranged a book tour in Portugal for me. I talked about what autism was and what parents could do to help their child. After each talk, there were almost no questions or discussion, no matter where I went. Parents would chat with me before and after my talks—but asked no questions about what I had said. I asked Dr. Miranda why he thought this was. He said that in Portugal, there are no autism services, that Portuguese are largely quite religiously faithful, and Portuguese parents felt that whatever would happen to their child was in the hands of God. Most Americans view things a little differently: As a wealthy, advanced, first-world society, we should, indeed, do all that is possible. But, willy-nilly doing everything and anything for everyone is not an answer or a plan.

Resetting Priorities

DEVELOPING AUTISM FAMILY WELLNESS PROTOCOLS

There needs to be a will, and a way, to provide mental health resources to every family as they face the diagnosis of autism in their child. Yes, just after the diagnosis, parents are very busy trying to get help for their child. One parent, usually the father, is busy working extra long hours because the other parent, usually the mother, has not or has not fully returned to the workforce. Instead, she finds herself with a new job, coordinating care of their child with autism. The mothers are stressed by having home therapists and services going on for their child 20 to 35 hours a week, running off to speech therapy, fighting on the phone with an insurance provider, trying not to neglect older siblings, or feeling scared to death about their 6-month-old who was conceived before their 2½-year-old was diagnosed with autism, and wondering whether this child also might develop autism.

We have manualized therapy for breast cancer survivors, for vets with post-traumatic stress disorder, for the bereaved. Can't we, shouldn't we, come up with some comparable initiative for parents of children with autism? Some really are walking wounded. Some find their way to therapists they know before even having a child with autism, some to therapists known by friends. These may be good, excellent therapists, but they may not have resources to fully appreciate the complex dynamics of raising a child with autism. These parents need individual or couples therapy focused on the loss of their mutually hoped-for child.

SUPPORTING PARENTS

In the next chapter, as we talk about the anti-vaxxer movement in autism, we will talk more about what can go wrong when you put grieving parents together in mutual self-support groups. In their anxiety, they share the extremes of their child's uncontrolled behavior and their worst fears. They are not yet able to reassure themselves, let alone people they don't know who are similarly traumatized. I see parent support groups for autism as somewhat similar to a 10-step AA (Alcoholics Anonymous) or NA (Narcotics Anonymous) group where everyone seems to want to top one another with stories of how high they have been and what bad things they did while high. Nontherapeutically led parent "support" groups have a dangerous liability to become the breeding ground of the non–evidence-based CAM and antivaccine attitudes through the retelling of radical, angry, and unfounded tales.

Autism family wellness can be defined as supports for both caregivers and for children; for the other siblings; and for the mother and father as a couple. We also need to support the extended family, who need to understand the challenges imposed by a diagnosis of autism so they can provide both tactical and emotional support. How can we do this?

Since retiring from UCSF after 24 years, it was time for me to tackle this problem. In a medical center or other medical setting (pediatrics, child psychiatry) where many children with autism are diagnosed, the standard of care is to carry out a valid and reliable diagnosis and rule out other medical conditions, like a brain disorder or a genetic disorder. Then, off you go to deal with educational and behavioral treatments on your own.

Families need a place to go to talk about helping their children adapt, socialize, and be educated. An early ABA program may be a good starting point, but most ABA service is provided by young technicians who know nothing about how a particular child will likely develop. Parents need autism wellness centers where their child's development can be guided; where the child's changing educational, behavioral, and social needs can be addressed; and where their own emotional needs can be discussed. Parents need help with the challenges of balancing their work lives and their child's autism. Siblings and the "What about me?" question from the autistic child's siblings are on the minds of parents who want to ask not only about what else to do for their child with autism, but also gain reassurance and ideas about how to make sure that time spent on autism is not robbing their other children.

I now have what some have called an "encore career": After leaving academia, I founded a nonprofit center (the Autism Center of Northern California, www.acnc.org), which I hope can become a model for other regions. We provide a one-to-one week-long parent training crash course called JumpStart Learning to Learn designed to support parents in filling in all those hours where there is no formal intervention in place. Parents can make their lives more livable and make their child's ability to progress more robust by knowing how to find teachable moments around daily routines, as well as playtimes.

Our Neurodevelopmental Assessment Clinic provides diagnostic services, but is less focused on identifying possible (untreatable) causes and more on psychoeducation about how a child with autism learns differently and what supports can help compensate for what we call his or her "autistic learning disabilities."

Part of the center is our School and Behavior Consultation Clinic, which works closely with schools to bridge evidence-based educational practices and individualized implementation, using the life skills prognostic framework I talked about in Chapters 4 and 5. We act as docents for parents, visiting potential classrooms for their child, teaching parents how to "see" good programs that match their child's needs. Behavioral consultation is focused on teaching parents techniques they can use to manage their children themselves so they can feel more effective and so family life is not limited by where the child with autism "can" or "can't" go.

Finally, we offer an Autism Home Clinic—based on the idea of a medical home—a place where there is continuity of care from clinicians who have known a child since he or she was diagnosed. Many parents never return to the centers where their child was diagnosed because a majority of these centers focus on diagnosis, not assessing progress or collaborating on family-centric individualized treatment plans based on treatment responses. For "autism homes"/continuity-of-care clinics for autism to develop, medical insurers, now just beginning to see autism as a medical condition, will need to support care continuity, not just early intervention.

In terms of clinical facilities, there is almost nowhere for parents to go with their about-to-be-adults with autism and to explore potentially successful future roads for their life and work. I'd love to add a psychotherapeutic component to this model: individual therapy for parents, couple therapy as husband and wife, as they struggle to redefine their roles in relation to each other while caring for their child with autism, and cognitive behavioral therapy for teens and adults with autism who need a base where they can rehearse their entry into the social and work world.

My feeling is that much of what has fanned the flames of non–evidence-based treatment for autism is the lack of models for ongoing care such as we are trying to do. We, as a clinical care community, don't pull back from parents dealing with a child with a chronic physical condition after it's been diagnosed. There are places to go for continuity of care and for management if you have cystic fibrosis, juvenile rheumatoid arthritis, diabetes, or other chronic conditions. But this is not the case for autism, and also not the case for parents facing other lifelong neurodevelopmental disorders in their children.

What's Next?

In the next chapter, I talk about the autism vaccine wars; the most tragic autism CAM scam of all time that has led to unnecessary disease outbreaks, kids dying of chelation, exorcism, and other quackery. Autism charlatans promoting themselves and their lies have created an enormous public health debacle in America today that has affected much more than the population of families who live with autism. The autism vaccine wars are an extension of the CAM culture we've just been discussing, but unquestionably is the most prominent case example where public health has been negatively affected and some children harmed by the specific treatments we will discuss.

Notes

1. Rimland, B. (1964). *Infantile autism: The syndrome and its implications for a neural theory of behavior*. Englewood Cliffs, NJ: Prentice Hall.

2. Hyman, S. L., Stewart, P. A., Foley, J., Cain, U., Peck, R., Morris, D. D., . . . Smith, T. (2015). The gluten-free/casein-free diet: A double-blind challenge trial in children with autism. *Journal of Autism and Developmental Disorders, 46*(1), 205–220. http://doi.org/10.1007/s10803-015-2564-9

3. Sandler, A. D., Sutton, K. A., DeWeese, J., Girardi, M. A., Sheppard, V., & Bodfish, J. W. (1999). Lack of benefit of a single dose of synthetic human secretin in the treatment of autism and pervasive developmental disorder. *New England Journal of Medicine, 341*(24), 1801–1806. http://doi.org/10.1056/NEJM199912093412404

4. Tisdale, S. (2013, August 23). Voice of the voiceless [Review of book *The reason I jump*, by Naoki Higashida]. *The New York Times*, Sunday Book Review.

5. Siegel, B. (1995). Brief report: Assessing allegations of sexual molestation made through facilitated communication. *Journal of Autism and Developmental Disorders, 25*(3), 319–326.

6. Engber, D. (2015, October 20). The strange case of Anna Stubblefield. *The New York Times*. Retrieved from https://www.nytimes.com/2015/10/25/magazine/the-strange-case-of-anna-stubblefield.html

7. Ayres, J. (1979). *Sensory integration and the child*. Los Angeles, CA: Western Psychological.

8. Optometrists Network. (n.d.). *Vision therapy success stories*. Retrieved from http://www.visiontherapystories.org/vision_autism.html

9. Stewart, P. A., Hyman, S. L., Schmidt, B. L., Macklin, E. A., Reynolds, A., Johnson, C. R., . . . Manning-Courtney, P. (2015). Dietary supplementation in children with autism spectrum disorders: Common, insufficient, and excessive. *Journal of the Academy of Nutrition and Dietetics, 115*(8), 1237–1248.

10. Issacson, R. (2009). *The horse boy: A father's quest to heal his son.* New York, NY: Little Brown/Hachette Books.

11. Scott, M. O. (Director). (2009). *The horse boy* [Motion picture]. United States: Zeitgeist Films.

12. Da Paz, N., Siegel, B., Coccia, M. A., & Epel, E. (2018). Acceptance or despair? Caregiver responses to having a child with autism. *Journal of Autism and Developmental Disorders.* https://doi.org/10.1007/S10803-017-3450-4.

13. Siegel, B. (1997). Parent responses to the diagnosis of autism: Mourning, coping, and adaptation. In D. Cohen & F. Volkmar (Eds.), *Handbook of autism and pervasive developmental disorders* (2nd ed., pp. 745–766). New York, NY: Wiley.

14. Offit, P. A. (2010). *Autism's false prophets: Bad science, risky medicine, and the search for a cure.* New York, NY: Columbia University Press.

15. Siegel, B. (2008). *O Mundo da Crianca com Autismo* [The world of the autistic child]. Porto, Portugal: Porto Editora.

8 }

The Vaccine Wars

I am being proven right about massive vaccinations—the doctors lied. Save our children and their future.

—President Donald Trump, Republican presidential debate, September 2, 2015

To that I say: "Fake News! So sad!" How does the belief that vaccines could possibly cause autism live on? Who believes it? Why?

Do Vaccines Cause Autism?

When I find myself at a social gathering, chit-chat leads someone to ask me, "What kind of work do you do?" When I say I am an academic, a (now retired) professor, and that my field of study is autism, there are two questions I am asked: The first, we talked about in Chapter 2: "Is there more autism these days—or are we just hearing more about it?" The second question I am asked is the one I'll deal with here: "Do you think vaccines cause autism?" My response may be to initially demur and say, "It's not important what *I think*." But, I always continue and immediately add, "What's important is what *the science* shows. The science shows unequivocally that vaccines *do not* cause autism."

For some people who ask me, this question is an opening salvo in their personal war on science. Sometimes, I know it in advance. Say, for example, I am at an evening fundraiser for autism research, and my hostess has pointed out a particular guest as an antivaccine advocate who knows I am on the "other" side. Sometimes, I am outside the autism world and find myself talking to someone with an unvaccinated grandchild or two. She may have a bee in her bonnet about how nice it would be to call her daughter and reassure her that even an expert in autism is not sure vaccines are OK. I do not give her an inch.

Since the demise of the Omnibus Autism Proceedings (an attempt to have the federal government assume liability for hypothesized vaccine-related damage to children with autism), there *does* seem to be a *little* less antivaccine militancy out there. But, it is still out there, mostly dormant, but not dead.

Donald Trump, as he ran for the US presidency, sensed he could tap into this. In front of fellow primary candidates at the time, one of whom is a pediatrician, he asserted that he knew vaccines caused autism. (Apparently a woman who worked for him had told him about her son's autism, and, as she understood it, her son's autism was caused by vaccinations.) Aside from the sheer audacity of saying this, the calculation (or instinct) behind Trump's statement about vaccines and autism was designed to rally individuals with contempt for the scientific process and reach out to individuals lured by authoritarian leadership based simply on demagogic power. (Look what he's done with climate science.) Trump wanted us all to believe what he believes. If he said the woman in his employ was believable, everyone else should find her believable—because he said so. I am not a political scientist, but such a strident statement strikes me as fascism—insistence that you should believe this because I believe this, or you are wrong. It certainly does not rely on scientific reasoning.

Fascism and the Psychology of Bias Against Vaccines

Those against vaccinations often refer to themselves as *anti-vaxxers*. Like habitual complementary and alternative medicine (CAM) adopters, anti-vaxxers indicate that the whole truth about what causes autism and what can be done to help is, for some nefarious reason, being intentionally obscured by mainstream media and by scientists, all under the thrall of Big Pharma.

As we discussed in the last chapter, much of non–evidence-based CAM is harmless, with nothing to lose but one's money and hope that the treatment being pursued will be of benefit in some way. Largely, American individualism dictates that it's fine to spend your money on whatever foolishness you want—as long as you do it in the privacy of your own home and don't hurt others. It is on this basis that the American government doesn't, and in fact has no right to, stop us from taking all the vitamins we can stomach, sculpting our bodies by freezing fat, or spending hours in a hyperbaric oxygen chamber trying to get more oxygen into our brains in case it might make us smarter (or less autistic).

Not vaccinating a child, when study after study finds vaccinations to be nothing but beneficial, crosses a line: Parents of unvaccinated children will talk about how they are fine with taking the risk of their child contracting a disease a vaccine prevents. Such a statement neglects to factor in the social good conferred by herd immunity. (Herd immunity is an epidemiological factor wherein the vast majority of people are vaccinated, so lines of transmission of a contagious disease are few should the disease reach the unvaccinated population.) Vaccine NIMBY (not in my back yard) is a selfish attitude that disregards that there are some in any population who can't be vaccinated because of immune diseases or being immune suppressed because of conditions like cancer or HIV treatments. Imagine bringing your child with cancer to school, knowing he or she is immune suppressed and wondering how many nonvaccinated children at the school are cutting a wide path for infectious disease to easily infect your child. In schools with a significant number of unvaccinated children, your child in cancer treatment is basically forced to give up his or her right to go to school with friends.

Becoming an Anti-Vaxxer

For some families, their child with autism is a child whom Big Pharma negligently caused to be autistic to bolster their bottom line. The illogic is that vaccines unarguably prevent disease—so what would be the point of just causing another illness (autism) in the service of preventing others (measles, mumps, rubella, diphtheria, pertussis, tetanus, polio, etc.). A corollary of this reasoning is that if Big Pharma *caused* autism, Big Pharma should *pay* to treat and raise this child. To support this kind of faulty reasoning, it has been argued that the diseases prevented by vaccines aren't nearly as bad as autism. As a group, though, these diseases formed the main causes of childhood mortality in the nineteenth and earlier twentieth centuries. Additional fuel for the anti-vaxxers' engine is the cold comfort that Big Pharma and not one's own genes caused the child's autism.

In July 2015, Frank Bruni of the *New York Times* wrote an op-ed piece, entitled "California, Camelot, and Vaccines."[1] He railed against the antivaccine advocacy of Robert Kennedy, Jr., one of a slew of celebrities who would like us to believe that their beliefs are better beliefs, I guess, because they are celebrities. This must have been the common ground Kennedy and Trump shared during their preinauguration powwow at Trump Tower, both certain that vaccines cause autism—because they *know*. Bruni pointed also to how any not-famous parent can also "know" by googling around until he or she finds a website with "studies" that cite Kennedy and validate what he thinks and also just happens to confirm what that parent really also thinks. Bruni said, "This is the erudition in the age of cyberspace: You surf until you reach the conclusion you are after. You click your way to validation, confusing the presence of a website with the plausibility of an argument. Although the Internet could be making all of us smarter, it makes many of us stupider, because it is not just a magnet for the curious. It's a sinkhole for the gullible." He is absolutely right about this in reference to anti-vaxxers (and a few other things, too).

Vaccines Are the Only Cause of Autism That Really Has Been Ruled Out

DR. PAUL OFFIT

There is high-quality authoritative work out there that covers the autism vaccine wars. Anyone really interested in knowing the blow-by-blow story must read *Autism's False Prophets: Bad Science, Risky Medicine, and the Search for a Cure* (2008) by Dr. Paul Offit, a pediatrician, chief of infectious diseases at Children's Hospital Philadelphia and professor of medicine at the University of Pennsylvania School of Medicine.[2] Dr. Offit has devoted a lifetime of research to the science of vaccination and was affronted as he watched the American public turn against the measles-mumps-rubella (MMR) vaccine in particular and vaccination of children in general because of fear of autism. His second book on the topic, *Deadly Choices: How the Anti-Vaccine Movement Threatens Us All* (2011),[3] focused on what the American public learns about autism and vaccines through the American media. He covered how reporting on vaccine safety and effectiveness has been skewed by appearances of celebrities, diatribes by talk show hosts, and one-sided news interviews—all fueling TV ratings. Offit provided a chronology of protests, rallies, and government testimony by these media stars and by angry parents. He detailed websites and public events funded by wealthy angry dads.

In September 2014, Dr. Offit wrote about vaccines for the *Wall Street Journal* audience.[4] He noted that the very wealthy families living between Malibu and Marina del Rey in Los Angeles County, California, were about as likely to vaccinate their children as residents of the countries of Chad or South Sudan—only about 40 percent were vaccinated. He noted that, at the same time, over 8,000 California children had been hospitalized for whooping cough (also known as pertussis, the *P* in the ubiquitous DPT [diphtheria-pertussis-tetanus] vaccine) in 2014, with 250 of them hospitalized, 58 in intensive care. In 2010, there had been an earlier outbreak of whooping cough, larger than any since 1947—in this outbreak, 10 children died. If 8,000 California schoolchildren had been sickened by tainted boxes of school lunch milk or 8,000 had broken arms on a new type of jungle gym, there probably would have been a swifter demand for action. Only after a widely publicized 2015 outbreak of measles at Disneyland,[5] where kids infected there took measles back to their home states and countries, did California pass SB 277 mandating vaccination of California schoolchildren, while closing huge loopholes allowing personal and religious exemptions.[6]

ANTIVACCINE MOVEMENT AS CULTURE WAR

A very interesting analysis and counterpunch to the antivaccine movement has been provided by Dr. Roy Grinkler, who is an ethnologist and parent of a daughter with autism. Grinkler is a professor of anthropology at George Washington University, and his book, *Unstrange Minds: Remapping the World of Autism* (2007),[7] is a cultural anthropology of the autism community.

After his daughter, Isabel, was diagnosed with autism, Grinkler read as much as he could and talked to all sorts of people about their views on autism. He found himself bombarded by unexpectedly disparate and strong positions on what was going on with his daughter. His professional antennae as an ethnographer went up. It led him to focus his intellectual lens and academic methodology on understanding autism from where it sat at the intersection of culture and illness.

ANTI-VAXXERS: SOLDIERS IN A CULTURAL WAR

Offit's journey into autism started in medicine, not anthropology or sociology. As a physician and immunology researcher, he understood that the public health perspective, based on tenets of evidence-based medicine, was becoming distorted by all sorts of disinformation emanating from certain quarters of the online and print autism community. From Offit's perspective, the anti-vaxxers were antiscience. From Grinkler's perspective, as an anthropologist, he saw the vaccine wars as a culture war. He argued that the vaccine wars were both a war against science and a war against determinism. In Offit's war, the sides are clearly delineated: science versus antiscience. Grinkler's war was between those who accept the paternalism of science versus those whose own seeing is believing and may be equal in veracity to conclusions derived by the scientific method. Grinkler's perspective led me to consider subtitling this book "The Vulnerability of Truth." Especially important today is that the anti-vaxxer war against determinism by science epitomizes what seems to drive the president of the United States and has begun to drive all sorts of policy change in the United States. The vaccine wars can now be seen as the leading edge of thinking ascendant in the White House. In some ways, Grinkler's perspective on anti-vaxxers as litigating a culture war was a prescient analysis that now can broadly be observed in a more widespread struggle between mainstream media and what has come to be called "fake news," that is, facts that do not support a certain worldview.

Science and conclusions that are "scientific" are based on such complex and specialized analysis that most of us will readily accept what we are told is scientifically, empirically valid, much as Renaissance men accepted God as an article of faith. Most of us who might someday submit to chemotherapy for cancer will be satisfied to go ahead based on a fairly primitive idea of how agents of chemotherapy should affect cancer cell biology. The anti-vaxxers similarly can rely on such primitive ideas of cause and effect and are satisfied to allow them to stand for as much as they feel they need to know. If an anti-vaxxer feels he or she can trace their child's autism to the day, week, or month that a child was vaccinated or to a fever on the day or week of his or her last vaccination, the anti-vaxxer will be able to find a community on the Internet who report the same. Finding this undoubtedly reinforces the feeling that, indeed, there is substantial proof that mainstream science may well be engaged in a cover-up when it concludes vaccines are safe; you've now met many who are believing as you believe.

THE PSYCHOLOGY OF ANTI-VAXXERS

What I will try to add to what has already been said by Offit (the scientist) and Grinkler (the cultural anthropologist) is a psychology of parents of children with autism as it bears on the vaccine controversies. Why has it been autism, and why not intellectual disability, why not AIDS, why not some other public health scourge that engenders so much antipathy and downright distrust of the medical establishment?

My additions to this Offit's history of the science of the antivaccine movement, and Grinkler's cultural anthropology of it, will be to focus on the "why" and "how" of human nature that may have led to the narrative that has supported the fall in US vaccination rates. What drives anti-vaxxers to have such great doubt about the beneficence of public health agencies that promote vaccinations and outright disbelief in pronouncements by scientists that vaccines are safe?

The heart of this matter, I believe, comes from the anger and shame that some parents may experience when they start to imagine what it will feel like to tell others that their child has autism. It is a narcissistic injury because it can fracture one's sense of self-efficacy. Perhaps overly narcissistic people (or very highly successful people) are the most badly injured. Friends and family may have sensed something was wrong with this child, maybe even urged an autism evaluation. It can hurt that someone you resent was right. Maybe there are places you don't go or can't go because of your child's behavior. You may feel outcast, so you don't want to, or feel that you can't, be with others in your social network. The anti-vaxxer community offers a new home of fellow travelers you can talk to about all this.

HERD MENTALITY

The search for authority, especially a search for authority that bucks the norms, was what Grinkler saw as fundamental to the anti-vaxxer culture and that it appealed to certain personalities. (That's why I quoted Donald Trump on vaccines at the beginning of this chapter.) Once "inside the tent" of the new anti-establishment authority, not only are you free of what the mainstream expects you to say and do (like have your child vaccinated), but also you are now included in a new and accepting culture. This anti-vaxxer culture, with its own clear tenets, gives your life (upended by the eye-opening demands of parenting a child with autism) new direction. Identification with the antivaccine movement offers a new place where you can be vindicated that they, like you, understand the true story, that vaccines caused your child's autism—not your genetics, not the way you have raised your child, or anything else anyone might have said you had done wrong.

What do you all believe as a member of this new group? What and who do you worship inside your tent? You believed in those things that delineated you from the opposite (and wrong) beliefs of the autism mainstream still out there getting their children one vaccine after another. You believed the mainstream (which is now to be suspect about everything having to do with autism) was wrong (about vaccines, about diet, about CAM treatments), and that your new group is the one in the know, not them. Anti-vaxxers can comfortably talk among themselves on the Internet, away from the approbation of doctors and even family members who may disagree. Your reference point for social support shifts to this new group, from those you may have relied on before you had a child with autism. The more you interact on the Internet with other anti-vaxxers, the more entrenched your distance from conventional ideas becomes.

MEDICINE VERSUS ALCHEMY

Suspicion of vaccines is rooted in suspicion of medicine. One hundred years ago, most people knew much less about what went on inside their bodies than they know now. Awareness of what doctors understood (which also was much less) was not even faintly understood by most people who received medical care. A doctor's medical care was something that happened only after home remedies didn't work.

The idea of preventive health care, including vaccinations for feared and endemic diseases, just did not exist in the near past. Instead, a tremendous ersatz knowledge base guided much of what we now call wellness behavior and primary care. Historically, this knowledge base was culture specific and religion specific, and much was passed by word of mouth. These days, the old word-of-mouth way of knowing maps pretty well onto Internet knowing. For a scientifically minded person, word-of-mouth knowledge now can be subjected to verification by examining any objective research that has tested causal hypotheses for a word-of-mouth theory. The problem is that very few of us have PubMed accounts that can take us to primary research, and only a small number of Internet users explore Google Scholar articles as opposed to first-hit websites in a search to verify a speculative idea.

Another barrier to straightforward acceptance of science is American individualism and the right to self-determination. Increasingly, in the era of "fake news" awareness, this translates into a right to believe what you want to believe. But this is not new either. As examples, there are long-standing formal antimedicine movements, such as the Christian Scientists and the Jehovah's Witnesses. The Christian Scientists feel the Bible shows that cure comes from prayer alone. The Jehovah's Witnesses believe the Bible's words warn of loss of eternal life if you have a blood transfusion—taking the flesh (blood) of another. In some cases, American law may step in, removing a child needing a blood transfusion for life-saving treatment—and charging parents as accessories to murder if the child dies of a treatable illness. (Parents often are found guilty, but usually receive reduced charges, perhaps an indication of American reluctance to censure what goes on in the privacy of a home.)

The Children Act by Ian McEwan[8] is a fictional exploration of the issues brought up when an English High Court judge must decide whether a teen son of Jehovah's Witnesses should be ordered to undergo a likely life-saving transfusion against parental beliefs. The parents' religious faithfulness runs in tandem with an immutable antiauthoritarianism toward the state. In *The Children Act,* parents regard it as their right to make a decision that will likely kill their only child—but preserve his chance for an eternal life. The authoritarian strictures of religion echo in antivaccine parents willing to do whatever the leaders of their movement say will heal the autism (like chelation), even if there is a risk of it killing the child. Like Jehovah's Witnesses, the antivaccine movement has been built on strong faith. Much as most of us "believe" in science, anti-vaxxers believe just as fervently in antiscience—specifically, that science has cynically been used against their child to create a product (the vaccines) that will make Big Pharma money at the risk of knowingly damaging their child. This is what Grinkler saw as a culture war, rebellion against the paternalism of science playing out in refusal to vaccinate one's child.

THE HISTORY OF THE VACCINE WARS

With many thanks to Dr. Offit, I recap here some of the key events he has detailed, as he is really our key historian and witness to the vaccine wars. My goal is to tie the growing acrimony of anti-vaxxers to the unfolding of events in these vaccine wars.

Dr. Andrew Wakefield was the doctor who started the MMR exodus, in 1998, by publishing in the premier medical journal *Lancet*, a scientific article linking MMR, gastrointestinal problems, and autism.[9] The article was later retracted for misinterpretation of data, failure to obtain consents for some of the research procedures, and conflict of interest because Wakefield was receiving support for his work from lawyers litigating against UK vaccine manufacturers. Eventually, Wakefield lost his medical license in the United Kingdom; the *Lancet* editor, horrified by the irregularities associated with the publication of the Wakefield paper, worked with Wakefield's coauthors, the large majority of whom voted for and received an opportunity to retract the *Lancet* article in 2004 in an attempt to stave off falling vaccination rates. For those who may have wondered what Wakefield might be able to do after having his UK medical career abruptly ended, he's making movies. This is a perfectly understandable transition for someone who played on appearances and apparently cannot produce well-regarded science. In early 2016, Andrew Wakefield, the "deity" of the anti-vaxxers "religion," directed and premiered a new movie, *Vaxxed: From Cover Up to Catastrophe.*[10.] It was to be included in the prestigious New York

City Tribeca Film Festival—until a hullabaloo from the scientific community forced its withdrawal.

WAKEFIELD'S MOMENT

Dr. Andrew Wakefield, who is a gastroenterologist by training, was affiliated with Royal Free Hospital in London when he "discovered" the autism vaccine link. Wakefield had a history of striving to see obvious relationships others had not. The first one he had seen had to do with Crohn's disease. His Crohn's work made an initial big splash, and he even published a paper suggesting that the measles vaccine might cause Crohn's. Although he later admitted that subsequent data had not supported that assertion, first there was a measles vaccine scare that had arisen in reaction to his initial claims that the measles vaccine could cause Crohn's. This work got Wakefield, a gastroenterologist, into the ballpark of work on vaccines and the gut and potential adverse, unintended responses to vaccines. This likely made Wakefield the expert to meet for personal injury lawyers wondering if there was a vaccine-gut-autism connection.

In February 1998, Wakefield called a press conference in advance of publication of his small preliminary study in *Lancet,* the most prestigious of British medical journals, where he and colleagues reported showing autism in children who all had a similar pattern of gut findings. He attributed these differences to the MMR vaccine, particularly the measles component, as having caused autism and also hypothesized a mechanism—a leaky gut where virus proteins could roam free and ultimately do damage to the autistic brain. He really didn't have sufficient subjects (autistic or controls) to yet support this possible interpretation of his findings, but the prestige of *Lancet* and the Royal Free Hospital won the day, and journalists took him at his word. It is neither customary nor appropriate to publicize findings before publication in a scientific journal. If your work is deemed important, after publication the press should come to you, not you to the press.

HOW VACCINE HYSTERIA SPREAD

Nevertheless, as soon as Wakefield first announced his work in 1998, all sorts of parents suddenly were stepping forward talking about how *their* child had changed after receiving an MMR vaccine. On November 12, 2000, Ed Bradley of *60 Minutes* showed Wakefield addressing a room of parents, asking parents to stand if their child had first developed signs of autism after receiving the MMR vaccine.[11] One after another of the parents stood up, making for great TV. Parents began to talk about how bad and persistent their autistic child's diarrhea also was, presumably because Wakefield, as a gastroenterologist, had examined the intestines of his study subjects and posited that the whole thing could be explained by a brain-gut-vaccine connection.

Interestingly, prior to Wakefield, I'd heard much more concern from parents about chronic and recurring ear infections in their children with autism, not diarrhea. Diarrhea? I could see how fluid-filled ears might slow language development, but diarrhea? Leaky guts? I called my colleague at the University of California at San Francisco who headed pediatric gastroenterology, Dr. Mel Hayman, and asked if he could explain all this to me. I still couldn't get a convincing picture of how a gut might leak or how high gut permeability might then cause autism. I had never heard much about diarrhea in the years of developmental histories I'd taken from parents of children with autism. Nevertheless, the autism-gut-vaccine connection was all over the media: It was repeatedly said that autism was caused by the MMR vaccine. Vaccine rates in the United Kingdom and United States quickly plummeted. At the same time, rates of reported cases of autism continued to rise in both countries. If vaccines caused autism, how did fewer vaccinated children result in more children diagnosed with autism?

A couple of years after the *Lancet* paper, in April 2000, a US Congressman, Dan Burton, who has a grandson with autism, held US congressional hearings to explore this new public health crisis. Wakefield and several others testified, supporting Wakefield's "MMR-causes-autism" hypothesis. The evidence being presented to Congress seemed initially to support Wakefield's claims.

Then, one key witness who spoke against Wakefield's claims, Dr. Brent Taylor, actually a colleague of Wakefield at the Royal Free Hospital, referred to epidemiology from a large national data set. He testified that rates of autism had *climbed*, even as rates of vaccination had *declined* in the past 2 years—seriously bringing into question the relationship between the two. Importantly, Wakefield had reported on just a handful of children, but all sorts of national databases from different countries with thousands of cases of vaccinated children began to refute what Wakefield had argued and, instead, support what Dr. Taylor had reported to Congress: Vaccines and autism were not correlated.

Nevertheless, the rates of vaccination in the United States and United Kingdom continued to plummet, certainly buoyed by Burton's congressional hearings, which were seen by many as another of his witch hunts directed at Big Pharma. The circus-like publicity and notoriety the hearings brought to pediatric vaccinations had the result of making the general public more aware, more afraid, and vaccine rates fell further.

In addition to Wakefield, an assortment of purveyors of alternative biomedical autism treatments jumped on Wakefield's bandwagon with claims of new cures based on Wakefield's work. These ranged from the innocuous, but unsupported, treatments like the simple use of vitamin A, which had allegedly been depleted by vaccination, to extreme interventions like plasmapheresis, steroids, or intravenous gamma globulin to destroy harmful antibodies supposedly left by the vaccine, even when "live" vaccines were not given. All this exploited a psychology of fear: that maybe the vaccines *were* live, even though they were said not to be. If Big Pharma had told one lie about vaccines being safe, how could anyone be sure there were not more undiscovered lies about vaccines?

TREATING "HERD IMMUNITY" WITH IMPUNITY

Despite further studies showing that vaccination and autism rates were not correlated, fear of autism continued to drive vaccine rates down. The pediatric community was slow to realize the magnitude of what was happening and to take it seriously. As an illustration of this, I remember that in 2002, 4 years after Wakefield's *Lancet* paper but 2 years before its retraction, I was doing training on diagnostic procedures for autism with a community developmental disabilities agency in Fresno, California. A 2½-year-old was brought in for a demonstration assessment. He had two older brothers; the oldest had been vaccinated and had later developed autism; the second, had no vaccination and no autism. This child I was seeing, the third brother, also was not vaccinated, but he, too, clearly met criteria for autism. I wrote this case up in a letter to the editor for *Journal of Pediatrics*—which wrote back, thanking me, but rejecting it for publication because he did not see the topic of autism and vaccines as being of interest to his readership.

Vaccination rates continued to fall. Rates were falling so low in some areas where antivaccine sentiments were very strong (like Sacramento, California) that "herd immunity" for the population was compromised, and eventually, there was a measles outbreak there. Many antivaccine parents developed a selfish NIMBY mentality to vaccines—happy if others wanted to vaccinate, happy to accept the benefit that would accrue to their child as the rare unvaccinated member of his or her "herd," but not willing to take the perceived risk that their child might develop autism. Parents who would not vaccinate were resented by parents who did, and fear of autism became socially divisive. As a backdrop to what was going on, it is worthwhile to note that measles was all but eradicated in the United States in 2000. By 2014, the Centers for Disease Control and Prevention (CDC) reported 667 cases nationally. By 2016, it was reported that many American parents had a poor understanding of herd immunity, the importance of vaccines, and diseases vaccines prevented; in short, they didn't understand why it was critical to both their child's health and public health to be vaccinated.[12]

WAKEFIELD'S RECKONING

In February 2004, an investigative journalist for the *Sunday Times of London,* Brian Deer, broke a story about Wakefield's original research and its claims[13]: First, he revealed, Wakefield had never bothered to obtain full research permissions from his hospital's human subjects protection committee for his work, even though it had involved young children who received spinal anesthesia and had fiber-optic scopes inserted into their intestines from their anuses, intestinal biopsies, and significant blood collection. For me, as a researcher who has written and rewritten protocols to human research committees to justify why 40 minutes of answering questionnaires will not be too invasive for a parent of a child with autism, Wakefield's neglect of subjects' rights was egregious.

Second, Wakefield had mentioned in the *Lancet* article's publication that the study was supported financially by acceptable sources like his hospital, but this was not the complete story. It is customary to list funders, as he did, but also to disclose anything that might be perceived as a conflict of interest specifically to convince the reader that the conclusions were not subject to findings that may have been desired by a funder. Wakefield failed to note, in fact, that his *main* funder for his 1988 *Lancet* paper was a personal injury law firm. This law firm was then actively litigating that the MMR vaccine had caused autism in their plaintiffs. Moreover, 5 of the 12 children in Wakefield's 1998 study were plaintiffs in the law firm's suit. Wakefield had been retained as an "expert" to provide supportive data.

OFFIT'S "FALSE PROPHET"

As Offit tells the story, when Wakefield started his legal consultation on the MMR vaccine, there was no leaky gut theory that went with how the MMR vaccines might cause autism. Wakefield only later introduced this notion as a post hoc causal hypothesis as he attempted to link his gastrointestinal data, blood samples, and the clinical diagnosis of autism. Originally, Wakefield had asserted that his *Lancet* study had been inspired by the many children with autism having bowel disorders who had found their way to his practice. In fact, something closer to the opposite was true. When the plaintiffs' lawyers found another vaccinated child with autism with bowel problems, he was sent to Wakefield for potential inclusion in his study, which could bolster the legal claims. Wakefield was no autism specialist until brought into this lawsuit.

There had been 13 authors on the Wakefield paper. When Richard Horton, editor of *Lancet*, confronted Wakefield coauthors about what Wakefield had done, they were shocked. In academia, related professionals commonly list one another as authors, trusting the ethics of the lead author. For example, I have been listed as a coauthor of brain imaging studies on autism in children with IQs above 70 because my lab has done the IQ testing, not because I can read brain scans, and agree that the brain scans have been correctly interpreted. I'm just vouching for the IQ scores.

Looking back on the problems Wakefield created with his later-retracted *Lancet* paper on autism and vaccines, what happened was not completely surprising: Wakefield's earlier Crohn's disease study, and his subsequent acknowledgment that others could not replicate his assertion that there was a link between measles vaccine and Crohn's disease, makes it rather less surprising that, as Brian Deer, the *Times of London* journalist had revealed, Wakefield also misled readers about his MMR and autism findings, a second incident of alluding to findings that couldn't yet fairly be concluded from his data.

The Offit's book tells how after the *Lancet* paper, Wakefield had convinced his hospital to sponsor a video on serious concerns about the MMR vaccine, offering instead an alternative vaccine to which the hospital and Wakefield would hold the patent. This agreement fell apart, eventually, when the majority of Wakefield's coauthors agreed that they needed to call for a retraction of the *Lancet* paper. Nevertheless, Wakefield had profited from the paper, having received $800,000 from the law firm retaining him as an expert to link the MMR vaccine and autism. Five of Wakefield's autistic subjects in the *Lancet* paper were clients of this law firm.

But the damage was done; the vaccine scare had taken firm hold. Needless to say, a study to support a new vaccine market as a joint venture of Wakefield and the Royal Free Hospital never emerged. Instead, Wakefield left his position at the Royal Free and lost his license to practice medicine in the United Kingdom. He was unrepentant (and was soon embraced by a cult of his believers in Texas, where he moved after being drummed out of British medicine).

How had Wakefield's paper made it into *Lancet* in the first place? Richard Horton, *Lancet's* editor, who ultimately had been responsible for the paper's publication, did argue that the peer review process in which others in the field read a paper before it is published to determine whether methods are solid, as well as editorials (commentary published simultaneously) warning there were not enough data in the paper to support a change in vaccination practices, had been sufficient safeguards. Many saw this as a weak defense, given that *Lancet* publishes only 5 percent of its submissions each year and given that Wakefield earlier had produced work on Crohn's disease that no one could subsequently validate. It is hard to understand how Wakefield got as far as he did.

Fear of the MMR Vaccine Continues

One might think that the discrediting of Wakefield's work would have put an end to fear of the MMR vaccine. At the time, I thought it would. Instead, seeds of suspicion about vaccinations grew: The numbers of vaccines, the ages at which each was given, and great concern about the expected and transitory fevers after a vaccine became great sources of concern for many parents because other parents who linked their child's development of autism to vaccinations would have reported a fever after vaccination. This was all Internet chatter; nothing in the medical literature supported justification of these fears.

IT MUST BE THE MERCURY

Vaccine fear had become rampant after Wakefield's *Lancet* paper. What was it about the MMR vaccine, people wondered? Some speculated that the increase in autism was due to the fact that there were *so many* vaccines these days. But, all vaccines approved by the Food and Drug Administration (FDA) had undergone extensive safety testing before being licensed for manufacture. If it wasn't the vaccine itself, what else could it be?

Suspicion fell on mercury used to preserve vaccine vials. It was known that methyl-mercury was a bad actor, and after an industrial plant contaminated a bay in Japan with it, fish died, as did birds and animals who ate the fish. People who ate the fish also got sick, and some of them also died. Methyl-mercury in a high dose had acted as a neurotoxin.

But the mercury compound in vaccines was different: A different mercury compound, *ethyl-mercury,* was used. For a very long time, ethyl-mercury was in wide use on its own as an antiseptic. Most Americans know ethyl-mercury as the widely used antiseptic, Mercurochrome, that orangey stuff that comes in a little brown bottle with a stick applicator. You can still buy Mercurochrome and Merthiolate at any drugstore as a common, self-administered antiseptic. If you are over 50, your mother probably used it on you when you scraped your knee and, even used in pure form, did not cause you to develop signs of autism.

The vaccine manufacturers first tested and then used tiny amounts of ethyl-mercury to preserve vaccines. Later, they developed and tested a further version of ethyl-mercury, thimerosol, which was then shown to be equally effective in preserving the sterility of vaccines. The FDA approved thimerosol's safety after a study of adults who were given 10,000 times what babies got in all their vaccines. These subjects showed no symptoms of mercury poisoning, nothing like what had been seen in the poisoned Japanese living near the plant discharging methyl-mercury. Meanwhile, epidemiological studies from the United States and Scandinavian countries continued to show autism rising as vaccination rates fell and autism rising even after the ethyl-mercury preservative thimerosol (the original culprit) was removed as a vaccine preservative.

What started as a fear of thimerosol, the ethyl-mercury preservative in the MMR vaccine, has spread to a fear of vaccines without preservatives, a fear of too many vaccines, and a fear of vaccines given too close together. The fear that vaccines may be linked to autism has spread to a generalized fear that even a transitory and mild adverse response to a vaccine, like a fever, might lead to brain damage. Yes, this is scary. But this is why we have science—to reassure us that mild adverse events are not the same as catastrophic events. It is really hard for many anxious parents not to confabulate these when they don't really understand how vaccines work.

In the spirit of full disclosure, I must write that not long ago I accompanied my daughter to my granddaughter's 18-month pediatric well-check. I promised

I would keep my mouth shut and not make a peep about vaccines to her pediatrician. My daughter has been a shot separator/vaccine number minimizer. She knows I do not agree, but life is about picking battles. She does not know it, but the shot separation strategy appears to have originated with Wakefield himself when asked in an interview whether he would have vaccinated his own children given his research, and he said he would have separated the different vaccines.

CHELATION

Perhaps the most dangerous chapter of the antivaccine hysteria started in 2001 when two (nonphysician) mothers got a paper published in a small circulation bulletin called *Medical Hypotheses*.[14] *Medical Hypotheses* is not a peer-reviewed medical journal. *Medical Hypotheses* has published some fringe, unsupported commentary. The best thing about this journal is that no serious academic would ever consider publishing in it—or reading it. Nevertheless, these mothers, one with a child with autism, another with a child with language problems, asserted that they had searched the "literature" and concluded that dysphasia, autism, and mercury poisoning all had the same symptoms. Both their children had received thimerosol-containing vaccines. The two moms who had published their concerns about the relation between autism and mercury had gone on to suggest that chelation, administration of more chemicals designed to bind to and then eliminate mercury from the body, could remedy the problem they had speculated was caused by thimerosol preservative in vaccines.

Chelation is a rarely used technique—called into use when a child, for example, manages to ingest a large amount of lead-containing paint chips. Recently in the United States, children in Flint, Michigan, have been lead poisoned from a thoughtless change to their community's water supply. Some of these children may be chelated, but even in this instance, there is no public health initiative to do so for all children because chelation removes not only the "bad" metals like methyl-mercury, but also iron, potassium, and other metals the body needs for its homeostasis.

THE GEIRERS

However, based on the *Medical Hypotheses* paper, the Geiers, a father-and-son team (Mark, a physician, and David, a biology major, respectively) working apart from any regulated laboratory, gave DMSA (dimercaptosuccinic acid, a chelating agent) to 200 children with autism and analyzed the results. Drawing specious conclusions from their data, they became heralded as the "scientists" who had proved chelation worked. Basically, they classified any improvement a parent could report as due to chelation, irrespective of other interventions a child was also receiving. (If you want to produce a placebo effect, rely on parent report of whether that parent saw any kind of gains from a treatment mainstream doctors have counseled him or her would be dangerous and ineffective.)

The same physician-and-son team and their colleagues met with similar "success" doing other peculiar things, like giving Lupron to reduce testosterone. The thought was maybe that males with autism were "too male" (there was "male brain" research, observations of supposedly unprovoked aggression and agitation) that might be helped by Lupron's effect—essentially chemical castration (as might be used in a male-to-female gender transition). What they did was to bring a new angle to the old vitamin B_{12} treatment, which was to "correct" alterations in presumably defective cellular metabolism; in this case, the defects were presumably caused by the ethyl-mercury (heretofore considered a biologically benign compound, but which they considered just as "bad" as methyl-mercury, the kind in the drinking water in Flint, Michigan).

The Geiers had not waited on basic immunological research on vaccines or the CDC for more epidemiological reports to be sure there was a relationship between vaccines and autism. Correlational studies such as what the *Medical Hypotheses* paper had relied on were misleading because saying that children with autism had very largely been vaccinated is equivalent to saying that children with autism have very largely been breastfed—so maybe breastfeeding should be examined as a cause of autism. (Correlation does not confirm causation.) Despite the fallacious logic behind their work, the Geiers were seen in the anti-vaxxers web space as able to cure vaccine-damaged children by using chelation.

Popular media interviews helped spread the word. One jewel in this crown of growing evidence against vaccines was a disinformative *Rolling Stone* article by Robert Kennedy, Jr., who had joined the fray via his interest in cleaning rivers polluted by "bad" mercury.[15] His *Rolling Stone* article was later subject to retractions on several points, but the battle had been joined as a popular cause, and by the mid-2000s, there were few American parents who didn't have a pang of anxiety about vaccinating their babies.

LESS THAN MINISCULE

The amount of thimerosol in vaccines, which, remember, is the "good" mercury, is so tiny it can be hard to imagine. I was discussing this one night over dinner in Honolulu with a Johns Hopkins–trained pediatric epidemiologist who directed early intervention programs for the state of Hawaii, Dr. Linda Rosen. In Hawaii, compared to the rest of the United States, everyone, including pregnant women, eat a lot more fish. Fish is obviously abundant, and the room to grow even chicken, let alone beef cattle, is pretty limited. This pediatric epidemiologist wanted to study methyl-mercury (bad mercury) levels in pregnant Hawaiian women to see if it presented a public health risk. She was quick to point out, as I already knew, that the vast majority of Hawaiian babies are healthy. She continued by pointing out that even the ahi poke appetizer (fresh tuna marinated in soy) I was eating at our dinner probably had more bad mercury than the amount of good mercury babies get in all the vaccines they receive in the first year of life—very reassuring.

Since I have written to tell this tale, I believe I was not harmed by my appetizer that night or by all the other mercury-containing fish I have eaten in the intervening 10 or so years. Nevertheless, thimerosol became the focus of big-time litigation brought by parents of children with autism against vaccine manufacturers.

THE AMERICAN ACADEMY OF PEDIATRICS RESPONDED COUNTERPRODUCTIVELY

Around 1999, vaccine makers actually had begun to remove thimerosol from vaccines at the behest of the American Academy of Pediatrics (AAP). Although thimerosol had been tested as safe and its ethyl-mercury was not the bad methyl-mercury, all of that had become conflated in the minds of the public, and even in the minds of some primary care health practitioners, as public hysteria around vaccines had increased. The idea behind the removal was that the risk of vaccines becoming contaminated (and needing a preservative like thimerosol in the first place) was so very small that they didn't need a preservative after all.

Unsurprisingly, this was received by the public as an admission that maybe thimerosol was *not* as safe as it had been said to be. Maybe there *was* something to worry about in having one's child vaccinated. The effect was that vaccination rates continued to fall even after the vaccines became preservative free. Interestingly, some Scandinavian countries had gone thimerosol free even earlier than the United States, and their rates of autism climbed in tandem with rates in the United States, with no blip in incidence rates when thimerosol was removed. (In Chapter 2, I detailed how changes in diagnostic practices during this period better account for the rise in autism diagnosis than any factor related to vaccines.)

THE TEXAS TAPES

In the mid-2000s, at the apex of the vaccine furor, I was contacted by a legal group representing some of the vaccine manufacturers. One plaintiff had submitted evidence of the MMR vaccine having caused his child's autism, and the lawyers were very interested to have this evidence examined carefully. The evidence was a box of VHS tapes. A father in Texas had videotaped 3 minutes of his child's life every day for the first 3 years. He had reasoned that we do not remember our first 3 years, so the videos would be a great gift to his son someday. The lawyers wanted me to watch the tapes. This was north of 50 hours of videotapes. There were not enough hours in the day for me to do this project as they ideally conceived it. We agreed that a student finishing his MA in early childhood special education who worked in my clinic and taught preschool children with autism could watch all the tapes. We agreed that both the grad student and I would remain blind to the boy's vaccination schedule. My student watched all 50 hours of the tapes and abstracted 2½ hours to an executive summary tape that he and I watched together. The 2½-hour tape was to focus on anything that could show behavior that clearly was or was not consistent with autism across the age span of the tapings.

The summary tape was amazing. The little fellow starts out strong: He hams for the camera from an early age, loves being read a story, and looks for how he can be the center of attention. He is jubilant when everyone claps for him at his first birthday, and all eyes are on him.

Between 21 and 22 months of age there is a change—crash and burn. He does not make eye contact any more, even when asked. He does not enjoy being read a book any longer, just squirms away. By his second birthday party, he does not want to get near that burning cake. He covers his ears, shrieks, and rocks in his high chair when sung "Happy Birthday." Along with other things we could see, he clearly met autism criteria by 24 months of age.

My student and I then met with the lawyers. We showed them 20 minutes of the 2½-hour tape—with excerpts from birth to his third birthday—focusing on the period of the boy's critical changes, 21 to 22 months of age. The boy is clearly among those with autism who has experienced significant developmental regression—his at 21 to 22 months. A typical time for regression seems to be 16–28 months—if that is to occur according to the literature. We told the lawyers that our best guess would be that if this little boy developed autism as a result of the MMR vaccine, he must have received it at 21 to 22 months old. They unblinded us. It turns out he was given the bolus of his vaccinations on schedule—with the MMR vaccine at 15 months of age, right on schedule. We go back and look at the tapes some more. Nothing special at the 15-month mark is noted, just chugging along his developmental trajectory at that point—looking just fine, even though he was just vaccinated with the MMR vaccine. For me, this intensive single-case study confirmed that the age range for autistic regression (for reasons still only hypothesized) and age range during which a child receives many of his or her vaccinations just happen to overlap. In this case, the regression with onset of autism happened 6 or 7 months after the MMR vaccination—with no changes observed between 15 and 21 months, the half-year after the MMR was administered and signs of autism were first evident.

NO STATISTICAL CORRELATION

Meanwhile, back at my clinic circa 2006, I endlessly fielded questions about the safety of vaccines from virtually every parent who came in. I was endlessly frustrated having to say, for the umpteenth time: "Vaccinations are the most prominent pediatric public health milestone of the twentieth century." (I got some solace from fellow professionals at national pediatric, child psychiatry, and education meetings, who all were having the same experience.)

When I listen carefully to parents concerned about a correlation between vaccination and autism, I hear (a) my child's development was a little slow, he [or she] got vaccinated, and it got slower; or (b) he [or she] made sounds, maybe they were words, he got vaccinated, sounds did not become words; or (c) he [or she] got vaccinated, no problems for 6 months, then signs of autism became apparent; or (d) signs of autism were mild, he [or she] got vaccinated, signs of autism got more marked, and so on. Both onset of symptoms and vaccinations are always included in the narrative, but with no consistent relationship—which is what a correlation is.

Vaccines: Their Days in Court

OMNIBUS AUTISM PROCEEDINGS (2007)

Before Wakefield's *Lancet* paper, before any concerns about vaccines and autism, the US National Childhood Vaccine Injury Act in 1986 had set up a special compensation program (the Vaccine Injury Compensation Program) for the very rare cases (like six to eight cases per year in the United States) who might be harmed by certain specific vaccines. Average compensation from the compensation program was about $900,000 per plaintiff. The vaccine court was not set up to handle a class action suit.

So many thousands of suits had been filed in this court about vaccines and autism (about 5,000) that a virtual class action group was created to hear it in the vaccine court. The trials were to be called the Omnibus Autism Proceedings. The Omnibus Autism Proceedings came to trial in the summer of 2007, before a panel of three vaccine court judges, all of whom were lawyers, but none of whom had previous experience with litigation involving medical evidence. A very large cadre of immunologists, epidemiologists, physical chemists, and some autism experts testified. My favorite part of the scientifically valid testimony at the Omnibus Autism Proceedings was that of a colleague, Dr. Eric Frombonne from McGill University in Montreal, who testified that the lead plaintiff's 1-year-old birthday party video showed that she had already met criteria for autism—months before her MMR vaccine. His findings were much like my analysis of my Texas tapes.

As for the rest of the story, Dr. Paul Offit's book retells in fascinating detail the blow-by-blow story of what happened. The bottom line is that good lab science, good clinical science, and good epidemiology duked it out against bad science represented by quacks, pseudoscientists, parent antivaccine advocacy organizations, the odd antivaccine celebrity, and powerful public relations firms. Thankfully, science won out!

A PERSONAL WINDOW ONTO THE VACCINE LITIGATION

Prior to the start of the Omnibus Autism Proceedings, other litigation on vaccines was afoot as well. One plaintiff, no longer a minor, was too old to qualify for the Omnibus Autism Proceedings class. He had allegedly developed autism prior to 1986, which is when the protection offered to vaccine manufacturers by the vaccine court had started and so was an important exception to the class action group—as he exemplified older individuals with autism who had been vaccinated prior to the vaccine court's existence—and before thimerosol was removed from the MMR vaccine.

I was engaged as a clinical expert in this case, as follow-on from my earlier involvement with analyzing the 50 hours of those Texas videos. This case was known as the *Blackwell v. Sigma-Aldrich* case. The respondent was Wyeth, the vaccine manufacturer; the venue was Baltimore, Maryland. My job was to review records and develop an opinion about Jamarr Blackwell's autism and his onset of autism symptoms.

I had been involved in legal matters involving children with autism many times before, though most of my work has been in the educational sector. A number of cases I'd involved with had been in front of civil and criminal judges, when it came to autism child abuse, autism custody, or wrongful death. But I had never experienced anything quite like the Blackwell case before or since, and suspect I will not again: *Blackwell* was heard by Judge Berger in the circuit court for Baltimore City (Maryland) at the same time the Omnibus Autism Proceedings were unfolding in nearby Washington, DC.

I flew into Baltimore on March 6, 2007, the night before my testimony. On checking in, a packet had been left at the hotel desk by defendant's counsel, asking me to come to the "war room" at 7:30 a.m. the next morning. The war room, it turned out, was a large suite in the Baltimore Intercontinental Hotel that had been stripped of all hotel property. Orrick, Herrington, and Sutcliffe, the law firm representing the respondent, had brought a truckload of material from their offices in Manhattan. This included 10 personal computer stations that had been set up around the suite, shelves with about 100 boxes of documents, and two copy machines installed in the walk-in shower stalls of the suite's two bathrooms. (Remember, this was before slim, powerful laptops, 10-terabyte external hard drives, AirDrop, DropBox, and even the iPhone.) Later, in the courtroom, I saw a huge audiovisual system that Orrick had installed, including an enormous video screen on which to project their exhibits and highlight paragraphs they wished witnesses to read and comment on. Coordinating and supporting this massive effort were four law partners, four legal associates, four paralegals, a bank of phones, and two people who appeared to be making PowerPoint slides all day.

For *Blackwell*, the plaintiff was represented by a sole-practice plaintiff's attorney who from time to time in court would ask to use Orrick's exhibits—so much more attractive and authoritative than his own three-ring binders. It was like the 101st Airborne had parachuted in and surrounded the Taliban mayor of a small Afghan village. However, to me, this mayor was clearly Taliban, and I was glad that this overwhelming force seemed likely, finally, to tip the odds in favor of science.

The *Blackwell* case judge, after a 10-day evidentiary hearing, granted Wyeth's request to exclude the testimony of all five of the "experts" offered by the plaintiff (which included the Geiers of chelation and Lupron notoriety). No one presented by the plaintiff's counsel rose to the level of credibility or expertise to have their testimony judged as valid evidence to be considered by a court of law. All the experts presented by the defendant's counsel were deemed indeed to be experts, and their testimony valid for the judge's consideration as evidence. The vaccine court activities were still ongoing, but now it would be highly improbable that the three judges in vaccine court would view the testimony of these same antivaccine "experts" as any more valid than Judge Berger in Baltimore had.

At the time, I thought that would be that, just as I had when Wakefield had to retract his *Lancet* paper. But it wasn't—irrational fear lived and continues to live on.

NOT QUITE HAPPILY EVER AFTER

I was more than ready to be able to stop endlessly discussing vaccines at my clinic, declaring an armistice, and erasing the battle lines drawn between doctor and patient that could so easily form when discussing vaccines. I wanted to get back to the real work of talking about things that would actually help a child with autism. I envisioned, with satisfaction, the staunching of the flow of angst that poured from parents terrified they had harmed their child by having their child vaccinated. It was not that simple.

By 2008, after a 10-year rollercoaster of vaccine hysteria, the link between rates of autism with thimerosol and the MMR vaccine had been dealt several blows, the final one being the dismissal of claims made in the Omnibus Autism Proceedings in federal vaccine court. Nevertheless, the antivaccine sentiments stubbornly live on.

WHERE HAS THE VACCINE WAR LEFT US?

Autism has certainly had its false prophets preaching a mean-spirited gospel about vaccines. While the antivaccine movement has been at it, it has promoted a culture of cynical disbelieving about the scientific method. Disbelieving anything and believing in a government conspiracy instead is readily fostered by googling "vaccines" on the Internet to see if there are others who still may share your suspicions. As Frank Bruni, who I quoted at the beginning of this chapter said, you can "click your way to validation." The paranoid suspicion that the federal government and vaccine manufacturers may have stood "shoulder to shoulder," as Paul Offit characterized it, guarding Big Pharma's apparently profit-driven motive to poison America's children with bad vaccines, is just one example of the fear that what is now sometimes called "the deep state" is out to harm the "little guy." If you believe vaccines are a conspiracy between the government and Big Pharma to help Big Pharma get rich, might you also believe educators are encouraged to neglect kids because it is cheaper? Might you also believe that the goal of affordable health care is not to entitle everyone to the opportunity to be healthy, but to make sure "government death panels" can end care when it gets "too" costly?

Arguably, the autism vaccine wars reflect, in a smaller way, a cultural sea change in some Americans today, from being more altruistic to becoming more self-seeking. The attitude of "let the herd immunity" protect *my* child embodies that perfectly. There are those who take herd immunity for granted, and not just literally, but more broadly as an entitlement to a good life.

What's Next?

The final leg of our journey examining the politics of autism takes us to its furthest frontier, neuroscience and gene sciences. This is what I examine in Chapter 9 of this book. While I have made a clear case for the importance for science in defining policy and progress for the autism community, in this last chapter, I'll reach for a new definition of autism science.

Notes

1. Bruni, F. (2014, July 4). California, Camelot and vaccines. *New York Times*, p. SR3 (NY edition).

2. Offit, P. (2008). *Autism's false prophets: Bad science, risky medicine, and the search for a cure*. New York, NY: Columbia University Press.

3. Offit, P. (2011). *Deadly choices: How the anti-vaccine movement threatens us all*. New York, NY: Basic Books.

4. Offit, P. (2014, September 14). The anti-vaccine epidemic. *Wall Street Journal*. Retrieved from https://www.wsj.com/articles/paul-a-offit-the-anti-vaccination-epidemic-1411598408

5. Ellis, R., Levs, J., & Hamasaki, S. (2015, January 23). *Outbreak of 51 measles cases linked to Disneyland*. Retrieved from http://www.cnn.com/2015/01/21/health/disneyland-measles/

6. National Vaccine Information Center. (2017). *California State vaccine requirements*. Retrieved from http://www.nvic.org/Vaccine-Laws/state-vaccine-requirements/california.aspx

7. Grinkler, R. R. (2007). *Unstrange minds: Remapping the world of autism.* New York, NY: Basic Book/Perseus.

8. McEwan, I. (2014). *The children act.* New York, NY: Nan A. Talese/Doubleday/ Random House.

9. Wakefield, A., Murch, S. H., Anthony, A., Linnell, J., Casson, D. M., Malik, M., . . . Walker-Smith, J. A. (1998). Ileal-lymphoid-nodular hyperplasia, non-specific colitis, and pervasive developmental disorder in children. *Lancet, 351*(9103), 637–641. Retracted.

10. Wakefield, A. (Director). (2016). *Vaxxed: From cover up to catastrophe.* United States: Cinema Libre Studios. Retrieved from http://vaxxedthemovie.com/

11. Bradley, E. (2000). The MMR vaccine. *60 Minutes*, Season 33, Episode 7.

12. Sobo, E. J. (2016). What is herd immunity, and how does it relate to pediatric vaccination uptake? US parent perspectives. *Social Science and Medicine, 165*, 187–195. https:// doi.org/10.1016/j.socscimed.2016.06.015

13. Deer, B. (2004). MMR: The truth behind the crisis. *Sunday London Times*, pp. 2, 22.

14. Bernard, S., Enayati, A., Redwood, H., Roger, H., & Binstock, T. (2001). Autism: A novel form of mercury poisoning. *Medical Hypotheses, 56*(4), 462–471.

15. Kennedy, R. F. (2005, February 9). Deadly immunity. *Rolling Stone Magazine.*

9 }

False Prophets of the Human Genome

There are known knowns; there are things we know we know.
We also know there are known unknowns; that is to say we know
there are some things we do not know. But there are also unknown
unknowns, the ones we don't know we don't know.
   —Donald Rumsfeld, 2002

Testimonial and Disclaimer

Advances in the medical fields of genetics and neuroscience have been among
the most remarkable accomplishments of the late twentieth century and will
continue to serve as foundations in building the tools needed to diagnose and
treat human disease in the future. It is unquestionable such work needs to
continue apace.

The topic for this chapter is to consider how we might balance basic research
funded as autism research with the need for high-quality autism treatment
research, which includes the development of new methods for educating and
caring for people with autism.

The message in this chapter is simple: Most dollars that have been spent
on autism research in the United States over the last four decades actually have been spent on basic research in genetics and basic brain science.
Virtually none of this work, this very important work, which no one
questions needs to be undertaken, is likely to help any child with autism
alive today (Table 9.1).[1]

Just less than 1 in 5 dollars is spent on treatment research, studies that
can guide us on which treatment may be best, for whom, and when. The
lion's share (over 60 percent) goes to work on basic biology and etiology
(e.g., genetics) and infrastructure (e.g., national genetics databases). To prepare children with autism to realize their potential as adults, understanding
of how autism develops over the life span is needed; this is the type of
research discussed in Chapter 5, which garners about 1 percent of autism
funding.

TABLE 9.1 } Estimated Public and Private Autism Research Funding for 2012

Category	Total Funding	% of Funding
Diagnosis	$36,856,119.01	11
Biology	$100,254,413.69	30
Causes	$56,487,025.27	17
Treatments	$64,149,899.90	19
Services	$22,827,101.20	7
Life span	$3,859,177.30	<1
Infrastructure	$47,516,196.72	14

We still cannot test genetically for autism in any meaningful way, let alone do any kind of "gene therapy." We still cannot look at the brain of an individual with autism, find something to alter, alter it, and have improvements in the symptoms of autism. It's not even clear that the brain regions that are implicated in autism, and can be seen on functional or structural neuroimaging, can systematically be modified through behavioral or biological interventions. Why aren't we spending more to help children and their families?

This state of affairs is opaque to families with children newly diagnosed with autism. They rush to get genetics panels and brain scans that diagnosing doctors recommend. Most often, they have no idea there is a near nil chance they will learn anything at all, let alone anything that will help their child. If diagnostic assessment takes place in a major academic center, parents of means are quickly identified as potential donors to basic research. Short of that, a diagnosing clinician is unlikely to have a reason to see a child and family again.

The treatments a family's child needs are often met with cookie-cutter recommendations like applied behavior analysis (ABA), speech therapy, and a social skills group. Attention to *which* ABA methods, *where* to start in speech therapy, or whether social skills training should start with one peer or a group and the many other ways in which these treatments need to be individualized can't be reliably discussed because we do not have adequate research on responder characteristics. Parents often receive short shrift on how much of these different therapies is likely to be beneficial, how to judge adequate treatment provision, what response to intervention can be expected in the short term, and how to factor in the child's individual strengths and weaknesses to individualize his or her treatment. After a diagnostic assessment visit, from which parents often leave, shell-shocked, the only follow-up is a report that may enumerate which of the current *Diagnostic and Statistical Manual of Mental Disorders (DSM)* criteria the child meets, may give results of some cognitive and language testing, and has some recommendations that are cut and pasted from a prior assessment. It is of questionable usefulness to direct a parent with limited education to the Autism Speaks website for their kit for the first 100 days, let alone give a mother who uses English as a second language the URL to the National Institute of Mental Health page on autism. I see reports like this all the time.

My concern is that parents are being thrown under the bus. Their child is diagnosed. The geneticist on the diagnostic team may draw blood to "rule out" rare conditions or look for a handful of target gene markers he or she is most interested in studying. Similarly, the neurologist on a diagnostic team may look to see if the child has a hypertrophied corpus callosum or small fusiform gyrus—and if the child does, there will be studies the family can participate in. Otherwise, there is nothing further.

BIOLOGICAL MARKERS OF DIAGNOSIS DO NOT LEAD TO TREATMENT

This state of affairs—attention to diagnosis, genetics, and brain imaging and then little else—is what also happens for families with a child with another childhood neurodevelopmental condition, such as intellectual disability, attention deficit disorder/attention deficit hyperactivity disorder (ADD/ADHD), communication disorder, and sensory processing problems. The doctor–patient relationship in neurodevelopmental disorders tends to end just where it began—with the diagnosis.

It also is true that diagnosis and treatment of any neuropsychiatric disorder, to the extent treatment is effective, has not been the result of any basic research in genetics and other neuroscience. The hope is that cataloging and classifying clinical symptoms may help *someday* to produce a road map to genes or brain regions with enough specificity that an intervention *can* be targeted. However, the likelihood of medical science getting to the point of identifying specific gene mutations, or specific brain regions, and then being able to alter a gene or brain structure for today's patients with a *DSM* psychiatric disorder is still not in their foreseeable futures. Genetically targeting specific kinds of cancer cells is still cutting-edge treatment. We are very far from doing that for neurodevelopmental or other psychiatric disorders, where the boundaries of just what defines each disorder shifts around every 5 or 10 years, as I explained in Chapter 3.

WHAT COMPRISES AUTISM RESEARCH?

The majority of funds that have been directed to autism research have not helped children, adults, and families living with autism, but instead have furthered basic research in the name of autism. Many investigators heading basic science grants "in autism" have no more familiarity with actual children or adults with autism than the average child psychiatry resident (which isn't much). Many basic science autism researchers have not clinically "seen" a child with autism for years. If you are a researcher with a basic science autism grant, your working office is most likely in a bench research laboratory or "wet lab," not in a place where patients come. This is even more likely if you are a basic scientist who is not a medical doctor (like a geneticist, neuroscientist, or neuro-chemist). Such researchers may see individuals with autism only when they draw their blood, scan their brains, or collect neurophysiological data. It will have been a clinician/researcher who would have had to tell such researchers whether the patient was autistic or not or whether the patient had an IQ above or below 70.

This almost complete disconnect between science and autism treatment may sound unbelievable to a general reader, but to a reader who is in any field of academic medicine, saying that autism researchers who get most of the au-tism research funding very seldom see children with autism is not likely to be considered a particularly remarkable statement. Indeed, collaborative research involves some researchers "working up" the subject clinically, collecting clin-ical data directly from interviews and observations of the patient with autism or through interviewing the subject's parents. As a clinical researcher myself, I have collected a great deal of such data. There is interdependence among clin-ical and basic researchers: I understand only a little of what goes on in the basic science labs, just as my basic science colleagues know little about how varied cases of autism can be. Basic scientists have their eyes on a biological treat-ment for autism beyond the horizon. I have my eyes on today's families coming for help. They are not beyond the horizon. They are sitting right in front of me and have lots of questions about what to do. I have spent my career doing what is essentially palliative care. The basic scientists have spent their careers advancing work toward a cure. I am pretty sure what I do will never come to the point of significantly alleviating most signs of autism in most individuals that have them. I am asserting that this is also true for the basic researchers. We follow different paths. Both types of work need to be done. But, one path, the biological science path, accrues many more resources than the clinical research path. Clinical research, which could be examining how to help individuals and their families living with autism today, is the research dollars stepchild, and I'd like to see her become more of a Cinderella. Balancing the aims of basic and clinical research is what I want to examine here.

"IF YOU'VE SEEN ONE CHILD WITH AUTISM, YOU'VE SEEN ONE CHILD WITH AUTISM"

For many autism advocates, "if you've seen one child with autism, you've seen one child with autism" is a mantra. But basic scientist autism researchers may start a lecture with an oft-used 30-second video clip from an "interesting" pa-tient with autism or a clip from a *60 Minutes* type television segment to show what autism is about, as if to say that what is talked about here is *this*. Linking such clinical vignettes to the first 3 minutes of a basic science lecture on autism can create the false impression that the lecturer's basic science research methods are able to deconstruct the wide clinical variation that defines the autism spectrum, when the opposite is true. Both genetics and neuroimaging offer only blunt tools for forging a clinical description of any single clinical symptom, let alone any multisymptom syndrome. Most autism "genes" correlate in a broad and nonspecific way with a range of interrelated clinical phenotypes that are associated with the autism spectrum, among other syndromes. For example, a particular gene deletion may have been reported in cases of autism—as well as cases with communication disorders or intellectual disability—and be marked by language abnormalities that can range from odd speech to complete lack of language.

It is important to keep in mind that for families with a child newly diagnosed with autism, belief in the limitless power of science is a very seductive idea, and one factor that has powered work in the biological science of autism compared to work in clinical research. The idea of a cure for autism is very powerful for parents of newly diagnosed children (as well as their wealthier grandparents, who have supported a good deal of nongovernment-funded biological studies on autism). Conversely, the idea of funding clinical treatment research is to acknowledge that palliation may be the path rather than cure.

IS BASIC RESEARCH ON AUTISM REALLY AUTISM RESEARCH?

Much basic research that is characterized as autism research could just as easily be characterized as research for any other neurodevelopmental disorder. How could that be? Let's say a grant proposal asserts that mapping the development of the somatosensory cortex in one genetic strain of fetal mouse may help us "in the future" better elucidate auditory processing abnormalities like auditory hypersensitivity—a diagnostic hallmark of autism. But not all children with autism have auditory hypersensitivity; not all children with auditory hypersensitivity are autistic.

Here's the part I can agree with: The more we know about how early arising regions of the brain are formed and how their connections to later emerging higher cortical regions work, the better. However, I could argue with equal conviction that research on formation of the somatosensory cortex focusing on the auditory cortex may elucidate sensorineural deafness (another big clinical problem), sensory processing disorder (a smaller clinical problem), tone deafness (annoying to some), and perfect pitch (not a problem at all).

The findings from this hypothetical research could arguably help us understand any other conditions for which there is congenital atypicality in how sound is processed, like language disorders or learning disabilities. Such unquestionably important basic research like this proposed work on the somatosensory cortex definitely should be carried out. But should it be carried out as autism research? Just to be clear here, less money is spent on the neural bases of language disorders and the neural bases of learning disabilities than on the neural bases for autism. Somehow, autism makes for "sexy" basic science.

CLINICAL QUESTIONS RELEVANT TO TREATMENT NOW

There are plenty of clinical questions to be asked and answered about how best to promote development in autism and how to help children and adults with autism best fulfill their potential. How do we teach and train individuals with autism so 90 percent are not unemployed or underemployed as adults? What can we or should we be doing to help families cope with the psychological and economic burdens imposed by autism? What would be the best models for long-term living arrangements for people with autism when parents are gone?

I am arguing that these questions also deserve empirical study. I am putting out for consideration that work that would provide answers to these questions is more uniquely, more specifically, autism research than is answering basic questions about the formation of a specific brain region or function of gene mutation present in individuals with autism, among others.

If, for example, we want to make a case for public funding to support one method of autism education over another or one type of congregate adult autism lifestyle over another, we would need research. It would be great to have simple data from testing subjects before and after targeted interventions or any educational or behavioral type. We have spent millions on early ABA therapy that has crept into instruction in classrooms and into the instruction of older children. Is it still differentially effective in older children or effective when administered in group settings? Are there other models that are comparably effective? How can we vocationally profile individuals with autism the way we can with vocational aptitude tests for nonautistic young people?

We don't know all that much about creating autism wellness in families, and there have not been any autism mental health initiatives: What about help for autism caregivers? Should they be entitled to individual therapy? Would group therapy be just as effective? What about marital therapy? Family therapy? What outcomes should we be measuring?

Mental health, education, and any services research on autism have received only a sliver of the autism research funding pie. Most autism research funding is directed through the National Institutes of Health (NIH) funding mechanisms, with much less consideration to nonmedical, nonbasic science studies. Despite 20 years of work by the Office of Autism Research Coordination (OARC) and the Interagency Autism Coordinating Committee (IACC), the public–consumer interfaces for prioritizing an autism research agenda, most autism research dollars are still directed to programs unlikely to help individuals or their families who are living with autism. Advocacy organizations demand diagnosis, then cure. Palliation is a back-burner priority for most.

There are conspicuous ethical questions here that apply not only to the field of autism research but also to the study of any psychiatric disorder: How do we value the acquisition of knowledge that can help us with individuals currently affected by the disorder we study versus placing emphasis on gaining knowledge that hypothetically will prevent or cure the disorder in the future? How do we (should we) prioritize research on interventions that are essentially palliative? Would we just be wasting money studying them because we are so confident that in the near future we will be able to just prevent or cure these conditions? How do we prioritize addressing autism through answering medical questions versus through answering psychological, sociological, and political questions? I would stipulate that all this work should be carried out, but that we need to reexamine how we prioritize work in these areas. Why? For one thing, we just haven't learned that much from the last 35 years of basic research in autism when it comes to furthering our understanding of exactly what autism is.

Slip Sliding Away

THE ONCE AND FUTURE AUTISM GENE(S)

In 1982, I was a postdoctoral fellow in psychiatry and behavioral sciences at the Stanford University School of Medicine. My postdoctoral research was focused on statistical methods in psychiatric research in general, and models for clinically subtyping autism in particular. In 1982, the new "cutting edge" in autism research was looking for neurobiological markers—neurotransmitters like serotonin was one being worked on by the psychiatric neurochemistry laboratory I was affiliated with. The holy grail in autism neuropsychiatry, though, already was to find "the" autism gene, the gene that made the neurotransmitter(s) go awry. In those early days, autism was seen as possibly a single-gene disorder and as possibly the most highly heritable of all psychiatric disorders with a familial basis.

The first real evidence for a genetic basis for autism had come from studies by London-based researchers Michael Rutter (now Sir Michael) and Dr. Susan Folstein. They had found that when one identical twin had autism, there was a 90 percent or greater chance the other twin would also have autism. Further, in fraternal twins, the rate fell to 15 percent; in full siblings, it fell again, to something closer to 5 percent.

It was clear as a bell: Autism was in the genes, and there was something going on prenatally as well, as sharing a pregnancy (like fraternal twins do) upped the risk of sharing autism by three-fold, and sharing the same amniotic sac (like identical twins usually do) increased the risk to an almost certainty that both infants would be affected. The thought at the time was "Wow! Childhood psychiatric disorders really *are* genetic! This is going to be easy."

My postdoctoral supervisor in 1982, Roland Ciaranello, an MD child psychiatrist who headed the NIH-funded lab that I worked with, had confidently told me, "We'll have the gene for autism in 10 years." At the time, as a newly minted psychologist trained in clinical research design, not a physician, not a bench researcher, I believed him. I really was excited as well.

WHERE ARE WE NOW?

Nearly 35 years on, we have a much more nuanced vocabulary and understanding of autism genetics and environmental modulators of genetic expression. We talk about autism genetics and, in the same breath, autism epigenetics. Epigenetics is the study of changes caused by alterations in gene expression rather than in the genetic code itself. Neuropsychiatric disorders, including autism, now are regarded as the result of many genes and multiple determining factors. Our 1980s optimism for finding *the* gene for autism has been replaced by a much more complex understanding: For starters, we now realize many paths for heritability—gene copy number variations (CNVs) characterized by either gene deletions and gene duplications, suspect "bad" genes that have spontaneously mutated and are not inherited (de novo mutations), and single-nucleotide polymorphisms (SNPs)—small abnormalities in the expected structure of a gene that may predispose to a disorder. Figure 9.1 is a Circos plot taken from a comprehensive review by the leading French autism genetics team.[2] Circos is used for the identification and analysis of similarities and differences arising from comparisons of genes. Around 150 genes have currently been implicated as having a possible role in at least some cases of autism (Figure 9.1).

Look at that Circos plot! No wonder the genetics of autism has not been sorted out: Our understanding includes more and more possibilities for genetic abnormality as our ability to look ever more closely at the human genome improves. It is expected that there may be more to come. Also, remember that some of the genes in this Circos plot may be found in children with intellectual disabilities or language disorders, just to name a couple of other broadly defined conditions. There has not been comparable genetics research on language disorder, for example, so we actually can't say whether some of the genes enumerated on the Circos plot are more often associated with pedigrees with language-disordered individuals than autistic individuals. This is why I am concerned that genetics research funded as "autism research" is really more basic science than research on autism per se.

Autism genetics research slowly chips away at the percentage of cases with at least one known type of genetic abnormality or another. We are at about 15 percent these days, with most single genetic abnormalities accounting for less than 2 percent of cases. Among these "15 percenters," where a genetic abnormality is detected, the abnormalities may be inherited, but the carrier parent may not be similarly affected, or the identified gene may result from a nonheritable mutation.

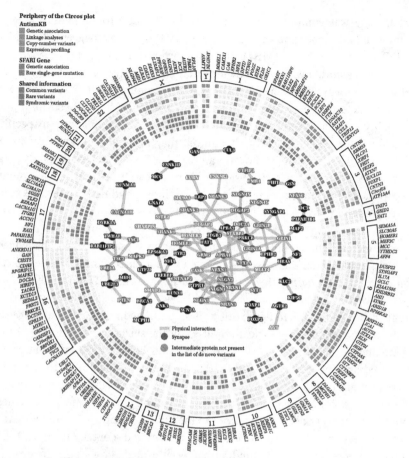

FIGURE 9.1 Periphery of a Circos plot for autism genetics.

What does that mean for clinical genetic testing, the one potential clinical implication from present-day autism genetics? What would you do if you found out that the fetus you were carrying had the same "autism gene" that your son with autism has *and* that your apparently completely normal husband also has? The answer is not clearly actionable. Some syndromes for intellectual disability have solid gene markers (like trisomy 21 for Down syndrome), but nothing of similar significance has been found yet for autism or for any *DSM* psychiatric disorder.

AUTISM AND THE BRAIN

The story is much the same when we look at the laboratory science of the brain. Over the last 45 years, neuroscience as a field has exploded: The first meeting of the Society for Neuroscience in 1971 had a little over 1,000 attendees; in 2014, over 30,000, attendees were on hand—a 30-fold growth. In 1971, the brain could be studied via autopsy or with electroencephalography (EEG), little else.

Then, there was computerized tomography (CT), positron emission tomography (PET), magnetic resonance imaging (MRI), magnetoencephalography (MEG), functional MRI (fMRI), and diffuser tensor imaging (DTI). As in genetics, the resolution with which the brain and its activity can be examined gets better and more comprehensive with each new scanner. As in genetics, where a specific defective gene cannot be linked to a specific clinical behavioral abnormality, specific neuroimaging abnormalities cannot be linked to a specific clinical behavioral abnormality, though our map of localization and function of different brain structures improves all the time. Today, localization only gets better with the use of specific physical probes that can be used in open cranium surgery as well as real-time imaging of the brain responding to different kinds of simple stimuli (like a click, not a conversation).

As in genetics, the brain, which once seemed relatively simpler, now is being seen as increasingly complex. Studying the brain presents special challenges because, unlike genes that can be harvested with a blood sample or even a saliva swab, we can't biopsy the brain short of neurosurgery. That means for autism, as well as for all psychiatric disorders, we are limited to looking at this organ in situ and trying to figure out what is going on in there. We have moved from looking simply at electrical impulses on the surface of the brain (EEG) to looking at morphology (MRI), to where and how quickly information is registered and moved (MEG and fMRI), to DTI with the ability to examine microstructural changes in tissue (like ischemia, inflammation, edema, myelination, or axonal damage). Nevertheless, neuroimaging still offers only clues about how the trillions of connections in the brain develop and become organized. Like genetics, there are obviously more exciting discoveries to come. Like autism genetics, much more funding has been available for autism neuroimaging than for neuroimaging in other conditions—like learning disabilities or ADHD. Some might argue this is because we have such well-developed instrumentation for diagnosing autism compared to, say, ADHD. I would counter by saying, as I did in Chapter 2, that establishing reliability of assessment tools in the absence of validity (like biomarkers) is just so much arranging and reupholstering the deckchairs on a sinking ship (a functional taxonomy of psychiatric disorders). Again, like autism genetics research, autism neuroimaging research has invaluable implications for understanding the brain, though much can be argued is not uniquely informative about autism.

In children, especially children with autism, the requirement to hold pretty darn still in any kind of brain scanner presents a significant barrier to being able to study a full range of ages and individuals with different levels of autism severity. In addition, in some forms of more advanced imaging, the subject needs to be awake and have enough receptive and expressive language and motivation to cooperate in order to collect data from the test stimuli (like sound or touch thresholds or whether a voice is saying "ba" or "pa"). This basically excludes study of the rapidly developing brains of toddlers, where it would be very interesting to see the likely architectural "faults" in the process of being created, and of more moderately to severely impaired individuals with autism, who may well have the most clearly marked neural abnormalities.

While families of children with autism by the thousands have volunteered their children for neuroimaging studies with these complex machines that can look at the brain in incredible detail, no findings save for epilepsy and tumors, which are rare (and unrelated) in autism, are likely to be detected, diagnosed, or treated as the result of any neuroimaging. As I have already stated, autism neuroimaging work, like work in autism genetics, is incredibly interesting, incredibly high yield in furthering our understanding of the brain, but it is not helping us specifically treat autism. Again, I would stipulate that all this work absolutely must be carried out, but that we need to reexamine how we prioritize autism funding for neuroimaging versus allocating resources to address clinical questions with answers that can be expected to improve the quality of life for individuals and families now living with autism.

THE SEDUCTION OF THE AUTISM COMMUNITY BY BASIC SCIENCE RESEARCH

In many fields of medicine, discoveries from basic laboratory work, often called "bench" or "wet lab" research, is often considered more groundbreaking than discoveries uncovered by systematically examining patients. Bench research attracts the biggest donors with its promises and generates many publications with each incrementally new experiment. It's what one needs to do in the publish-or-perish world of academic medicine. What many in the lay public do not know is that the heads of these huge, well-funded basic research laboratories at university medical centers seldom to never see living human patients (unless one is also a potential donor).

Never "having" to see patients in academic medicine says that your research is well funded and therefore very well regarded and important. These heads of basic research laboratories are, of course, professors of some medical specialty or another. Most do not teach classes in their specialty or teach medical students to become doctors to treat the disease they study. Such faculty are mainly interested in, and interact with, medical students eager to apprentice in their labs. If you head a serious wet lab, teaching medical students, even supervising residents in a clinic, is generally understood to be a misuse of the time that could better be spent analyzing data (collected by medical students and research associates), writing up research papers, or writing more grants.

BENCH TO BEDSIDE

Nevertheless, in academic medicine, there is much deference to the notion of "bench-to-bedside" science. For me, this catchphrase conjures the image of a doctor in a white lab coat rushing with his or her newly discovered agent, still in a test tube, to the patient's bedside. There, the doctor draws the newly compounded liquid up into a syringe and injects it into a mortally ill patient, who then does much better. This is not so, of course. There are miles of clinical trials, human research protocols, and such that stand between any bench research and any patient. The allegory is meant to be compelling, though.

But many academic medicine labs don't even have to worry about getting caught up in any literal bench-to-bedside activity, human clinical trials, or human research protocols because they work with mice, not people. Certainly, there are review boards that prevent too much cruelty to mice, but then there are slugs, fruit flies, and bacteria that can be used in research, too. Luckily, they also have genes; the slugs and fruit flies have neurons as well.

THE KNOCKOUT AUTISTIC MOUSE

Mice, however, tend to present the most compelling animal model to basic science autism researchers: Behold the knockout mouse. This is not a mouse that boxes well, but rather a genetically altered mouse that is said to be "autistic."[3] One knockout variant is known as the whiskered or disheveled mouse; another is the BTBR mouse.

"Are they autistic?" I was once asked this over the snack buffet in the hallway of an NIH grant review study section. I was a grant reviewer focusing on clinical characterization of autism; the questioner was there to evaluate animal model studies. From her, I learned the disheveled mouse is so called because it does not let the dominant mouse groom its whiskers—apparently the socially appropriate thing to do when a more dominant mouse approaches you. The BTBR mouse is characterized by its learning and attentional impairments. (This sounds more like ADHD to me, but there is not as much basic research funding for neural substrates of ADHD as for autism, as I have said already.) The BTBR mouse also may make repetitive vocalizations unlike other mouse-like sounds and that, I have been told by mouse researchers, are analogous to echolalia in autistic children. Honestly, language is so multidetermined, autism is so multifaceted, that I would argue, as a basic science approach, this knockout mouse approach may be too reductionist to model the complexities of autism, but they are trying (Table 9.2).[4]

The knockout mice (autistic as they may or may not be) get a lot closer to the bench-to-bedside ideal than other lines of basic autism research. I have a colleague who works in a glass-towered building full of very modern, basic science labs; his has an impressive light- and temperature-controlled wall of stacked Lucite boxes, at least 10 boxes high and 20 boxes wide, comprising different mice colonies. He looks at things like forebrain neuronal migration from gestational Day 6 to gestational Day 10 in the fetal mouse. I admire what he

TABLE 9.2 } **Are Mice a Good Model for Autism? Clinical Aspects of Autistic Disorder and Relevant Behaviors in Animal Models**

Behavioral Impairments	Behavior Measures in Rats and Mice
Social interaction	Decreased huddle, groom, barber, and play (chasing, sparring, wrestling, pinning) behavior; social exploration (approach, nose grooming); sexual activity (following, sniffing, mounting, genital grooming); aggression (threatening, attacking, biting, etc.)
Cognitive and communication	Decreased pup distress calls, mating calls, submissive calls
Stereotypical behaviors	Increased repeated motor activities (spontaneous activity, exploration, circling, digging, jumping, etc.)
	Increased self-injurious behaviors and other self-involved behaviors (self-grooming, scratching, washing, etc.)

Source: Based on Tordjman, S., Drapier, D., Bonnot, O., Graignic, R., Fortes, S., Cohen, D., . . . Roubertoux, P. L. (2007). Animal models relevant to schizophrenia and autism: Validity and limitations. *Behavior Genetics, 37*(1), 61–78.

does. I try to more fully understand what he does. I do know this kind of work is needed to understand how brains develop, become organized, and do the things brains do. But, is it autism research?

The process to obtain funding for autism research is worth describing here: An RFP (request for proposal) is issued by an NIH funding agency for work that addresses (more or less specifically) possible causes and cures for autism. The proposal that is submitted includes an introduction with support for the idea that the neurobiology leading to this devastating condition, to autism, has long been understood to start prenatally. (Remember how identical and fraternal twins, fetuses sharing the same pregnancy, were so much more likely both to have autism than singleton brothers and sisters?) This leads to the justification for studying fetal mice. Their brains can be sliced open at different numbers of days of fetal development (which conveniently are far fewer than in a human), at which time we can check out how things are going under different teratogenic conditions or with different genes "knocked out."

From that first paragraph of the grant proposal, referring to studies of "twins with autism," the word *autism* is likely to never appear in the grant proposal again until the concluding paragraph, which addresses the potential significance of the proposed work. The final paragraph notes that a better understanding of how early structures in the mouse forebrain are formed will have important implications for understanding early maldevelopment in the human brain, which will contribute to elucidation of the fundamental neurological underpinnings of autism. I agree we may learn about the development of the forebrain, but I do not agree we will learn anything more about autism than about any other neurodevelopmental disorders, such as ADHD, where problems with the prefrontal cortex are also implicated.

WHAT WE CALL AUTISM

What we call autism is very complex indeed. What we call autism clinically has now been studied in so many ways, has called into question so many mechanisms and pathways of expression, it is hard to believe we will ever have a complete answer to what autism is—especially if we keep studying this multifaceted autism "spectrum" as if there is a nugget of "pure" autism in there somewhere.

For example, Figure 9.2 is a diagram from one study hypothesizing that valproate, an anticonvulsant contraindicated in pregnancy, might cause autism. The mediators and pathways between valproate ingestion and an autism phenotype are so numerous, there is no possibility of measuring all hypothesized influences to show clear cause (valproate) and effect (autism) in any one case. Instead, such research simply makes us aware of how complex the road to expression of autism, or any condition with biological underpinnings, can be (Figure 9.2).[2]

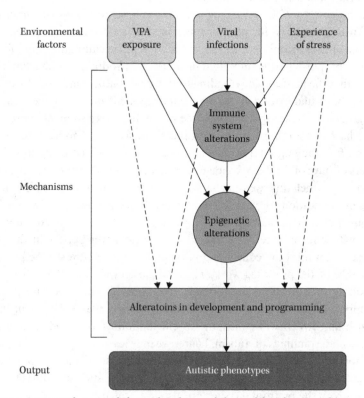

FIGURE 9.2 Autism etiology: A multifactorial road to a multifactorial disorder. VPA, valproic acid.

Reprioritizing Research

As I have already said, as clearly as I can, basic medical research is needed. It is essential. It is the only way we move forward in the important work of preserving quality of life, prolonging life, and saving lives. However, we need a course correction or at least a reexamination: From where I sit as someone who very much wants to improve outcomes and quality of life for people with autism and their families, I can't help feeling a little jealous of basic science researchers in my field.

We clinical researchers who want to help families currently living with autism are not considered in the same league and, most often, not invited into the same room when it comes to shaking hands with big donors. Over the last 30 plus years, whenever new research initiatives for autism are announced by government agencies, or by private foundations, it is almost always clear that the priority is to fund more basic research. It is a better time to be an autism geneticist or an autism neuroimaging researcher than an autism educator or an autism psychologist.

CLINIC TO KITCHEN AND CLINIC TO CLASSROOM

Clinic to kitchen and clinic to classroom, I know, just do not sound as interesting or catchy as bench to bedside, and they are not. In the clinic, we sit with parents and listen carefully to their problems. Each child, each family, has slightly different issues, has tried slightly different solutions, and had varying degrees of success or failure. There is very little direct research I can draw on to formulate truly individual recommendations to the everyday problems I am being asked to address.

I understand stages of child development well. I understand principles of behavioral analysis well. I have spent time in autism classrooms. I draw on those theories and experience. It would be absolutely stupid to respond to a family's query about what to do when their child undoes his or her seat belt and tries to open the door while the car is moving, by saying that the only experimentally valid, possibly relevant, research I can think of applying to this situation would be giving the child an atypical antipsychotic, as that has been approved by the FDA as a treatment for autism.

Instead, we need to research solutions that move from clinic to kitchen (or car seat), not bench to bedside. When a mother of a child with autism asks, for example, "How do we get him to eat noncrunchy foods? Do I just let him go without dinner if he won't eat what we eat?" or "Should I be hand feeding him?" All I can do is go to my autism treatment toolbox and pull out some basic tools: I go to behaviorism; I can use a desensitization/exposure paradigm and maybe it works. Wouldn't it be nice to have some research on food refusal in autism that systematically compared motivational strategies and could tell me something about which approaches might work best with a preverbal child versus a nonverbal child versus one who can argue and yell. This is not sexy research but would provide answers to questions that might improve a family's life by getting their toddler to eat a well-balanced diet and reduce overall instructional control battles in that family with the noncompliant, not socially motivated to please, child.

We also need solutions that move from clinic to classroom. If my group is doing an assessment that is going to be sent to an individualized education program (IEP) team and I am asked, "Should this child be in a full-inclusion first grade or in a special education classroom?" there are virtually no case-controlled or even observational studies to which I can refer. Instead, I again go to my autism treatment toolbox and this time pull out a developmental tool: Is the child "in reach" of the first-grade curriculum, or for this particular child, would first grade be like sticking a bright 5-year-old who loves math in a high school algebra course? It would be very helpful to answer this question with simple empirical data on comparable groups of children who had received either special education or inclusion and bypass the emotional and political arguments for one or the other.

Setting Social Policy Priorities in the Age of Genetics and Neuroscience

Both sides of this chasm between basic medical research and the world of helping patients face their own difficulties. For basic researchers, the number of things to measure grows and grows. First, there was epigenetics. A gene's modulation can be multidetermined. There are CNVs, SNPs, and de novo mutations that muck up what was once thought to be a simple model of heritable autism. As Rumsfeld said, there are known knowns, known unknowns, and unknown unknowns. That pretty much sums up discoveries in autism genetics in the last 30 years.

Brain researchers need to decide whether to look for a problem that is on the cellular level or may be regional or systemic or all three. There is plasticity and transfer of function that, as the child gets good treatment, might advantageously reorganize the brain or brain networks and we have little idea how that looks pre- to postintervention from what we can look at with present neuroimaging tools.

HEDGING OUR BETS

Basic researchers who focus on genes, cells, nerves, or brains like to think there is an "autism." Well, now they accept there is an "autism spectrum," but truthfully, that only muddies their waters. Try talking to one of these basic genetics or neuroimaging researchers about the issues I discussed in the first few chapters, the arbitrary and ever-changing boundaries between diagnostic classifications in *DSM* and changing incidence. This kind of moving target makes their work that much more difficult.

Basic researchers were not happy when after 20 years of accumulating databases with ASD subjects diagnosed according to the *DSM-IV* or *DSM-IV-TR*,[5] the subjects faced reclassification with new *DSM-5*[6] criteria in 2013. What were they supposed to do with their *DSM-IV-TR* Asperger's cases who were the best at holding still in a scanner? Now, Asperger's isn't necessarily "on the spectrum" unless you read the fine print in *DSM-5*, which basically says that if the *DSM-IV-TR* diagnosed individual with Asperger's still identifies as Asperger's, so be it (a political compromise made for the sake of those diagnosed with *DSM-IV* Asperger's afraid they would lose services if they "fell off" the spectrum). This is not exactly a classification with the same degree of scientific "resolution" you get from a DTI scan. Should neuroimaging researchers just drop Asperger's-diagnosed subjects out of future studies? What about the generalizability of findings from earlier studies where many of their subjects on the autism spectrum were on the spectrum because of an Asperger's diagnosis?

There sure are striking similarities among individuals with autism, but as the spectrum has become broader and broader, as the spectrum has encompassed more and more individuals who are "high functioning" with fewer and less marked traits that tend to get even less marked with maturation and good supports, who are they going to be studying if the individuals clinically come "off" the spectrum? Will they still have the same neuropathology they did when they met criteria for an autism spectrum disorder at age 8? People with autism are not a horde of genetically identical knockout mice. We might want to assume that positive change in a human with autism has biological correlates that would distort sample characteristics if still counted as autistic.

THE VIEW FROM FAMILIES LIVING WITH AUTISM

As I said previously, I am "down in the trenches," every week, with parents who have children with autism. At the University of California at San Francisco, I worked for 24 years in a boxy stucco building in tired clinic rooms with poorly functioning radiators. Now, in my nonprofit autism center for the benefit of families living with autism, the Autism Center of Northern California, I at least work in an architectural gem of early pre-WWI cast iron construction with marble hallways (but even older 1903 cast iron radiators). I describe these settings because, in other clinics, and in special education classrooms for autism, the trenches are seldom prime real estate. For every portable classroom or other grade "C" facility that I have visited that houses services for children with autism, I wish my nonprofit center had $100 to spend on caring for families living with autism. Clinical care for autism, like clinical study of autism, does not receive the funding that biological research on autism does.

Down in the trenches, we are fine with lousy real estate, but at the top of our wish list is research that could help us guide treatment decision-making. We wish for research to better guide educators in program development that reflects evidence-based practice. We wish for research to better train home ABA providers with a manual more recent than Lovaas's 1981 *The Me Book* (discussed in previous chapters). We wish for research that would support empirical guidelines for moving away from teaching spoken language to children who cross-sectional studies tell us will remain mute. There are hundreds more issues where research on methods, treatment outcomes, or longitudinal change would be very helpful.

In general, there needs to be much more careful study of how to teach children with autism at different stages of mental development. For the growing numbers of adults with autism, we need clinical trials of cognitive behavioral therapies, mindfulness, and group therapies to see what can best support social adjustment and workability.

How do we prioritize research when we have this divide between basic research on genes and the brain on the one hand and the desperately needed autism research designed and carried out expressly with the intent of producing findings that will help the children and adults with autism today?

Resetting Priorities

REBALANCE FUNDING ON AUTISM RESEARCH

Autism receives a lot of research funding already. I know my ADHD-studying colleagues are jealous. Most of this money is going to important basic research, but that has virtually no chance of helping anyone who currently has autism. If you are a private donor, and that is what you want to do, that's your choice, of course. I certainly have met some private donors to autism research who have not had basic studies pitched to them quite that way. Perhaps the answer is not quite "No" when asked if this particular line of bench science is close enough to the bedside that it will reach a loved family member with autism before it is "too late."

A substantial portion of autism research funding, however, is federal funding. I think we need to reexamine autism research dollars and consider whether to instead designate these basic science studies as basic neuroscience studies, not autism studies. Many have just as much of a chance of furthering our understanding of other neurodevelopmental disorders, so perhaps the cost of such studies should be shared with efforts to uncover the genetics and neurology of learning disorders, language disorders, early onset mood disorders, ADHD, and so on.

In Chapter 3, I talked about the work of Dr. Christopher Gillberg, who has conceptualized a superordinate designation (ESSENCE, early symptomatic syndromes eliciting neurodevelopmental clinical examination) as a more useful, meaningful approach to studying childhood neuropsychiatric disorders as an amalgam given the overlap in clinical signs among childhood neuropsychiatric disorders and the low specificity of biomarkers (like all those genes enumerated in the Circos plot at the beginning of this chapter).[7] Study of symptoms rather than diagnoses using a model like his could allow for more refined and meaningful clinical outcome research designs. There is room for collaboration between the goals of basic researchers and clinical researchers, such as in brain imaging studies that characterize structural or functional brain changes that might arise in response to intervention.

Reprioritized funding should be put toward efforts to improve early teaching, early parent training, autism educational strategies, vocational training, viability of adult community models, and strategies for supporting the mental health of families living with children and adults on the autism spectrum. We need to commit resources to families living with autism today, not just aim at preventing future autism, as we should all be able to agree that is still a ways off.

Notes

1. Interagency Autism Coordinating Committee. (2016, April). *2011–2012 IACC autism spectrum disorder research portfolio analysis report.* Retrieved from https://iacc.hhs.gov/publications/portfolio-analysis/2012/

2. Bourgeron, T. (2016). The genetics and neurobiology of ESSENCE: The third Birgit Olsson lecture. *Nordic Journal of Psychiatry, 70*(1), 1–9. doi:10.3109/08039488.2015.1042519

3. Iwata, K., Matsuzaki, H., Takei, N., Manabe, T., & Mori, N. (2010). Animal models of autism: An epigenetic and environmental viewpoint. *Journal of Central Nervous System Disease, 2,* 37–44. Retrieved from https://www.ncbi.nlm.nih.gov/pmc/articles/PMC3661233/

4. Tordjman, S., Drapier, D., Bonnot, O., Graignic, R., Fortes, S., Cohen, D., . . . Roubertoux, P. L. (2007). Animal models relevant to schizophrenia and autism: Validity and limitations. *Behavior Genetics, 37*(1), 61–78.

5. American Psychiatric Association. (2000). *Diagnostic and statistical manual of mental disorders* (4th ed., text revision; *DSM-IV-TR*). Washington, DC: APA Press.

6. American Psychiatric Association. (2013). *Diagnostic and statistical manual of mental disorders* (5th ed.; *DSM-5*). Washington, DC: APA Press.

7. Gillberg, C. (2010). The ESSENCE in child psychiatry: Early symptomatic syndromes eliciting neurodevelopmental clinical examinations. *Research in Developmental Disabilities, 31,* 1543–1551.

CONCLUSIONS: PRIORITIES FOR OUR AUTISM COMMUNITY

Where do we go from here? In the preceding nine chapters, I detailed things amiss in our efforts to understand and treat autism. These issues not only are problems experienced by the autism community, but also, and just as important, are symptomatic of a broader disorder and lack of direction in American social policy toward families and any of their children who are born with significant enough disability that they may require supports. Americans dwell on myths of autistic geniuses and miraculous recoveries, ignoring the autism most families face.

The politics of autism is a case study in American values and the increasing vulnerability of truth. Where we get our information, what we come to believe, our priorities, and what we want and why are reflected not only in autism policy, but also in all the ways we form consensus on any topic and how our culture may be changing with increasing permission to ignore science in favor of personal experience. (This can be seen in believing that your child has autism because you are convinced symptoms emerged a couple of months after receiving the measles, mumps, and rubella vaccine, or that you are convinced there is no global warming because you were in the biggest snowstorm in your memory this winter.)

This shift in what people believe about autism and what they believe about all kinds of issues comes from bombardment with more information than ever. As I said in the introduction, information and knowledge are not the same thing. On a sociological level, we grapple with data, the media, the Internet and politics; on a personal level, we deal with altruism and hope and false beliefs—whenever we try to form an opinion or an action plan about anything. Integration of information into knowledge has made truth vulnerable.

What has been said in this book about autism and the issues faced by the autism community is also true for families of children with intellectual disabilities, borderline intellectual functioning, attention and learning disorders, inborn psychiatric disorders, as well as families with a member with a chronic mental health disorder. These conditions mostly do not make for humorous sitcoms or heartwarming investigative TV reports looking voyeuristically into the life of artistic savants or mentally ill mathematicians. The autism community is not well served by viral Internet posts announcing new cures. The issues raised here about autism are ones that affect families and communities who are trying to deal with the difficulties they face and a society with priorities that do not mesh with readily giving them the help their children need now or in the future for which they need to plan.

We Americans are an optimistic bunch. We love stories about children with moms who were once told their child should be "put away," would never speak, or would never go to a school with "normal" children, who have defeated the odds, producing a child who now is out there with the rest of us. Occasionally, this is true, and it is wonderful that it can be true. However, such tales do nothing to orient us to the reality most families living with autism face.

To say such children are "differently abled" not "disabled," to say they are "neurodiverse" not "atypical" or "handicapped," or even to refer to children without disabilities as "neurotypical" (as if it is just one more variant) is to sweep under the rug that there is indeed a core set of social, communicative, and adaptive competencies that really are not optional if one is to "make it" in the American mainstream.

Yes, there is room for plenty of variation. There are niches into which individuals with specific strengths and weakness can fit, thrive, and be happy. Some families have the perspicacity or luck to find them, but it is seldom easy. What is not particularly helpful are public relations pieces in newspapers, on radio, and on TV asserting that companies like SAP, Oracle, and Microsoft have plans to hire hundreds with Asperger's syndrome because they are such good coders. Surely some are, but most have social and other issues that make work on a time schedule, in an office, or as part of a team very problematic. I applaud these companies for their good intentions and for the employment they will provide for perhaps a few. I very seriously doubt they will fulfill their announced quotas. The thought of 500 people with Asperger's or high-functioning autism coding away at these three companies makes it sound like having autism is not so much of a handicap. Feel-good public relations short-circuit what any company or employer really needs to commit to do, which is to understand who can do what job and provide access for needed apprenticeships, on-the-job training, employment coaches, cognitive behavioral therapy, and the like, to ensure success. Accommodating people with autism is much more difficult than installing wheelchair ramps with the right grade or making space for hand-icapped restrooms.

For individuals with autism, the chain is often only as strong as its weakest link. I have seen some smart adults with autism fail because they basically are expected to be like the rest of us when they work. I have seen lovely not-as-smart people with autism fail because they are given ill-suited jobs that rely on speed or the ability to chit-chat and may have too much going on around them. It is time we acknowledge that *neurodiversity* is not just an interesting new concept, but a term that obfuscates the real difficulties with which people with some strengths and some inherent, autistic weaknesses struggle. We need programs that can result from policy that creates schools and training programs and incentivizes special workplaces that can best foster success for anyone who will carry an autism diagnosis into adulthood.

I have argued here that our social policy regarding children with autism and other disabilities is in many cases the result of public policy and practice that is not "in the best interest of the child." This is certainly true in much of special education for autism today, as I discussed in Chapters 4 and 5. Our sense of political correctness, our growing tendency to be swayed by ignorant yet mellif-luous voices on the Internet proclaiming cures, and our belief that misdirected "can-do"-spirited efforts will someday solve the problem do not get us where we need to go. Much of today's policy toward children with disabilities does not prepare them for lives with meaning and does a disservice to their families, who just want the best for their kids—like everyone else.

In each chapter, I offered some solutions for the problems I have laid out. Some proposals may make you think I am surely a Democrat, others that I am a Republican. Compared to present polices and practices, some of my proposals would cost money; some would likely save money. These recommendations as a whole are independent of any party ideology. Overall, I do not advocate getting the government into, or out of, the lives of children and their families, but simply to support access to evidence-based practice for affected individuals be-cause it is the right thing to do and that, done well, may even be cost-effective. My perspective is as an advocate for children with autism and for the adults they become.

Best Interest of the Child. In 1998, a remarkable book, *The Best Interests of the Child: The Least Detrimental Alternative*,[1] was written by a preeminent group of Yale University child advocates: Joseph Goldstein (a law professor); Dr. Albert Solnit (a child psychiatrist, professor, and director of the Yale Child Study Center); Sonja Goldstein (a lawyer and mental health advocate); and Anna Freud (a child psychoanalyst and daughter of Sigmund Freud). This book has had far-reaching effects on social policy affecting children in the United States and in the United Kingdom, among other places. These authors did not have children with autism in mind, but everything they had to say was spot on for the autism community.

The "Best Interest" Burden in Autism. Acting in the best interest of (typi-cally developing) children as laid out by Goldstein et al. already is a substantial societal burden. Acting in the best interest of children with developmental disa-bility is even more of a burden. Parents of children with disabilities must invest a sizable amount of time and effort learning about what their child needs and getting it. This is a task that basically never ends. It starts with arranging diag-nostic assessments and early interventions; continues through the school years by making annual decisions about education with IEPs and other treatments; continues as parents figure out how to help their adult child get and stay employed, creating adult living arrangements in or out of the family home, and overseeing that everything works for the rest of their lives.

My social policy recommendations in this book have fallen into three areas: helping families do better, helping children do better, and helping adults with disabilities do better. Among families dealing with a less than fully able offspring, there is a tremendous range of possible outcomes. A relatively small number will need supervised care for their entire lives. Others may function in semisheltered living and work settings, with able adults supervising home and work activities. An increasingly large group are those who get out in the mainstream (those with Asperger's, high-functioning autism, borderline intellectual functioning, those dually diagnosed with developmental and mental health conditions) but will need significant supports and much more time to "grow up." This means extra support until the point where such a person can take care of personal daily needs, have a job, live separately from their families of origin, form mutual and nonexploitive social relationships, make viable education and employment choices, manage money, and stay physically healthy. The people with autism that I have focused on in this book largely are not the college-educated self-advocates for the autism community, but rather those unable to voice self-advocacy. But even the most highly educated autism self-advocates will talk about the ways in which they continue to struggle to fully adapt to what is expected of them.

Autism can't really be understood from a TV cameo, a newspaper column about one amazing mom, or a website for an autism advocacy organization, although each will contain kernels of some important truths about autism. My hope is that my readers here will have gained a new portal for evaluating all kinds of things that are true about autism.

Note

1. Goldstein, J., Solnit, A., Goldstein, S., & Freud, A. (1996). *The best interests of the child: The least detrimental alternative*. New York, NY: Free Press, Simon & Schuster.

ACKNOWLEDGMENTS

There are many to thank whose tangible and indescribable efforts moved me to complete this work. First, I thank my husband, David Bradlow. I know this sounds too "California"—but one night, in our hot tub, I was rambling about a loosely connected set of ideas, and he said, "I think you have another book." Then he suggested the title: *The Politics of Autism*. He has been my audience for ideas throughout this long, 6-year process, longer than it has taken for me to write anything else.

Initially, I wrote a prospectus, showed it to my long-time University of California at San Francisco (UCSF) Psychiatry Department mentor, Dr. Paul Ekman, who urged me to write it and to seriously consider living beyond academia to write it, and I did both—thank you Paul!

Thanks also to current colleagues who listened to my ideas and suggested further resources: Dr. Elysa Marco at UCSF Pediatric Neurology; Lina Fancy, executive director of our Autism Center of Northern California's (ACNC) JumpStart Learning to Learn; and Dr. Mariam King, my close colleague and chief psychologist at ACNC.

My long line of clinic coordinators make my life possible, and the ones with me through this project have been Tahle Sendowski (almost PhD), Olivia Park (almost MD), Tahle Leibovitz (PhD in the works), and Raizel DeWitt, my current medical school–bound coordinator and also the fine researcher who worked on the compilation of the References and Notes sections of each chapter of this book.

Thanks to reviewers of the initial draft of this work: Dr. Laura Schriebman, emeritus professor of psychology, University of California at San Diego; Dr. Susan Holloway of the University of California at Berkeley; and John Elder Robison, autist extraordinaire. My long-time Oxford University Press editor, Joan Bossert, has been my "voice coach" for getting the "voice" of this book just right. I sincerely thank her for the tremendous editorial work she did, shaping this work to go beyond my earlier audiences of parents, teachers, and therapists of children with autism and allowing me to speak to policymakers, political scientists, sociologists, ethnographers, and the rest of you.

There are many more friends and colleagues in the United States and world-wide whose own talk and work inspired me to complete this project. I especially value those of you who shared my passion for my perspectives on the *Diagnostic and Statistical Manual of Mental Disorders*, autism education, the autism sociology of complementary and alternative medicine, and the vaccine wars, as well as my voice for more research to help those living with autism and their families.

I thank all the families I have met in my work with autism in the last 40 years. (I wonder where many of you are today. Come visit!) I am especially grateful to the children and adults with autism whom I have tried to help—because your very being has helped me know things that could be known no other way.

REFERENCES AND SUGGESTED READING

These references are also available online as a PDF at http://www.brynasiegel.com/politicsofautism/ to facilitate access to cited hyperlinks.

Introduction

Bettelheim, B. (1967). *The empty fortress: Infantile autism and the birth of the self.* New York, NY: Free Press/Simon & Schuster.

Kanner, L. (1943). Autistic disturbances of affective contact. *Nervous Child, 2,* 217–250. Reprinted 1968: *Acta Paedopsychiatrica, 35*(4), 100–136.

Lovaas, I. (1987). Behavioral treatment and normal educational and intellectual functioning in young autistic children. *Journal of Consulting and Clinical Psychology, 55*(1), 3–9.

Sheinkopf, S., & Siegel, B. (1998). Effects of very early intensive behavioral intervention for autistic children. *Journal of Autism and Developmental Disorders, 28*(1), 15–23.

Siegel, B. (1996). *The world of the autistic child: Understanding and treating autistic spectrum disorders.* New York, NY: Oxford University Press.

Siegel, B. (2001). *The Pervasive Developmental Disorders Screening Test–II.* San Antonio, TX: Psychological Corporation.

Siegel, B. (2003). *Helping children with autism learn: Treatment approaches for parents and professionals.* New York, NY: Oxford University Press.

Siegel, B. (2008). *Getting the best for your child with autism: An expert's guide to treatment.* New York, NY: Guilford Press.

Siegel, B., Anders, T., Ciaranello, R. D., Bienenstock, B., & Kraemer, H. C. (1985). Empirical of the autistic syndrome. *Journal of Autism and Developmental Disorders, 16*(3), 475–491.

Siegel, B., & Silverstein, S. (2001). *What about me? Growing up with a developmentally disabled sibling.* Cambridge, MA: Perseus Press.

Siegel, B., Vukicevic, J., & Spitzer, R. L. (1990). Using signal detection theory to revise *DSM-III-R*: Reanalysis of the *DSM-III-R* field trials data for autistic disorder. *Journal of Psychiatric Research, 4,* 301–311.

Solomon, A. (2013). *Far from the tree: Parents, children and the search for identity.* New York, NY: Scribner/Simon & Schuster.

Spitzer, R. L., & Siegel, B. (1990). The *DSM-III-R* field trials for pervasive developmental disorders. *Journal of the American Academy of Child and Adolescent Psychiatry, 26*(6), 855–862.

Volkmar, F., Klin, A., Siegel, B., Szatmari, P., Lord, C., Campbell, M., . . . Towbin, K. (1994). Field trial for autistic disorder in *DSM-IV. American Journal of Psychiatry, 151*(9), 1361–1367.

Chapter 1
POPULAR MEDIA

Barnbaum, D. (2008). *The ethics of autism: Among them, but not of them.* Indianapolis, IN: Indiana University Press.

Douthat, R. (2016, May 21). Facebook's subtle empire. *New York Times.* Retrieved from http://www.nytimes.com/2016/05/22/opinion/sunday/facebooks-subtle-empire.html

Facts and statistics. (n.d.). Retrieved August 23, 2016, from Autism Speaks website: http://www.autism-society.org/what-is/facts-and-statistics/. Last updated August 25, 2015.

Five inspiring success stories of people with autism finding employment. (2015, May 29). Retrieved August 23, 2016, from Autism Speaks website: https://www.autismspeaks.org/news/news-item/5-inspiring-success-stories-people-autism-finding-employment

Fox, M. (2010, August 22). O. Ivar Lovaas, pioneer in developing therapies for autism, dies at 83. *The New York Times.* Retrieved from http://www.nytimes.com/2010/08/23/health/23lovaas.html

JumpStart: Learning to Learn (JSLTL). (n.d.). Retrieved from Autism Center of Northern California website: http://www.acnc.org/our-four-programs/jumpstart-learning-to-learn-jsltl/

Leigh, S. (2007, August 19). A force of nurture: Bryna Siegel's pragmatic approach to autism. *San Francisco Chronicle Magazine*, pp. 19–21, 27.

Norton, A. (2012, May 15). Autistic children less likely to go to college. *Chicago Tribune.* Retrieved August 23, 2016, from http://articles.chicagotribune.com/2012-05-15/lifestyle/sns-rt-us-adult-autismbre84e13t-20120515_1_young-adults-asd-autism-spectrum-disorder

Ostrow, N. (2014, June 10). Autism costs more than $2 million over patient's life. *Bloomberg.* Retrieved August 23, 2016, from http://www.bloomberg.com/news/articles/2014-06-09/autism-costs-more-than-2-million-over-patient-s-life

Peters, J. W. (2016, December 26). Wielding claims of "fake news," conservatives take aim at mainstream media. *New York Times.* Retrieved from https://www.nytimes.com/2016/12/25/us/politics/fake-news-claims-conservatives-mainstream-media-.html

Sacks, O. (1993, December 27). An anthropologist on Mars. *The New Yorker.* Retrieved August 23, 2016, from http://www.newyorker.com/magazine/1993/12/27/anthropologist-mars

Singal, J. (2016, May 9). John Oliver took on junk science on *Last Week Tonight,* and it was great. *New York Magazine.* Retrieved from https://www.thecut.com/2016/05/john-oliver-took-on-junk-science-last-night-and-it-was-glorious.html

Social Security Administration. (n.d.). *Disability planner: Benefits for a disabled child.* Retrieved August 23, 2016, from https://www.ssa.gov/planners/disability/dqualify10.html

US Department of Labor, Bureau of Labor Statistics. (n.d.). Table A-6. Employment status of the civilian population by sex, age, and disability status, not seasonally adjusted [Economic news release]. Retrieved August 23, 2016, from http://www.bls.gov/news.release/empsit.t06.htm. Last modified January 5, 2018.

SCIENTIFIC READINGS

Economics

Buescher, A. S., Cidav, Z., Knapp, M., & Mandell, D. S. (2014). Costs of autism spectrum disorders in the United Kingdom and the United States. *JAMA Pediatrics, 168*(8), 721–728. http://doi.org/10.1001/jamapediatrics.2014.210

Cimera, R. E., & Cowan, R. J. (2009). The costs of services and employment outcomes achieved by adults with autism in the US. *Autism, 13*(3), 285–302. http://doi.org/10.1177/1362361309103791

A. J. Drexel Autism Institute. (n.d.). *National autism indicators report series.* Retrieved from http://drexel.edu/autisminstitute/research-projects/research/ResearchPrograminLifeCourseOutcomes/IndicatorsReport/#sthash.WqMvOWCQ.dpuf

Lavelle, T. A., Weinstein, M. C., Newhouse, J. P., Munir, K., Kuhlthau, K. A., & Prosser, L. A. (2014). Economic burden of childhood autism spectrum disorders. *Pediatrics, 133*(3), e520–e529. http://doi.org/10.1542/peds.2013-0763

Leigh, J. P., & Du, J. (2015). Brief report: Forecasting the economic burden of autism in 2015 and 2025 in the United States. *Journal of Autism and Developmental Disorders, 45*(12), 4135–4139. http://doi.org/10.1007/s10803-015-2521-7

Parent Involvement and Intervention

Abbott, M., Bernard, P., & Forge, J. (2013). Communicating a diagnosis of autism spectrum disorder—A qualitative study of parents' experiences. *Clinical Child Psychology and Psychiatry, 18*(3), 370–382. http://doi.org/10.1177/1359104512455813

Chevallier, C., Kohls, G., Troiani, V., Brodkin, E. S., & Schultz, R. T. (2012). The social motivation theory of autism. *Trends in Cognitive Sciences, 16*(4), 231–239. http://doi.org/10.1016/j.tics.2012.02.007

Corcoran, J., Berry, A., & Hill, S. (2015). The lived experience of US parents of children with autism spectrum disorders. A systematic review and meta-synthesis. *Journal of Intellectual Disabilities, 19*(4), 356–366. http://doi.org/10.1177/1744629515577876

Crane, L., Chester, J. W., Goddard, L., Henry, L. A., & Hill, E. (2016). Experiences of autism diagnosis: A survey of over 1,000 parents in the United Kingdom. *Autism*, 20(2), 153–162. http://doi.org/10.1177/1362361315573636

Foxx, R. M. (2008). Applied behavior analysis treatment of autism: The state of the art. *Child and Adolescent Psychiatric Clinics of North America, 17*(4), 821–834. http://doi.org/10.1016/j.chc.2008.06.007

Grindle, C. F., Kovshoff, H., Hastings, R. P., & Remington, B. (2008). Parents' experiences of home-based applied behavior analysis programs for young children with autism. *Journal of Autism and Developmental Disorders, 39*(1), 42–56. http://doi.org/10.1007/s10803-008-0597-z

KasariLab. (n.d.). *JASPER.* Retrieved from http://www.kasarilab.org/treatments/jasper/

Langan, M. (2011). Parental voices and controversies in autism. *Disability & Society, 26*(2), 193–205. http://doi.org/10.1080/09687599.2011.544059

Matson, J. L., Benavidez, D. A., Stabinsky Compton, L., Paclawskyj, T., & Baglio, C. (1996). Behavioral treatment of autistic persons: A review of research from 1980 to the present. *Research in Developmental Disabilities, 17*(6), 433–465. http://doi.org/10.1016/S0891-4222(96)00030-3

Mattingly, D. J., Prislin, R., McKenzie, T. L., Rodriguez, J. L., & Kayzar, B. (2002). Evaluating evaluations: The case of parent involvement programs. *Review of Educational Research, 72*(4), 549–576. http://doi.org/10.3102/00346543072004549

McConachie, H., & Diggle, T. (2007). Parent implemented early intervention for young children with autism spectrum disorder: a systematic review. *Journal of Evaluation in Clinical Practice, 13*(1), 120–129. http://doi.org/10.1111/j.1365-2753.2006.00674.x

Peters-Scheffer, N., Didden, R., Korzilius, H., & Sturmey, P. (2011). A meta-analytic study on the effectiveness of comprehensive ABA-based early intervention programs for children with autism spectrum disorders. *Research in Autism Spectrum Disorders, 5*(1), 60–69. http://doi.org/10.1016/j.rasd.2010.03.011

Pickles, A., Le Couteur, A., Leadbitter, K., Salomone, E., Cole-Fletcher, R., Tobin, H., . . . Green, J. (2016). Parent-mediated social communication therapy for young children with autism (PACT): Long-term follow-up of a randomised controlled trial. *Lancet, 388*(10059), 2501–2509. http://dx.doi.org/10.1016/S0140-6736(16)31229-6

Pivotal response treatment. (n.d.). Retrieved from Gevirtz School, Graduate School of Education, University of California at Santa Barbara, website: https://education.ucsb.edu/autism/pivotal-response-treatment

Siegel, B. (1996). *The world of the autistic child: Understanding and treating autistic spectrum disorders.* New York, NY: Oxford University Press.

Siegel, B. (2003) *Helping children with autism learn: Treatment approaches for parents and professionals.* New York, NY: Oxford University Press.

Siegel, B., & Bernard, A. (2009). JumpStart Learning-to-Learn: First intervention and training parents to promote generalization of children's early interventions. In C. Whalen (Ed.), *Real life, real progress for children with autism spectrum disorders: Strategies for successful generalization in natural environments* (pp. 149–172). Baltimore, MD: Brookes.

Siegel, B., Homen, A., & Mayes, L. (2014). Evidence-based treatment of autism spectrum disorders. In E. Weller, J. McDermott, & G. Gabbard (Eds.), *Gabbard's treatment of psychiatric disorders* (5th ed., Chapter 3). Washington, DC: American Psychiatric Association Press.

US Department of Labor. (2015, December 9). *FMLA (Family & Medical Leave).* Retrieved September 15, 2016, from https://www.dol.gov/general/topic/benefits-leave/fmla

Virués-Ortega, J. (2010). Applied behavior analytic intervention for autism in early childhood: Meta-analysis, meta-regression and dose–response meta-analysis of multiple outcomes. *Clinical Psychology Review, 30*(4), 387–399. http://doi.org/10.1016/j.cpr.2010.01.008

Wage and Hour Division (WHD), US Department of Labor. (n.d.). *Family and Medical Leave Act.* Retrieved September 15, 2016, from https://www.dol.gov/whd/fmla/

Chapter 2
POPULAR MEDIA

Autism and infertility treatment: Your questions answered. Retrieved from Autism Speaks website: https://www.autismspeaks.org/science/science-news/autism-and-infertility-treatment-your-questions-answered

CAR Autism Roadmap. (n.d.). *Medical diagnosis vs. educational eligibility for special services: Important distinctions for those with ASD.* (n.d.). Retrieved from https://www.carautismroadmap.org/medical-diagnosis-vs-educational-eligibility-for-special-services-important-distinctions-for-those-with-asd/. Last updated June 15, 2016.

Carey, B. (2014, March 27). Rate of diagnosis for autism grows. *The New York Times.* Retrieved from http://www.nytimes.com/2014/03/28/us/rate-of-diagnosis-for-autism-grows.html

Centers for Disease Control and Prevention. (n.d.-a). Birth rate data and statistics: Reproductive health. Retrieved September 15, 2016, from http://www.cdc.gov/reproductivehealth/data_stats/

Centers for Disease Control and Prevention. (n.d.-b) *Facts about ASDs*. Retrieved September 15, 2016, from http://www.cdc.gov/ncbddd/autism/facts.html

Centers for Disease Control and Prevention, National Center for Health Statistics. (2016, January). *Mean age of mothers is on the rise: United States, 2000–2014* (NCHS Data Brief 232). http://www.cdc.gov/nchs/products/databriefs/db232.htm

Delivery and payment models: Patient-centered medical home. (n.d.). Retrieved September 15, 2016, from ACP website: https://www.acponline.org/practice-resources/business-resources/payment/models/pcmh

Donovan, J., & Zucker, C. (2016). *In a different key: The story of autism*. New York, NY: Crown.

Educational vs. medical autism diagnosis. (2013, June 27). *Spectrums Magazine*. Retrieved from http://spectrumsmagazine.com/educational-vs-medical-autism-diagnosis/

Genzlinger, N. (2016, July 12). Review: "The A word" takes unblinking look at autism. *The New York Times*. Retrieved from http://www.nytimes.com/2016/07/13/arts/television/review-the-a-word-takes-unblinking-look-at-autism.html

Patient-centered medical home: Understanding the patient-centered medical home. (n.d.). Retrieved September 15, 2016, from ACP website: https://www.acponline.org/practice-resources/business-resources/payment/models/pcmh/understanding

Ratey, J. J., & Johnson, C. (1997). *Shadow syndromes: Recognizing and coping with the hidden psychological disorders that can influence your behavior and silently determine the course of your life*. New York, NY: Pantheon Books.

Senior, J. (2015, August 17). *NeuroTribes*, by Steve Silberman [Book review]. *The New York Times*. Retrieved from http://www.nytimes.com/2015/08/23/books/review/neurotribes-by-steve-silberman.html

Silberman, S. (2015). *NeuroTribes: The legacy of autism and the future of neurodiversity*. New York, NY: Avery/Penguin Random House.

Sowell, T. (2001). *The Einstein syndrome: Bright children who talk late*. New York, NY: Basic Books.

Steinberg, P. (2012, January 31). Asperger's history of overdiagnosis. *The New York Times*. Retrieved from http://www.nytimes.com/2012/02/01/opinion/aspergers-history-of-over-diagnosis.html

Yanofsky, J. (2014, July 31). *The kids who don't beat autism*. *New York Times*. Retrieved September 15, 2016, from http://parenting.blogs.nytimes.com/2014/07/31/the-kids-who-dont-beat-autism/

SCIENTIFIC READINGS

Autism Rates, Screening, and Diagnosis

Buxbaum, J. D., & Hof, P. R. (2013). *The neuroscience of autism spectrum disorders*. New York, NY: Academic Press.

CAR Autism Roadmap. (n.d.). *Medical diagnosis vs. educational eligibility for special services: Important distinctions for those with ASD*. Retrieved from https://www.carautismroadmap.org/medical-diagnosis-vs-educational-eligibility-for-special-services-important-distinctions-for-those-with-asd/. Last updated June 15, 2016.

Centers for Disease Control and Prevention (CDC). (n.d.-a). *Autism spectrum disorder: Facts about ASDs*. Retrieved September 15, 2016, from http://www.cdc.gov/ncbddd/autism/facts.html

Centers for Disease Control and Prevention (CDC). (n.d.-b). *Reproductive health: Data and statistics*. Retrieved September 15, 2016, from http://www.cdc.gov/reproductivehealth/data_stats/

Charman, T., & Gotham, K. (2013). Measurement issues: Screening and diagnostic instruments for autism spectrum disorders—lessons from research and practise. *Child and Adolescent Mental Health, 18*(1), 52–63. http://doi.org/10.1111/j.1475-3588.2012.00664.x

Christensen, D. L., Baio, J., Braun, K. V., Bilder, D., Charles, J., Constantino, J. N., . . . Yeargin-Allsopp, M. (2016). Prevalence and characteristics of autism spectrum disorder among children aged 8 years—Autism and Developmental Disabilities Monitoring Network, 11 sites, United States, 2012. *MMWR Surveillance Summaries, 65*(SS-3), 1–23. doi:http://dx.doi.org/10.15585/mmwr.ss6503a1

Daniels, A. M., Halladay, A. K., Shih, A., Elder, L. M., & Dawson, G. (2014). Approaches to enhancing the early detection of autism spectrum disorders: A systematic review of the literature. *Journal of the American Academy of Child & Adolescent Psychiatry, 53*(2), 141–152. http://doi.org/10.1016/j.jaac.2013.11.002

Educational vs. medical autism diagnosis. (2013, June 27). *Spectrums Magazine*. Retrieved from http://spectrumsmagazine.com/educational-vs-medical-autism-diagnosis/

Elsabbagh, M., Divan, G., Koh, Y.-J., Kim, Y. S., Kauchali, S., Marcín, C., . . . Fombonne, E. (2012). Global prevalence of autism and other pervasive developmental disorders. *Autism Research, 5*(3), 160–179. http://doi.org/10.1002/aur.239

Falkmer, T., Anderson, K., Falkmer, M., & Horlin, C. (2013). Diagnostic procedures in autism spectrum disorders: A systematic literature review. *European Child & Adolescent Psychiatry, 22*(6), 329–340. http://doi.org/10.1007/s00787-013-0375-0

Hansen, S. N., Schendel, D. E., & Parner, E. T. (2015). Explaining the increase in the prevalence of autism spectrum disorders: The proportion attributable to changes in reporting practices. *JAMA Pediatrics, 169*(1), 56–62. http://doi.org/10.1001/jamapediatrics.2014.1893

Huguet, G., Ey, E., & Bourgeron, T. (2013). The genetic landscapes of autism spectrum disorders. *Annual Review of Genomics Human Genetics, 14*, 191–213.

Iwata, K., Matsuzaki, H., Takei, N., Manabe, T., & Mori, N. (2010). Animal models of autism: An epigenetic and environmental viewpoint. *Journal of Central Nervous System Disease, 2*, 37–44. Retrieved from https://www.ncbi.nlm.nih.gov/pmc/articles/PMC3661233/

Jonge, M. de, Parr, J., Rutter, M., Wallace, S., Kemner, C., Bailey, A., . . . Pickles, A. (2014). New interview and observation measures of the broader autism phenotype: Group differentiation. *Journal of Autism and Developmental Disorders, 45*(4), 893–901. http://doi.org/10.1007/s10803-014-2230-7

Kim, Y. S., Fombonne, E., Koh, Y.-J., Kim, S.-J., Cheon, K.-A., & Leventhal, B. L. (2014). A comparison of *DSM-IV* pervasive developmental disorder and *DSM-5* autism spectrum disorder prevalence in an epidemiologic sample. *Journal of the American Academy of Child & Adolescent Psychiatry, 53*(5), 500–508. http://doi.org/10.1016/j.jaac.2013.12.021

Kulage, K. M., Smaldone, A. M., & Cohn, E. G. (2014). How will *DSM-5* affect autism diagnosis? A systematic literature review and meta-analysis. *Journal of Autism and Developmental Disorders, 44*(8), 1918–1932. http://doi.org/10.1007/s10803-014-2065-2

Lord, C., Petkova, E., Hus, V., Gan, W., Lu, F., Martin, D. M., . . . Risi, S. (2012). A multisite study of the clinical diagnosis of different autism spectrum disorders. *Archives of General Psychiatry, 69*(3), 306–313. http://doi.org/10.1001/archgenpsychiatry.2011.148

Luhrmann, T. M. (2001). *Of two minds: An anthropologist looks at american psychiatry.* New York, NY: Vintage.

Mayes, S. D., Calhoun, S. L., Murray, M. J., Pearl, A., Black, A., & Tierney, C. D. (2014). Final *DSM-5* under-identifies mild autism spectrum disorder: Agreement between the *DSM-5*, CARS, CASD, and clinical diagnoses. *Research in Autism Spectrum Disorders, 8*(2), 68–73. http://doi.org/10.1016/j.rasd.2013.11.002

Ozonoff, S., Young, G. S., Belding, A., Hill, M., Hill, A., Hutman, T., . . . Iosif, A.-M. (2014). The broader autism phenotype in infancy: When does it emerge? *Journal of the American Academy of Child & Adolescent Psychiatry, 53*(4), 398–407.e2. http://doi.org/10.1016/j.jaac.2013.12.020

Salazar, F., Baird, G., Chandler, S., Tseng, E., O'Sullivan, T., Howlin, P., . . . Simonoff, E. (2015). Co-occurring psychiatric disorders in preschool and elementary school-aged children with autism spectrum disorder. *Journal of Autism and Developmental Disorders, 45*(8):2283–2294.

Sandin, S., Hultman, C. M., Kolevzon, A., Gross, R., MacCabe, J. H., & Reichenberg, A. (2012). Advancing maternal age is associated with increasing risk for autism: A review and meta-analysis. *Journal of the American Academy of Child & Adolescent Psychiatry, 51*(5), 477–486.e1. http://doi.org/10.1016/j.jaac.2012.02.018

Wigham, S., Rodgers, J., South, M., McConachie, H., & Freeston, M. (2014). The interplay between sensory processing abnormalities, intolerance of uncertainty, anxiety and restricted and repetitive behaviours in autism spectrum disorder. *Journal of Autism and Developmental Disorders, 45*(4), 943–952. http://doi.org/10.1007/s10803-014-2248-x

Zablotsky, B., Black, L. I., Maenner, M. J., Schieve, L. A., & Blumberg, S. J. (2015, November 13). *Estimated prevalence of autism and other developmental disabilities following questionnaire changes in the 2014 National Health Interview Survey.* National Health Statistics Report No. 87. Retrieved from https://pdfs.semanticscholar.org/92c2/2987bdb4397ef53b8e2b0b8a7bda432a0900.pdf

Laws, Policies, Economics

Buescher, A. S., Cidav, Z., Knapp, M., & Mandell, D. S. (2014). Costs of autism spectrum disorders in the United Kingdom and the United States. *JAMA Pediatrics, 168*(8), 721–728. http://doi.org/10.1001/jamapediatrics.2014.210

Harpe, D. L., & Baker, D. L. (2007). Financial issues associated with having a child with autism. *Journal of Family and Economic Issues, 28*(2), 247–264. http://doi.org/10.1007/s10834-007-9059-6

Leigh, J. P., & Du, J. (2015). Brief report: Forecasting the economic burden of autism in 2015 and 2025 in the United States. *Journal of Autism and Developmental Disorders, 45*(12), 4135–4139. http://doi.org/10.1007/s10803-015-2521-7

US Department of Labor. (2015, December 9). *FMLA (Family & Medical Leave).* Retrieved September 15, 2016, from https://www.dol.gov/general/topic/benefits-leave/fmla

US Department of Labor, Wage and Hour Division. (n.d.). *Family and Medical Leave Act.* Retrieved September 15, 2016, from https://www.dol.gov/whd/fmla/

Psychology of Autism Diagnosis

American Psychiatric Association. (1987). *Diagnostic and statistical manual of mental disorders* (3rd ed., rev.; *DSM-III-R*). Washington, DC: APA Press.

American Psychiatric Association. (1994). *Diagnostic and statistical manual of mental disorders* (4th ed.; *DSM-IV*). Washington, DC: APA Press.

Cascio, M. A. (2012). Neurodiversity: Autism pride among mothers of children with autism spectrum disorders. *Intellectual and Developmental Disabilities, 50*(3), 273–283. http://doi.org/10.1352/1934-9556-50.3.273

Clifford, T., & Minnes, P. (2012a). Logging on: Evaluating an online support group for parents of children with autism spectrum disorders. *Journal of Autism and Developmental Disorders, 43*(7), 1662–1675. http://doi.org/10.1007/s10803-012-1714-6

Clifford, T., & Minnes, P. (2012b). Who participates in support groups for parents of children with autism spectrum disorders? The role of beliefs and coping style. *Journal of Autism and Developmental Disorders, 43*(1), 179–187. http://doi.org/10.1007/s10803-012-1561-5

Corcoran, J., Berry, A., & Hill, S. (2015). The lived experience of US parents of children with autism spectrum disorders A systematic review and meta-synthesis. *Journal of Intellectual Disabilities, 19*(4), 356–366. http://doi.org/10.1177/1744629515577876

Crane, L., Chester, J. W., Goddard, L., Henry, L. A., & Hill, E. (2016). Experiences of autism diagnosis: A survey of over 1000 parents in the United Kingdom. *Autism,* 20(2), 153–162. http://doi.org/10.1177/1362361315573636

Evans, B. (2012). *Understanding autism: Parents, doctors and the history of a disorder* (Princeton, NJ: Princeton University Press, 2012; 340 pp) [Book review]. *Psychoanalysis and History, 15*(1), 116–119. http://doi.org/10.3366/pah.2013.0126

Fernández-Alcántara, M., García-Caro, M. P., Pérez-Marfil, M. N., Hueso-Montoro, C., Laynez-Rubio, C., & Cruz-Quintana, F. (2016). Feelings of loss and grief in parents of children diagnosed with autism spectrum disorder (ASD). *Research in Developmental Disabilities, 55,* 312–321. http://doi.org/10.1016/j.ridd.2016.05.007

Gray, D. E. (2002). Ten years on: A longitudinal study of families of children with autism. *Journal of Intellectual & Developmental Disability, 27*(3), 215–222. http://doi.org/10.1080/1366825021000008639

Harpe, D. L., & Baker, D. L. (2007). Financial issues associated with having a child with autism. *Journal of Family and Economic Issues, 28*(2), 247–264. http://doi.org/10.1007/s10834-007-9059-6

Hayes, S. A., & Watson, S. L. (2012). The impact of parenting stress: A meta-analysis of studies comparing the experience of parenting stress in parents of children with and without autism spectrum disorder. *Journal of Autism and Developmental Disorders, 43*(3), 629–642. http://doi.org/10.1007/s10803-012-1604-y

Hidalgo, N. J., McIntyre, L. L., & McWhirter, E. H. (2015). Sociodemographic differences in parental satisfaction with an autism spectrum disorder diagnosis. *Journal of Intellectual & Developmental Disability, 40*(2), 147–155. http://doi.org/10.3109/13668250.2014.994171

Ivey, J. K. (2004). What do parents expect? A study of likelihood and importance issues for children with autism spectrum disorders. *Focus on Autism and Other Developmental Disabilities, 19*(1), 27–33. http://doi.org/10.1177/10883576040190010401

Jones, L., Goddard, L., Hill, E. L., Henry, L. A., & Crane, L. (2014). Experiences of receiving a diagnosis of autism spectrum disorder: A survey of adults in the United

Kingdom. *Journal of Autism and Developmental Disorders, 44*(12), 3033–3044. http://doi.org/10.1007/s10803-014-2161-3

Langan, M. (2011). Parental voices and controversies in autism. *Disability & Society, 26*(2), 193–205. http://doi.org/10.1080/09687599.2011.544059

Rocque, B. (2009). Science fictions: Figuring autism as threat and mystery in medico-therapeutic literature. *Disability Studies Quarterly, 30*(1). Retrieved from http://dsq-sds.org/article/view/1064

Russell, G., & Norwich, B. (2012). Dilemmas, diagnosis and de-stigmatization: Parental perspectives on the diagnosis of autism spectrum disorders. *Clinical Child Psychology and Psychiatry, 17*(2), 229–245. http://doi.org/10.1177/1359104510365203

Siegel, B. (2004). *Pervasive Developmental Disorders Screening Test-II.* San Antonio, TX: Psychological Corporation/Harcourt Assessment/Pearson.

Siegel, B. (2010). Reconceptualizing autistic spectrum disorders as autism-specific learning disabilities and learning styles. In T. Millon, Krueger, & Simonsen (Eds.), *Contemporary directions in psychopathology* (pp. 553–564). New York, NY: Guilford Press.

Siklos, S., & Kerns, K. A. (2006). Assessing need for social support in parents of children with autism and Down syndrome. *Journal of Autism and Developmental Disorders, 36*(7), 921–933. http://doi.org/10.1007/s10803-006-0129-7

Solomon, A. (2012). *Far from the tree: Parents, children and the search for identity.* New York, NY: Scribner/Simon & Schuster.

Watters, E. (2011). *Crazy like us: The globalization of the American psyche* (Reprint edition). New York, NY: Free Press.

Chapter 3

POPULAR MEDIA

American Psychiatric Association. *DSM history.* (n.d.). Retrieved September 15, 2016, from https://www.psychiatry.org/psychiatrists/practice/dsm/history-of-the-dsm

Beautiful minds, wasted. (2016, April 16). *The Economist.* Retrieved from http://www.economist.com/news/leaders/21696944-how-not-squander-potential-autistic-people-beautiful-minds-wasted

Bray, J. H. (2009). President's column: Psychology, politics, APA and you. *Monitor on Psychology, 40*(4). Retrieved September 15, 2016, from http://www.apa.org/monitor/2009/04/pc.aspx

Carey, B. (2012, January 19). New definition of autism may exclude many, study suggests. *The New York Times.* Retrieved from http://www.nytimes.com/2012/01/20/health/research/new-autism-definition-would-exclude-many-study-suggests.html

Centers for Disease Control and Prevention. (n.d.) *Facts about ASDs.* Retrieved September 15, 2016, from http://www.cdc.gov/ncbddd/autism/facts.html

Disability Rights California. (2014, November). *What does SB 946 (which requires private health plans to provide some services for people with autism) mean for me?* (F071.01). Retrieved September 15, 2016, from http://www.disabilityrightsca.org/pubs/F07101.pdf

Drug-fuelled couplings. (2015, November 5). *The Economist.* Retrieved from http://www.economist.com/news/business/21677637-why-giant-mergers-are-especially-popular-among-drugmakers-drug-fuelled-couplings?zid=318&ah=ac379c09c1c3fb67e0e8fd1964d5247f

DSM-5 *diagnostic criteria.* (2013, July 29). Retrieved September 15, 2016, from Autism Speaks website: https://www.autismspeaks.org/what-autism/diagnosis/dsm-5-diagnostic-criteria

Frances, A. (2013). *Saving normal.* New York, NY: William Morrow/HarperCollins.

Hamblin, J. (2014, March 7). What it's like on the autism spectrum. *The Atlantic.* Retrieved from http://www.theatlantic.com/health/archive/2014/03/what-its-like-on-the-autism-spectrum/284268/

In praise of misfits. (2012, June 2). *The Economist.* Retrieved from http://www.economist.com/node/21556230

Laing, R. D. (1967). *The politics of experience.* New York, NY: Pantheon Books.

Larsen, A. (Filmmaker). (2013, July 29). Timeline: A cultural history of autism: Neurotypical [Television series episode]. *POV.* United States: PBS. Retrieved from http://www.pbs.org/pov/neurotypical/timeline-autism-history/

Locker, R. (2015, February 4). Pentagon 2008 study claims Putin has Asperger's syndrome. *USA Today.* Retrieved from http://www.usatoday.com/story/news/politics/2015/02/04/putin-aspergers-syndrome-study-pentagon/22855927/

McGuire, A. (2013, August 14). *The war on autism: On normative violence and the cultural production of autism advocacy* (Doctoral dissertation). Retrieved from https://tspace.library.utoronto.ca/handle/1807/36211

McQuiston, J. T. (1989, August 24). R. D. Laing, rebel and pioneer on schizophrenia, is dead at 61. *The New York Times.* Retrieved from http://www.nytimes.com/1989/08/24/obituaries/rd-laing-rebel-and-pioneer-on-schizophrenia-is-dead-at-61.html

Nugent, B. (2012, January 31). I had Asperger syndrome. Briefly. *The New York Times.* Retrieved from http://www.nytimes.com/2012/02/01/opinion/i-had-asperger-syndrome-briefly.html

Ratey, J. J., & Johnson, C. (1997). *Shadow syndromes: Recognizing and coping with the hidden psychological disorders that can influence your behavior and silently determine the course of your life.* New York, NY: Pantheon Books.

Reese, H. (2013, May 2). The real problems with psychiatry. *The Atlantic.* Retrieved from http://www.theatlantic.com/health/archive/2013/05/the-real-problems-with-psychiatry/275371/

Rosin, H. (2014, March). Letting go of Asperger's. *The Atlantic.* Retrieved from http://www.theatlantic.com/magazine/archive/2014/03/letting-go-of-aspergers/357563/

Schwarz, A. (2015, December 10). Still in a crib, yet being given antipsychotics. *The New York Times.* Retrieved from http://www.nytimes.com/2015/12/11/us/psychiatric-drugs-are-being-prescribed-to-infants.html

Simpson, D. E., Hanley, J. J., & Quinn, G. (Filmmakers). (2002, July 16). History of autism blame: Refrigerator mothers [Television series episode]. *POV.* United States: PBS. Retrieved from http://www.pbs.org/pov/refrigeratormothers/fridge/

Spectrum shift. (2016a, April 16). *The Economist.* Retrieved from http://www.economist.com/news/briefing/21696928-children-rich-world-are-far-more-likely-be-diagnosed-autism-past-why

Wallis, C. (2009, November 2). A vanishing diagnosis for Asperger's syndrome. *The New York Times.* Retrieved from http://www.nytimes.com/2009/11/03/health/03asperger.html

Weintraub, K. (2016, April 28). Asperger's Are Us offers comedy for all. *The New York Times.* Retrieved September 15, 2016, from http://well.blogs.nytimes.com/2016/04/28/aspergers-are-us-offers-comedy-for-all/

Yale School of Medicine, Child Study Center: Research. (n.d.). *Pervasive developmental disorder—Not otherwise specified*. Retrieved September 15, 2016, from http://childstudycenter.yale.edu/autism/information/pddnos.aspx

SCIENTIFIC READINGS

American Psychiatric Association. (1950). *Diagnostic and statistical manual of mental disorders*. Washington, DC: APA Press.

American Psychiatric Association. (1952). *Diagnostic and Statistical Manual of Mental Disorders (DSM)*. Washington, DC: APA Press.

American Psychiatric Association. (1968). *Diagnostic and statistical manual of mental disorders* (2nd ed.; *DSM-II*). Washington, DC: APA Press.

American Psychiatric Association. (1974). *Diagnostic and statistical manual of mental disorders* (2nd ed.; *DSM-II*). Washington, DC: APA Press.

American Psychiatric Association. (1980). *Diagnostic and statistical manual of mental disorders* (3th ed.; *DSM-III*). Washington, DC: APA Press.

American Psychiatric Association. (1987). *Diagnostic and statistical manual of mental disorders* (3rd ed., revised; *DSM-III-R*). Washington, DC: APA Press.

American Psychiatric Association. (1994). *Diagnostic and statistical manual of mental disorders* (4th ed.; *DSM-IV*). Washington, DC: APA Press.

American Psychiatric Association. (2000). *Diagnostic and statistical manual of mental disorders* (4th ed., text revision; *DSM-IV-TR*). Washington, DC: APA Press.

American Psychiatric Association. (2013). *Diagnostic and statistical manual of mental disorders* (5th ed.; *DSM-5*). Washington, DC: APA Press.

DSM Criteria and APA Politics

Collier, R. (2012). Person-first language: Noble intent but to what effect? *Canadian Medical Association Journal, 184*(18), 1977–1978. http://doi.org/10.1503/cmaj.109-4319

Dunn, D. S., & Andrews, E. E. (2015). Person-first and identity-first language: Developing psychologists' cultural competence using disability language. *American Psychologist, 70*(3), 255–264. http://doi.org/10.1037/a0038636

Elsabbagh, M., Divan, G., Koh, Y.-J., Kim, Y. S., Kauchali, S., Marcín, C., . . . Fombonne, E. (2012). Global prevalence of autism and other pervasive developmental disorders. *Autism Research, 5*(3), 160–179. http://doi.org/10.1002/aur.239

Falkmer, T., Anderson, K., Falkmer, M., & Horlin, C. (2013). Diagnostic procedures in autism spectrum disorders: A systematic literature review. *European Child & Adolescent Psychiatry, 22*(6), 329–340. http://doi.org/10.1007/s00787-013-0375-0

Gillberg, C. (2010). The ESSENCE in child psychiatry: Early symptomatic syndromes eliciting neurodevelopmental clinical examinations. *Research in Developmental Disabilities, 31*, 1543–1551.

Gillberg, C., Fernell, E., & Minnis, H. (2014). Early symptomatic syndromes eliciting neurodevelopmental clinical examinations (ESSENCE). *Scientific World Journal, 2014*, 710570. http://doi.org/10.1155/2013/710570. eCollection

Hansen, S. N., Schendel, D. E., & Parner, E. T. (2015). Explaining the increase in the prevalence of autism spectrum disorders: The proportion attributable to changes in reporting practices. *JAMA Pediatrics, 169*(1), 56–62. http://doi.org/10.1001/jamapediatrics.2014.1893

Insel, T. R. (2014a). Mental disorders in childhood: Shifting the focus from behavioral symptoms to neurodevelopmental trajectories. *JAMA, 311*(17), 1727–1728. http://doi.org/10.1001/jama.2014.1193

Insel, T. R. (2014b). The NIMH Research Domain Criteria (RDoC) Project: Precision medicine for psychiatry. *American Journal of Psychiatry, 171*(4):395–397. http://doi.org/10.1176/appi.ajp.2014.14020138

Johnson, R. A., Barrett, M. S., & Sisti, D. A. (2013). The ethical boundaries of patient and advocate influence on *DSM-5. Harvard Review of Psychiatry, 21*(6), 334–344. http://doi.org/10.1097/HRP.0000000000000010

Kanner, L. (1943). Autistic disturbances of affective contact. *The Nervous Child, 2,* 217–250.

Kanner, L. (1949). Problems of nosology and psychodynamics in early childhood autism. *American Journal of Orthopsychiatry, 19*(3), 416–426. doi:10.1111/j.1939-0025.1949.tb05441.x

Kanner, L. (1968). Autistic disturbances of affective context. *Acta Paedopsychiatrica, 35*(4), 100–136.

Kanner, L., & Eisenberg, L. (1956). Early infantile autism 1943–1955. *American Journal of Orthopsychiatry, 26*(3), 556–566. doi:10.1111/j.1939-0025.1956.tb06202.x

Katz, N., & Zemishlany, Z. (2006). Criminal responsibility in Asperger's syndrome. *Israel Journal of Psychiatry and Related Sciences, 43*(3), 166–173.

Kawa, S., & Giordano, J. (2012). A brief historicity of the *Diagnostic and Statistical Manual of Mental Disorders*: Issues and implications for the future of psychiatric canon and practice. *Philosophy, Ethics, and Humanities in Medicine: PEHM, 7,* 2. http://doi.org/10.1186/1747-5341-7-2

Kim, Y. S., Fombonne, E., Koh, Y.-J., Kim, S.-J., Cheon, K.-A., & Leventhal, B. L. (2014). A comparison of *DSM-IV* pervasive developmental disorder and *DSM-5* autism spectrum disorder prevalence in an epidemiologic sample. *Journal of the American Academy of Child & Adolescent Psychiatry, 53*(5), 500–508. http://doi.org/10.1016/j.jaac.2013.12.021

Kulage, K. M., Smaldone, A. M., & Cohn, E. G. (2014). How will *DSM-5* affect autism diagnosis? A systematic literature review and meta-analysis. *Journal of Autism and Developmental Disorders, 44*(8), 1918–1932. http://doi.org/10.1007/s10803-014-2065-2

Lyons, V., & Fitzgerald, M. (2007). Asperger (1906–1980) and Kanner (1894–1981), the two pioneers of autism. *Journal of Autism and Developmental Disorders, 37*(10), 2022–2023. http://doi.org/DOI 10.1007/s10803-007-0383-3

Mallett, R., & Runswick-Cole, K. (2012). Commodifying autism: The cultural contexts of "disability" in the academy. In D. Goodley, B. Hughes, & L. Davis (Eds.), *Disability and social theory* (pp. 33–51). London: Palgrave Macmillan UK. Retrieved from http://link.springer.com/chapter/10.1057/9781137023001_3

Matson, J. L., Dempsey, T., LoVullo, S. V., Fodstad, J. C., Knight, C., Sevin, J. A., & Sharp, B. (2013). The moderating effects of intellectual development on core symptoms of autism and PDD-NOS in toddlers and infants. *Research in Developmental Disabilities, 34*(1), 573–578. http://doi.org/10.1016/j.ridd.2012.03.031

Mattison, R., Cantwell, D. P., Russell, A. T., & Will, L. (1979). A comparison of *DSM-II* and *DSM-III* in the diagnosis of childhood psychiatric disorders II. Interrater agreement. *Archives of General Psychiatry, 36*(11), 1217–1222. doi:10.1001/archpsyc.1979.01780110071008

Mayes, S. D., Black, A., & Tierney, C. D. (2013). *DSM-5* under-identifies PDDNOS: Diagnostic agreement between the *DSM-5, DSM-IV*, and Checklist for

Autism Spectrum Disorder. *Research in Autism Spectrum Disorders, 7*(2), 298–306. http://doi.org/10.1016/j.rasd.2012.08.011

McGuire, A. E. (2013). Buying time: The S/pace of advocacy and the cultural production of autism. *Canadian Journal of Disability Studies, 2*(3), 98–125. http://doi.org/10.15353/cjds.v2i3.102

McPartland, J. C., Reichow, B., & Volkmar, F. R. (2012). Sensitivity and specificity of proposed *DSM-5* diagnostic criteria for autism spectrum disorder. *Journal of the American Academy of Child & Adolescent Psychiatry, 51*(4), 368–383. http://doi.org/10.1016/j.jaac.2012.01.007

Ohan, J. L., Ellefson, S. E., & Corrigan, P. W. (2015). Brief report: The impact of changing from *DSM-IV* "Asperger's" to *DSM-5* "autistic spectrum disorder" diagnostic labels on stigma and treatment attitudes. *Journal of Autism and Developmental Disorders, 45*(10), 3384–3389. http://doi.org/10.1007/s10803-015-2485-7

Orsini, M., & Smith, M. (2010). Social movements, knowledge and public policy: The case of autism activism in Canada and the US. *Critical Policy Studies, 4*(1), 38–57. http://doi.org/10.1080/19460171003714989

Pennington, M. L., Cullinan, D., & Southern, L. B. (2014). Defining autism: Variability in state education agency definitions of and evaluations for autism spectrum disorders. *Autism Research and Treatment, 2014*, e327271. http://doi.org/10.1155/2014/

Sheinkopf, S., & Siegel, B. (1998). Effects of very early intensive behavioral intervention for autistic children. *Journal of Autism and Developmental Disorders, 28*(1), 15–23.

Shorter, E. (2015). The history of nosology and the rise of the *Diagnostic and Statistical Manual of Mental Disorders. Dialogues in Clinical Neuroscience, 17*(1), 59–67.

Spitzer, R. L., & Siegel, B. (1990). The *DSM-III-R* field trials for pervasive developmental disorders. *Journal of the American Academy of Child and Adolescent Psychiatry, 26*(6):855–862.

Tsai, L. Y., & Ghaziuddin, M. (2013). *DSM-5* ASD moves forward into the past. *Journal of Autism and Developmental Disorders, 44*(2), 321–330. http://doi.org/10.1007/s10803-013-1870-3

Viding, E., & Blakemore, S.-J. (2006). Endophenotype approach to developmental psychopathology: Implications for autism research. *Behavior Genetics, 37*(1), 51–60. http://doi.org/10.1007/s10519-006-9105-4

Volkmar, F. R., & McPartland, J. C. (2014). From Kanner to *DSM-5*: Autism as an evolving diagnostic concept. *Annual Review of Clinical Psychology, 10*(1), 193–212. http://doi.org/10.1146/annurev-clinpsy-032813-153710

Volkmar, F. R., State, M., & Klin, A. (2009). Autism and autism spectrum disorders: Diagnostic issues for the coming decade. *Journal of Child Psychology and Psychiatry, 50*(1–2), 108–115. http://doi.org/10.1111/j.1469-7610.2008.02010.x

Wigham, S., Rodgers, J., South, M., McConachie, H., & Freeston, M. (2014). The interplay between sensory processing abnormalities, intolerance of uncertainty, anxiety and restricted and repetitive behaviours in autism spectrum disorder. *Journal of Autism and Developmental Disorders, 45*(4), 943–952. http://doi.org/10.1007/s10803-014-2248-x

Medication Trends

Anderson, G. M. (2014). Autism biomarkers: Challenges, pitfalls and possibilities. *Journal of Autism and Developmental Disorders, 45*(4), 1103–1113. http://doi.org/10.1007/s10803-014-2225-4

Chirdkiatgumchai, V., Xiao, H., Fredstrom, B. K., Adams, R. E., Epstein, J. N., Shah, S. S., . . . Froehlich, T. E. (2013). National trends in psychotropic medication use in young children: 1994–2009. *Pediatrics, 132*(4), 615–623. peds.2013–1546. http://doi.org/10.1542/peds.2013-1546

Comer, J. S., Olfson, M., & Mojtabai, R. (2010). National trends in child and adolescent psychotropic polypharmacy in office-based practice, 1996–2007. *Journal of the American Academy of Child and Adolescent Psychiatry, 49*(10), 1001–1010. http://doi.org/10.1016/j.jaac.2010.07.007

Hunsinger, D. M., Nguyen, T., Zebraski, S. E., & Raffa, R. B. (2000). Is there a basis for novel pharmacotherapy of autism? *Life Sciences, 67*(14), 1667–1682. http://doi.org/10.1016/S0024-3205(00)00763-3

Schwarz, A. (2015, December 10). Still in a crib, yet being given antipsychotics. *The New York Times.* Retrieved from http://www.nytimes.com/2015/12/11/us/psychiatric-drugs-are-being-prescribed-to-infants.html

Chapter 4

POPULAR MEDIA

Response to intervention. (n.d.). Retrieved from Special Education Guide website: http://www.specialeducationguide.com/pre-k-12/response-to-intervention/

US Department of Education. (2010, November). *Thirty-five years of progress in educating children with disabilities through IDEA.* Retrieved September 14, 2016, from https://www2.ed.gov/about/offices/list/osers/idea35/history/idea-35-history.pdf

SCIENTIFIC READINGS

Behavior Analysis and Education

Grindle, C. F., Hastings, R. P., Saville, M., Hughes, J. C., Huxley, K., Kovshoff, H., . . . Remington, B. (2012). Outcomes of a behavioral education model for children with autism in a mainstream school setting. *Behavior Modification, 36*(3), 298–319. http://doi.org/10.1177/0145445512441199

Harris, S. L., & Delmolino, L. (2002). Applied behavior analysis: Its application in the treatment of autism and related disorders infants & young children. *Infants and Young Children, 14*(3), 11–17. Retrieved September 26, 2016, from http://journals.lww.com/iycjournal/Fulltext/2002/01000/Applied_Behavior_Analysis__Its_Application_in_the.6.aspx

Hilton, J. C., & Seal, B. C. (2006). Brief report: Comparative ABA and DIR trials in twin brothers with autism. *Journal of Autism and Developmental Disorders, 37*(6), 1197–1201. http://doi.org/10.1007/s10803-006-0258-z

Larsson, E. (n.d.). *Is applied behavior analysis (ABA) and early intensive behavioral intervention (EIBI) an effective treatment for autism? A cumulative history of impartial independent reviews.* The Lovaas Institute. Retrieved from http://www.behavior.org/resources/649.pdf

Mohammadzaheri, F., Koegel, L. K., Rezaee, M., & Rafiee, S. M. (2014). A randomized clinical trial comparison between pivotal response treatment (PRT) and structured applied behavior analysis (ABA) intervention for children with autism. *Journal of Autism and Developmental Disorders, 44*(11), 2769–2777. http://doi.org/10.1007/s10803-014-2137-3

Romanczyk, R. G., Callahan, E. H., Turner, L. B., & Cavalari, R. N. S. (2014). Efficacy of behavioral interventions for young children with autism spectrum disorders: Public policy, the evidence base, and implementation parameters. *Review Journal of Autism and Developmental Disorders, 1*(4), 276–326. http://doi.org/10.1007/s40489-014-0025-6

Domains of Intervention

Chevallier, C., Kohls, G., Troiani, V., Brodkin, E. S., & Schultz, R. T. (2012). The social motivation theory of autism. *Trends in Cognitive Sciences, 16*(4), 231–239. http://doi.org/10.1016/j.tics.2012.02.007

D'Elia, L., Valeri, G., Sonnino, F., Fontana, I., Mammone, A., & Vicari, S. (2013). A longitudinal study of the TEACCH program in different settings: The potential benefits of low intensity intervention in preschool children with autism spectrum disorder. *Journal of Autism and Developmental Disorders, 44*(3), 615–626. http://doi.org/10.1007/s10803-013-1911-y

Foxx, R. M. (2008). Applied behavior analysis treatment of autism: The state of the art. *Child and Adolescent Psychiatric Clinics of North America, 17*(4), 821–834. http://doi.org/10.1016/j.chc.2008.06.007

Foxx, R. M., & Mulick, J. A. (2015). *Controversial therapies for autism and intellectual disabilities: Fad, fashion, and science in professional practice.* Abingdon-on-Thames, England: Routledge.

Grindle, C. F., Kovshoff, H., Hastings, R. P., & Remington, B. (2008). Parents' experiences of home-based applied behavior analysis programs for young children with autism. *Journal of Autism and Developmental Disorders, 39*(1), 42–56. http://doi.org/10.1007/s10803-008-0597-z

Leonard, H. C., Bedford, R., Pickles, A., & Hill, E. L. (2015). Predicting the rate of language development from early motor skills in at-risk infants who develop autism spectrum disorder. *Research in Autism Spectrum Disorders, 13–14*, 15–24. http://doi.org/10.1016/j.rasd.2014.12.012

Matson, J. L., Benavidez, D. A., Stabinsky Compton, L., Paclawskyj, T., & Baglio, C. (1996). Behavioral treatment of autistic persons: A review of research from 1980 to the present. *Research in Developmental Disabilities, 17*(6), 433–465. http://doi.org/10.1016/S0891-4222(96)00030-3

Peters-Scheffer, N., Didden, R., Korzilius, H., & Sturmey, P. (2011). A meta-analytic study on the effectiveness of comprehensive ABA-based early intervention programs for children with autism spectrum disorders. *Research in Autism Spectrum Disorders, 5*(1), 60–69. http://doi.org/10.1016/j.rasd.2010.03.011

Schreibman, L., & Stahmer, A. C. (2013). A randomized trial comparison of the effects of verbal and pictorial naturalistic communication strategies on spoken language for young children with autism. *Journal of Autism and Developmental Disorders, 44*(5), 1244–1251. http://doi.org/10.1007/s10803-013-1972-y

Schuele, C. M. (2013). Adequacy and accessibility. *Language Speech and Hearing Services in Schools, 44*(4), 325. http://doi.org/10.1044/0161-1461(2013/ed-04)

Smith, T., Groen, A. D., & Wynn, J. W. (2000). Randomized trial of intensive early intervention for children with pervasive developmental disorder. *American Journal of Mental Retardation, 105*, 269–285.

Snyder, N. (2016). The new education law and ASHA members: The Every Student Succeeds Act gives school-based audiologists and speech-language pathologists a greater role in literacy efforts and more funding to carry them out. *ASHA Leader, 21*(2), 26. http://doi.org/10.1044/leader.PA.21022016.26

Virués-Ortega, J. (2010). Applied behavior analytic intervention for autism in early childhood: Meta-analysis, meta-regression and dose–response meta-analysis of multiple outcomes. *Clinical Psychology Review, 30*(4), 387–399. http://doi.org/10.1016/j.cpr.2010.01.008

Zablotsky, B., Bradshaw, C. P., Anderson, C. M., & Law, P. (2014). Risk factors for bullying among children with autism spectrum disorders. *Autism, 18*(4), 419–427. http://doi.org/10.1177/1362361313477920

Early Intervention

McConachie, H., & Diggle, T. (2007). Parent implemented early intervention for young children with autism spectrum disorder: a systematic review. *Journal of Evaluation in Clinical Practice, 13*(1), 120–129. http://doi.org/10.1111/j.1365-2753.2006.00674.x

McLean, M., Sandall, S. R., & Smith, B. J. (2016). A history of early childhood special education. In B. Reichow, B. A. Boyd, E. E. Barton, & S. L. Odom (Eds.), *Handbook of early childhood special education* (pp. 3–19). New York, NY: Springer International. Retrieved from http://link.springer.com/chapter/10.1007/978-3-319-28492-7_1

Reichow, B. (2016). Evidence-based practice in the context of early childhood special education. In B. Reichow, B. A. Boyd, E. E. Barton, & S. L. Odom (Eds.), *Handbook of early childhood special education* (pp. 107–121). New York, NY: Springer International. Retrieved from http://link.springer.com/chapter/10.1007/978-3-319-28492-7_7

Inclusive Education

Al-Yagon, M., Aram, D., & Margalit, M. (2016). Early childhood inclusion in Israel. *Infants & Young Children, 29*(3), 205–213. http://doi.org/10.1097/IYC.0000000000000063

Armstrong, F., Armstrong, D., & Barton, L. (2016). *Inclusive education: Policy, contexts and comparative perspectives.* Abingdon-on-Thames, England: Routledge.

Danforth, S., & Jones, P. (2015). From special education to integration to genuine inclusion. In P. Jones & S. Danforth (Eds.), *Foundations of inclusive education research* (Vol. 6, pp. 1–21). West Yorkshire, England: Emerald Group. Retrieved from http://www.emeraldinsight.com/doi/abs/10.1108/S1479-363620150000006014

Kasari, C., Freeman, S. F. N., Bauminger, N., & Alkin, M. C. (n.d.). Parental perspectives on inclusion: Effects of autism and Down syndrome. *Journal of Autism and Developmental Disorders, 29*(4), 297–305. http://doi.org/10.1023/A:1022159302571

Kauffman, J. M., & Hallahan, D. P. (Eds.). (1994). *The illusion of full inclusion: A comprehensive critique of a current special education bandwagon.* Austin, TX: Pro Ed.

Lindsay, S., Proulx, M., Thomson, N., & Scott, H. (2013). Educators' challenges of including children with autism spectrum disorder in mainstream classrooms. *International Journal of Disability, Development and Education, 60*(4), 347–362. http://doi.org/10.1080/1034912X.2013.846470

Pennington, M. L., Cullinan, D., & Southern, L. B. (2014). Defining autism: Variability in state education agency definitions of and evaluations for autism spectrum disorders. *Autism Research and Treatment, 2014*, e327271. http://doi.org/10.1155/2014/327271

Rodriguez, C. C., & Garro-Gil, N. (2015). Inclusion and integration on special educa-tion. *Procedia—Social and Behavioral Sciences, 191*, 1323–1327. http://doi.org/10.1016/j.sbspro.2015.04.488

Siegel, B. (1996). Is the emperor wearing clothes? Social policy and the empirical support for full inclusion of children with disabilities in the preschool and early elementary grades. *Monograph of the Society for Research in Child Development, 2/3*, 2–17.

Laws and Policies

Giordano, C. (2012). Uses of the class action device in autism health benefits litigation. *Wayne Law Review, 58*, 157.

Kurth, J. A. (2015). Educational placement of students with autism: The impact of state of residence. *Focus on Autism and Other Developmental Disabilities, 30*(4), 249–256. http://doi.org/10.1177/1088357614547891

Martin, E. W., Martin, R., & Terman, D. (1996). The legislative and litigation history of special education. *Special Education for Students With Disabilities, 6*(1), 25–39. Retrieved September 14, 2016, from https://www.princeton.edu/futureofchildren/publications/docs/06_01_01.pdf

Mead, J. F. (2014). The right to an education or the right to shop for schooling: Examining voucher programs in relation to state constitutional guarantees. *Fordham Urban Law Journal, 42*, 703.

Powell, J. J. W. (2015). *Barriers to inclusion: Special education in the United States and Germany*. Abingdon-on-Thames, England: Routledge.

Pudelski, S. (2016). *Rethinking special education due process: A proposal for the next reau-thorization of the Individuals With Disabilities Act*. Alexandria, VA: AASA, the School Superintendents Association.

US Department of Education. (n.d.). IDEA—Building the legacy: IDEA 2004. (n.d.). Retrieved September 14, 2016, from http://idea.ed.gov/

Special Education Models and Methods

Boyd, B. A., Hume, K., McBee, M. T., Alessandri, M., Gutierrez, A., Johnson, L., . . . Odom, S. L. (2013). Comparative efficacy of LEAP, TEACCH and non-model-specific special education programs for preschoolers with autism spectrum disorders. *Journal of Autism and Developmental Disorders, 44*(2), 366–380. http://doi.org/10.1007/s10803-013-1877-9

Cook, B. G., & Cook, S. C. (2013). Unraveling evidence-based practices in special ed-ucation. *The Journal of Special Education, 47*(2), 71–82. http://doi.org/10.1177/0022466911420877

Dawson, G., Rogers, S., Munson, J., Smith, M., Winter, J., Greenson, J., . . . Varley, J. (2010). Randomized, controlled trial of an intervention for toddlers with autism: The early start Denver model. *Pediatrics, 125*(1), e17–e23. http://doi.org/10.1542/peds.2009-0958

Dempsey, I., & Foreman, P. (2001). A review of educational approaches for individuals with autism. *International Journal of Disability, Development and Education, 48*(1), 103–116. http://doi.org/10.1080/10349120120036332

Hess, K. L., Morrier, M. J., Heflin, L. J., & Ivey, M. L. (2007). Autism treatment survey: Services received by children with autism spectrum disorders in public school classrooms. *Journal of Autism and Developmental Disorders, 38*(5), 961–971. http://doi.org/10.1007/s10803-007-0470-5

Hourigan, R. M. (2014). Intersections between school reform, the arts, and special education: The children left behind. *Arts Education Policy Review, 115*(2), 35–38. http://doi.org/10.1080/10632913.2014.883892

Howlin, P. (1998). Psychological and educational treatments for autism. *The Journal of Child Psychology and Psychiatry and Allied Disciplines, 39*(3), 307–322.

Locke, J., Rotheram-Fuller, E., Xie, M., Harker, C., & Mandell, D. (2014). Correlation of cognitive and social outcomes among children with autism spectrum disorder in a randomized trial of behavioral intervention. *Autism, 18*(4), 370–375. http://doi.org/10.1177/1362361313479181

Mattingly, D. J., Prislin, R., McKenzie, T. L., Rodriguez, J. L., & Kayzar, B. (2002). Evaluating evaluations: The case of parent involvement programs. *Review of Educational Research, 72*(4), 549–576. http://doi.org/10.3102/00346543072004549

Mesibov, G., Howley, M., & Naftel, S. (2015). *Accessing the curriculum for learners with autism spectrum disorders: Using the TEACCH program to help inclusion.* Abingdon-on-Thames, England: Routledge.

Nahmias, A. S., Kase, C., & Mandell, D. S. (2014). Comparing cognitive outcomes among children with autism spectrum disorders receiving community-based early intervention in one of three placements. *Autism, 18*(3), 311–320. http://doi.org/10.1177/1362361312467865

O'Connor, R. E., Bocian, K. M., Beach, K. D., Sanchez, V., & Flynn, L. J. (2013). Special education in a 4-year response to intervention (RtI) environment: Characteristics of students with learning disability and grade of identification. *Learning Disabilities Research & Practice, 28*(3), 98–112. http://doi.org/10.1111/ldrp.12013

Olson, A. J., Roberts, C. A., & Leko, M. M. (2015). Teacher-, student-, and peer-directed strategies to access the general education curriculum for students with autism. *Intervention in School and Clinic, 21*(1), 37–44. http://doi.org/10.1177/1053451214546406

Palmer, R. (2013). The top 10 iPad apps for special education: Empowering independence in SPED learners: There's an app for that! *T H E Journal (Technological Horizons in Education), 40*(6), 10.

Ruble, L., & McGrew, J. H. (2013). Teacher and child predictors of achieving IEP goals of children with autism. *Journal of Autism and Developmental Disorders, 43*(12), 2748–2763. http://doi.org/10.1007/s10803-013-1884-x

Stahmer, A. C., Reed, S., Suhrheinrich, J., & Schreibman, L. (2013). *Working with teachers to adapt an evidence-based intervention for children with autism.* Society for Research on Educational Effectiveness. Retrieved from http://eric.ed.gov/?id=ED564053

Tomlinson, S. (2012). *A sociology of special education (RLE Edu M).* Abingdon-on-Thames, England: Routledge.

Travers, J. C., Tincani, M. M., Thompson, J. L., & Simpson, R. L. (2016). Picture exchange communication system and facilitated communication: Contrasting an evidence-based practice with a discredited method. In B. G. Cook, M. Tankersley & T. J. Landrum (Eds.), *Instructional practices with and without empirical validity* (Vol. 29, pp. 85–110). West Yorkshire, England: Emerald Group. Retrieved from http://www.emeraldinsight.com/doi/abs/10.1108/S0735-004X20160000029005

Wei, X., Wagner, M., Christiano, E. R. A., Shattuck, P., & Yu, J. W. (2014). Special education services received by students with autism spectrum disorders from preschool through high school. *The Journal of Special Education, 48*(3), 167–179. http://doi.org/10.1177/0022466913483576

Werts, M. G., & Carpenter, E. S. (2013). Implementation of tasks in RTI perceptions of special education teachers. *Teacher Education and Special Education: The Journal of the Teacher Education Division of the Council for Exceptional Children, 36*(3), 247–257. http://doi.org/10.1177/0888406413495420

Chapter 5
POPULAR MEDIA

Beautiful minds, wasted: How to deal with autism. (2016, April 16). *The Economist*, p. 9.

Camphill Association of North America. (n.d.). Home page. Retrieved September 15, 2016, from http://www.camphill.org/

CIP. (n.d.). CIP Berkeley. Retrieved from https://cipworldwide.org/2017site/wp-content/cache/page_enhanced/cipworldwide.org//cip-berkeley/berkeley-overview//_index.html_gzip

College-bound and living with autism. (2014, April 20). *The New York Times*. Retrieved September 15, 2016, from http://consults.blogs.nytimes.com/2011/04/20/college-bound-and-living-with-autism/

Cook, G. (2012, November 29). The autism advantage. *The New York Times*. Retrieved from http://www.nytimes.com/2012/12/02/magazine/the-autism-advantage.html

Creamer, J. (2015). *Programming hope: Changing the face of autism* [Motion picture]. P. Hollingswood & J. Craemer, producers; J. Craemer, writer/director. United States: Kickstarter funded.

Goehner, A. L. (2011, April 13). A generation of autism, coming of age. *The New York Times*. Retrieved from http://www.nytimes.com/ref/health/healthguide/esn-autism-reporters.html

Gottlieb, E. (2015, September 5). Adult, autistic and ignored. *The New York Times*. Retrieved from http://www.nytimes.com/2015/09/06/opinion/sunday/adult-autistic-and-ignored.html

Grandin, T. (2006). *Thinking in pictures: My life with autism.* New York, NY: Vintage.

Greenfeld, K. T. (2009, May 24). Growing old with autism. *The New York Times*. Retrieved from http://www.nytimes.com/2009/05/24/opinion/24greenfeld.html

Harmon, A. (2011, September 17). Autistic and seeking a place in an adult world. *The New York Times*. Retrieved from http://www.nytimes.com/2011/09/18/us/autistic-and-seeking-a-place-in-an-adult-world.html

Lewis and Clark Community College. (n.d.). Disability services. Retrieved September 14, 2016, from http://www.lc.edu/disability/

Mounting evidence of critical need for adult transition support. (2012, December 18). Retrieved September 14, 2016, from Autism Speaks website: https://www.autismspeaks.org/science/science-news/top-ten-lists/2012/mounting-evidence-critical-need-adult-transition-support

Park, C. C. (1982). *The siege: A family's journey into the world of a child with autism.* Boston, MA: Little Brown.

Park, C. C. (2002). *Exiting Nirvana: A daughter's life with autism.* Boston, MA: Little Brown.

Peabody College, Vanderbilt University. (n.d.). Next steps at Vanderbilt University. Retrieved September 14, 2016, from http://peabody.vanderbilt.edu/departments/nextsteps/

Programming Hope. (n.d.). Home page. Retrieved from http://programminghope.com/

Report: 1 in 3 young adults with autism disconnected from work and school. (2015, April 21). Retrieved September 14, 2016, from Autism Speaks website: https://www.autismspeaks. org/blog/2015/04/21/report-1-3-young-adults-disconnected-work-and-school

Robison, J. E. (2007). *Look me in the eye.* Pittsburgh, PA: Three Rivers Press.

Siegel, B. (2003). *Helping children with autism learn: Treatment approaches for parents and professionals.* New York, NY: Oxford University Press.

Siegel, B., & Silverstein, S. (2001). *What about me? Growing up with a developmentally disabled sibling.* Cambridge, MA: Perseus Press.

Solomon, A. (2012). *Far from the tree: Parents, children and the search for identity.* New York, NY: Scribner/Simon & Schuster.

Sweetwater Spectrum. (n.d.). Home page. Retrieved September 15, 2016, from https:// sweetwaterspectrum.org/

Tammet, D. (2006). *Born on a blue day.* New York, NY: Free Press, Simon & Schuster.

TEACCH autism program home page. (n.d.). Retrieved from UNC School of Medicine website: https://www.teacch.com/

UCLA Extension. (n.d.). Welcome to Pathway. Retrieved from http://education. uclaextension.edu/pathway/

SCIENTIFIC READINGS

Chevallier, C., Kohls, G., Troiani, V., Brodkin, E. S., & Schultz, R. T. (2012). The social motivation theory of autism. *Trends in Cognitive Sciences, 16*(4), 231–239. http://doi. org/10.1016/j.tics.2012.02.007

de Bruin, C. L., Deppeler, J. M., Moore, D. W., & Diamond, N. T. (2013). Public school–based interventions for adolescents and young adults with an autism spectrum disorder: A meta-analysis. *Review of Educational Research, 83*(4), 521–550. http://doi.org/ 10.3102/0034654313498621

Fleury, V. P., Hedges, S., Hume, K., Browder, D. M., Thompson, J. L., Fallin, K., . . . Vaughn, S. (2014). Addressing the academic needs of adolescents with autism spectrum disorder in secondary education. *Remedial and Special Education, 35*(2), 68–79. http://doi.org/ 10.1177/0741932513518823

Adult Employment

Andersson, R., Nabavi, P., & Wilhelmsson, M. (2014). The impact of advanced vocational education and training on earnings in Sweden. *International Journal of Training and Development, 18*(4), 256–270. http://doi.org/10.1111/ijtd.12040

Baldwin, S., Costley, D., & Warren, A. (2014). Employment activities and experiences of adults with high-functioning autism and Asperger's disorder. *Journal of Autism and Developmental Disorders, 44*(10), 2440–2449. http://doi.org/10.1007/s10803-014-2112-z

Burgess, S., & Cimera, R. E. (2014a). Employment outcomes of transition-aged adults with autism spectrum disorders: A state of the states report. *American Journal on Intellectual and Developmental Disabilities, 119*(1), 64–83. http://doi.org/10.1352/1944-7558-119.1.64

Chiang, H.-M., Cheung, Y. K., Li, H., & Tsai, L. Y. (2012). Factors associated with participation in employment for high school leavers with autism. *Journal of Autism and Developmental Disorders, 43*(8), 1832–1842. http://doi.org/10.1007/s10803-012-1734-2

Cimera, R. E., & Cowan, R. J. (2009). The costs of services and employment outcomes achieved by adults with autism in the US. *Autism, 13*(3), 285–302. http://doi.org/ 10.1177/1362361309103791

Hanushek, E. A., Schwerdt, G., Woessmann, L., & Zhang, L. (2017). General education, vocational education, and labor-market outcomes over the life-cycle. *Journal of Human Resources, 52*(1), 48–87. http://doi.org/10.3368/jhr.52.1.0415-7074R

Hedley, D., Uljarević, M., Cameron, L., Halder, S., Richdale, A., & Dissanayake, C. (2017). Employment programmes and interventions targeting adults with autism spectrum disorder: A systematic review of the literature. *Autism, 21*(8), 929–941. http://doi.org/10.1177/1362361316661855

Jacob, A., Scott, M., Falkmer, M., & Falkmer, T. (2015). The costs and benefits of employing an adult with autism spectrum disorder: A systematic review. *PLOS One, 10*(10), e0139896. http://doi.org/10.1371/journal.pone.0139896

Orsmond, G. I., Shattuck, P. T., Cooper, B. P., Sterzing, P. R., & Anderson, K. A. (2013). Social participation among young adults with an autism spectrum disorder. *Journal of Autism and Developmental Disorders, 43*(11), 2710–2719. http://doi.org/10.1007/s10803-013-1833-8

Roux, A. M., Shattuck, P. T., Cooper, B. P., Anderson, K. A., Wagner, M., & Narendorf, S. C. (2013). Postsecondary employment experiences among young adults with an autism spectrum disorder. *Journal of the American Academy of Child & Adolescent Psychiatry, 52*(9), 931–939. http://doi.org/10.1016/j.jaac.2013.05.019

Sanches-Ferreira, M., Lopes-dos-Santos, P., Alves, S., Santos, M., & Silveira-Maia, M. (2013). How individualised are the individualised education programmes (IEPs): An analysis of the contents and quality of the IEPs goals. *European Journal of Special Needs Education, 28*(4), 507–520. http://doi.org/10.1080/08856257.2013.830435

Shattuck, P. T., Narendorf, S. C., Cooper, B., Sterzing, P. R., Wagner, M., & Taylor, J. L. (2012). Postsecondary education and employment among youth with an autism spectrum disorder. *Pediatrics, 129*(6), 1042–1049. http://doi.org/10.1542/peds.2011-2864

Taylor, J. L., & Seltzer, M. M. (2011). Employment and post-secondary educational activities for young adults with autism spectrum disorders during the transition to adulthood. *Journal of Autism and Developmental Disorders, 41*, 566. http://link.springer.com/article/10.1007/s10803-010-1070-3

Vogeley, K., Kirchner, J. C., Gawronski, A., van Elst, L. T., & Dziobek, I. (2013). Toward the development of a supported employment program for individuals with high-functioning autism in Germany. *European Archives of Psychiatry and Clinical Neuroscience, 263*(2), 197–203. http://doi.org/10.1007/s00406-013-0455-7

Laws and Policies

ADA.gov. (n.d.). Home page. Retrieved September 14, 2016, from https://www.ada.gov/

Buescher, A. S., Cidav, Z., Knapp, M., & Mandell, D. S. (2014). Costs of autism spectrum disorders in the United Kingdom and the United States. *JAMA Pediatrics, 168*(8), 721–728. http://doi.org/10.1001/jamapediatrics.2014.210

Fleury, V. P., Hedges, S., Hume, K., Browder, D. M., Thompson, J. L., Fallin, K., . . . Vaughn, S. (2014). Addressing the academic needs of adolescents with autism spectrum disorder in secondary education. *Remedial and Special Education, 35*(2), 68–79. http://doi.org/10.1177/0741932513518823

Sanches-Ferreira, M., Lopes-dos-Santos, P., Alves, S., Santos, M., & Silveira-Maia, M. (2013). How individualized are the individualized education programs (IEPs): An analysis of the contents and quality of the IEPs goals. *European Journal of Special Needs Education, 28*(4), 507–520. http://doi.org/10.1080/08856257.2013.830435

Shattuck, P., Narendorf, S. C., Cooper, B. P., Sterzing, P. R., Wagner, M., & Taylor, J. L. (2012, May 14). Postsecondary education and employment among youth with an autism spectrum disorder. *Pediatrics, 129*, 1042–1049. Retrieved September 14, 2016, from http://pediatrics.aappublications.org/content/pediatrics/early/2012/05/09/peds.2011-2864.full.pdf

School Outcomes

Anderson, D. K., Liang, J. W., & Lord, C. (2014). Predicting young adult outcome among more and less cognitively able individuals with autism spectrum disorders. *Journal of Child Psychology and Psychiatry, 55*(5), 485–494. http://doi.org/10.1111/jcpp.12178

Bowler, D. M. (Panel chair). (2016, May 13). *Growing older with autism: Co-morbidity and quality of life.* Paper presentation at International Meetings for Autism Research, Baltimore.

Ciullo, S., Ortiz, M. B., Otaiba, S. A., & Lane, K. L. (2016). Psychiatric co-occurring symptoms and disorders in young, middle-aged, and older adults with autism spectrum disorder. Advanced reading comprehension expectations in secondary school considerations for students with emotional or behavior disorders. *Journal of Disability Policy Studies, 27*(1), 54–64. http://doi.org/10.1177/1044207315604365

Davis, K. J. (2014). Autism in the schools: IEP best practices at work. *Perspectives on School-Based Issues, 15*(1), 32. http://doi.org/10.1044/sbi15.1.32

Gillberg, I. C., Helles, A., Billstedt, E., & Gillberg, C. (2016). Boys with Asperger's syndrome grow up: Psychiatric and neurodevelopmental disorders 20 years after initial diagnosis. *Journal of Autism & Developmental Disorders, 46*(1), 74–82.

Gray, K. M., Keating, C. M., Taffe, J. R., Brereton, A. V., Einfeld, S. L., Reardon, T. C., & Tonge, B. J. (2014). Adult outcomes in autism: Community inclusion and living skills. *Journal of Autism and Developmental Disorders, 44*(12), 3006–3015. http://doi.org/10.1007/s10803-014-2159-x

Henninger, N. A., & Taylor, J. L. (2013). Outcomes in adults with autism spectrum disorders: A historical perspective. *Autism, 17*(1), 103–116. http://doi.org/10.1177/1362361312441266

Howlin, P. (2005) Outcomes in autism spectrum disorders. In F. Volkmar, A. Klin, R., Paul, & D. Cohen (Eds.), *Handbook of autism and pervasive developmental disorders* (3rd ed., pp. 201–222). Hoboken, NJ: Wiley.

Howlin, P., Moss, P., Savage, S., & Rutter, M. (2013). Social outcomes in mid- to later adulthood among individuals diagnosed with autism and average nonverbal IQ as children. *Journal of the American Academy of Child & Adolescent Psychiatry, 52*(6), 572–581.e1. http://doi.org/10.1016/j.jaac.2013.02.017

Lever, A. G., & Geurts, H. M. (2016). Psychiatric co-occurring symptoms and disorders in young, middle-aged, and older adults with autism spectrum disorder. *Journal of Autism and Developmental Disorders, 46*(6), 1916–1930.

Magiati, I., Tay, X. W., & Howlin, P. (2014). Cognitive, language, social and behavioural outcomes in adults with autism spectrum disorders: A systematic review of longitudinal follow-up studies in adulthood. *Clinical Psychology Review, 34*(1), 73–86. http://doi.org/10.1016/j.cpr.2013.11.002

Mavranezouli, I., Megnin-Viggars, O., Cheema, N., Howlin, P., Baron-Cohen, S., & Pilling, S. (2014). The cost-effectiveness of supported employment for adults with autism in the United Kingdom. *Autism, 18*(8), 975–984. http://doi.org/10.1177/1362361313505720

McCoy, S., Maître, B., Watson, D., & Banks, J. (2016). The role of parental expectations in understanding social and academic well-being among children with disabilities in Ireland. *European Journal of Special Needs Education, 31*(4), 535–552. http://doi.org/10.1080/08856257.2016.1199607

McKenney, E. L. W., Stachniak, C., Albright, J., Jewell, J. D., & Dorencz, J. M. (2016). Defining success for students with autism spectrum disorder: Social academic behavior in secondary general education settings. *Education and Training in Autism and Developmental Disabilities, 51*(3), 318–327. Retrieved September 14, 2016, from http://search.proquest.com/openview/b0123aee324aca62eafb96bb35457221/1?pq-origsite=gscholar&cbl=2032023

Miller, V. (2013). *The quality and effects of secondary transition plans on special education graduates' postsecondary outcomes and their effects on secondary transition* (Doctoral dissertation, Gardner Webb University, Boiling Springs, NC, accession number 3589100). Retrieved from http://www.proquest.com/en-US/products/dissertations/individuals.shtml

Poon, K. K., Koh, L., & Magiati, I. (2013a). Parental perspectives on the importance and likelihood of adult outcomes for children with autism spectrum disorders, intellectual disabilities or multiple disabilities. *Research in Autism Spectrum Disorders, 7*(2), 382–390. http://doi.org/10.1016/j.rasd.2012.10.006

Roux, A. M., Rast, J. E., Anderson, K. A., & Shattuck, P. T. (2016). *National autism indicators report: Vocational rehabilitation.* Philadelphia: Life Course Outcomes Research Program, A. J. Drexel Autism Institute, Drexel University.

Roux, A. M., Shattuck, P. T., Rast, J. E., Rava, J. A., & Anderson, K. A. (2015). *National autism indicators report: Transition into young adulthood.* Philadelphia, PA: Life Course Outcomes Research Program, A. J. Drexel Autism Institute, Drexel University. http://drexel.edu/autisminstitute/research-projects/research/ResearchPrograminLifeCourseOutcomes/IndicatorsReport/#sthash.WqMvOWCQ.dpuf

Shattuck, P. (2015). *National autism indicators report: Transition into young adulthood.* Philadelphia, PA: Life Course Outcomes Research Program, A. J. Drexel Autism Institute, Drexel University.

Wei, X., Wagner, M., Hudson, L., Yu, J. W., & Javitz, H. (2016). The effect of transition planning participation and goal-setting on college enrollment among youth with autism spectrum disorders. *Remedial and Special Education, 37*(1), 3–14. http://doi.org/10.1177/0741932515581495

Chapter 6

POPULAR MEDIA

Department of Health and Human Services, Aging and Disability Services Division. (n.d.). Disability services: Autism Treatment Assistance Program (ATAP). (n.d.). Retrieved September 26, 2016, from http://adsd.nv.gov/Programs/Autism/ATAP/ATAP/

High-quality early intervention for autism more than pays for itself. (2012, July 25). Retrieved September 26, 2016, from Autism Speaks website: https://www.autismspeaks.org/science/science-news/high-quality-early-intervention-autism-more-pays-itself

Lovaas, O. I. (1981). *Teaching developmentally disabled children: The me book.* Austin, TX: University Park Press.

Medicaid: States cannot "delay or deny" autism treatment. (2014, September 29). Retrieved September 26, 2016, from Autism Speaks website: https://www.autismspeaks.org/advocacy/advocacy-news/medicaid-states-cannot-delay-or-deny-autism-treatment

Sacks, O. (1993, December 27). An anthropologist on Mars. *The New Yorker*. Retrieved August 23, 2016, from http://www.newyorker.com/magazine/1993/12/27/anthropologist-mars

US Department of Education. (n.d.). IDEA—Building the legacy: IDEA 2004. (n.d.). Retrieved September 14, 2016, from http://idea.ed.gov/

SCIENTIFIC READINGS

Cost of ASDs

Croen, L. A., Najjar, D. V., Ray, G. T., Lotspeich, L., & Bernal, P. (2006). A comparison of health care utilization and costs of children with and without autism spectrum disorders in a large group-model health plan. *Pediatrics, 118*(4), e1203–e1211. http://doi.org/10.1542/peds.2006-0127

Feldman, N. (2017, January 16). US Supreme Court attempts to delimit special education costs. *Hartford Courant*. Retrieved from http://www.courant.com/opinion/op-ed/hc-op-feldman-supreme-court-special-education-0115-20170113-story.html

Jacobson, J. W., Mulick, J. A., & Green, G. (1998). Cost–benefit estimates for early intensive behavioral intervention for young children with autism—General model and single state case. *Behavioral Interventions, 13*(4), 201–226. doi:10.1002/(SICI)1099-078X(199811)13:4<201::AID-BIN17>3.0.CO;2-R

Lindgren, S., Wacker, D., Suess, A., Schieltz, K., Pelzel, K., Kopelman, T., . . . Waldron, D. (2016). Tele-health and autism: Treating challenging behavior at lower cost. *Pediatrics, 137*(Supplement 2), S167–S175. http://doi.org/10.1542/peds.2015-2851O

Morgan-Besecker, T. (2015, December 20). Special education legal fees major hit to local schools. *The Times-Tribune*. Retrieved from http://thetimes-tribune.com/news/special-education-legal-fees-major-hit-to-local-schools-1.1985439

Motiwala, S. S., Gupta, S., Lilly, M. B., Ungar, W. J., & Coyte, P. C. (2006). The cost-effectiveness of expanding intensive behavioral intervention to all autistic children in Ontario. *Healthcare Policy, 1*(2), 135–151.

Penner, M., Rayar, M., Bashir, N., Roberts, S. W., Hancock-Howard, R. L., & Coyte, P. C. (2015). Cost-effectiveness analysis comparing pre-diagnosis autism spectrum disorder (ASD)-targeted intervention with Ontario's Autism Intervention Program. *Journal of Autism and Developmental Disorders, 45*(9), 2833–2847. http://doi.org/10.1007/s10803-015-2447-0

Peters-Scheffer, N., Didden, R., Korzilius, H., & Matson, J. (2012). Cost comparison of early intensive behavioral intervention and treatment as usual for children with autism spectrum disorder in the Netherlands. *Research in Developmental Disabilities, 33*(6), 1763–1772.

Wei, X., Wagner, M., Christiano, E. R. A., Shattuck, P., & Yu, J. W. (2014). Special education services received by students with autism spectrum disorders from preschool through high school. *The Journal of Special Education, 48*(3), 167–179. http://doi.org/10.1177/0022466913483576

Economics

Brachlow, A. E., Ness, K. K., McPheeters, M. L., & Gurney, J. G. (2007). Comparison of indicators for a primary care medical home between children with autism or asthma and other special health care needs: National survey of children's health. *Archives of Pediatrics & Adolescent Medicine, 161*(4), 399–405.

Buescher, A. V. S., Cidav, Z., Knapp, M., & Mandell, D. S. (2014). Costs of autism spectrum disorders in the United Kingdom and the United States. *JAMA Pediatrics, 168*(8), 721–728. doi:10.1001/jamapediatrics.2014.210

Cimera, R. E., & Cowan, R. J. (2009). The costs of services and employment outcomes achieved by adults with autism in the US. *Autism, 13*(3), 285–302. http://doi.org/10.1177/1362361309103791

D'Elia, L., Valeri, G., Sonnino, F., Fontana, I., Mammone, A., & Vicari, S. (2013). A longitudinal study of the TEACCH program in different settings: The potential benefits of low intensity intervention in preschool children with autism spectrum disorder. *Journal of Autism and Developmental Disorders, 44*(3), 615–626. http://doi.org/10.1007/s10803-013-1911-y.

Harpe, D. L., & Baker, D. L. (2007). Financial issues associated with having a child with autism. *Journal of Family and Economic Issues, 28*(2), 247–264. http://doi.org/10.1007/s10834-007-9059-6

Kirkland, A. (2012). Credibility battles in the autism litigation. *Social Studies of Science, 42*(2), 237–261. http://doi.org/10.1177/0306312711435832.

Krauss, M. W., Gulley, S., Sciegaj, M., & Wells, N. (2003). Access to specialty medical care for children with mental retardation, autism, and other special health care needs. *Mental Retardation, 41*(5), 329–339. http://doi.org/10.1352/0047-6765(2003)41<329:ATSMCF>2.0.CO;2

Lavelle, T. A., Weinstein, M. C., Newhouse, J. P., Munir, K., Kuhlthau, K. A., & Prosser, L. A. (2014). Economic burden of childhood autism spectrum disorders. *Pediatrics, 133*(3), e520–e529. http://doi.org/10.1542/peds.2013-0763

Leigh, J. P., & Du, J. (2015). Brief report: Forecasting the economic burden of autism in 2015 and 2025 in the United States. *Journal of Autism and Developmental Disorders, 45*(12), 4135–4139. http://doi.org/10.1007/s10803-015-2521-7

Lovaas, I (1987). Behavioral treatment and normal educational and intellectual functioning in young autistic children. *Journal of Consulting & Clinical Psychology, 55*(1), 3–9.

Mavranezouli, I., Megnin-Viggars, O., Cheema, N., Howlin, P., Baron-Cohen, S., & Pilling, S. (2014). The cost-effectiveness of supported employment for adults with autism in the United Kingdom. *Autism, 18*(8), 975–984. http://doi.org/10.1177/1362361313505720

Orsini, M., & Smith, M. (2010). Social movements, knowledge and public policy: The case of autism activism in Canada and the US. *Critical Policy Studies, 4*(1), 38–57. http://doi.org/10.1080/19460171003714989

Pudelski, S. (2016). *Rethinking special education due process.* Alexandria, VA: AASA, School Superintendents Association.

Ruble, L. A., Heflinger, C. A., Renfrew, J. W., & Saunders, R. C. (n.d.). Access and service use by children with autism spectrum disorders in Medicaid managed care. *Journal of Autism and Developmental Disorders, 35*(1), 3–13. http://doi.org/10.1007/s10803-004-1026-6

Smith, T., Groen, A., & Wynn, J. (2000). Randomized trial of intensive early intervention for children with pervasive developmental disorder. *American Journal on Mental Retardation. 105*(4):269–285. Retrieved from http://analisicomportamentale.com/media/Smith%20Groen%20and%20Wynn%202000.pdf

Chapter 7

POPULAR MEDIA

Adams, J. (2012, March 12). *Stories of hope: Autism*. California Stem Cell Agency. Retrieved September 27, 2016, from https://www.cirm.ca.gov/our-progress/stories-hope-autism

Autism Center of Northern California. (n.d.). Home page. Retrieved September 27, 2016, from http://www.acnc.org/

Autism Key. (2011, January 1). *DAN doctor directory offers alternatives for parents of children with autism*. Retrieved from http://www.autismkey.com/dan-doctor-directory/

Autism Watch. (n.d.). Home page. Retrieved September 27, 2016, from https://www.autism-watch.org/

Barrett, S. (2015, June 1) *A critical look at Defeat Autism Now! and the "DAN! protocol."* Quackwatch. Retrieved from http://www.quackwatch.org/04ConsumerEducation/Nonrecorg/dan/overview.html

Bauer, S. C., & Roberts, M. Y. (2016, July 15). There's no one-size-fits-all way to treat autism. *Scientific American*. Retrieved September 27, 2016, from http://blogs.scientificamerican.com/guest-blog/there-s-no-one-size-fits-all-way-to-treat-autism/

Broader autism phenotype. (2015, June 17). Retrieved September 27, 2016, from Autism Speaks website: https://www.autismspeaks.org/site-wide/broader-autism-phenotype

Brownstein, J., and *ABC News* Medical Unit. (2010, March 11). Father sues doctors over autism therapy. *ABC News*. Retrieved September 27, 2016, from http://abcnews.go.com/Health/TheLaw/doctors-sued-autism-chelation-therapy/story?id=10045951

Chelation and autism—Talk About Curing Autism (TACA). (2016, September 9). Retrieved September 27, 2016, from TACA website: http://www.tacanow.org/family-resources/chelation-and-autism/

Complementary approaches for treating autism. (2012, July 25). Retrieved September 27, 2016, from Autism Speaks website: https://www.autismspeaks.org/what-autism/treatment/complementary-treatments-autism

Dawson, M. (2015, June 17). The miracle that cured my son's autism was in our kitchen. *New York Post*. Retrieved from http://nypost.com/2015/06/17/is-diet-the-key-to-curing-autism/

Defeat Autism Now. (n.d.). *Your guide to information, resources, and help*. Retrieved September 27, 2016, from http://www.defeatautismnow.net/

Engber, D. (2015, October 20). The strange case of Anna Stubblefield. *The New York Times*. Retrieved from https://www.nytimes.com/2015/10/25/magazine/the-strange-case-of-anna-stubblefield.html

Engber, D. (2016, February 3). What Anna Stubblefield believed she was doing. *The New York Times*. Retrieved from http://www.nytimes.com/2016/02/03/magazine/what-anna-stubblefield-believed-she-was-doing.html

English, J. (2013, April 26). *Saving Eli: One family's struggle with autism*. Nutrition Review. Retrieved from http://nutritionreview.org/2013/04/saving-eli-one-familys-with-struggle-autism/

Gladwell, M. (2005). *Blink: The power of thinking without thinking*. Boston, MA: Back Bay Book/Little Brown.

Higashida, N. (2013). *The reason I jump: The inner voice of a thirteen-year-old boy with autism* (K. A. Yoshida & D. Mitchell, Trans.). New York, NY: Random House.

Interlandi, J. (2016, September). Supplements: A complete guide to safety. *Consumer Reports*, ppp. 20–33.

Issacson, R. (2009). *The horse boy: A father's quest to heal his son.* New York, NY: Little Brown/Hachette Books.

Johannes, L (1999, December 9). Autism treatment fails to top placebo in study of secretin hormone's effects. *Wall Street Journal.* Retrieved from http://www.wsj.com/articles/SB944701250710205201

Laidler, J. R. (n.d.). The "refrigerator mother" hypothesis of autism. (n.d.). Autism Watch. Retrieved September 27, 2016, from http://www.autism-watch.org/causes/rm.shtml. Revised September 15, 2004.

Mayo Clinic. (n.d.). *Complicated grief.* Retrieved September 27, 2016, from http://www.mayoclinic.org/diseases-conditions/complicated-grief/basics/definition/con-20032765

Michaels, D. (2008). *Doubt is their product: How industry's assault on science threatens your health.* New York, NY: Oxford University Press.

Moyer, M. W. (2014, September 1). Gut bacteria may play a role in autism. *Scientific American.* Retrieved September 27, 2016, from http://www.scientificamerican.com/article/gut-bacteria-may-play-a-role-in-autism/

Padawer, R. (2014, July 31). The kids who beat autism. *The New York Times.* Retrieved from http://www.nytimes.com/2014/08/03/magazine/the-kids-who-beat-autism.html

Peterson, P. E. (2016, June 23). Please don't take away my autistic son's treatment. *Wall Street Journal.* Retrieved from http://www.wsj.com/articles/please-dont-take-away-my-sons-treatment-1466722896

Ryan, F. (2016, July 13). The fake cures for autism that can prove deadly. *The Guardian.* Retrieved from https://www.theguardian.com/society/2016/jul/13/fake-cures-autism-prove-deadly

Simpson, D. E., Hanley, J. J., & Quinn, G. (Filmmakers). (2002, July 16). History of autism blame: Refrigerator mothers [Television series episode]. *POV.* United States: PBS. Retrieved from http://www.pbs.org/pov/refrigeratormothers/fridge/

Sonya. (2015, March 31). Autism and methylation—Are you helping to repair your child's methylation cycle? Retrieved September 27, 2016, from Treat Autism website: http://treatautism.ca/2015/03/31/autism-and-methylation-are-you-helping-to-repair-your-childs-methylation-cycle/

Specter, M (2009). *Denialism: How irrational thinking hinders science progress, harms the planet, and threatens our lives.* New York, NY: Penguin Press.

Stem Cell Institute. (n.d.). *Stem cell therapy for autism.* Retrieved September 27, 2016, from https://www.cellmedicine.com/stem-cell-therapy-for-autism/

Stewart, J. (2015, August 6). Final broadcast [Television series episode]. *The Daily Show.* New York, NY: Comedy Central.

Thimerosal and autism: Reviewing the evidence (2007). (n.d.). Autism Watch. Retrieved September 27, 2016, from http://www.autism-watch.org/rsch/thimerosal.shtml

Tisdale, S. (2013, August 23). Voice of the voiceless [Review of book *The reason I jump,* by Naoki Higashida]. *The New York Times,* Sunday Book Review.

US Food and Drug Administration. (n.d.). *Beware of false or misleading claims for treating autism.* Retrieved September 27, 2016, from http://www.fda.gov/ForConsumers/ConsumerUpdates/ucm394757.htm. Updated April 12, 2017.

Wang, S. S. (2015, September 14). Gluten-free diet has no benefit for children with autism, study finds. *Wall Street Journal*. Retrieved from http://www.wsj.com/articles/gluten-free-diet-has-no-benefit-for-children-with-autism-study-finds-1442244486

Willingham, E. (2013, October 29). The 5 scariest autism "treatments." *Forbes*. Retrieved September 27, 2016, from http://www.forbes.com/sites/emilywillingham/2013/10/29/the-5-scariest-autism-treatments/

Yanofsky, J. (2014, July 31). The kids who don't beat autism. *The New York Times*. Retrieved September 27, 2016, from http://parenting.blogs.nytimes.com/2014/07/31/the-kids-who-dont-beat-autism/

SCIENTIFIC READINGS

Authoritative Reviews

Corcoran, J., Berry, A., & Hill, S. (2015). The lived experience of US parents of children with autism spectrum disorders: A systematic review and meta-synthesis. *Journal of Intellectual Disabilities, 19*(4), 356–366. http://doi.org/10.1177/1744629515577876

Hanson, E., Kalish, L. A., Bunce, E., Curtis, C., McDaniel, S., Ware, J., & Petry, J. (2006). Use of complementary and alternative medicine among children diagnosed with autism spectrum disorder. *Journal of Autism and Developmental Disorders, 37*(4), 628–636. http://doi.org/10.1007/s10803-006-0192-0

Klein, N., & Kemper, K. J. (2016). Integrative approaches to caring for children with autism. *Current Problems in Pediatric and Adolescent Health Care, 46*(6), 195–201. http://doi.org/10.1016/j.cppeds.2015.12.004

Levy, S. E., & Hyman, S. L. (2008). Complementary and alternative medicine treatments for children with autism spectrum disorders. *Child and Adolescent Psychiatric Clinics of North America, 17*(4), 803–820. http://doi.org/10.1016/j.chc.2008.06.004

Offit, P. A. (2010). *Autism's false prophets: Bad science, risky medicine, and the search for a cure.* New York, NY: Columbia University Press.

Owen-Smith, A., Bent, S., Lynch, F., Coleman, K., Yau, V., Freiman, H., . . . Croen, L. (2013). PS2-47: Complementary and alternative medicine use among children with autism spectrum disorders: Findings from the Mental Health Research Network Autism Registry Web Survey. *Clinical Medicine & Research, 11*(3), 163–163. http://doi.org/10.3121/cmr.2013.1176.ps2-47

Owen-Smith, A. A., Bent, S., Lynch, F. L., Coleman, K. J., Yau, V. M., Pearson, K. A., . . . Croen, L. A. (2015). Prevalence and predictors of complementary and alternative medicine use in a large insured sample of children with autism spectrum disorders. *Research in Autism Spectrum Disorders, 17*, 40–51. http://doi.org/10.1016/j.rasd.2015.05.002

Biological CAM Treatment for ASD

Bolman, W. M., & Richmond, J. A. (n.d.). A double-blind, placebo-controlled, crossover pilot trial of low dose dimethylglycine in patients with autistic disorder. *Journal of Autism and Developmental Disorders, 29*(3), 191–194. http://doi.org/10.1023/A:1023023820671

Cartwright, C., & Power, R. (2003). Alternative biological treatments for autism. In E. Hollander (Ed.), *Autism spectrum disorders* [e-book] (pp. 347–367). Boca Raton, FL: Taylor & Francis Group, CRC Press. Available from http://www.crcnetbase.com/doi/10.3109/9780203911723-17

Edelson, S. M. (2014). *Infantile autism: The syndrome and its implications for a neural theory of behavior by Bernard Rimland, PhD.* London, England: Kingsley.

Esch, B. E., & Carr, J. E. (2004). Secretin as a treatment for autism: A review of the evidence. *Journal of Autism and Developmental Disorders, 34*(5), 543–556. http://doi.org/10.1007/s10803-004-2549-6

Frustaci, A., Neri, M., Cesario, A., Adams, J. B., Domenici, E., Dalla Bernardina, B., & Bonassi, S. (2012). Oxidative stress-related biomarkers in autism: Systematic review and meta-analyses. *Free Radical Biology and Medicine, 52*(10), 2128–2141. http://doi.org/10.1016/j.freeradbiomed.2012.03.011

Goldani, A. A. S., Downs, S. R., Widjaja, F., Lawton, B., & Hendren, R. L. (2014). Biomarkers in autism. *Frontiers in Psychiatry, 5.* http://doi.org/10.3389/fpsyt.2014.00100

Goldfarb, C., Genore, L., Hunt, C., Flanagan, J., Handley-Derry, M., Jethwa, A., . . . Anagnostou, E. (2016). Hyperbaric oxygen therapy for the treatment of children and youth with autism spectrum disorders: An evidence-based systematic review. *Research in Autism Spectrum Disorders, 29–30,* 1–7. http://doi.org/10.1016/j.rasd.2016.05.004

Heberling, C. A., Dhurjati, P. S., & Sasser, M. (2013). Hypothesis for a systems connectivity model of autism spectrum disorder pathogenesis: Links to gut bacteria, oxidative stress, and intestinal permeability. *Medical Hypotheses, 80*(3), 264–270. http://doi.org/10.1016/j.mehy.2012.11.044

Hsiao, E. Y., McBride, S. W., Hsien, S., Sharon, G., Hyde, E. R., McCue, T., . . . Mazmanian, S. K. (2013). The microbiota modulates gut physiology and behavioral abnormalities associated with autism. *Cell, 155*(7), 1451–1463. http://doi.org/10.1016/j.cell.2013.11.024

Hunsinger, D. M., Nguyen, T., Zebraski, S. E., & Raffa, R. B. (2000). Is there a basis for novel pharmacotherapy of autism? *Life Sciences, 67*(14), 1667–1682. http://doi.org/10.1016/S0024-3205(00)00763-3

Hyman, S. L., Stewart, P. A., Foley, J., Cain, U., Peck, R., Morris, D. D., . . . Smith, T. (2015). The gluten-free/casein-free diet: A double-blind challenge trial in children with autism. *Journal of Autism and Developmental Disorders, 46*(1), 205–220. http://doi.org/10.1007/s10803-015-2564-9

Ichim, T. E., Solano, F., Glenn, E., Morales, F., Smith, L., Zabrecky, G., & Riordan, N. H. (2007). Stem cell therapy for autism. *Journal of Translational Medicine, 5,* 30. http://doi.org/10.1186/1479-5876-5-30

Lloyd-Thomas, P. (2013, April 3). Placebo effect in autism. Retrieved from Epiphany website: https://epiphanyasd.blogspot.com/2013/04/placebo-effect-in-autism.html

Marí-Bauset, S., Zazpe, I., Mari-Sanchis, A., Llopis-González, A., & Morales-Suárez-Varela, M. (2014). Evidence of the gluten-free and casein-free diet in autism spectrum disorders: A systematic review. *Journal of Child Neurology, 29*(12), 1718–1727. http://doi.org/10.1177/0883073814531330

Navarro, F., Pearson, D. A., Fatheree, N., Mansour, R., Hashmi, S. S., & Rhoads, J. M. (2015). Are "leaky gut" and behavior associated with gluten and dairy containing diet in children with autism spectrum disorders? *Nutritional Neuroscience, 18*(4), 177–185. http://doi.org/10.1179/1476830514Y.0000000110

Nitkin, C. R., & Bonfield, T. L. (2017). Concise review: Mesenchymal stem cell therapy for pediatric disease: Perspectives on success and potential improvements. *Stem Cells Translational Medicine, 6*(2), 539–565. http://doi.org/10.5966/sctm.2015-0427

Rossignol, D. A., & Frye, R. E. (2012). A review of research trends in physiological abnormalities in autism spectrum disorders: Immune dysregulation, inflammation, oxidative stress, mitochondrial dysfunction and environmental toxicant exposures. *Molecular Psychiatry, 17*(4), 389–401. http://doi.org/10.1038/mp.2011.165

Sampanthavivat, M., Singkhwa, W., Chaiyakul, T., Karoonyawanich, S., & Ajpru, H. (2012). Hyperbaric oxygen in the treatment of childhood autism: A randomized controlled trial. *Diving and Hyperbaric Medicine, 42*(3), 128–133.

Sandler, A. D., & Bodfish, J. W. (2000). Placebo effects in autism: lessons from secretin. *Journal of Developmental and Behavioral Pediatrics: JDBP, 21*(5), 347–350.

Sandler, A. D., Sutton, K. A., DeWeese, J., Girardi, M. A., Sheppard, V., & Bodfish, J. W. (1999). Lack of benefit of a single dose of synthetic human secretin in the treatment of autism and pervasive developmental disorder. *New England Journal of Medicine, 341*(24), 1801–1806. http://doi.org/10.1056/NEJM199912093412404

Stewart, P. A., Hyman, S. L., Schmidt, B. L., Macklin, E. A., Reynolds, A., Johnson, C. R., . . . Manning-Courtney, P. (2015). Dietary supplementation in children with autism spectrum disorders: Common, insufficient, and excessive. *Journal of the Academy of Nutrition and Dietetics, 115*(8), 1237–1248. Epub 2015 Jun 04.

Clinical CAM Treatments for Autism

Ayres, J. (1979). *Sensory integration and the child.* Los Angeles, CA: Western Psychological.

Ayres, A. J. (2005). *Sensory integration and the child: 25th anniversary edition.* Los Angeles, CA: Western Psychological Services.

Bettelheim, B. (1959). Feral children and autistic children. *American Journal of Sociology, 64*(5), 455–467.

Case-Smith, J., Weaver, L. L., & Fristad, M. A. (2015). A systematic review of sensory processing interventions for children with autism spectrum disorders. *Autism, 19*(2), 133–148. http://doi.org/10.1177/1362361313517762

Lang, R., O'Reilly, M., Healy, O., Rispoli, M., Lydon, H., Streusand, W., . . . Giesbers, S. (2012). Sensory integration therapy for autism spectrum disorders: A systematic review. *Research in Autism Spectrum Disorders, 6*(3), 1004–1018. http://doi.org/10.1016/j.rasd.2012.01.006

Lang, R., Tostanoski, A. H., Travers, J., & Todd, J. (2014). The only study investigating the rapid prompting method has serious methodological flaws but data suggest the most likely outcome is prompt dependency. *Evidence-Based Communication Assessment and Intervention, 8*(1), 40–48. http://doi.org/10.1080/17489539.2014.955260

Lanning, B. A., Baier, M. E. M., Ivey-Hatz, J., Krenek, N., & Tubbs, J. D. (2014). Effects of equine assisted activities on autism spectrum disorder. *Journal of Autism and Developmental Disorders, 44*(8), 1897–1907. http://doi.org/10.1007/s10803-014-2062-5

Lilienfeld, S. O., Marshall, J., Todd, J. T., & Shane, H. C. (2014). The persistence of fad interventions in the face of negative scientific evidence: Facilitated communication for autism as a case example. *Evidence-Based Communication Assessment and Intervention, 8*(2), 62–101. http://doi.org/10.1080/17489539.2014.976332

McDaniel, B. C., Osmann, E. L., & Wood, W. (2015, October 2*A systematic mapping review of equine-assisted activities and therapies for children with autism: Implications for occupational therapy.* Paper presentation at CommonKnowledge—SSO:USA Annual Research Conference, Fort Lauderdale, FL. Retrieved from http://commons.pacificu.edu/sso_conf/2015/2/34/

O'Haire, M. E. (2012). Animal-assisted intervention for autism spectrum disorder: A systematic literature review. *Journal of Autism and Developmental Disorders, 43*(7), 1606–1622. http://doi.org/10.1007/s10803-012-1707-5

Optometrists Network. (n.d.). *Vision therapy success stories.* Retrieved from http://www.visiontherapystories.org/vision_autism.html

Schlosser, R. W., Balandin, S., Hemsley, B., Iacono, T., Probst, P., & von Tetzchner, S. (2014). Facilitated communication and authorship: A systematic review. *Augmentative and Alternative Communication, 30*(4), 359–368. http://doi.org/10.3109/07434618.2014.971490

Siegel, B. (1995). Brief report: Assessing allegations of sexual molestation made through facilitated communication. *Journal of Autism & Developmental Disorders, 25*(3), 319–326.

Siegel, B. (2000). Commentary on "Lack of benefit of a single dose of synthetic human secretin in the treatment of autism and pervasive developmental disorder" (in *New England Journal of Medicine*). *Evidence-Based Mental Health, 3,* 2.

Siegel, B., & Zimnitsky, B. (1998). Facilitated communication and auditory integration training: A critical review of two non-mainstream treatments for language disorder associated with autistic spectrum disorders. *Journal of Speech-Language Pathology & Audiology, 22*(2), 61–70.

Sokhadze, E. M., Casanova, M. F., Tasman, A., & Brockett, S. (2016). Electrophysiological and behavioral outcomes of Berard Auditory Integration Training (AIT) in children with autism spectrum disorder. *Applied Psychophysiology and Biofeedback, 41*(4), 405–420. http://doi.org/10.1007/s10484-016-9343-z

Tostanoski, A., Lang, R., Raulston, T., Carnett, A., & Davis, T. (2014). Voices from the past: Comparing the rapid prompting method and facilitated communication. *Developmental Neurorehabilitation, 17*(4), 219–223. http://doi.org/10.3109/17518423.2012.749952

Travers, J. C., Tincani, M. M., Thompson, J. L., & Simpson, R. L. (2016). Picture exchange communication system and facilitated communication: Contrasting an evidence-based practice with a discredited method. In B. G. Cook, M. Tankersley & T. J. Landrum (Eds.), *Instructional practices with and without empirical validity* (Vol. 29, pp. 85–110). West Yorkshire, England: Emerald Group. Retrieved from http://www.emeraldinsight.com/doi/abs/10.1108/S0735-004X20160000029005

Wigham, S., Rodgers, J., South, M., McConachie, H., & Freeston, M. (2014). The interplay between sensory processing abnormalities, intolerance of uncertainty, anxiety and restricted and repetitive behaviours in autism spectrum disorder. *Journal of Autism and Developmental Disorders, 45*(4), 943–952. http://doi.org/10.1007/s10803-014-2248-x

Psychological Experiences With ASD Diagnosis and Treatment

Cascio, M. A. (2012). Neurodiversity: Autism pride among mothers of children with autism spectrum disorders. *Intellectual and Developmental Disabilities, 50*(3), 273–283. http://doi.org/10.1352/1934-9556-50.3.273

Clifford, T., & Minnes, P. (2012a). Logging on: Evaluating an online support group for parents of children with autism spectrum disorders. *Journal of Autism and Developmental Disorders, 43*(7), 1662–1675. http://doi.org/10.1007/s10803-012-1714-6

Clifford, T., & Minnes, P. (2012b). Who participates in support groups for parents of children with autism spectrum disorders? The role of beliefs and coping style. *Journal of Autism and Developmental Disorders, 43*(1), 179–187. http://doi.org/10.1007/s10803-012-1561-5

Corcoran, J., Berry, A., & Hill, S. (2015). The lived experience of US parents of children with autism spectrum disorders: A systematic review and meta-synthesis. *Journal of Intellectual Disabilities, 19*(4), 356–366. http://doi.org/10.1177/1744629515577876

Crane, L., Chester, J. W., Goddard, L., Henry, L. A., & Hill, E. (2016). Experiences of autism diagnosis: A survey of over 1,000 parents in the United Kingdom. *Autism,* 20(2), 153–162. http://doi.org/10.1177/1362361315573636

Da Paz, N., Siegel, B., Coccia, M. A., & Epel, E. (2018). Acceptance or despair? Caregiver responses to having a child with autism. *Journal of Autism and Developmental Disorders.* https://doi.org/10.1007/S10803-017-3450-4.

Evans, B. (2012). *Understanding autism: Parents, doctors and the history of a disorder* (Princeton, NJ: Princeton University Press, 2012; 340 pp) [Book review]. *Psychoanalysis and History, 15*(1), 116–119. http://doi.org/10.3366/pah.2013.0126

Fernańdez-Alcántara, M., García-Caro, M. P., Pérez-Marfil, M. N., Hueso-Montoro, C., Laynez-Rubio, C., & Cruz-Quintana, F. (2016). Feelings of loss and grief in parents of children diagnosed with autism spectrum disorder (ASD). *Research in Developmental Disabilities, 55,* 312–321. http://doi.org/10.1016/j.ridd.2016.05.007

Foxx, R. M., & Mulick, J. A. (2015a). *Controversial therapies for autism and intellectual disabilities: Fad, fashion, and science in professional practice.* Abingdon-on-Thames, England: Routledge.

Gray, D. E. (2006). Coping over time: The parents of children with autism. *Journal of Intellectual Disability Research, 50*(12), 970–976. http://doi.org/10.1111/j.1365-2788.2006.00933.x

Luhrmann, T. M. (2001). *Of two minds: An anthropologist looks at American psychiatry.* New York, NY: Vintage.

Rimland, B. (1964). *Infantile autism: The syndrome and its implications for a neural theory of behavior.* Englewood Cliffs, NJ: Prentice Hall.

Siegel, B. (1997). Parent responses to the diagnosis of autism: Mourning, coping, and adaptation. In D. Cohen & F. Volkmar (Eds.), *Handbook of autism and pervasive developmental disorders* (2nd ed., pp. 745–766). New York, NY: Wiley.

Siegel, B. (2008). *O Mundo da Crianca com Autismo* [The world of the autistic child]. Porto, Portugal: Porto Editora.

Siegel, B. (2012, July 5). Siblings of children with autism spectrum disorders. In F. Volkmar (Ed.), *Autism and autism spectrum disorders: History, diagnosis, neurobiology, treatment and outcomes.* Henry Stewart Talks [Webcast]. Retrieved from http://hstalks.com/main/browse_talk_info.php?talk_id=2352&series_id=444&c=252

Siegel, B., & Silverstein, S. (1994). *What about me? Growing up with a developmentally disabled sibling.* New York, NY: Insight Books, Plenum Press.

Chapter 8
POPULAR MEDIA

Adams, J. (2012, March 12). *Stories of hope: Autism.* California Stem Cell Agency. Retrieved September 27, 2016, from https://www.cirm.ca.gov/our-progress/stories-hope-autism

Autism Watch. (n.d.). Home page. Retrieved September 27, 2016, from http://www.autism-watch.org/

Bauer, S. C., & Roberts, M. Y. (2016, July 15). There's no one-size-fits-all way to treat autism. *Scientific American.* Retrieved September 27, 2016, from http://blogs.scientificamerican.com/guest-blog/there-s-no-one-size-fits-all-way-to-treat-autism/

Bradley, E. (2000). The MMR vaccine. *60 Minutes*, Season 33, Episode 7.

Brownstein, J., and *ABC News* Medical Unit. (2010, March 11). Father sues doctors over autism therapy. *ABC News*. Retrieved September 27, 2016, from http://abcnews.go.com/ Health/TheLaw/doctors-sued-autism-chelation-therapy/story?id=10045951

Bruni, F. (2014, July 4). California, Camelot and vaccines. *The New York Times*, p. SR3 (NY edition).

Chelation and autism—Talk About Curing Autism (TACA). (2016, September 9). Retrieved September 27, 2016, from TACA website: http://www.tacanow.org/family-resources/ chelation-and-autism/

Complementary approaches for treating autism. (2012, July 25). Retrieved September 27, 2016, from Autism Speaks website: https://www.autismspeaks.org/what-autism/treat-ment/complementary-treatments-autism

Dawson, M. (2015, June 17). The miracle that cured my son's autism was in our kitchen. *New York Post*. Retrieved from http://nypost.com/2015/06/17/ is-diet-the-key-to-curing-autism/

Deer, B. (2004). MMR: The truth behind the crisis. *Sunday London Times*, pp. 2, 22.

Defeat Autism Now. (n.d.). *Your guide to information, resources, and help*. Retrieved September 27, 2016, from http://www.defeatautismnow.net/

Engber, D. (2015, October 20). The strange case of Anna Stubblefield. *The New York Times*. Retrieved from http://www.nytimes.com/2015/10/25/magazine/the-strange-case-of-anna-stubblefield.html

Engber, D. (2016, February 3). What Anna Stubblefield believed she was doing. *The New York Times*. Retrieved from http://www.nytimes.com/2016/02/03/magazine/what-anna-stubblefield-believed-she-was-doing.html

Ellis, R., Levs, J., & Hamasaki, S. (2015, January 23). *Outbreak of 51 measles cases linked to Disneyland*. Retrieved from http://www.cnn.com/2015/01/21/health/ disneyland-measles/

English, J. (2013, April 26). *Saving Eli: One family's struggle with autism*. Nutrition Review. Retrieved from http://nutritionreview.org/2013/04/saving-eli-one-familys-with-struggle-autism/

Isaacson, R. (2009). *The horse boy: A father's quest to heal his son*. New York, NY: Little, Brown.

Johannes, L. (1999, December 9). Autism treatment fails to top placebo in study of secretin hormone's effects. *Wall Street Journal*. Retrieved from http://www.wsj.com/articles/ SB944701250710205201

Kennedy, R. F. (2005, February 9). Deadly immunity. *Rolling Stone Magazine*.

Laidler, J. R. (n.d.). The "refrigerator mother" hypothesis of autism. Autism Watch. Retrieved September 27, 2016, from http://www.autism-watch.org/causes/rm.shtml

Mayo Clinic. (n.d.). *Complicated grief*. Retrieved September 27, 2016, from http://www. mayoclinic.org/diseases-conditions/complicated-grief/basics/definition/con-20032765

Moyer, M. W. (2014, September 1). Gut bacteria may play a role in autism. *Scientific American*. Retrieved September 27, 2016, from http://www.scientificamerican.com/ article/gut-bacteria-may-play-a-role-in-autism/

National Vaccine Information Center. (2017). *California State vaccine requirements*. Retrieved from http://www.nvic.org/Vaccine-Laws/state-vaccine-requirements/ california.aspx

Padawer, R. (2014, July 31). The kids who beat autism. *The New York Times*. Retrieved from http://www.nytimes.com/2014/08/03/magazine/the-kids-who-beat-autism.html

Peterson, P. E. (2016, June 23). Please don't take away my autistic son's treatment. *Wall Street Journal*. Retrieved from http://www.wsj.com/articles/please-dont-take-away-my-sons-treatment-1466722896

Ryan, F. (2016, July 13). The fake cures for autism that can prove deadly. *The Guardian*. Retrieved from https://www.theguardian.com/society/2016/jul/13/fake-cures-autism-prove- deadly

Siegel, B. (1996). *The world of the autistic child: Understanding and treating autistic spectrum disorders*. New York, NY: Oxford University Press.

Simpson, D. E., Hanley, J. J., & Quinn, G. (Filmmakers). (2002, July 16). History of autism blame: Refrigerator mothers [Television series episode]. *POV*. United States: PBS. Retrieved from http://www.pbs.org/pov/refrigeratormothers/fridge/

Sonya. (2015, March 31). Autism and methylation—Are you helping to repair your child's methylation cycle? Retrieved September 27, 2016, from Treat Autism website: http://treatautism.ca/2015/03/31/autism-and-methylation-are-you-helping-to-repair-your-childs-methylation-cycle/

Stem Cell Institute. (n.d.). *Stem Cell Therapy for Autism*. Retrieved September 27, 2016, from https://www.cellmedicine.com/stem-cell-therapy-for-autism/

Thimerosal and autism: Reviewing the evidence (2007). (n.d.). Autism Watch. Retrieved September 27, 2016, from http://www.autism-watch.org/rsch/thimerosal.shtml

US Food and Drug Administration. (n.d.). Autism: Beware of false or misleading claims for treating autism. Retrieved September 27, 2016, from http://www.fda.gov/ForConsumers/ConsumerUpdates/ucm394757.htm. Updated April 12, 2017.

Wang, S. S. (2015, September 14). Gluten-free diet has no benefit for children with autism, study finds. *Wall Street Journal*. Retrieved from http://www.wsj.com/articles/gluten-free-diet-has-no-benefit-for-children-with-autism-study-finds-1442244486

Willingham, E. (2013, October 29). The 5 scariest autism "treatments." *Forbes*. Retrieved September 27, 2016, from http://www.forbes.com/sites/emilywillingham/2013/10/29/the-5-scariest-autism-treatments/

Yanofsky, J. (2014, July 31). The kids who don't beat autism. *The New York Times*. Retrieved September 27, 2016, from http://parenting.blogs.nytimes.com/2014/07/31/the-kids-who-dont-beat-autism/

SCIENTIFIC READINGS

Authoritative Reviews

Doja, A., & Roberts, W. (2006). Immunizations and autism: A review of the literature. *Canadian Journal of Neurological Sciences, 33*(4), 341–346. http://doi.org/10.1017/S031716710000528X

Grinkler, R. R. (2007). *Unstrange minds: Remapping the world of autism*. New York, NY: Basic Book/Perseus.

National Vaccine Information Center. (2017). *California State vaccine requirements*. Retrieved from http://www.nvic.org/Vaccine-Laws/state-vaccine-requirements/california.aspx

Offit, P. A. (2008). *Autism's false prophets: Bad science, risky medicine, and the search for a cure*. New York, NY: Columbia University Press.

Offit, P. (2011). *Deadly choices: How the anti-vaccine movement threatens us all.* New York, NY: Basic Books.

Offit, P. (2014, September 14). The anti-vaccine epidemic. *Wall Street Journal.* Retrieved from https://www.wsj.com/articles/paul-a-offit-the-anti-vaccination-epidemic-1411598408

Sobo, E. J. (2016). What is herd immunity, and how does it relate to pediatric vaccination uptake? US parent perspectives. *Social Science and Medicine, 165,* 187–195. https://doi.org/10.1016/j.socscimed.2016.06.015

CAM for Autism Based on Vaccine Fears

Aaseth, J., Skaug, M. A., Cao, Y., & Andersen, O. (2015). Chelation in metal intoxication—Principles and paradigms. *Journal of Trace Elements in Medicine and Biology, 31,* 260–266. http://doi.org/10.1016/j.jtemb.2014.10.001

Bernard, S., Enayati, A., Redwood, H., Roger, H., & Binstock, T. (2001). Autism: A novel form of mercury poisoning. *Medical Hypotheses, 56*(4),462–471.

Crisponi, G., Nurchi, V. M., Lachowicz, J. I., Crespo-Alonso, M., Zoroddu, M. A., & Peana, M. (2015). Kill or cure: Misuse of chelation therapy for human diseases. *Coordination Chemistry Reviews, 284,* 278–285. http://doi.org/10.1016/j.ccr.2014.04.023

Geier, D. A., & Geier, M. R. (n.d.). A prospective assessment of porphyrins in autistic disorders: A potential marker for heavy metal exposure. *Neurotoxicity Research, 10*(1), 57–63. http://doi.org/10.1007/BF03033334

Sinha, Y., Silove, N., & Williams, K. (2006). Chelation therapy and autism. *BMJ: British Medical Journal, 333*(7571), 756.

Wakefield, A. (Director). (2016). *Vaxxed: From cover up to catastrophe.* United States: Cinema Libre Studios. Retrieved from http://vaxxedthemovie.com/

Wakefield, A., Murch, S. H., Anthony, A., Linnell, J., Casson, D. M., Malik, M., . . . Walker-Smith, J. A. (1998). Ileal-lymphoid-nodular hyperplasia, non-specific colitis, and pervasive developmental disorder in children. *Lancet, 351*(9103), 637–641. Retracted.

Chapter 9

POPULAR MEDIA

Blakeslee, S. (1997, September 2). Some biologists ask "Are genes everything?" *The New York Times.* Retrieved from http://www.nytimes.com/1997/09/02/science/some-biologists-ask-are-genes-everything.html

Broader autism phenotype. (2012, July 25). Retrieved September 27, 2016, from Autism Speaks website: https://www.autismspeaks.org/site-wide/broader-autism-phenotype

Debunking animal autism. *Scientific American.* Retrieved September 27, 2016, from http://www.scientificamerican.com/podcast/episode/3e744d29-dd5a-eb39-ec70f5438254a14a/

Interagency Autism Coordinating Committee. (2018, February). 2016–2017 IACC strategic plan for autism spectrum disorder. Retrieved from https://iacc.hhs.gov/publications/strategic-plan/2017/

Murphy, K. (2016, August 28). Do you believe in God or is that a software glitch? *The New York Times.*

NIH Clinical Center. (n.d.). *Bench-to-bedside program.* Retrieved September 27, 2016, from http://clinicalcenter.nih.gov/ccc/btb/. Last updated December 13, 2017.

Satel, S., & Lilienfeld, S. O. (2013). *Brainwashed: The seductive appeal of mindless neuroscience.* New York, NY: Basic Books.

Wade, N. (1997, September 9). First gene for social behavior identified in whiskery mice. *The New York Times.* Retrieved from http://www.nytimes.com/1997/09/09/science/first-gene-for-social-behavior-identified-in-whiskery-mice.html

SCIENTIFIC READINGS

American Psychiatric Association. (2000). *Diagnostic and statistical manual of mental disorders* (4th ed., text revision; *DSM-IV-TR*). Washington, DC: APA Press.

American Psychiatric Association. (2013). *Diagnostic and statistical manual of mental disorders* (5th ed.; *DSM-5*). Washington, DC: APA Press.

Autism Biomarker Research

Anderson, G. M. (2014). Autism biomarkers: Challenges, pitfalls and possibilities. *Journal of Autism and Developmental Disorders, 45*(4), 1103–1113. http://doi.org/10.1007/s10803-014-2225-4

Frustaci, A., Neri, M., Cesario, A., Adams, J. B., Domenici, E., Dalla Bernardina, B., & Bonassi, S. (2012). Oxidative stress-related biomarkers in autism: Systematic review and meta-analyses. *Free Radical Biology and Medicine, 52*(10), 2128–2141. http://doi.org/10.1016/j.freeradbiomed.2012.03.011

Goldani, A. A. S., Downs, S. R., Widjaja, F., Lawton, B., & Hendren, R. L. (2014). Biomarkers in autism. *Frontiers in Psychiatry, 5.* http://doi.org/10.3389/fpsyt.2014.00100

Hunsinger, D. M., Nguyen, T., Zebraski, S. E., & Raffa, R. B. (2000). Is there a basis for novel pharmacotherapy of autism? *Life Sciences, 67*(14), 1667–1682. http://doi.org/10.1016/S0024-3205(00)00763-3

Ichim, T. E., Solano, F., Glenn, E., Morales, F., Smith, L., Zabrecky, G., & Riordan, N. H. (2007). Stem cell therapy for autism. *Journal of Translational Medicine, 5*, 30. http://doi.org/10.1186/1479-5876-5-30

Raugh, V. A., & Margolis, A. E. (2016). Research review: Environmental exposures, neurodevelopment, and child mental health—new paradigms for the study of brain and behavioral effects. *Journal of Child Psychology & Psychiatry*, 57(7), 775–793. doi:10.1111/jcpp.12537

Rossignol, D. A., & Frye, R. E. (2012). A review of research trends in physiological abnormalities in autism spectrum disorders: Immune dysregulation, inflammation, oxidative stress, mitochondrial dysfunction and environmental toxicant exposures. *Molecular Psychiatry, 17*(4), 389–401. http://doi.org/10.1038/mp.2011.165

Autism Brain Research

Amaral, D. G. (2011). The promise and the pitfalls of autism research: An introductory note for new autism researchers. *Brain Research, 1380*, 3–9. http://doi.org/10.1016/j.brainres.2010.11.077

Poldrack, R. A., Mumford, J. A., & Nichols, T. E. (2011). *Handbook of functional MRI analysis.* New York, NY: Cambridge University Press.

Raichle, M. E. (1998). Behind the scenes of functional brain imaging: A historical and physiological perspective. *Proceedings of the National Academy of Sciences of the United States of America, 95*(3), 765–772.

Autism Epigenetics

Flashner, B. M., Russo, M. E., Boileau, J. E., Leong, D. W., & Gallicano, G. I. (2013). Epigenetic factors and autism spectrum disorders. *NeuroMolecular Medicine, 15*(2), 339–350. http://doi.org/10.1007/s12017-013-8222-5.

Hall, L., & Kelley, E. (2013). The contribution of epigenetics to understanding genetic factors in autism. *Autism, 18*(8), 872–881. http://doi.org/10.1177/1362361313503501

Lahvis, G. P. (2016). Rodent models of autism, epigenetics, and the inescapable problem of animal constraint. In J. C. Gewirtz & Y.-K. Kim (Eds.), *Animal models of behavior genetics* (pp. 265–301). New York, NY: Springer. Retrieved from http://link.springer.com/chapter/10.1007/978-1-4939-3777-6_9

Miyake, K., Hirasawa, T., Koide, T., & Kubota, T. (2012). Epigenetics in autism and other neurodevelopmental diseases. In S. I. Amad (Ed.), *Neurodegenerative diseases* (pp. 91–98). New York, NY: Springer US. Retrieved from http://link.springer.com/chapter/10.1007/978-1-4614-0653-2_7

Rangasamy, S., D'Mello, S. R., & Narayanan, V. (2013). Epigenetics, autism spectrum, and neurodevelopmental disorders. *Neurotherapeutics, 10*(4), 742–756. http://doi.org/10.1007/s13311-013-0227-0

Schanen, N. C. (2006). Epigenetics of autism spectrum disorders. *Human Molecular Genetics, 15*(Supplement 2), R138–R150. http://doi.org/10.1093/hmg/ddl213

Autism Genetics and Mouse Models

Crawley, J. N. (2007). Mouse behavioral assays relevant to the symptoms of autism. *Brain Pathology, 17*(4), 448–459. http://doi.org/10.1111/j.1750-3639.2007.00096.x

Davies, G. (2010). Captivating behavior: mouse models, experimental genetics and reductionist returns in the neurosciences. *The Sociological Review, 58*, 53–72. http://doi.org/10.1111/j.1467-954X.2010.01911.x

Iwata, K., Matsuzaki, H., Takei, N., Manabe, T., & Mori, N. (2010). Animal models of autism: An epigenetic and environmental viewpoint. *Journal of Central Nervous System Disease, 2*, 37–44. Retrieved from https://www.ncbi.nlm.nih.gov/pmc/articles/PMC3661233/

McFarlane, H. G., Kusek, G. K., Yang, M., Phoenix, J. L., Bolivar, V. J., & Crawley, J. N. (2008). Autism-like behavioral phenotypes in BTBR T+tf/J mice. *Genes, Brain and Behavior, 7*(2), 152–163.

Moy, S. S., Nadler, J. J., Magnuson, T. R., & Crawley, J. N. (2006). Mouse models of autism spectrum disorders: The challenge for behavioral genetics. *American Journal of Medical Genetics Part C: Seminars in Medical Genetics, 142C*(1), 40.

Moy, S. S., Nadler, J. J., Young, N. B., Perez, A., Holloway, L. P., Barbaro, R. P., . . . Crawley, J. N. (2007). Mouse behavioral tasks relevant to autism: Phenotypes of 10 inbred strains. *Behavioural Brain Research, 176*(1), 4–20. http://doi.org/10.1016/j.bbr.2006.07.030

Silverman, J. L., Yang, M., Lord, C., & Crawley, J. N. (2010). Behavioral phenotyping assays for mouse models of autism. *Nature Reviews Neuroscience, 11*(7), 490–502. http://doi.org/10.1038/nrn2851

Yoo, J., Bakes, J., Bradley, C., Collingridge, G. L., & Kaang, B.-K. (2014). Shank mutant mice as an animal model of autism. *Philosophical Transactions of the Royal Society of London B: Biological Sciences, 369*(1633), 20130143. http://doi.org/10.1098/rstb.2013.0143

Autism Genetics Research

Bourgeron, T. (2016). The genetics and neurobiology of ESSENCE: The third Birgit Olsson lecture. *Nordic Journal of Psychiatry, 70*(1), 1–9. doi:10.3109/08039488.2015.1042519

de Jonge, M., Parr, J., Rutter, M., Wallace, S., Kemner, C., Bailey, A., . . . Pickles, A. (2014). New interview and observation measures of the broader autism phenotype: Group differentiation. *Journal of Autism and Developmental Disorders, 45*(4), 893–901. http://doi.org/10.1007/s10803-014-2230-7

de la Torre-Ubieta, L., Won, H., Stein, J. L., & Geschwind, D. H. (2016). Advancing the understanding of autism disease mechanisms through genetics. *Nature Medicine, 22*(4), 345–361. http://doi: 10.1038/n071.m.4

Ecker, C. (2017). The neuroanatomy of autism spectrum disorder: An overview of structural neuroimaging findings and their translatability to the clinical setting. *Autism, 21*(1), 18–28. pii: 1362361315627136

Folstein, S., & Rutter, M. (1977). Infantile autism: A genetic study of 21 twin pairs. *Journal of Child Psychology and Psychiatry, 18*(4), 297–321. http://doi.org/10.1111/j.1469-7610.1977.tb00443.x

Gillberg, C. (2010). The ESSENCE in child psychiatry: Early symptomatic syndromes eliciting neurodevelopmental clinical examinations. *Research in Developmental Disabilities, 31*, 1543–1551.

Huguet, G., Ey, E., & Bourgeron, T. (2013). The genetic landscapes of autism spectrum disorders. *Annual Review of Genomics & Human Genetics, 14*, 191–213.

Sanders, S. J., He, X., Willsey, A. J., Ercan-Sencicek, A. G., Samocha, K. E., Cicek, A. E., . . . State, M. W. (2015). Insights into autism spectrum disorder genomic architecture and biology from 71 risk loci. *Neuron, 87*(6), 1215–1233. doi:10.1016/j.neuron.2015.09.016

Singh, J., Illes, J., Lazzeroni, L., & Hallmayer, J. (2009). Trends in US autism research funding. *Journal of Autism and Developmental Disorders, 39*(5), 788–795. http://doi.org/10.1007/s10803-008-0685-0

Tordjman, S., Drapier, D., Bonnot, O., Graignic, R., Fortes, S., Cohen, D., . . . Roubertoux, P. L. (2007). Animal models relevant to schizophrenia and autism: Validity and limitations. *Behavior Genetics, 37*(1), 61–78.

Viding, E., & Blakemore, S.-J. (2006). Endophenotype approach to developmental psychopathology: Implications for autism research. *Behavior Genetics, 37*(1), 51–60. http://doi.org/10.1007/s10519-006-9105-4

Conclusions

Goldstein, J., Solnit, A., Goldstein, S., & Freud, A. (1996). *The best interest of the child: The least detrimental alternative.* New York, NY: Free Press, Simon & Schuster.

INDEX

References to figures, tables and boxes are indicated with an italicized *f, t*, and *b.*

Applied Behavior Analysis Association, 185
apprenticeship learning
  creating opportunities in autism, 149–50
  incentivizing employers to train and hire
    individuals with ASD, 150
  for youth with ASDs, 139–40
arbitration
  potential for replacing due process, 117–18
  special education due process, 113–14
Armed Services Vocational Aptitude Battery
  (ASVAB), 148
ASHA. *See* American Speech and Hearing
  Association (ASHA)
Asperger's disorder, *xvii–xviii*, 15, 272
  autism shadow syndrome *vs.*, 78
  criminality and, 79–80
  diagnosis, 73–74, 80–81, 82
  DSM-IV adding, 60–61
  online, 81
  PDD diagnosis of, 27
  politics of diagnosis of, 78–82
  self-diagnosis, 78, 80–81
Aspies, 27, 78, 139
assessment
  American problem with identifying
    autism, 42–43
  diagnosis through developmental
    lens, 83–89
  lens of psychologists and
    psychiatrists, 34–36
  lens of speech and language
    pathologists, 36
  occupational therapist lens, 36–37
  parents and trust, 32–33
  pediatric lens, 34
  responsiveness to sensory stimuli, 39–40
  screening checklists, 40–42
  teachers lens, 37
attention deficit disorders (ADHD/ADDs),
  74*t*, 253
attention deficit hyperactivity disorder
  (ADHD), 2, 17*f*, 21*f*, 22, 29, 51, 172,
  260, 262–63
auditory integration training (AIT), autism
  treatment, 207–8
autism, *ix*
  American, 4
  American experience of, *xviii*
  assessment, 31–37
  best interest of child, 273–74
  Big Pharma as stakeholder, 67–69
  biological factors contributing to rise
    in, 22–23
  concept of, 54
  culture of, *xviii*

Dark Ages of, *xi*
diagnoses history, 16–31
"diagnosing for dollars" phenomenon,
  21–22, 24
diagnostic overshadowing, 28–30
dietary treatment for, 210–12
dimensions of, *xiii–xiv*
as disorder, 51–52
early infantile, *xi*
etiology, 264, 264*f*
hype, hope and hyperbole, 77–78
incidence, 16*f*
increased awareness of, 18–20
increasing prevalence, 28–30
information *vs.* knowledge, 2–3
with intellectual disability, 131–32
misdiagnosis and informant bias, 37–45
our information about, 3
"pie chart" children, 20–21, 21*f*
political correctness, 6
politics of, 4–6
prevalence, 22*t*, 30
priorities for autism community, 271–74
public advocacy of, 70–71
resetting priorities for diagnosis, 82–84
service entitlements ending with
  graduation, 123*f*
social policy recommendations, 45–48
spectrum, 18–20
treatment providers as stakeholders, 69–70
as wanted diagnosis, 23–24
young adult outcomes in, 124*f*
Autism and Developmental Disabilities
  Monitoring Network (ADDMN), 15,
  21, 22*t*
autism aware, 70–71
Autism Center of Northern California, *xvii*,
  223, 267
Autism Centers of Excellence, 202
Autism Diagnostic Interview-Revised (ADI-
  R), 30, 31, 35
Autism Diagnostic Observation Schedule
  (ADOS), 20*f*, 30–31, 33, 35, 40, 62
autism family wellness, 6–7
autism gatekeepers, 71–76
  DSM and diagnosing the brain, 71–72
  Saving Normal (Frances), 73, 75–76
Autism Home Clinic, 223
autism research
  advocates of, 254–55
  animal models, 262–63
  autism etiology, 264, 264*f*
  basic research and, 255–56, 261
  "bench-to-bedside" science, 261–62
  brain science, 259–61